FILIPINO AMERICANS

Transformation and Identity

Maria P. P. Root

Editor

SAGE Publications
International Educational and Professional Publisher
Thousand Oaks   London   New Delhi

WITHDRAWN

For information address:

SAGE Publications, Inc.
2455 Teller Road
Thousand Oaks, California 91320
E-mail: order@sagepub.com

SAGE Publications Ltd.
6 Bonhill Street
London EC2A 4PU
United Kingdom

SAGE Publications India Pvt. Ltd.
M-32 Market
Greater Kailash I
New Delhi 110 048 India

Printed in the United States of America

Library of Congress Cataloging-in-Publication Data

Main entry under title:
Filipino Americans: transformation and identity / edited by Maria
P. P. Root.
p.   cm.
Includes bibliographical references and index.
ISBN 0-7619-0578-2. — ISBN 0-7619-0579-0 (pbk.)
1. Filipino Americans—History. 2. Filipino Americans—Ethnic
identity. 3. Filipino Americans—Social conditions. I. Root,
Maria P. P.
E184.F4F385 1997
973'.049921—dc21   97-4591

This book is printed on acid-free paper.

98 99 00 01 02 03 10 9 8 7 6 5 4 3 2

Acquiring Editor:	C. Deborah Laughton
Editorial Assistant:	Eileen Carr
Production Editor:	Diana E. Axelsen
Production Assistant:	Denise Santoyo
Typesetter:	Danielle Dillahunt
Indexer:	Mary Mortensen
Cover Designer:	Candice Harman
Print Buyer:	Anna Chin

Contents

Foreword

It is time that a book like this gathers authoritative Filipino Americans to discuss, in scholarly fashion, their issues of the day.

It is a propitious time when throughout the United States many Filipino Americans, and particularly Filipino American students, are beginning to want to know more about themselves, their past, and their future. All this is happening despite the minimal transmission of knowledge, ideas, and values about Filipino Americans in American schools.

Most academics have believed that Filipino Americans and/or Filipinos have made no substantial contribution to the history and development of the United States and, therefore, perceive that Filipino American and/or Philippine ethnic studies are inferior, valueless, not essential to education, and not marketable to the general public. In this era, most academics continue to believe that if something is Filipino American and/or Philippine, it is inferior. Everything Filipino American has been denied its intrinsic value. Such an omission has led much to the ignorance of all.

Beginning with the Black Power movement, minority and ethnic studies—notably African American, Chicano, Native American, and Asian American studies—were introduced into some higher education curricula. Yet in the first two decades, there was hardly a page of history of which Filipino Americans might be proud. In academe, Filipino

Americans among American minorities were entirely miscast in every-one's minds, including their own.

Among the authoritative contributors to this vital publication are a dozen from the "family" of the Filipino American National Historical Society, which has been responsible, I believe, for helping to share and to provide some pages of history of which Filipino Americans and all others seeking the full story of U.S. history might be proud.

However, there is still much to research and publish in the process of discovering Filipino American history, legacy, and pride. In this pro-cess, scholarly discussion is essential for understanding contemporary issues facing Filipino Americans and erasing the "inferiorizing" of Fili-pino Americans as well as Filipinos.

This is not a matter of being politically correct. It is a matter of educational, sociological, cultural, and spiritual urgency for the good of the country—our country, the United States.

Through these ensuing pages of contemporary issues, I see the fruition of scholarly work that has extended the frontiers of knowledge, ideas, and values through critical and exhaustive investigation of Amer-ica's forgotten Filipino Americans.

It is time—our Pinoy Time!

Fred Cordova
Founding President Emeritus
Filipino American National Historical Society
and Affiliate Assistant Professor
of American Ethnic Studies,
University of Washington

Introduction

Maria P. P. Root

S panning five centuries, colonization ravaged the souls and psyche of the indigenous people of the archipelago dubbed *Las Islas Filipinas* by Spain in 1565. The traumas associated with colonization that lasted almost 400 years scarred us all, regardless of our nativity, language, class, or gender. Trauma fragments and fractures the essence of our being and self-knowledge; it disconnects us from each other. And whether consciously or unconsciously, we mark elapsed emotional time since a trauma with anniversary responses. Thus, millions of Filipino Americans and Filipinos anticipate the numerous centennial anniversaries that are upon us beginning in 1996 and continuing through the end of this millenium. Anniversary memories and responses typically allow us to rework and transcend the events of the past.

It is my hope that these pages will offer challenging questions, some refreshing analysis, and new paradigms for interpreting the Filipino American experience. Thus, we may continue gradually healing ourselves, mitigating and eventually terminating the fractionalization and fragmentation that result from the divisive meanings applied to the economic, social, phenotypic, language, and nativity differences among us. Although this book offers discussion on contemporary issues, it more specifically transforms Filipino American history and experience, and therefore identity.

This volume is a constructive anniversary response by 30 contributors. Compiled during 1996, it marks the centennial anniversary of the beginning of the decline of Spanish rule of Las Islas Filipinas from Spain in 1896. This revolution is marked with other centennial anniversaries. The national figures Jose Rizal and Andres Bonifacio were killed—one executed and the other assassinated. On June 12, 1898, the Philippines declared a short-lived independence from Spain. The contest for imperial expansion by two significant colonial powers led to the beginning of the Spanish-American War later that year on Philippine soil. Despite bitter resistance by Filipinos, William Howard Taft, the subsequent 27th president of the United States, became the first governor general of the Philippines on July 4, 1901. In claiming wardship of the archipelago of over 7,000 islands, the United States would anglicize the name to *The Philippines* (Pido, 1986). The Philippines' and the United States' histories and fates fused.

The pages of this book, filled with pride, sorrow, anger, and courage, analyze and interpret the far-reaching impact of the insidious traumas euphemistically called "history" on contemporary Filipino Americans, although they are generations removed from the original traumas (Root, 1992). The resilience and perseverance characteristic of Filipinos across nations emerge from these pages despite the scars of dislocation, relocation, and exclusion that have left many Filipino Americans perpetually in search of symbols, locations, and definitions of the ancestral home.

By the simple revolutionary acts of telling our story and reinterpreting them within cultural and trauma survivor frameworks, these contributors continue to propel us forward in our healing and empowerment. Healing is a process composed of the acts of many people across time as well as across space. Necessarily, the contributors represent diversity among Filipino Americans. Some of the authors were born in the United States, some have immigrated from the Philippines, and still others have come to the United States by circuitous routes. Most are citizens, some are not. Some are multilingual, others are not. Some prefer the use of *Pilipino,* others prefer the use of *Filipino* (see Chapter 2, p. 37, Note 1, and Chapter 7, p. 106, this volume). Although the geographic location of home for most Filipino Americans may be in the United States or the Philippines (or both), the ancestral home for those in the second, third, fourth, and later generations may reside in the psyche and soul. This symbolic home is nurtured by family stories and historical accounts that document the tragic, heroic, and ordinary ancestors who make our lives possible now. These pages could not have been produced without gratitude to and appreciation of those Filipinos who have come before us. Related by blood or not, we are connected to the trials and successes of those who have been here before us. This connection may be the *balikbayan* (homecoming) vehicle or ticket for those who still search for home.

People of Filipino heritage have experiences very different from those of other Asian American groups who are part of the fabric of this country. Not dominated by Confucian philosophy, oral in tradition, coming from societies that have matriarchal structures and bilateral kinship systems, intersected and invaded by seafarers, traders, military, missionaries, and colonizers, Filipinos of America are seldom accurately situated in history or culture and are therefore often misinterpreted. We share cultural affinities with people from Mexico, Central and South America, Cuba, and Puerto Rico because of Spain. We share shamanic and animistic traditions with indigenous peoples throughout the world. We share cultural patterns of communication with Japanese, Chinese, Vietnamese, and Koreans. An archipelago of Malayan people, our braiding of cultures and phenotypes creates affinities with Pacific Island people, who clearly are recipients of the African diaspora. A century of American contact provides Filipinos with a familiarity, if only in distorted images, of America and European American values.

Through all of this, our response to the question, "What does it mean to be Filipino American?" continues to evolve. We are likely both to agree and to disagree on the answer to this question because we are a dynamic people with diverse origins whose experiences change with time. This perspective suggests that the paradigm in which a single response is expected will only pathologize our continually changing and diverse meanings of *Filipino American*. Thus, this volume, instead of attempting to offer a single resolution, affirms that there are many. We suggest that for Filipinos, as for Native American (Indian and Hawaiian) people and people of the Caribbean, Mexico, and Central and South America, U.S. paradigms of race are useless.

The resilience of Filipinos defies the images in which colonists cast Filipinos to justify domination: stereotypically "feminine" images of the country and its conquered people, stereotypically "masculine" images of potential or actual threats to colonial and imperial control. The female needs protection, the male needs watching. Thus we see, through history and up to the present, that those in a position of domination describe Filipinos and Filipino Americans as gentle and passive but capable of aggressiveness, childlike but threatening, and compliant but stubborn.

None of these stereotypes are evoked when we define our own image. Rather, there is an insider expectation of strength and resilience. The reader may glimpse this through the challenges we offer to each other. Thus, at times, contributors are brutally frank in naming the ways in which Filipinos usurp the methods of the colonizer, such as racism and patriarchy, in their behavior toward other people, including other Filipinos.

As editor, I have taken the liberty of defining *Filipino American* in the most inclusive sense. We are immigrants-now-citizens, American born, immigrant spouses awaiting eligibility for green cards, mixed-heritage Filipinos, students or workers on visa, *tago ng tago* (undocumented), and transnationals moving between the Philippines and the United States. Thus, *Filipino American* is a state of mind rather than of legality or geography. Under the same roof, family members hold different meanings for and attachments to being Filipino American.

Throughout this book, there will not be a uniform use of *Filipino* or *Filipino American*. This ambiguity is in itself a challenge to those who assume dichotomous paradigms; many Filipinos have overlapping and simultaneous identities that necessitate different paradigms for identity, nationalism, and authenticity. The contributor's context determines the meaning of the term. Furthermore, the text makes the assumption, unless otherwise denoted by context, that the use of *Filipino* in an American text assumes *American*.

We offer the reader *Filipino Americans: Transformation and Identity* as a *balikbayan* ticket that may transcend citizenship, generation, nativity, and diversity of social locations one might occupy. In the Philippines, many of the indigenous healers were priestesses who possessed sacred knowledge for transformation: the *babaylan* of the Visayas, *catalonan* of Central Luzon, and *baglan* of the northern Philippines (Enriquez, 1992). Throughout these pages, the strength of the original feminine voice of the healers is abundantly available to the women and men who make this volume possible. We seek to establish connection and respect amidst and despite our differences. Through inclusion, we can find our home with each other. With our diversity, we can achieve a formidable voice. Because of our resourcefulness, we can transform our past. We hope that in traveling these pages, the reader finds heart, hope, and home in Filipino American experiences.

References

Enriquez, V. G. (1992). *From colonial to liberation psychology: The Philippine experience.* Manila: De La Salle University Press.

Pido, A. J. A. (1986). *The Pilipinos in America.* New York: Center for Migration Studies.

Root, M. P. P. (1992). The impact of trauma on personality: The second reconstruction. In L. Brown & M. Ballou (Eds.), *Complexity and diversity in feminist theory and therapy* (pp. 191-211). New York: Haworth.

1

The Tragic Sense
of Filipino History

Peter Bacho

The sorrow and downright tragedy of Filipino history have long been the main components of the engine that drives Filipino literature. As we approach any number of centennials (1896—the start of the war against Spain and Jose Rizal's execution; 1897—the signing of the short-lived Pact of Biak na Bato; 1898—the arrival of the Americans; 1899—the start of the American war against Filipinos), it is appropriate to understand that the bloody crushing of dreams at the turn of the century was simply a harbinger of worse hardships to come. Some of these were triggered by foreigners, such as the devastation caused by the Japanese occupation. Others, however, had domestic origins: the Huk Rebellion, the Marcos era, the twin insurrections led by the Marxist New People's Army and Muslim secessionists.

For many Filipinos, the major good to emerge from this litany of instability and war was the enduring link to the United States. For most of that colonial period, it meant a chance to escape to America. Left behind was the Philippines' rural poverty, a condition that would only worsen as landlords distanced themselves from their tenants and—

operating within the lucrative context of the tariff-free American market—
began to pay more attention to increased profits. Yet even here, among
the fabled "Manong generation," there is a particular sadness to their
stories.

In the 1920s and 1930s, they arrived in the United States full of hope.
They were, after all, American nationals and products of a Thomasite
school system[1] that preached only the best of American ideals. America,
young Filipinos believed, was a meritocracy, a social ideal that the
Philippines—with its emphasis on inherited wealth and European blood—
was most assuredly not. Somewhere—whether in an asparagus field in
Stockton, a hotplate room in Seattle, or a cannery in Alaska—a part of
that ideal died. Restricted by race, these men were forced into a life of
migrant labor, doing menial jobs most white workers would never touch.
Keep moving, they were told in one hostile West Coast town after
another. And so they did, living a life of constant motion; on the West
Coast, they ranged from California's Imperial Valley to the northernmost
Alaskan cannery, and to all points in between.

In the literature gleaned from Filipino authors in the Philippines and
in America, the shadow of Sisyphus, the Greek king condemned by the
gods to everlasting failure, looms exceedingly large. He is embodied in
Crisostomo Ibarra, a mestizo idealist who seeks a modest reform—the
establishment of a Spanish academy—in his homeland, the Philippines.

Yet even that advance proves too much for the friars, the true powers
who govern the archipelago on behalf of Spain. The political and economic power of the friars, medieval in its scope and authority, is built on
the passivity and blind obedience of the Filipino masses. Any reform,
ranging from Philippine representation in the Cortes to trimming of the
extent of the friars' secular powers, is quickly crushed by religious
authorities. Even as modest a reform as the teaching of Spanish smacks
of "progress" and merits condemnation by the friars and worse. Such is
the case in Jose Rizal's first great propaganda novel, *Noli Me Tangere*
(1887/1961), in which forces led by the friars appear to have killed the
luckless Ibarra by the novel's end.

Of course, Rizal is not finished with his protagonist; his pedagogical
value has not been exhausted. Ibarra does not die; rather, as in any good
melodrama, he returns a number of years later, as the jaded, wealthy, and
mysterious Simoun, to haunt his old foes in Rizal's sequel, *El Filibusterismo* (1891/1965). Simoun's purpose is simple: to provoke Filipinos to

rise against Spain. He fails and, in his final confession to Father Florentino, a Filipino priest, Rizal, through Florentino, speaks out against violence (revolution) as a means of promoting a social good.

By this time, of course, Florentino/Rizal's protest against violence is a bit too late. Indelibly etched in the minds of the book's Filipino audience is an encyclopedia of legitimate Filipino grievances and Spanish cruelties. In *Noli,* one example of the latter is the execution of Tarsilo, a captured rebel, who is lowered head first into the town well. The prospect is so horrific that Tarsilo pleads, not for life, but for a quicker death: "If you're Christians, if you have hearts . . . lower me fast or hit my head against the wall and kill me. God will reward you for this good deed. Think, maybe some day you will find yourselves where I am" (p. 358).

Surely, among Rizal's audience, Tarsilo's admonition—that others might someday find themselves sharing his fate—must have struck a resonant chord, leading some to an inevitable conclusion: that reform was insufficient. Those who held this view gathered within the ranks of the Katipunan, a secret organization under the leadership of Andres Bonifacio. Their goal was revolution, which erupted against Spain in 1896.

The Spaniards blamed Rizal for the revolt and executed him that same year. Rizal, up to his death, protested his innocence, claiming that his intent was reform, not rebellion, and, to a degree, he was correct. To a larger degree, however, the logical product of Rizal's works was revolution. What his writing unleashed, aside from revulsion at Spanish injustice, was a growing sense that the Philippines' myriad cultural and linguistic groups, despite a history of competition and even violence, had a common bond, and that collectively they stood separate from their Spanish overseers. The former is best summarized in a scene from F. Sionil Jose's great novel *Po-on* (1984).

In that scene, Istak, the protagonist, has been assigned the task of delivering a letter to General Gregorio del Pilar, leader of the rear guard of the retreating Presidente of the infant republic, Emilio Aguinaldo. Fast on the entourage's heels are American forces, who intend to succeed the Spaniards as colonial masters of the Philippines. By agreeing to this task, Istak makes an existential choice and accepts the consequence (his death). He declines safety and the welfare of his family in favor of a call to a larger loyalty, Filipinas, a nation in concept if not in fact. As Istak mounts his horse, his nationalist patron, Don Jacinto, declares that by doing this task, Istak is "no longer Ilocano [i.e., with loyalty to the Ilocos region of the Philippines and its people specifically], [he is] Filipino" (p. 162). This leap in loyalty—from the specific and narrow to the general—is one that many Filipinos have tried and are still trying to make. In the classic Filipino American work *America Is in the Heart,* Carlos Bulosan (1973) noted that a "tribal" orientation had "obstructed all efforts toward Filipino unity in America" (p. 98).

Nonetheless, Bulosan, as the narrator of the Manong generation's story, confronts not just the frustrating problems of internal disunity but also a society openly hostile to Filipinos. Bulosan and his Filipino American colleagues accepted the challenge; they chose to struggle against entrenched economic and violently racist forces in the America of the 1930s. In the process, that generation manages to participate effectively in a powerful movement of organized labor: Filipinos were the main force behind the creation of the United Cannery, Agricultural, Packing and Allied Workers of America, a union affiliated with the militant Congress of Industrial Organizations (CIO). By responding in this fashion, these young Filipino Americans hoped to create nothing less than a new America, or to revise the old one to the point that it would resemble the gossamer Thomasite vision of a meritocratic society, one still held "in the heart."

Although Ibarra/Simoun, Istak, and Bulosan as narrator all exist in separate literary contexts, a number of themes are common. Each text is the writer's interpretation of historic conditions; such conditions are dismal (colonial oppression, war, racism, class consciousness) and inevitably force the main character to choose whether or not to act; the choice of action carries with it no guarantee of success. For writers such as Rizal, Jose, and, later, Ninotchka Rosca (*State of War;* 1988) and Jessica Hagedorn (*Dogeaters;* 1990), this entails identification of the enemy—whether foreign or native—followed by action against that enemy. Although not quite so dramatic, Bulosan identified the foe of all workers (including Filipinos) as fascism. The Filipino American response was militant labor organizing.

In that sense, the inclusion of Filipino literature—whether Philippine or Filipino American—in the occasional Asian American literature class is, at best, a very ill fit. The focus of Japanese and Chinese American literature is different, whether it is Maxine Kingston's or Amy Tan's

exploration of relations between immigrant mothers and citizen daughters, Frank Chin's outrage at the theft of Chinese American history, or
John Okada's depiction of a community's attempts to heal divisions
caused by the Japanese American internment. These are, by the nature
of their topics, quieter, more introspective stories that at the very least
hold out hope of resolution.

In contrast, such hope is often missing from the fiction of Filipino
writers. Given the penchant of many Filipino writers to use in their
works substantial doses of Philippine and Filipino American reality, it is
hardly any wonder that success is such an elusive goal. Instead, such
writers tend to celebrate the protagonist's decision to act as we readers
applaud the choice while bracing ourselves for the inevitable disappointment or demise. Even in a work as wonderfully understated as Bien-
venido Santos's collection *Scent of Apples* (1979), a melancholy mood
pervades many of the stories. Who, for example, can forget Santos's
description of his reaction to the devastation of post-war Manila, as seen
by the narrator from a ship returning from America:

> How indeed . . . rebuild the other ruins? Could old men do it by dying
> in a land they had decided to call their own? Or was it done by
> scattering toys all over the land, rattlers and kiddie cars, balloons and
> electric trains, guns, grimacing clowns and dolls with upswept lashes,
> that childhood might start with laughter and kindness? Or would it
> help if the dumb were made to speak at least and the deaf hear and
> understand? Or would songs do it; wisdom, perhaps? Or, maybe
> prayer? There is a way, but it could not be the way of trembling hands
> with so many things to hide, nor could it be the way of that woman,
> holding a fatherless child in her arm, dragging a duffle bag by her side,
> now walking slowly toward the ruins of the city. (p. 107)

The most cohesive group of Santos's stories focuses on Filipino
students living in Washington, D.C., during World War II. Unlike Bulosan's characters, many of these Filipinos come from the Philippine
elite. Also, unlike many of their impoverished countrymen on the West
Coast, they are purely sojourners: They have something to return to.

The students are temporarily in the United States for the sole purpose of achieving a prestigious American degree, after which they are
expected to return and help run the various family enterprises. Ironically,
separated from their families' wealth by enemy occupation and by

distance, they are forced to sample a bit, but not all, of the desperation endured by West Coast Filipinos. For example, although both Bulosan and Santos write about Filipinos in America during roughly the same period of time, American racism is a dominant theme in Bulosan's work; that element is missing from Santos's depictions.

Ironically as well, the "savior" of Santos's privileged characters comes in the humble form of Ambo, a working-class old-timer similar to those characters found in Bulosan. Ambo's tireless efforts prompt one elite beneficiary to utter the following:

> The boys look up to him. I have heard . . . he had a whole household of Filipinos, feeding on everything he could give them, and he was tireless. Now those whom he saw through those years will fight for him, will die for him. He is well loved by the Filipino community. (p. 51)

Still, Ambo's integrity and his unqualified kindness are not enough; they are several rungs short of bridging the socioeconomic gap and prompt the same beneficiary to add a caveat: "If he [Ambo] had only been educated, he would have been an articulate leader of our countrymen in this country" (p. 51).

This disdainful view of Ambo, expressed in the United States but having Philippine roots, explains Bulosan's class consciousness and his hostility toward the Philippines' elite. The Philippine-centered works of later writers such as Jose, Rosca, and Hagedorn continuously examine the problem of class division and extreme turmoil prompted, in large part, by the insular arrogance of the elite.

For Santos's wealthy sojourners, the question arises: Is their professed affection for Ambo in any way genuine, or more a matter of need? In his collection, Santos provides the answer in "Letter: The Faraway Summer." Ambo returns to the Philippines, but the wartime devastation has forced him to reconsider his move. He wants to come back to the United States and hopes that one of his "boys"—Steve, now a successful Manila doctor—can pull the right strings at the U.S. Embassy. He visits Steve's office; Steve is embarrassed by his presence and treats Ambo like "a stranger" (p. 112). Ambo then inadvertently overhears Steve's telephone conversation with (presumably) his wife or lover and recounts it in a letter to a stateside friend: "Darling, I should have called earlier, but

I just got rid of a visitor. . . . No, no, it wasn't a girl . . . a man, a *Pino.*
I said *Pinoy* just one of those *Pinoys* I had met in the States" (p. 112)

Here, the term *Pinoy* needs some explanation. As used by Steve, *Pinoy* is a pejorative. If so, it is one that has been proudly worn by thousands. As I recall from my Pinoy childhood, the term had class (poor, working), geographic (American), and attitudinal (aggressive) connotations. Thus, it was applied to the Manong generation and to their American-born offspring. It most surely does not apply to Steve or to others of his status. But it does apply to the proletarian Ambo, and it is he that the Tondo-born Santos celebrates, not the shallowness of Steve or the other high-born "boys." It is a criticism of the elite that Bulosan, Santos's blunter contemporary, would have warmly endorsed.

What future directions, then, for Filipino literature? In the Philippines, the wars against the Americans and the Japanese are, respectively, almost a century and more than half a century old. In recent years, the most obvious problem, the dictatorship of Ferdinand Marcos, has been removed, and democracy has been restored. Still, endemic corruption, the gap between wealthy and poor, and ongoing insurrections remain both as severe national problems and as grist for writers/social critics. Undoubtedly, the tradition of using fiction as social/political/historical commentary will continue. However, there is also evidence that other themes may assume prominence. Even F. Sionil Jose departed somewhat from his position as writer/rebel in his recent novel *Viajero* (1993). Here, the focus is on Buddy, a Filipino orphan adopted by an African American officer serving in the Philippines during World War II. Although the protagonist finds himself returning to familiar ground—the unstable Philippines—the novel is as much a depiction, through Buddy's young eyes, of life in America and the state of American race relations in the 1960s and 1970s as it is a comment on the root causes of Philippine turmoil.

Another fascinating variation can be found in Jessica Hagedorn's gritty and gripping new novel *Gangster of Love* (1996); the plot follows the life of Rocky, an immigrant Filipina who attempts to "make it" as a poet/singer/performance artist in the often seamy realm of the New York City arts scene. Hagedorn is unique; although born in the Philippines, she spent her youth in San Francisco, where, in the 1970s, she became an emerging voice in what was then a promising Filipino American (mostly second-generation) literary arts scene. Because of the novel's setting, based to a certain degree on the author's own experiences (Hagedorn was a performance artist/poet/writer who moved to New York City and still lives there), the settings and the characters are fascinating, unique, and credible. Undoubtedly, a large part of *Gangster of Love* will be revelatory to many Filipino readers. However, Hagedorn's observations on the impact of America on Filipino culture resonate affectionate humor and easy familiarity. For example, Voltaire, Rocky's younger brother, while still in the Philippines, decides to honor his late hero, Jimi Hendrix.

> Voltaire grew his bushy hair out and teased it into what he called a "Filipino Afro." Voltaire caused a sensation whenever he appeared in his royal purple bell-bottoms and gauzy shirts from India. My parents were appalled, especially when Voltaire took the next logical step and adopted an "indigenous Filipino" hippie look . . . batik fabric . . . carabao horns, scapulars, and amulets he purchased from bemused marketplace vendors in front of Baclaran Church. (p. 5)

Gangster of Love is a significant step in the evolution of Filipino literature produced either by writers born outside of the Philippines or by those whose life experiences are tied to other lands. Realistically, this means mainly Filipino American writers, and of this small core, two—Bulosan and Santos—paint a picture of America that is also decades old. Among the younger American-born writers, the poet Jeff Tagami (*October Light;* 1987) and I (*Cebu;* Bacho, 1991) portray the lives of poor working-class Filipino Americans. Between the aging of the first generation and the maturation of the second came a third, starting in 1968: new waves of Filipino immigrants, beneficiaries of dramatically liberalized U.S. immigration laws. Their children now constitute the majority of Filipino America.

Unlike Bulosan and his peers, they do not come to a land that permits legal discrimination. Unlike Bulosan's generation, many of the newcomers are highly educated and have put that education to profitable use in America. Unlike my generation, many have not raised their families in racially segregated, economically disadvantaged neighborhoods. Unlike the first two generations, many profess never to have felt the sting of racism.

How will these later, less hostile conditions affect the literature their children produce? What will these new, younger voices say? A partial answer can be gleaned from Evelina Galang's collection of short stories, *Her Wild American Self* (1996). Not only is the geographic locale different—the Midwest as opposed to the traditional West Coast setting of Bulosan, Bacho, Tagami, Jose, and Santos (to a lesser degree in *Scent of Apples*)—but so, too, are the perspective (female) and the issues stressed (sexism, identity, and generational friction between immigrant parent and American-born child).

The setting of the stories and poems of these different authors is important. Up until the recent demographic changes wrought by U.S. immigration law, the West Coast had been the population center of Filipino America; it had also been the cauldron of overt racial hostility, extreme poverty, and class tension.

For later Filipino arrivals, the same has not been true in other parts of America. Galang's work reflects a different Filipino American reality, one infused with gender-based, generational, and geographic insights. Suffice it to say that this expansion of the shallow pool of literary themes was inevitable and, quite possibly, overdue. That said—and although it is premature to suggest what other added works will deepen the pool—it is clear that one adjustment will be made: Sisyphus, long the main icon of Filipino literature, must move to make room.

Note

1. American teachers and officials staffing the Philippine school system during the period of American colonization were called "Thomasites" because of their arrival on the transport *Thomas*.

References

Bacho, P. (1991). *Cebu*. Seattle: University of Washington Press.
Bulosan, C. (1973). *America is in the heart*. Seattle: University of Washington Press.
Galang, M. E. (1996). *Her wild American self*. Minneapolis: Coffee House.
Hagedorn, J. (1990). *Dogeaters*. New York: Houghton Mifflin.
Hagedorn, J. (1996). *Gangster of love*. New York: Pantheon.
Jose, F. S. (1984). *Po-on*. Manila: Solidaridad.

Jose, F. S. (1993). *Viajero*. Manila: Solidaridad.

Rizal, J. P. (1961). *Noli me tangere* (L. M. Guerrero, Trans.). London: Longman. (Original work published 1887)

Rizal, J. P. (1965). *El filibusterismo* (L. M. Guerrero, Trans.). London: Longman. (Original work published 1891)

Rosca, N. (1988). *State of war*. New York: Norton.

Santos, B. N. (1979). *Scent of apples*. Seattle: University of Washington Press.

Tagami, J. (1987). *October light*. San Francisco: Kearny Street Workshop.

2

Demographic Changes Transforming the Filipino American Community

Juanita Tamayo Lott

There is a sugar plantation on the outskirts of Honolulu called the Waipahu Plantation Village. It is a step back in time to the turn of the 20th century when sugar plantations were the main industry of Hawaii. Visitors are guided by former camp residents through a time tunnel that emerges into a multiethnic village housing some 400,000 immigrants circa 1910. What is striking about the village is that it is divided into separate camps for each ethnic immigrant group—Chinese, Filipino, Japanese, Korean, Portuguese, Puerto Rican, Okinawan, and Spaniard.

The centerpiece of the Chinese camp is a two-story pagoda with a social hall on the first floor and a temple with several altars on the second floor. The Japanese camp features a communal bathhouse. The Portuguese camp is noted for its outdoor stone oven, which was used for baking *malasadas*, Portuguese donuts. All the camps except for one are composed of three- and four-room cabins that contain a kitchen, a living room, and one or two bedrooms. The cabins reflect the status of the

11

workers. Those from Asia were temporary contract laborers, so the Chinese, Japanese, Korean, and Okinawan cabins were sparsely furnished, holding only basic utensils. On the other hand, the Portuguese and Puerto Ricans went to Hawaii as permanent settlers, and their cabins were decorated with china, lace curtains, artwork, and knickknacks.

In lieu of a camp of cabins, the Filipino camp was distinguished by a long dormitory-style building with a common living area and rows upon rows of single beds. This captures the prevailing first image of the Filipino community in the United States, the romanticized "Manong generation."

It was a mobile population of young, primarily single males from the barrios and farms of the Ilocos and Visayan regions of the Philippines. They were recruited as contract workers and manual laborers initially for the Hawaiian sugar and pineapple fields and subsequently for the Alaskan canneries and California agriculture.

The 1910 census enumerated 2,767 Filipinos, of whom 90% were male (see Table 2.1). Females made up only 1 out of every 10 Filipinos. By 1930, the census enumerated 108,424 Filipinos (U.S. Department of Commerce, 1980, Table 40). Between 1920 and 1929, 31,092 Filipinos were admitted to the state of California alone. Of these, about 85% arrived from the Philippines and the Hawaiian Islands in vessels operated by two California steamship companies (State of California, 1930, p. 11). The numbers of Filipinos subsequently diminished with the end of contract immigration and the passage of stringent immigration laws that virtually barred immigration from Asia (Lott, 1995; Shinagawa, 1996). By 1940, Filipinos in the United States had decreased to 98,535 (U.S. Department of Commerce, 1980, Table 40).

Although this generation did not intend to settle in the United States, economic opportunities in the Philippines were not conducive to returning. Many men had worked long hours without saving much money. Returning home broke could be embarrassing. Simultaneously, the political and social climate in the United States was not encouraging for permanent settlement. Although the Philippines was a colony of the United States at this time, Filipinos could not become naturalized citizens. State antimiscegenation laws abounded. Filipinos could not be property owners. Many of their struggles during this period were directed to survival and improved working conditions. Filipinos were

TABLE 2.1   Numbers of Filipino Males and Females in the United States, 1910 to 1990

Year	Males	Females
1910	2,502	265
1920	22,083	4,551
1930	94,973	13,451
1940	80,835	17,700
1950	89,658	33,049
1960	112,286	64,024
1970	189,498	153,562
1980	374,191	400,461
1990	656,765	765,946

SOURCE: For 1910 to 1980, U.S. Department of Commerce (1980, Table 40). For 1990, U.S. Department of Commerce (1993, Table 1).

involved in the labor movement and organized Filipino unions in the 1920s and 1930s (Bulosan, 1943; Cordova, 1983).

From 1930 to 1960, the Filipino population experienced slow growth, with a trickle of immigration for spouses of World War II servicemen and of Filipino sailors recruited into the U.S. Navy. By 1960, there were 176,310 Filipinos in the United States. Almost two thirds (64%) were males (U.S. Department of Commerce, 1980, Table 40).

Only as recently as 1983 has a broader view of the Filipino community been documented. In his book *Filipinos: Forgotten Asian Americans,* Fred Cordova (1983) described three other little-known segments of the Filipino community: the Manila men who established a 1763 Louisiana settlement; the *pensionados,* Filipino leaders and intellectuals of the 1900s who were sent by the Philippine government for higher education in the United States; and the Filipino Americans or second generation (between 1930 and 1965). The Filipino American community grew as some bachelors did marry and raise families. They established community centers in Hawaii; Alaska; Seattle; Washington; and Stockton, California. The socioeconomic status of this population in the period between 1941 and 1959 was still primarily lower income and lower occupation. Over half of the Filipino labor force (58%) were farmworkers and domestics. Roughly one third (32%) worked in restaurants and hotels. Six percent were semiskilled or in the armed forces, and a mere 4% were professionals (Morales, 1974, p. 138).

Despite this diversity within the Filipino community, this population was still a primarily male, working-class community with a sizable rural population in 1960. Although it was a small community, it was a stable community.

In the post-World War II era, the political and social climate changed and became more receptive to a permanent community. Civil rights for all residents was a national goal. Filipinos, like other Asian Americans, were allowed to be naturalized. Discriminatory housing, education, and antimiscegenation statutes and policies were replaced by laws of nondiscrimination in the third quarter of this century. Of equal importance in affecting the composition of Filipinos in the United States was the abolishment of restrictive immigration quotas in 1965.

With the passage of the Immigration and Nationality Act of 1965, which resulted in increased immigration, especially from Asia and Latin America (Kim & Kim, 1977, p. 392), the Filipino community experienced profound demographic changes. These changes were first apparent and documented in the 1970 census. The 1990 census reaffirmed these changes.

Numbers and Distribution

Asian Americans are considered the fastest-growing population in the United States, doubling their numbers between 1970 and 1980 and again between 1980 and 1990. This doubling phenomenon was observed earlier in the Filipino population. Between 1960 and 1970, the number of Filipinos in the United States about doubled, from 176,310 to 343,060 (U.S. Department of Commerce, 1980, Table 40). It more than doubled between 1970 and 1980, from 343,060 to 774,652 (U.S. Department of Commerce, 1980, Table 40). It nearly doubled again between 1980 and 1990, from 774,652 to 1,422,711 (U.S. Department of Commerce, 1993, Table 3).

In 1970, Filipinos were the third-largest Asian American group after the Japanese and Chinese (U.S. Department of Health, Education and Welfare, 1974). Two thirds of the additional population were new immigrants, and the remaining third was due to new births of Filipinos in the United States.

By 1990, Filipinos were the second-largest Asian group in the United States (U.S. Department of Commerce, 1993, Table 3). Filipinos already are the largest Asian group in the largest state of California. This continuing growth is due to both high immigration rates and high birth rates. In 1990, almost two thirds of the Filipino population (64.4%) were foreign born.

In 1970, over two thirds of the Filipino population lived on the West Coast, with 40% in California and 28% in Hawaii (U.S. Department of Health, Education and Welfare, 1974, Table B-1). Whereas in 1960 over a quarter (26%) lived in rural areas, by 1970 this had decreased to about one fifth (22%), although a sizable number of elderly Filipinos were still rurally located.

Locality was associated with nativity in the 1970 Filipino population. In Hawaii, almost two thirds (65%) of the population were American born. In California, fewer than half (42%) were born in the United States. Outside of these two states that had the highest number of Filipinos, 63% were foreign born (U.S. Department of Health, Education and Welfare, 1974, Table B-4).

In 1990, the majority of the Filipino population continued to live on the West Coast. About one half (51%) resided in Hawaii or California. Seventy-one percent lived in the West, with the remainder distributed almost equally among the Northeast (10%), the Midwest (8%), and the South (11%). With the continued urbanization and suburbanization of the U.S. population in the 1980s and 1990s, many Filipinos settled in suburban areas rather than central cities or rural areas.

Families

By 1970, Filipino families were firmly established. The image of this population as the Manong generation was replaced by a generation of families and a more balanced sex ratio. In 1910, the ratio of Filipino males to Filipino females was over 10 to 1. By 1980, Filipinas constituted over half of the Filipino population (see Table 2.1).

Among all Filipino families in 1970, married-couple families were the majority at 86%, which was the same proportion as U.S. families in general (U.S. Department of Health, Education and Welfare, 1974, Table C-1). The percentage of Filipino female-headed households in 1970 was 9% compared to 11% for female-headed households in the general U.S. population (U.S. Department of Health, Education and Welfare, 1974, Table C-2).

These patterns held in 1990 (U.S. Department of Commerce, 1993, Table 3). Married-couple families constituted 78.3% of all Filipino families. The comparable proportion of all U.S. families was 78.6%. Female-headed households increased among both Filipino and U.S. families between 1980 and 1990. In 1990, female-headed households constituted 15.4% of all Filipino families. The U.S. proportion was slightly higher, at 16.5%.

Filipino families are larger than other families.[1] In 1990, the average Filipino family was composed of 4.02 persons, compared to an average of 3.8 persons for all Asian American families and an average of 3.16 persons for all U.S. families (U.S. Department of Commerce, 1993, Table 3).

Education, Occupation, and Socioeconomic Status

Educational Attainment

Although the majority of the first generation of Filipinos in the United States had very little formal education, subsequent generations have been and are highly educated, especially women. In 1970, 64% of all Filipino women had completed high school, compared to 48% of Filipino men. Over one fourth of Filipino women (27%) had 4 or more years of college, compared to 15% of Filipino men. Median schooling for Filipino men was less than a high school degree, at 11.9 years, whereas for Filipino women it was greater, at 12.6 years (U.S. Department of Health, Education and Welfare, 1974, Table D-6).

By 1990, with the passing of many of the Manong generation and the entry of educated male immigrants, the proportions of highly educated Filipino men and women were similar. Their levels of education exceeded those of the general U.S. population (U.S. Department of Commerce, 1993, Table 3). Among persons 25 years and older, about four out of five Filipino males (82.5%) and females (81.4%) were high school graduates or higher. This compares with three fourths of the general population. Filipino proportions of college and higher-level graduates for both men and women were double those of the total U.S. population: 39.3% for Filipino males and 41.4% for Filipino females, compared with 20.3% for all U.S. males and 17.6% for all U.S. females. This high achievement in part reflects the immigration of Filipino health professionals, particularly nurses.

Given this high educational attainment, it is not surprising that Filipinos exhibit a high labor force participation rate. In 1970, about four out of five (79%) Filipino men were in the labor force. Over half (55%) of Filipino women were in the labor force. They had the highest labor force participation of all groups of women (U.S. Department of Health, Education and Welfare, 1974). By 1990, the labor force participation rate was similar for Filipino males and females, with a drop to 75.4% for males and a rise to 72.3% for females. By comparison, the labor force participation rate for all U.S. males was 65.3% and for all U.S. females was 56.8%. Among all females, Filipinas had the highest labor force participation rate (U.S. Department of Commerce, 1993, Table 3).

Occupational Distribution

Greater occupational distribution has accompanied the higher education and labor force participation rates of Filipinos.

By 1970, there was already a shift from working-class to professional occupations. Over one fourth (26.8%) of Filipinos in 1970 were in managerial, professional, and technical occupations. Almost one fifth (18.9%) were in sales or clerical positions. Nevertheless, the largest proportion, one third (33.5%), were service workers and farmworkers. About one fifth held positions as craftsmen and operatives (U.S. Department of Health, Education and Welfare, 1974).

In 1990, in contrast, almost two thirds (63.3%) of all Filipinos in the labor force were in managerial, professional, and technical occupations. Only 9.5% were in sales and clerical work. The proportion of service workers and farmworkers had diminished to 18.3%, and the proportion of craftsmen and operatives to 8.9% (U.S. Department of Commerce, 1993, Table 3).

In addition to federal affirmative action policies in education and employment, this shift from working class to professional class was directly related to immigration patterns for this period. Of all immigrants from the Philippines reporting an occupation at their time of entry into the United States between 1965 and 1973, the vast majority (69%) were professional, technical, and managerial workers. Service workers and farmworkers constituted less than one fifth of immigrants at 17%. Clerical and sales workers constituted 8%, and craftsmen and operatives constituted 6% (U.S. Department of Health, Education and Welfare, 1974, Table E-5).

Although entrepreneurship is associated less with Filipinos than with other Asian American groups, businesses are thriving in this community. There has been an increase in Filipino businesses over the past two decades. In 1977, the Department of Commerce identified 10,000 Filipino businesses. Within 5 years, this had more than doubled to 23,359 in 1982. By 1987, Filipino businesses increased to 40,412. Business receipts in 1982 were $747 million, and in 1987 they more than doubled to $1.9 billion (U.S. Department of Commerce, 1991, Table A). For 1992, it was estimated that there were 60,289 Filipino-owned businesses, with estimated gross receipts of $4.5 billion (U.S. Department of Commerce, 1996, Table A).[2]

Socioeconomic Status

Representation in higher-education and higher-status occupations has resulted in higher socioeconomic status for Filipinos than for the total U.S. population. The income distribution of Filipino families in 1970 was similar to American families in general. During this period, the median family income of Filipinos was $9,318. Of all Filipino families, 14% made less than $4,000, similar to 15% of all U.S. families. Almost half, (46%) made more than $10,000, which was comparable to 47% of all families in the United States. By 1990, median family income was $46,698, compared to a U.S. median family income of $35,225. Although median family income for Filipinos is higher than that of the general U.S. population, their per capita income of $13,616 is less than the $14,143 of the general population. This is due in part to larger families and a greater number of workers per household among Filipinos. As noted previously, in 1990, the average number of Filipinos per family was 4.02. By comparison, the average number of persons in U.S. families was lower, at 3.16 (U.S. Department of Commerce, 1993, Table 3). Furthermore, among all Asian American groups, Filipinos had the greatest proportion of three or more workers per family, at 29%. This is more than twice the proportion for all U.S. families with three or more workers, 13.4% (U.S. Department of Commerce, 1993, Table 3).

Conclusion

No longer can the demographic profile of Filipinos in the United States be captured by a long dormitory in a Hawaiian plantation. The present and future profiles of Filipinos depict a cosmopolitan and complex community—one with mixed neighborhoods of renters and property owners, primarily in major cities and suburbs. This community is distributed across all income and occupational groups and diverse living arrangements. The issue facing this community is whether this demographic profile can be transformed into an effective political constituency and economic force in and of itself and in unison with other population groups under a pan-ethnic coalition.

Notes

   1. According to the Bureau of the Census, "families" are groups of persons related by blood, adoption, or marriage and living in the same household. "Households" are housing units of related or unrelated persons living at the same address.
   2. Dollar values are expressed in current dollars: Thus, for example, 1992 data are expressed in 1992 dollars and 1987 data in 1987 dollars.

References

Bulosan, C. (1943). *America is in the heart.* Seattle: University of Washington Press.
Cordova, F. (1983). *Filipinos: Forgotten Asian Americans.* Dubuque, IA: Kendall/Hunt.

Immigration and Nationality Act of 1965. 8 U.S.C. § 1101 *et seq.*

Kim, C., & Kim, B. L. (1977). Asian immigrants in American law: A look at the past and the challenge which remains. *American University Law Review, 26,* 373-407.

Lott, J. T. (1995). Population growth and distribution. In S. Gall (Ed.), *The Asian American almanac* (pp. 275-298). Detroit: Gale Research.

Morales, R. (1974). *Makibaka: The Pilipino American struggle.* Los Angeles: Mountainview.

Shinagawa, L. (1996). The impact of immigration on the demography of Asian Pacific Americans. In B. O. Hing & R. Lee (Eds.), *Reframing the immigration debate* (pp. 59-126). Los Angeles: LEAP Asian Pacific American Public Policy Institute and University of California-Los Angeles Asian American Studies Center.

State of California, Department of Industrial Relations. (1930). *Facts about Filipino immigration into California.* San Francisco: R & E Research Associates.

U.S. Department of Commerce, Bureau of the Census. (1980). *1980 census of population: General population characteristics, United States summary* (PC80-1-81). Washington, DC: Government Printing Office.

U.S. Department of Commerce. (1991). *Survey of minority-owned business enterprises: Asian Americans, American Indians, and other minorities* (MB87-3). Washington, DC: Government Printing Office.

U.S. Department of Commerce, Bureau of the Census. (1993). *We, the American Asians.* Washington, DC: Author.

U.S. Department of Commerce. (1996). *Survey of minority-owned business enterprises: Asian Americans, American Indians, and other minorities* (MB92-3). Washington, DC: Government Printing Office.

U.S. Department of Health, Education and Welfare, Office of the Secretary. (1974). *A study of selected socio-economic characteristics of ethnic minorities based on the 1970 census: Vol. 2. Asian Americans.* Washington, DC: Author.

3

Macro/Micro Dimensions of Pilipino Immigration to the United States

Antonio J. A. Pido

Issues and Perspectives

On October 21, 1995, national, state, and chapter officials of the Filipino American National Historical Society (FANHS), as well as civic officials of Morro Bay, California, celebrated the first landing of Pilipinos[1] in what is now the United States of America, in Morro Bay, California, in 1587. On that day, a Spanish galleon entered Morro Bay. A party was sent ashore in which there were four Pilipinos, referred to in the chronicles as *Indios Luzones* (Luzon Indians). The party claimed the area for Spain. A few days later, they were attacked by the Indians, and two of the Pilipinos were killed. The rest of the party returned to the ship, which then sailed out of Morro Bay.

The first Pilipino settlement in the United States was established in 1765 in what is now Jefferson Parish, near New Orleans, Louisiana (Espina, 1988). It was an all-male settlement, which eventually died out. Note that these two incidents occurred when these areas (California and

Louisiana) were not U.S. territories. In fact, the Morro Bay incident occurred before there was a United States—about a century before the Mayflower. I have no doubt that future research will reveal similar chronicles of Pilipinos having been in what is now the American continent at the same and earlier periods.

However, immigration of Pilipinos to the United States in large numbers occurred from the early 1900s to 1935 and again from the late 1960s up to the present (Pido, 1986, pp. 74-77). This chapter will focus on these migrations. Those who immigrated from the early part of this century up to the late 1960s will be referred to as "early immigrants" and those after as the "new immigrants."[2]

The immigrants and the host peoples are the principal actors in the process of immigration and integration. The term *host society* or country (people and institutions) refers to the original settlers, starting with the indigenous population, who are followed by newer settlers—immigrants. Over time, the latter become the host society to other waves of settlers (immigrants). Prior to the colonization by Europeans of what is now the United States, the natives were the host society and the colonizers the immigrants. When the European settlers were firmly established politically, militarily, economically, socially, and culturally, they became the host society. They were then followed by succeeding voluntary and involuntary (slaves from Africa) immigrants.

There are certain macro historical, political, economic, and sociological dimensions over which the immigrants and host peoples have little or no control. Nevertheless, these macro dimensions, which change across time and space, to a great extent influence the interaction at the micro level between the immigrants and the host peoples and institutions. This chapter will examine this proposition by use of the example of Pilipino immigration to the United States.

In a comparison of the three major groups of Asian immigrants to the United States (Chinese, Japanese, and Pilipinos), the following issues may be relevant to Pilipinos:

1. Since the promulgation of the Immigration and Nationality Act of 1965, the Philippines has supplied and continues to supply the largest number of immigrants after Mexico. Yet the Philippines is not the largest country source of immigrants, nor does the 1965 act favor the Philippines particularly.

2. The Pilipinos, among the three Asian groups, were the only ones that had a long colonial experience—four centuries under Spain and half a century under the United States.

3. They were the last to immigrate to the United States, following the Chinese and Japanese.

4. Compared to the Chinese and Japanese, the Pilipinos had the lowest socioeconomic status, as reported in the U.S. censuses of population for 1970, 1980, and 1990.

Macro Dimensions of Emigration:
The Philippines

The major concerns of average Pilipinos at the turn of the century were economic survival and security (through land reform), educational opportunities for themselves and their children, social justice, and some political participation. The inequities of the system that kept them in bondage did not provide any hope for themselves and their children in the foreseeable future. Some attempted to supplement their income by off-season employment by sending family members to urban centers for low-wage employment or as domestic servants.

The short-lived republic at the end of Spanish rule in 1898 was followed by 4 years of conventional and guerrilla-type warfare against the Americans. The end of the war and establishment of a civil government in which Pilipino participation was maximized provided some political stability. However, the pre-American agrarian economic deprivation and unrest persisted. The Spanish *encomienda*—a feudal type of land tenure system—was officially abolished. But a similar oppressive and exploitative system under a new name—the *hacienda*, a type of agricultural plantation—continued—this time, under the native elite in collaboration with American economic and political interests. Most of the American administrators and politicians (in the Philippines and the United States) looked the other way because this was considered an "internal" Philippine problem. This was consistent with the pattern of American colonial administration of the Philippines. The attitude was, Let the Pilipinos govern themselves and solve their own problems (i.e., with the native elites having near absolute economic and political control over the whole country) as long as they do not interfere or threaten American economic, geopolitical, and military interests in the country and region.

There was a marked improvement in the general economy in the country with the building of new infrastructures and increased revenues from domestic and international trade. But these were mostly confined to the metropolis, and the beneficiaries were mostly the elites and the middle class emerging from commercial and governmental bureaucracies. The majority who lived on the land continued to be economically deprived, and many migrated to urban areas, adding to the large numbers of underemployed and unemployed laborers.

Some of the agrarian pressure was relieved when new lands were opened for settlement and former tenant sharecroppers were given homesteads there. Unfortunately, this was the era before agricultural extension, rural credit, and the support that small and starting farmers need. A good number of would-be landowners had to abandon their homesteads, and many became victims of *compradores* (buyers) who provided supplies at their own price and credit at high interest and who bought the farmers' products, also at the *compradores'* price. Many of the homesteaders drifted back to the cities to become urban proletariat, and some became sharecroppers again or agricultural workers.

The United States established a massive nationwide public school system in which many of the initial teachers and officials were Americans. They were popularly known as the "Thomasites" because they arrived on the transport St. Thomas (Agoncillo & Alfonso, 1967, pp. 330-331). The medium of instruction was English. Aside from the basics, the thrust was inculcating Pilipinos with American values and the Coca-Cola culture. But the system did open educational opportunities for all, whereas previously this had been a luxury that only the children of the rich could previously afford (Agoncillo & Alfonso, 1967, pp. 330-331). The education opened more opportunities for employment in government and private bureaucracies, and in some instances for higher education. Availability of educational opportunities in addition to information and propaganda about America as the land of milk and honey for the poor resulted in higher or different life expectations for a coming generation of Pilipinos. Many no longer wanted to make a living from the land as their parents did, even if the land was available. The old land

tenure system continued to prevail. In addition to having a diff\
occupational outlook, this generation of Pilipinos also had diffe.
lifestyle expectations. They were becoming oriented as consumers
ward American products. At the same time, the national economy was
not developing fast enough to satisfy real or perceived needs. It was
perceived that the only way to live like Americans was to be in America.

In brief, the general conditions of the average Pilipino did not change
much under American tutelage. Those American and Pilipino leaders
attempting social, economic, and political reforms (especially on land
tenure) were no match for the entrenched landed elite. The Americans
could have instituted changes, especially in the distribution (or redistri-
bution) of land, because they were in total control of the country. But as
long as Philippine problems did not interfere with U.S. concerns, the
Americans turned the other way—and legitimately claimed that the
Pilipinos should solve their own "internal" problems. The situation was
building up to a boiling point when across the Pacific a safety valve was
opened to ease the pressure. Before 1900, very few wealthy Pilipinos had
come to the United States as students and tourists compared to those
who went to Europe, especially Spain. Then, in the early 1900s, the
United States conducted a massive recruitment of Filipino farm labor,
complete with round-trip fares (to the United States and back to the
Philippines). In the case of the Hawaiian plantations, whole families
were recruited and given passage. This helped defuse a potential agrarian problem (Agoncillo & Alfonso, 1967; Alcantara, 1981; Karnow, 1989;
Lasker, 1969; Wolfe, 1961).

World War II brought massive destruction. Postwar reconstruction
and political independence from the United States in 1946 did not change
the situation much. Land tenure continued to be a problem, and the best
perceived way of making a decent living was getting off the land and
into higher-paid urban occupations or professions. And this could only
be done by gaining more education. Thus, the Philippines experienced
an educational boom in the decades following World War II. By the 1960s,
the Philippines had the second-highest number of college students (1,500
per 100,000 of population), exceeded only by the United States (United
Nations Educational, Scientific, and Cultural Organization, 1969). The
Philippines was showing some improvement in terms of gross national
product (GNP)-type data. But for the rest of the population, especially
for the majority who lived on the land, conditions were just as bad as

before the war. Moreover, the economy was not growing fast enough to provide jobs for the growing college-trained labor force.

Once again, emigration was perceived as a way out. Only this time, it was for a large pool of "educated proletariat" that had been building up during the decades following World War II. However, only 100 Pilipinos a year were allowed to immigrate to the United States. Once again, the situation in the Philippines was coming to a boiling point when a safety valve was opened across the Pacific to relieve some of the economic, social, and political pressure. This was the promulgation of the Immigration and Nationality Act of 1965, which raised the annual quota of immigrants from the Philippines from 100 to 20,000, plus additional quotas for certain types of immigrants. Moreover, the act was selective of the college educated and highly skilled (Pido, 1986, pp. 72-78). The act precipitated massive immigration of Filipinos to the United States—only this time, of the college educated and those with high occupational skills.

Macro Structural Dimensions of Immigration:
The United States

Toward the end of the 19th century, structural macro changes were occurring in the United States that led to the immigration of free (non-slave) nonwhites, including Pilipinos. Among these changes were the abolition of slavery, the expansion of industry and family-type farms in the North and Midwest, the expansion of the U.S. frontier to the West, the development of large-scale agribusinesses in Hawaii and the West Coast, and the development of the fish-canning industry in Alaska. The need for cheap labor was initially filled by poor, unskilled, and highly mobile white males—the "hobos" and some native Americans. Later, they were supplemented and supplanted by aliens: Mexicans, Chinese, and Japanese.

However, when these people started to demand better conditions—or worse, demand jobs and compete in businesses—they became or were perceived to be a threat to the competitive advantage of the majority and thus became problems. Their immigration had to be stopped or limited.

This resulted in the first U.S. immigration law in 1882, passed to stop or limit the immigration of nonwhites in general but the Chinese in particular (McWilliams, 1964, pp. 91-94; Takaki, 1989, pp. 111-112). This created labor shortages, especially in the plantations of Hawaii and the West Coast.

The Japanese had a policy of restricting the emigration of their people. The U.S. government convinced the Japanese government to ease this restriction and allow those who wanted to immigrate to the United States. And they did, by the thousands (McWilliams, 1964, pp. 140-144; Takaki, 1989, p. 186). They worked at the plantations for long hours, after which they still found time to cultivate plots and clear unwanted land. It did not take long for the Japanese to compete with farmers in the sale of fresh produce and horticultural products. They also wanted into the American dream, which included no longer being satisfied with the socioeconomic status accorded to them. It did not take long for anti-Japanese feelings to stir up the fears of a "Yellow Peril" left over from the anti-Chinese era.

The "Gentlemen's Agreement" in 1907 (in which Japan agreed not to issue passports to U.S.-bound Japanese) limited the immigration of the Japanese until the Immigration Act of 1924, which stopped it altogether. This racist perspective persisted in all succeeding immigration policies, laws, and actions until 1965, exacerbating the need for agricultural and cannery low-wage labor (McWilliams, 1964, pp. 144-146; Takaki, 1989, pp. 202-211, 209-210; Title 8, U.S.. Code § 1151 et. seq.).

The acquisition of the Philippines from Spain by the United States as a result of the Spanish-American War of 1896 helped meet the American demand for cheap labor. Here were a people who came from the Orient but were not exactly Orientals in the "Yellow Hordes" sense. In fact, they were dubbed "little brown brothers" by their American masters and were considered to be a mostly "primitive" people willing to work at a fraction of American wages. Moreover, because the Philippines was a colony of the United States, the Pilipinos were not, strictly speaking, aliens. Therefore, the movement of Pilipinos to the U.S. mainland and territories was an internal U.S. matter that did not involve dealing with foreign governments such as those of Mexico, China, and Japan (Lasker, 1969; McWilliams, 1939, 1964; Takaki, 1989).

Like their predecessors, the Pilipinos did not take long to realize the status accorded them by Americans. Indeed, they became acutely aware of it because they had been led to believe by their American tutors that everyone was equal in America. As the Depression of the late 1920s and early 1930s worsened, feelings and actions against the Pilipinos became more vicious. This led to a proposed law excluding Pilipinos from the United States, which did not pass. A law that did pass (An Act to Provide Means by Which Certain Filipinos Can Emigrate From the United States, 1935) was one that provided a free fare to Pilipinos who voluntarily returned to the Philippines but then were not allowed to return to the United States. Very few Pilipinos took advantage of this law. This was partly due to the improvement of the U.S. economy and partly because returning Pilipinos who were not rich were looked on as failures by their families, their friends, and the community (Bogardus, 1936; Catapusan, 1940).

The political relationships between the United States and the Philippines at the macro level that had facilitated the immigration of Pilipinos made it difficult to exclude them because, unlike the Mexicans, Chinese, and Japanese, the Pilipinos were not aliens. To have excluded the Pilipinos not only would have violated U.S. laws but also would have been inconsistent with the policy of keeping the Philippines a U.S. territory. It was therefore argued that the best way of keeping Pilipinos out of the United States was to grant the Philippines political independence. Then Pilipinos would be subject to anti-Oriental immigration laws. There were other reasons that the Philippines wanted to be independent of the United States. The elites wanted independence because they would be in charge when the colonial administrators left. The oppressed hoped that with independence they might be able to effect changes in the economic and political structures. However, a major reason for granting Philippine independence was that this would reduce the immigration of Pilipinos to the United States.

In 1935, the Philippines became a commonwealth, ostensibly an almost autonomous state, except for defense and control of the currency. Pilipino immigration to the United States was then subjected to existing quotas of national origin of 50 persons a year. After gaining "full independence" from the United States in 1946, a bilateral agreement between the Philippines and the United States increased this number to 100 a year (Grunder & Livezey, 1951, pp. 205, 226-264).

Until 1965, the "brain drain" to the United States was mostly a European problem. After 1965, it also became a problem of Third World countries such as the Philippines, which since then had the highest number of immigrants classified as "professional, technical, and kindred workers." Whether by design or not, the Immigration and Nationality Act of 1965 radically liberalized the immigration of nonwhite immigrants from the Eastern Hemisphere. But the act was also selective of immigrants with high educational and occupational credentials. For the Philippines, by definition these were those who came from the middle to upper socioeconomic classes (Bello, Lynch, & Makil, 1969; Gupta, 1973).

In general, U.S. current immigration laws are no longer racially exclusive. However, with the exception of refugees, they have the tendency to "cream off" the best from the hundreds of thousands that want to immigrate to the United States—no longer admitting "the poor and huddled masses," as the inscription at Ellis Island proclaims. During the fall election campaign of 1996, conservative (mostly Republican) politicians again used immigrants (legal and illegal) as scapegoats for real and perceived economic and social problems. None had the courage to say categorically whether they were against all immigration—including that from Europe and Canada. However, by sheer numbers, the largest targets would be Pilipinos, other Asians, and those coming from south of the U.S. border (Mexicans and others).

The Macro Implications of Pilipino Immigration to the Philippines and to the United States

Whether by design and collusion or not, the large-scale migration of the early immigrants from the Philippines to the United States benefited certain segments of the Philippines and the United States. The Philippine body politic was relieved of the pressure to effect radical social and economic reforms that would have removed the conditions that precipitated the emigration of Pilipinos, thereby maintaining the status quo to the advantage of the elite. At the same time, segments of the U.S. economy were provided with a cheap source of labor whenever and wherever there were shortages, or in jobs that Americans did not want, without having to deal with foreign governments.

The post-1965 Pilipino immigration had similar effects. Again, it relieved the Philippine leadership of undertaking economic, social, and political reforms to satisfy the demands of a large, overeducated, under-employed, and unemployed labor force. With other countries, it also provided the United States with the services of a highly skilled labor force at a time they were needed most, at a lower cost than that of hiring Americans—if the latter were even available. Thus, in collaboration with their American colleagues, combined with U.S. resources and organization, the brain-drain immigrants contributed to moving the United States ahead technologically. In the meantime, the contributing countries such as the Philippines lost the type of labor force they needed most, thereby contributing to their continued state of underdevelopment.

The Micro Ramifications of the Macro Structural Dimensions of Immigration

As posited earlier, interactions between immigrants and a host people are to some extent determined by the structural relationships between the immigrants' country of origin and the host country, as well as by the changing international situations across time.

The colonizers/immigrants, even if they are fewer in population than the host society, almost always dictate the terms on which the colonizers/immigrants interact with the host society. The European settlers, due to superiority in weapons and other factors, dominated the interaction between themselves and the natives, who either resisted or simply minimized their contact with the white settlers. Over time, the white population became the majority in population as well as economically and politically. In the case of South Africa, until recently, the original white settlers continue to control power and resources over a nonwhite population much larger than they.

Involuntary immigrants (e.g., slaves and refugees) interact on the host or dominant society's terms. Voluntary immigrants, except for a few who are wealthy or have some political power or fame (performers, scientists, etc.), almost always consciously or unconsciously immigrate and interact on the host society's terms, regardless of the macro structure between their countries of origin and the host country and the conditions on which they are allowed to immigrate. However, the more homogeneous the immigrants' culture with the host culture, the less conflict is encountered in adjusting to the host culture's terms. For example, WASP (white Anglo-Saxon Protestant) immigrants did not have the same experience in adjusting to America as the Irish, non-English-speaking immigrants from southern and eastern Europe, who were mostly Catholics. Nonwhite immigrants with non-European cultures and non-Christian religious backgrounds have had more difficulties in adjusting to the American system.

Pilipino immigration to the United States involved considerable adjustment difficulties. First, immigration was seldom fully voluntary because the alternative of not emigrating so often resulted in actual or perceived deprivation. To put it another way, barring some individual exceptions, most migrants would not have migrated if they had not had to. Second, once the Pilipinos opted to immigrate, they were not as free to participate fully in the American system as they had thought they would be. Thus, the actual or perceived necessity to immigrate on the host (American) society's terms hardly put them on an equal status with their hosts. Third, the Pilipinos had been colonized by the United States in their own land. Migration to the United States merely transferred their colonial subordinate position from their native land to that of the colonizer. In other words, if Pilipinos did not fare as well as the Americans in the Philippines, one could hardly expect them to do any better in America.

The Chinese and Japanese were allowed—in fact, induced—to immigrate to the United States for similar economic reasons and were then subjected to almost the same prejudice and discrimination. Yet among the three, the Japanese seem to have "made it" in the United States in terms of socioeconomic status (U.S. Bureau of the Census, 1972, 1983, 1993). This may be partly due to ethnic-based cultural and other factors. However, the different relationships that the United States has had with Japan, China, and the Philippines and the different socioeconomic statuses of the three Asian groups in the United States are more than just a coincidence. Among the three, the Japanese nation has had the most political, economic, and military leverage to protest the treatment of their nationals in the United States, and the Philippines has had the least.

Pilipino Responses

There may have been differences between Pilipinos and other Asian immigrants. Many of the Asian immigrants were what was referred to as "birds of passage." They came to the United States only to earn enough money to bring back to where they came from so that they could buy a farm or start a business, or to get an education in the United States so that they could get better jobs where they came from. Indeed, the Pilipino plantation workers in Hawaii were given 3-year contracts that were renewable and included the cost of fares. In effect, these immigrants were sojourners rather than settlers.

The American body politic and institutions were at least ambivalent about this. Sojourners certainly were not expected to have equal status with the majority. For as long as the nonwhite immigrants were satisfied with the status accorded them and not perceived as threats to the competitive advantage of the white majority, they were tolerated—in fact, in many cases sought after.

As sojourners, many of the Pilipinos were not concerned with their future in the United States. Their main objective was to earn a lot of money and get an education or both and return to the Philippines, the sooner the better. Discrimination, insults, and any activity short of outright violence were to be tolerated. The economic, social, and political problems of other minorities (Native Americans, African Americans, Latino Americans, and others) were not their concern. Consequently, they kept political participation, such as protests against racism, to a minimum, except in work-related activities and to protect themselves against violence. These overt political activities were reduced when wages and working conditions improved and when violence, or the threat of it, was reduced. There was some anxiety among Pilipinos that to be politically active, especially in coalition with other groups, would cause the dominant white society to associate Pilipinos with those groups. Being allowed to be temporarily or permanently in the United States was more important than being right on political and civil rights issues.

Pilipinos made conscious or unconscious attempts to be an invisible minority. The less they were noticed, the less they were perceived as threats, and the more freedom they had to pursue their goals. Or, as old immigrants who made the rounds working in Hawaii, California, Alaska, and Chicago informed many of them, they needed to develop the skills for acting, or "Uncle Tomming," to accomplish their goals. It meant taking the position that if the white Americans want to feel superior, let them, as long as we get better paid and subjected to less overt discrimination and violence. Play the role of an inferior "little brown brother" to the fullest advantage.

However, in general, U.S.-born Pilipinos no longer engage in this kind of posturing. Unlike their grandparents and parents, who behaved as "guests" lest they be deported by their hosts, and like their Asian and other minority counterparts, this generation of Pilipinos is now more assertive and demonstrative about its rights as "true Americans," in addition to being assertive about its racial, ethnic, and cultural roots.

In contrast to such American-born Pilipinos, the new "brain-drain" type of immigrants often have the same orientation to be politically invisible as the earlier, less educated immigrants had. However, unlike the early immigrants, they had a very good idea of the racial issues in the United States before they immigrated. They were more aware that they were not coming to the land of equal opportunity, at least between the races. They hoped that the improvements in civil rights in the United States and their educational and occupational credentials would place them on a better footing than the earlier immigrants. They are conscious of being nonwhite immigrants in a white-dominated society. From being a racial majority in the Philippines, they have become a racial minority among competing minorities. This puts them in an uncomfortable position in dealing with the majority and with other minority groups.

For example, many are not completely informed about and are sometimes ambivalent about affirmative action. On the basis of the inaccurate but popular perception that unqualified minorities and women can get jobs and promotions only by affirmative action, they feel that they do not need affirmative action because many are overqualified for many jobs. This perception is further based on the assumption of a real equality of opportunity or a "level playing field." There is also apprehension that affirmative action based on the percentage of a minority group in the population of an area may militate against them as well as other Asians.

Pilipinos are classified in the category of Asians and Pacific Islanders (API). The size of the API population ranges from 3% to less than 1% of the population of a geopolitical area. On several occasions, Asian state employees of Michigan expressed concerns that they could not get promoted to jobs for which they were qualified because there were already Asians in similar positions. Rightly or wrongly, they believed that the state had already reached the "quota" of Asians (somewhere under 2%). There were similar concerns due to the perception that some colleges and universities were worried that the number of Asians admitted was far exceeding their percentage of the population.

At the same time, some sympathize with other minorities who have been and continue to be deprived. They are often faced with a clash of perspectives. As individuals, they are qualified or even overqualified for the jobs they apply for or have. But as immigrants, do they have rights to jobs that other "true Americans" fought so hard for, only to have taken from them by later arrivals to this country? The situation is exacerbated by subtle and not-so-subtle attempts to pit them and other Asians (i.e., "model minorities") against blacks, Hispanics, and Native Americans.

Most post-1965 Pilipino immigrants tend to be settlers rather than sojourners, at least in initial intent. Even among those who are here on special work permits (in effect, legal sojourners), most might want to be settlers if given the opportunity. Indeed, many on student, business, or tourist visas overstay and disappear into the crowd, with the hope of being here permanently. In some circles, they are referred to as "TNTs" (*tago ng tago*, roughly translated as "playing hide-and-seek" with immigration authorities; Morales, 1974; Pido, 1986).

One of the primary goals of immigrants is to be accepted by and integrated with the host people and institutions as soon as possible. This requires compliance with the host people's codes of acceptable behavior. Such compliance may include collaboration with the host's economic and social stratification systems, as well as with overt and covert racism, by accepting the racism and other forms of discrimination they are subjected to and practicing it toward other minorities, at least temporarily.

It is not surprising that many immigrants who have not yet learned English already practice (or pretend to practice) discrimination against other minorities. In comparing notes with other Asian colleagues, it seems that Pilipinos' (and other Asians') propensity to show some form of discrimination against Africans (particularly), Hispanics, and Indians somewhat follows socioeconomic status. Thus, the more affluent one is, the greater one's tendency to show some discrimination (whether one is actually prejudiced or not). Pilipinos learn to use code words and phrases such as "welfare cheats," "teenage single mothers," and "drug addicts." They tend (or pretend) to be conservatives and to support the reactionary elements and agenda of the Republican Party. A few go to the extent of denying their racial, ethnic, and cultural heritage. Anecdotal information indicates that this syndrome of denying one's racial, ethnic, and cultural heritage can be found across the U.S. mainland. (This does not mean that it does not exist in Hawaii.) In general, it is more prevalent among first-generation immigrants and in areas with larger Pilipino as well as Asian populations. The declared motives vary from very traumatic political and emotional reasons for leaving the Philippines to a desire to "Americanize" as completely and quickly as possible, whether for perceived or actual better occupational opportunities and access to better residential communities, or simply as the price of acceptance in the white suburban cocktail circuit. Indeed, this pattern of behavior can also be observed among some of the nouveau riche in the Philippines who want to disassociate themselves from their humbler (and perhaps rural) origins and affirm their new occupational and social associations.

Setting New Perspectives

There has been a tendency among younger Pilipinos—those who immigrated as children and those who were born and raised in the United States—to perceive themselves as Americans and Pilipinos. They tend to drop the linguistic and regional origins that their parents and grandparents tried to maintain. This has also to do with the fact that the body politic and society in general have tended to accept them as Filipino Americans. Even when the earlier immigrants wanted to assimilate, they were not allowed to. They had no choice but to group themselves on the basis of their origins—language and region. Today's younger Pilipinos do not need to group themselves as Ilocanos, Bicolanos, or Warrays. They are able and allowed to integrate as one of America's ethnic groups.

Moreover, the civil rights movement of the 1950s and 1960s demonstrated the power of coalitions to promote assertiveness. Unlike their grandparents and parents, who perceived themselves as "guests" (no one forced them to come here) who were at most tolerated and at times unwelcome, Pilipino Americans are now more conscious and assertive of their place and rights in the United States. The civil rights movement also brought new civil and voting rights laws. The youth perceive themselves as legitimate members of the American household, with the same rights and privileges as other Americans. But whatever their emotional allegiance to their ethnicity and culture, it does not prevent them from full participation in America.

Nothing remains static, including racial attitudes. The 1960s brought in new opportunities for minorities, legal and otherwise. But such opportunities have appeared in the past, only to be withdrawn again and again. Starting with the mid-1990s election process, politicians again began fanning ancient prejudices that have not disappeared but merely receded. Civil rights laws and those favoring immigration, such as affirmative action, are again being questioned and indeed being changed. Immigrants are again a major target—but not all immigrants, only the nonwhites.

From recent and not-too-recent experience, there is hope that the younger Pilipino Americans can stand up to new challenges and that it is not a long leap from being Pilipino Americans to being Asian Americans. Unlike their predecessors, they will not perceive the problems of other minorities as "Negro," Chinese, Japanese, or, more recently, Vietnamese problems and therefore shy away from them. Any form of discrimination against other minorities will eventually affect all minorities, even the darlings of white suburbia. At the micro level, the issue is not just whether the immigrants (particularly racial minorities) want to integrate with American society but also to what extent they are allowed to do so by the white dominant society.

The issue, then, may be viewed at the macro level—the American body politic and institutions. Starting from the Emancipation Proclamation up to the latest civil and equal rights laws, history has demonstrated that laws alone will not change people's minds and attitudes (prejudice). However, the laws help prevent having the acting out of prejudice in forms of discrimination. Change at the macro level structures can happen, even just gradually by people acting in unison. "In unison" means not only with other minority groups but also with those in the white majority who share similar values about equality of opportunity. Indeed, there are white Americans who do not like minorities at all at the micro level. They are prejudiced. But at the macro level, they strongly believe in the ideal of equality of opportunity under the law. These individuals can be valuable allies as well.

There are virtually no Pilipino or Asian publications in the United States that do not have news items on the "first" Pilipino (or other Asian) who is appointed or elected to a position at the local, state, or national level: in government, a corporation, or a nonprofit organization. These people did not achieve this recognition merely by the support of fellow ethnics, but rather by the support of a multicultural community. Such solidarity did not happen to the Pilipino Americans because they are Pilipinos who are in America, as their parents and grandparents were, but rather because they are Americans who are Pilipinos.

Notes

1. The Philippines was named *Las Islas Filipinas* (Philippine Islands) after Felipe (Philip) II of Spain (1527-1598). Spaniards born in the Philippines of pure Spanish parentage were called *Españoles Filipinos* or *Filipinos* for short, to distinguish them from the Spaniards born in Spain, who were *Españoles Peninsulares*, or simply *peninsulares*. Those of mixed (native and foreign) parentage were referred to as *mestizos*, and those with mixed Spanish blood specifically were *creollos*. When the United States took over the country from Spain, the name of the country was Anglicized to *Philippines*, and all the native born were called Filipinos. None of the seven major Philippine linguistic groups have an "f" sound. The people refer to their country as *Pilipinas* and themselves as *Pilipinos*. This chapter will use the latter term when referring to the people and will use the English term *Philippines* when referring to the country.

2. These terms should not be confused with similar ones used in describing the U.S. immigration experience. In that terminology, "old immigrants" were those who came as early as arrival on the Mayflower, up to the early part of this century, and who were mostly of Anglo-Saxon origin. The "new immigrants" were those who came in massive numbers from the start of this century up to the 1940s and beyond. They were mostly from Mediterranean, central, and southern Europe and from Ireland.

References

An Act to Provide Means by Which Certain Filipinos Can Emigrate From the United States. 48 U.S.C. §§ 1251-1257 (1935).

Agoncillo, T. A., & Alfonso, O. M. (1967). *History of the Filipino people.* Quezon City, Philippines: Malaya.

Alcantara, R. R. (1981). *Sakada: Filipino adaptation in Hawaii.* Washington, DC: University Press of America.

Bello, W. F., Lynch, F., & Makil, P. Q. (1969). *Brain drain in the Philippines.* In W. F. Bello & A. Guzman II (Eds.), *Modernization: Its impact in the Philippines* (Institute of Philippine Culture [IPC] Paper No. 7). Manila: Ateneo de Manila University Press.

Bogardus, E. S. (1936, September-October). Filipino repatriation. *Sociology and Social Research, 21,* 67-71.

Catapusan, B. T. (1940). *The social adjustment of Filipinos in the United States.* Unpublished doctoral dissertation, University of Southern California.

Espina, M. E. (1988). *Filipinos in Louisiana.* New Orleans: A. F. Laborde.

Grunder, G. A., & Livezey, W. E. (1951). *The Philippines and the United States.* Norman: University of Oklahoma Press.

Gupta, M. L. (1973, February). Overflow of high level manpower from the Philippines. *International Labor Review, 8,* 167-191.

Immigration and Nationality Act of 1965. 8 U.S.C. § 1101 *et seq.*

Karnow, S. (1989). *In our image.* New York: Ballantine.

Lasker, B. (1969). *Filipino immigration to continental United States and Hawaii.* New York: Arno and New York Times.

McWilliams, C. (1939). *Factories in the fields.* Boston: Little, Brown.

McWilliams, C. (1964). *Brothers under the skin.* Boston: Little, Brown.

Morales, R. F. (1974). *Makibaka: The Filipino-American struggle.* Los Angeles: Mountainview.

Pido, A. J. A. (1986). *Pilipinos in America.* New York: Center for Migration Studies.

Takaki, R. (1989). *Strangers from a different shore.* New York: Penguin.

United Nations Educational, Scientific, and Cultural Organization. (1969). *UNESCO statistical yearbook 1969.* Paris: Author.

U.S. Bureau of the Census. (1972). *United States census of population: 1970* (PC(1)-C1). Washington, DC: Government Printing Office.

U.S. Bureau of the Census. (1983). *United States census of population: 1983* (PC80-1-C). Washington, DC: Government Printing Office.

U.S. Bureau of the Census. (1993). *United States census of population: 1990* (CP-2-1). Washington, DC: Government Printing Office.

Wolfe, L. (1961). *Little brown brothers.* Manila: Erewhon.

4

Colonialism's Legacy
The Inferiorizing of the Filipino

Nilda Rimonte

You must look and look until you are blind with looking,
then out of this blindness will come illumination.

Art critic and historian Bernard Berenson, on
how to tell the genuine from the fake

For generations, historians, educators, culture critics, and just about everyone else have consistently represented the Spanish conquest and colonization of the Philippines as benevolent in intent and beneficial in effect. Typical of this view is writer Nick Joaquin (1965), who rhapsodized about it as nothing less than "one of the great civilizing labors in the history of mankind" (p. 72). To Joaquin and many like him, the

AUTHOR'S NOTE: I thank Doris and John Keiser for wading through this manuscript and for their suggestions and encouragement.

imposition of Christianity and the European culture that came with it were the work of culture heroes disguised as caring missionaries and brave conquistadors. American historian John Phelan (1959), whose work the nationalist Renato Constantino enshrined in a reprint series of historical works on the Philippines, asserted not only that contact with Spain produced little damage but that it was overwhelmingly advantageous to Filipinos. Constantino (1974) himself endorsed Spanish colonial assumptions, describing pre-Hispanic Filipino culture as a virtual tabula rasa, just waiting for Spanish inscription. Like his Left colleagues who echoed Marx's position, he equated the arrival of colonialism with the fortuitous onset of modernity. Many other privileged attitude shapers and myth makers, such as the Catholic Church and the educational system, not only endorse Spanish colonialist assessment of the pre-Hispanic *tao*[1] but also accept the necessity for cultural invasion. So pervasive and persistent is this golden legend that anyone growing up in the Philippines breathes it in with the air itself.

As a result, Filipinos have never doubted the dominant view that Europeans risked their lives to voyage thousands of miles from Mexico— over largely uncharted seas, in death-defying ships, enduring the hardships of legend and nightmare, at enormous cost to the Spanish king's personal treasury—just to bring the gift of their religion. *For our own good,* the colonizers did what nobility obliged them to do.

Not surprisingly, the violence of the conquest and the oppression it engendered have been normalized, or minimized when acknowledged at all, as the natural cost of progress. If the divine mission occasionally got mixed up with violence and greed, it was only because the colonizers were merely human, their misdeeds an unfortunate result of a civilization that was otherwise superior in every other respect (Nandy, 1983). Misdeeds, in any case, were incidental and should not detract from the achievements of Spanish colonialism (Noone, 1986). Given what Filipinos were said to be like before and what they became after the Spanish arrival, the Filipinos' deferential gratitude to the West is quite an appropriate reciprocal gift, the golden legend insists.

American colonialism has been much analyzed, but a settling of accounts with Spanish colonialism has yet to be made. After Rizal (1890/1972) in the 1890s, little or no assessment has been made of Spanish colonialism's damaging psychological and cultural effects. A hundred years after Spain's departure, Filipinos are only just beginning to question what four centuries of Spanish domination have meant to them.

The golden legend is a gross misrepresentation of Filipino history. Filipinos were the intended victims, not beneficiaries, of Spanish colonialism. Deconstructed, the motive to convert the Filipinos—origin of Filipino tenderness toward the Spanish Catholic Church and by extension the Western world—was subversive of colonial purposes. It could function only as a tool of the conquest and exploitation ideology. Nothing about colonialism's violence was either accidental or incidental, contrary to the "merely human" excuse. Not only was victimization inevitable, it was the only possible result of an ideology that had at its core the intent to devalue in order to conquer and to use the conquered for self-interested purposes. Conversion was but the "metaphor . . . for conquest" (Thomas, 1994, p. 73).

Filipinos were victimized on several fronts: by the assumptions and presumptions of colonial ideology, by the very act of cultural invasion itself, by coercive cultural transformations, and by the complicit collaboration of leaders and elders who perpetuated the violence of historical distortions. How they came to accept the representation of "conquest"— which implies an oppressor and a victim—as "civilizing" and "Christianizing" is the narrative of Filipino victimization.

Denial of this past has been the source of a crippling confusion about Filipino identity and obligations to the West. In a classic case of victim blaming and of identification with the aggressor, both Western and Filipino political discourses blame colonialism's victims for colonialism's legacies—the sin of not loving themselves enough and the resulting "inauthenticity" of their culture. Some Western anthropologists are even reported to speak of Filipinos as possessing no culture of their own (Rosaldo, 1989). At least one observer traced the failures of Filipino society to a "damaged culture" (Fallows, 1987, p. 49), while deftly side-stepping the questions of how damage was done and by whom. "*Tayo ang problema!*" Manila's Cardinal Jaime Sin accused—"We are the problem!"—as if Filipino difficulties were due to misshapen genes and were unrelated to historical realities (Rimonte, 1989, p. 24).

This is more than an inconvenient fiction. Filipinos do have a problem, that burden of persistent self-hate of which many acts of anti-Filipinism are the chiefest manifestations. The condition produces an acute, destabilizing, discomfiting self-awareness, akin to that situation in which one feels ashamed, *nahihiya*. Desperate to hide a stigmatizing defect, one nevertheless feels naked, if not transparent, before the seemingly omnipotent gaze of this observing, fully clothed, opaque other. The other is the colonizer, representative of everything one regards as superior and therefore longs for.

"It is a peculiar sensation," W. E. B. DuBois (1903/1961) wrote,

> this double-consciousness, this sense of always looking at one's self through the eyes of others, of measuring one's soul by the tape of a world that looks on in amused contempt and pity. One ever feels this twoness . . . two souls, two thoughts, two unreconciled strivings, two warring ideals in one dark body whose dogged strength alone keeps it from being torn asunder. (pp. 16-17)

As DuBois and many others, such as Allport (1958), Memmi (1965), Fanon (1965), Freire (1970), and Turnbull (1962), attest, the condition is not idiosyncratic to Filipinos. It is the common fate of the oppressed, though it preys more perniciously on the educated and the acculturated.

Like the monstrous parasite in the 1986 American sci-fi horror film *Alien*, this alien other devours what it inhabits. How did it usurp its way into the Filipino? In this chapter, and as a first step toward charting the trajectory of Filipino alienation, I deconstruct Spanish colonialism's conversion motive.

Hidalguismo and the Colonial Consciousness

The term *hidalgo*, meaning "son of God," is of Arabic origin. Hispanists such as Americo Castro (1970) agree that it is the "quintessential Spanish type" (p. 185) bred by the *reconquista* (series of Spanish crusades against Muslim kingdoms; see below). *Hidalguismo* is the obsessive pursuit of status and honor, the alpha and omega of the *hidalgo's* life. According to Castro (1970), every Hispano Christian, however humble his origin, regarded himself as a potential "member of the seignorial caste, a potential *hidalgo*" (p. 197). "He was born to life with the certainty of already being what he ought to be; the rest was a matter of time and confidence" (p. 191). This conviction of innate nobility that marked him as intrinsically superior to everyone is related to the famous Spanish indolence and parasitism, about which much has been written (Ellis, 1920; Roth, 1974).

Along with castism, the Hispano Christian traced his sense of inborn nobility to purity of blood, or *limpieza de sangre*. To be *limpia* or clean was to be an "Old Christian" or be descended from one, as opposed to the "New Christians"—recently converted Muslims and Jews, considered lower caste and locally known as "pigs" (Lea, 1968; Roth, 1974). The farther down in time one could trace one's lineage, the "purer" one was. This preoccupation with being rather than doing, the belief in the primacy of faith and the irrelevance of reason, yielded the defining values that honed the *hidalgo's* conviction of superiority: religiosity, valor, courage, and individualism. As Castro (1970) wrote, "The Spaniard is the only example in Western history of man whose purpose in life is founded on the idea that the only calling worthy of a man is to be a man and nothing more" (p. 202).

Romanticized, satirized, philosophized, and psychoanalyzed, *hidalguismo* has a hoary history in Spanish culture. Embedded in *hidalguismo* and in the *reconquista* are compelling economic motives for colonial expansion overseas, as well as its ideology and contradictions. For this very reason, historians regard Spanish colonialism as the extension of the *reconquista* (Johnson, 1970; Sanchez-Albornoz, 1970).

Begun in 800, the *reconquista* was represented by Christian Spain as a religious crusade against the Muslims, the concept and underpinnings of which were derived from the Muslim concept of *jihad*, holy war (Castro, 1970; Lea, 1968; Sanchez-Albornoz, 1970). A protracted and bloody political and military struggle against the various Muslim kingdoms on the Iberian peninsula, the prize was a "reunified" Christian kingdom. In pursuit of this prize, the young Christian male was persuaded to trade his life on earth for a virtual one in paradise. If he survived, *hidalguia*—status, glory, and wealth—awaited him in the bosom of his king.

Reunification was accomplished in 1492, but the effort had cost Spain its wealth and its most productive people, the Jews and Muslims who had been either driven out or killed (Lea, 1968; Roth, 1974). Also dissipated was the energy that once fueled the fighting Christian's frenzy. He would not or could not attend to his kingdom's rebuilding, feeling destined for better things. Not surprisingly, the military and the clergy were his preferred professions, but at the *reconquista*'s end, there no longer were kingdoms to conquer, and churches had overrun Spain. Another avenue to wealth and sinecure appropriate to his personality's requirements and the era's "booty capitalism" (Johnson, 1970, p. 18) had to be found. The colonial voyages provided the answer.

Doctrines of the Conquest

According to historians of the period, the act of conquest during the *reconquista* legitimized the expropriation of lands from the defeated Muslims, at that time considered mere heretics rather than practitioners of an entirely separate religion. The Hispano Christian saw himself as simply reclaiming possessions illegally usurped by Muslims from the Christian kings. "The defeated populations were considered to be without juridical rights, subject to the victor's will, and many of them were . . . enslaved" (Johnson, 1970, p. 25). This legal precedent justified the subsequent conquests and colonization of places occupied by Muslims, such as North Africa. Territories were annexed to the Spanish Crown as if they were "various parts of the peninsula, . . . [and] title was derived from discovery or conquest" (Johnson, 1970, p. 26). The same doctrine later served Spanish colonialism's claims of ownership over newly "discovered" lands. But if Muslims were fair game because they were apostates, the indigenes of the "New World" had never even heard of Christianity and therefore could not be considered heretics; they were simply nonbelievers. What right, then, did the Spaniards have in annexing their lands? This conundrum occupied the best and the brightest of the era's legal scholars and humanists. This in turn is cited by some as "proof" that Spanish imperialism was impelled by religious rather than mercantilistic concerns (Fast & Richardson, 1979; Sanchez-Albornoz, 1970; Thomas, 1994).

What followed was a search for a doctrine acceptable to the Christian conscience to justify Spanish predations. To review this search today is to observe the forging of an ideology that created the "legitimate victim." As defined by Weis and Borges (1973, p. 92) in connection with rape victims, a "legitimate" victim is a safe victim. She is "safe" because she does not pose any hazard to the assailant. She does not blame him and cannot claim retribution, nor does she have any reason to complain. If she blames anyone, it is herself; she feels she deserves what she got.

A "legitimate victim" is made, not born. The predator shapes her into one, using social and cultural processes reinforced by institutions. Shaping begins by naming her as inferior or attributing to her certain characteristics considered inferior. What is important is "to maintain a view [of her] . . . consistent with the image of the deserving victim" (Weis & Borges, 1973, p. 100). Often considered "legitimate victims" are the poor; members of designated out-groups such as gays, prostitutes, certain ethnicities; and women. Because they "deserve" their injuries, the predators' action is justified: "Violence against them is not a crime, and the [predators] cannot be criminals" (Rimonte, 1991, p. 1316). Thus can the predator, who of course regards himself superordinate, injure another without being inconvenienced by responsibility; he may even be rewarded.

The Hostiensis doctrine was first in the effort to establish non-Christians as legitimate victims. As formulated by Cardinal Henry of Susa, "Non-Christians . . . had no right to property and their governments were illegitimate" because "all human beings were first and foremost creatures of God, [and thus] their right to possess property and to govern themselves was dependent upon divine grace" (Johnson, 1970, p. 27). Obviously, non-Christians lacked this divine grace; "therefore, it was entirely proper for the Pope, as God's representative on earth, to distribute these peoples to suitable Christian princes for evangelization and governance as he saw fit" (Johnson, 1970, p. 27). European—that is, Christian—civilization was the standard against which to measure all others.

Helpful though it was, the Hostiensis doctrine posed a potential problem to the Crown: It gave the Pope an opening to claim suzerainty over the newly discovered territories. A more suitable doctrine had to be found, beginning with St. Thomas Aquinas's contrary stipulation that

> property and self-government were not the result of grace, not a "gift of God" handed down from above, but rather the natural response of men to their need to live together in society. Although non-Christian societies . . . were imperfect in the sense that they did not know Christ, they nevertheless had as "natural" a right to property and self-government as did Christians. (Johnson, 1970, pp. 27-28)

Aquinas's principle of noninterference was good for the infidels but not for the Crown. Attempting to synthesize these competing doctrines just before America's "discovery," Juan de Torquemada and Cardinal Cajetan identified three different types of non-Christians and their appropriate treatments in Christian hands. These were, first, heretical Muslims, who "could with good conscience, be enslaved"; second, non-Muslim infidels who were converting to Christianity and could be confirmed in their freedom after conversion; and third, infidels who, refusing conversion, "were therefore to be equated with Muslims, conquered and enslaved" (Johnson, 1970, p. 28).

Considered a great humanist of his time, Francisco de Vitoria refined this synthesis even further. Maintaining that *indios* "were free men, constituting legitimate societies as St. Thomas had taught," he justified Spanish presence in their territories "not from any right to conquer non-Christian peoples, but from the natural right of nations to engage in preaching the Gospel and to enter into mutually beneficial trade relationships with all nations of the world" (Johnson, 1970, p. 29). But as Todorov (1982) shrewdly pointed out, the principle of reciprocity in trade and travel apparently invoked by this doctrine was not truly reciprocal. It did not acknowledge the indigenes' reciprocal right to circulate their ideas or religious beliefs. Nor did it reflect the reality that indigenes did not share the European drive to proselytize the world. Above all, this was a doctrine proclaimed unilaterally by Europeans, without benefit of input from the indigenes. The doctrine was calculated to privilege the Europeans. True reciprocity in the freedom to disseminate ideas would have validated the principle of equality, rendering colonialism unthinkable.

Vitoria justified the European assumption of tutelary roles and wars over and against indigenes on the basis of the latter's self-evident moral and cultural inferiority—as defined by Europeans. "Although these barbarians [i.e., indigenes] are not altogether mad," continued Vitoria,

yet they are not far from being so. They are not, or are no longer, capable of governing themselves any more than madmen or even wild beasts and animals, seeing that their food is not anymore agreeable and scarcely better than that of wild beasts; [their stupidity] is much greater than that of children and madmen in other countries. (Todorov, 1982, p. 150)

If indigenes were found to be tyrannical—if they were inclined to eat humans or have them eaten by their gods, for example, as did the Aztecs in what is now Mexico—Europeans could intervene and punish such abominations. There was no mention of parity right for indigenes to punish Europeans for their murderous habits toward Jews, Muslims, and indigenes. Racist language and convoluted logic aside, the European as lawmaker, judge, and executioner all at once aimed for absolute control over the non-European (Todorov, 1982). Henceforth, the superordinate European could compel the transformation of the other through conversion, punishment, and teaching without consent—setting the terms for the power relationship in the dyad of indigene and European.

Duplicity, Surveillance, and Spanish Motives

Spaniards came because they believed the Philippines had something they wanted: spices and gold; access to China and Japan; and, for the greater glory of the Hispano Christian, a harvest of souls and a projection of European culture onto the non-Western world. Spain came for Spain.

The economic-political motive was paramount. It rested on the desire to capitalize on the then-recent discovery of spices and precious metals in what is now Central and North America—and to control their sources. Spain was in fierce competition with Portugal. Through trade concessions in Macao and missionaries in Nagasaki, Portugal was making inroads into China and Japan. To expand territorially and commercially into these fabled lands, Spain needed to find a safe and quick return route to Mexico (Bernal, 1967; Noone, 1986). To this end, four expeditions sailed to the Philippines after Magellan's 1521 visit, culminating with Legazpi's 1565 arrival in Samar-Leyte.

Was the religious mission ever articulated? In a letter written in 1559 to the president of the Royal Audiencia in Mexico, Philip II (1965) authorized the preparations for the voyages. He defined the voyages' goals as follows: One, bring back to New Spain "some spices as a test shipment" (p. 1); two, "ascertain the return voyage" (p. 1); and three, determine the cost of the return voyage. He also specifically ordered entry into "the Philippine Islands and the other islands, . . . which are said to have spices also" (p. 2). There was no mention of a religious mission. Unmistakably, trade was on his mind, though he could not, of course, overlook the conversion aspect of the enterprise, for in exchange for exclusive ownership rights to half the globe, Spain had committed itself to Alexander VI to evangelize newly discovered populations. The Catholic Church had given the colonizers the moral cover they needed, but the silence about the religious mission is quite striking.

Translating the king's will into action items for Legazpi, the Royal Audiencia's instructions, written in 1564, contain many highly detailed and often repetitious references to spices and "rich lands" (Instruction, 1965). But over and over again, Legazpi is urged to study and thoroughly investigate newly discovered territories, the surrounding waters, and the inhabitants and their customs, economies, and languages. His compliance has earned these 16th-century colonizers the appellation of "proto-anthropologists." And like latter-day anthropologists, they depended on surveillance to penetrate new territories to serve up later for the political and economic use of their government (Spurr, 1993; Todorov, 1982). As Said (1990) put it, "This Eurocentric culture relentlessly codified and observed everything about the non-European or presumably peripheral world, in so thorough and detailed a manner as to leave no item untouched, no culture unstudied, no people and land unclaimed" (p. 72).

By contrast, Legazpi's numerous instructions refer to the religious mission only twice. After 10 pages of highly detailed instructions about other matters, the first reference appears: "In order to reach those islands and obtain the principal goal His Majesty is after—to bring to the inhabitants of those places our holy Catholic faith and to discover the return route to this New Spain to the credit of the patrimony of the Royal Crown" (Instruction, 1965, p. 20). This reference is not preceded or followed by either a ringing call to a religious crusade or a flat declaration of commitment to world evangelization. Such understatement is so atypical of Spanish rhetorical style at the time that it is tantamount to indifference and hardly reflects devotion to a religious cause. Nor does the juxtaposing of the religious mission with the political-economic goal (of discovering the return route) compel belief that all that expeditionary energy was motivated primarily, or even less entirely, by a desire to serve God.

The second reference comes 14 pages later in connection with Legazpi's instruction to cooperate with the religious who were to travel with him: "As you well know, the most important thing His Majesty desires is the spread of our holy Catholic faith and the salvation of the souls of those infidels" (Instruction, 1965, p. 34). Almost immediately, this articulation of a religious-altruistic motive is subverted by the explanation for why Legazpi's support of missionary activities is re-quired—thus revealing conversion's strategic role and utility in achiev-ing the economic-political objectives of the voyage and destabilizing the notion of the conversion project's primacy:

> In any place you will settle you will strive to help the religious . . . to enable them to communicate with the natives . . . and to go to their villages . . . and in their contact with them they will learn the local language easily. Once the religious have learned the language, they can teach the natives our holy Catholic faith, convert them to it, and make them love and obey His majesty. (Instruction, 1965, p. 34)

In this context, another major Legazpi instruction now makes sense: "Either you yourself or those whom you will designate shall upon landing take possession in the name of His majesty of the lands, islands and places you discover; and decrees and documents shall be issued and attested by the notary" (Instruction, 1965, p. 25). If the goal was to convert, there was no need to seize the inhabitants' lands. But because the real intent was to possess—to control—notarizing the seizures would leave no legal doubt that by the act of conquest based on *reconquista* precedents, the king had become lord and owner of the new territories.

Deceit has been an unfortunate part of human negotiations and arrangements. Nevertheless, its use detracts from the European claim of moral superiority, their original justification for subjugating the differ-ent. Historical documents suggest that deceit was not only part of Spanish strategy—the conversion project being an integral part of it—but that from the beginning, the Spanish expedition was based on conscious duplicities, or what Todorov (1982) called, in a related context, "the discourse of seeming" (p. 174).

King Philip II knew that the Philippines "belonged" to Portugal by virtue of the Treaty of Zaragoza brokered by Pope Alexander VI. Never-theless, he instigated Legazpi's 1565 voyage originating from Mexico. Some historians insist that the erudite cartographer Urdaneta was trou-bled on learning of the king's determination to proceed "illegally" to the Philippines (Noone, 1986). In a letter written in 1560, Urdaneta did appear to decline the king's commission to join Legazpi unless a legal basis for the voyage could be found, but he himself promptly supplied it by return mail (Urdaneta, 1965a, 1965b). He simply reminded the king of his obligation to rescue Spaniards from earlier failed expeditions who were believed to have survived on the Philippine and nearby islands. Urdaneta's "legal basis" became Legazpi's instruction to deceive. To the Portuguese in the area, Legazpi was told to misrepresent his expedition as a mere rescue operation waylaid by foul weather (Instruction, 1965).

Legazpi strategically used deceit in many other ways. On contact with the tao, he offered friendship and protection again and again. "We told the king [Tupas] and his men that . . . His majesty [Philip II] had ordered us to help you in all that we could against your enemies. . . . You will become masters of all this land and all the natives will obey you" (Rodriguez, 1965, p. 71). We know now that the last thing they became was masters of their land, and, as we have seen, this was neither a friendship of equals nor a friendship they could refuse. To refuse was to invoke the third type of non-Christian according to the Torquemada-Cajetan typology: Those who refused to be Christianized were fit to be conquered and enslaved, as the redoubtable Queen Isabella of Castile had previously authorized. Against this backdrop, the Spaniards' description of the tao—entirely without a hint of irony—as "a crafty and treacherous race" (Legazpi, 1965, p. 94) while the tao was engaged after his arrival in what we now would call guerrilla tactics, must be satisfyingly risible to contemporary critics of colonialism.

The Audiencia did remind Legazpi to be nice to the natives, but only "so they will like you and tell you always the truth" (Instruction, 1965, p. 30)—sound advice for strangers in strange lands. Continuing in this pragmatic vein, Legazpi was not to allow any slaves in the ships, not out of concern for Spanish conscience but "in order not to increase those to be fed" (p. 32). Natives were to be treated with respect and courtesy, if they were "white like ourselves" (p. 24).

Five years after their landfall in Samar-Leyte, the Europeans remained unsure about the Philippines' fate: Was Spain going to stay or not? Conditions in the new territories were highly unsatisfactory, and talk of abandoning them was rife among the invaders. Legazpi found the islands worthless—except as a gateway to China and Japan—and only for such a purpose would he recommend staying on, as he did (Legazpi, 1965; Noone, 1986).

But this is not how colonialism's golden legend reads. Every Filipino schoolchild is taught instead that the Spaniards stayed in the interest of the *tao*'s welfare. "The missionaries could have given up and gone home. . . . They preferred to stay in an attempt to redress the wrongs, though tortured by the seeming hopelessness of the situation," asserted Noone (1986). Joaquin (1965) also suggested that Spain stayed for the sake of the colony rather than the mother country. Noone was referring to the cruel mistreatment of the indigenes by the soldiers as documented in the Augustinian missionaries' 1573 memorandum to the king (Augustinian Memoranda, 1965). Moreover, Philip II's grandiose proclamation "I am the instrument of Divine Providence" (Fast & Richardson, 1979, p. 4) to justify his willingness to tolerate financial loss on account of the nonproductive colony gilded the Spanish motive, allowing apologists to argue for a spiritual—that is, altruistic—mission.

Regardless of the missionaries' stated concern and the king's self-assigned, self-aggrandizing role, Spanish tolerance for the deficit did not diminish the Spanish purpose of territorial control. By hanging on to the Philippines, Spain accomplished the opening of new trade routes between Europe and the Far East, including the Manila-Cadiz route and the Manila-Acapulco galleon trade, which ran for 200 years and made Manila (and other cities later) a major trans-shipment port. This led to other ventures such as the Manila-California coast and the Manila-Peru trade routes in 1774 (Fast & Richardson, 1979). Not only were these enterprises consistent with the expedition's original goal of commercial expansion via newly discovered routes, but they reflected that Legazpi's and Martin de Rada's recommendation to use the Philippines as an opening to the Far East was the Spanish reason for staying in the Philippines. That these ventures were only marginally successful if they were not downright failures is a separate issue. As with the 19th-century imperialists, a failed investment did not make Spanish motives less economic and political (Nandy, 1983). Nor did it alter the fact that they intended to, and did, establish a colonial situation in the Philippines.

Contributing to the obfuscation of true Spanish motives is the economic underdevelopment of the Philippines after nearly 350 years of colonization. Instead of evidence of commercial development, Spain's most lasting tangible imprint on Filipinos has been the Spanish Catholic worldview and language. This thin overlay of European culture resulted in the hybridization of indigenous cultural, religious, and linguistic

practices, reproachably Western to neighboring Asians and confusing to
Filipinos. All these have helped shape the notion that Spain was interested only in saving souls, rather than in exploiting the Philippines.
Joaquin (1965), usually an ardent critic of American imperialism, converted a major Spanish failing into a badge of honor and proclaimed:
"Spain's economic legacy was as nearly disinterested as any act in this
selfish world can be" (p. 72).

Yet what Joaquin regarded as the results of Spanish selflessness are
more consistent with results one might expect from the legendary Spanish predilection for indolence and parasitism, combined with what
Spanish philosopher Unamuno deplored as "ideophobia" or lack of
intellectual curiosity among his people (Ellis, 1920, p. 410; also Castro,
1970; Roth, 1974). Until the mid-1800s, the Spaniards showed neither will
nor skill in developing the colony. Not until 1776, with the arrival of
Governor Basco y Vargas and with fierce pressures from English traders,
was there any attempt to begin to develop the country's agricultural
potentials (Constantino, 1975; Fast & Richardson, 1979). The only commercial enterprise organized with some success was the previously
mentioned galleon trade. For Spaniards in Manila, the galleon trade was
singularly suitable: It required only graft (plentiful), capital (frequently
borrowed or extorted from the local Chinese), and the luck of good
weather (courtesy of divine intervention). Of ingenuity and hard work
it had no need. The Spaniards, after all, did not come to the islands to
become merchants or farmers; they were *hidalgos*.

Conversion as Moral Cover

Perhaps most confusing about the conversion motive is its implication
of altruism. Filipinos regard themselves fortunate for having fallen into
the hands of the religious Spaniards instead of the sheerly mercantilistic
English or Dutch. Obscured by the claim of altruism is the compulsory
and consequently dehumanizing nature of conversion. The Spaniard, we
remember, was possessed by a peculiar sense of nobility, which convinced him that despite his unappeasable hunger for gold, he was a
hidalgo—son of God—intrinsically superior to everyone else and vested

with a special obligation and dispensation to shape and dominate his presumed inferiors (Castro, 1970).

Mirroring this tension between tyranny and altruism was the behavior of those charged with carrying out colonial intentions. Missionary and soldier-bureaucrat shared the will and the goal to dominate the tao, but pursuing separate and clashing priorities, they differed in strategies and constantly undermined each other. The history of Spain in the Philippines, as elsewhere—Yucatan, for example—is a history of this power struggle. Although this must have been confusing to the colonized, in the end both missionary and soldier won out. The missionary, through nearly exclusive control over the tao, kept the colony safe and secure for the soldier-bureaucrat to administer (Abella, 1971). Popular (and even scholarly) interpretation of this tension, however, favored the missionary—mythicized as the good guy defending the helpless tao against the villainous soldier-bureaucrat besotted with greed—thereby further burnishing the golden legend.

Could the Spaniards have represented the expeditionary voyages in terms less glorious than "Christianizing" and "civilizing"? Not very likely. Truth in advertising might have made it difficult to appeal to men whose skills were urgently needed, such as the cartographer Urdaneta and mathematician Martin de Rada, who also happened to be, in their fashion, men of conscience. The *hidalgo* in the Spaniard would have found no honor in a call to adventure that was openly predatory, even if his eye was riveted to the gold doubloon on the masthead. It is equally difficult to imagine how the Spaniards could have easily gained a toehold on the islands if they had been more transparent.

There were other pragmatic imperatives for the conversion motive.

Conversion as Ideology

Conversion as a moral cover was not just a strategy for establishing a colonial situation. It was an ideology that served an important function for the colonizer in resolving his ethical doubts. As I have used the concept throughout this chapter, ideology is a way of construing the world that gives justification to one's goals and motives, providing license to act on these goals and motives and legitimating actions and their consequences (Farganis, 1986). Commonly expressed in formulaic expressions such as "the rightness of our cause" and "God is on our side!" its purpose is to provide the confidence to wrest and to possess. It is a way of organizing reality that begins with the act of naming, defining, differentiating, to set apart a people or a culture or even an idea, using the gaze as "the active instrument of construction, order and arrangement" (Spurr, 1993, p. 15). In this sense, to formulate an ideology is to create a "legitimate" victim.

The self-styled representative of European civilization could not afford to be perceived as morally deficient by those he had come to punish and transform (Nandy, 1983). Besides giving him the moral cover he needed, conversion allowed him to possess the "inferior other" without violating his conscience excessively. Conversion was a means to mitigate the oppressiveness of colonization.

Indications of ethical reservations meant that the colonizer was not a total monster. A very small handful of individuals such as Las Casas stand out as defenders of the oppressed—though Las Casas' ideology is still questionable. In addition to softening the harshness of colonial rule, ethical reservations expressed through "the king's conscience" and the missionaries' paternalism had the effect of binding the colonized to the colonizer, as often happens to victims of oppression who experience kindness intermittent with cruelty (Graham, Rawlings, & Rimini, 1990). For 40 years after conquest, the debate about the right of the Spaniard to claim sovereignty over the indigenes raged in the Philippines, once again cited by some as argument for a religious Spanish colonialism (Fast & Richardson, 1979). Occasioned by the rivalry between the missionaries and the *encomenderos* over the collection of tributes or taxes, the debate did not concern issues such as the right of the indigenes to refuse conversion or the principle of noninterference. The debate's subtext was the proper guardian over the tao: Who should it be? The soldier-bureaucrat turned *encomendero* advanced the king's interest against the missionary's assertion of the pope's. To resolve the matter, Domingo de Salazar, first Bishop of Manila, convened the chiefs of the tao and asked them to seek "voluntarily" a pact with the Spanish king for mutual protection against the infidels and to elect him as natural sovereign (Bernal, 1967; Constantino, 1975). As in the Yucatan and Mexico, local chiefs who had turned Spanish agents received special privileges, such as exemption

from compulsory labor and payment of tributes. By this time in Ma
in 1591, about 600,000 of the estimated 800,000 tao then inhabiting the
islands had been converted, or in any case baptized (Bernal, 1967; Fast
& Richardson, 1979). Besides strengthening the Spanish pretensions
to a religious mission, it could now be claimed, as a result of the synod,
that the tao themselves asked for Christianity, in a sense colluding with
the colonizers and to that extent becoming responsible for their own
oppression.

Christianizing Versus Colonizing

Christianity rests on a belief in human equality and mutability; it must,
or it cannot be the universal church that it claims to be. Literally anyone
is eligible for membership and qualified for admission to heaven, assum-
ing compliance with published rules. In effect, conversion promises to
bridge distance and erase difference between the colonizer and the
colonized.

Hispanicizing/civilizing devolves on the same assumptions and
accomplishes the same objective. It means transforming the tao, re-creating
her in the image and likeness of the colonizer, or re-creating the European
in the tao, so that tao and colonizer can finally gaze at each other as
equals—even if only on European terms.

But both Christianizing and civilizing objectives clash directly with
colonialism's agenda. Colonial ideology is premised on establishing
hierarchies, on distancing and maintaining distance. To erase the indigenes through extermination is economically senseless—as the Spaniards learned to their regret from their slaughter of the Antilles Indians.
Nor does it serve their political purpose, as it leaves them no one to rule.
Exactly the same can be said of erasure by Europeanizing. Given the
relentlessly reciprocal (Sartre, 1965) nature of this convoluted relationship, the colonizer would vanish if the colonized perished. Conver-
sion/civilizing objectives, carried to their logical conclusion, would
subvert colonial purposes.

Conversion could be used to serve colonial purposes by only partly
transforming the tao. Partial transformation would render them more

intelligible to the colonizer, their opacity made transparent, their strangeness made familiar, but they would never be accorded European status, ensuring their perpetual subservience and prolonging their "spiritual childhood." Membership in the colonizer's church would partially transform the tao. It would give the tao a false sense of acceptance as the master's equals, rendering them more accepting of colonization. Plainly, to convert the indigene was to domesticate the "wild" or the "savage." Conversion was a strategy of appropriation—and containment.

Foregrounded in colonial ideology, Spanish racism could not have accommodated the assimilationist or egalitarian notions of the conversion motive. After nearly 350 years of Christianity in the Philippines, Rizal—wealthy, educated, Spanish speaking, and Europeanized—was caned and thrown into jail for failing to salute a member of the local police. Until the 1896 Revolution, Filipinos had to get off the sidewalk when encountering a Spaniard. Similarly, the Spaniards could not accept as their equals the converted Muslim and Jew, more kin to them than all the indigenes of the world. Though their work in Mexico and elsewhere must have desensitized them to indigenes as the embodiment of cultural and racial difference, the tao was still "more different" than either Muslim or Jew.

The colonizers sapped indigenous sources of cultural vitality by debasing those that had survived uprooting. In addition, by refusing to diffuse literacy and Spanish, the language of power, and by the active cultivation of anti-intellectualism, the colonizers impoverished the tao intellectually and culturally. Deliberately isolating the victim is a common tactic in oppression, as can often be seen in wife abuse, among other abuses. As well as reflecting colonizer anxiety about the colonized's emancipation, isolation ensured that the missionary, bilingual and in control of the tao's mind through the confessional and nearly all other aspects of life, remained the tao's only link to the outside world (Abella, 1971). Trapped in the colonial enclosure, the victims became dependent and docile, divided by language and retarded by illiteracy. Through conversion, the colonizers resolved the inherent contradiction in their colonial objectives in the only possible way: They Christianized without Hispanicizing.

Were one to accept the view that the Spaniards were impelled by a religious mission rather than by economics and the will to dominate, the claim of altruism would still remain insupportable. Labors for the greater glory of the Christian God translated into the greater glory of the *hidalgo* or the Hispano Christian. *Hidalguismo* is racist and self-regarding, the longing for glory twin to expectations of gold. This "undeterred and unrelenting Eurocentricism," as Said (1990) puts it, "subordinated the tao to the culture and indeed the very idea of white, Christian Europe (p. 72).

Conclusion

Colonialism or a colonial situation is the

> domination imposed by a foreign minority racially and culturally different, over a materially weaker indigenous majority in the name of a racial or ethnic and cultural superiority. . . . A set of relations is put into place between two different cultures, antagonized by the "instrumental role" the colonized is compelled to play. (Spurr, 1993, p. 6)

It begins with dehumanizing cultural invasion (Freire, 1970). First, the invader deprives the invaded of her freedom;[2] then he inscribes himself on the victim, whom he regards as no more than part of the environment. Cut off from her cultural memories yet not entirely deracinated, the victim becomes detribalized or "inauthentic" (p. 50), Freire's preferred word. In a complex and dynamic process that Memmi (1965) so lucidly described, the colonized develops for the colonizer both love and hate, mirroring her shame and hate for herself and leading to other grotesqueries. Such "traits due to victimization" (Allport, 1958, p. 138) are central to DuBois's (1903/1961) notion of "double-consciousness" (p. 16). However it is named, the condition describes the process of self-estrangement—of alienation—once, and for good reason, psychiatric parlance for insanity. Paralysis and other forms of maladaptations set in, as documented by anthropologists observing the effects of asymmetrical and violent culture contacts (Gillen, 1948; Redfield, 1953; Turnbull, 1962). Describing the sociocultural dislocation in the wake of colonization, Cushner (1971), alone among students of the Philippines under Spain, contradicted the hegemonic view of Filipino-Spanish entanglement as an unqualified boon to Filipinos.

Fanon (1965) summarized both process and effect eloquently: "Colonialism is not satisfied merely with holding a people in its grip and emptying the native's brain of all form and content. By a kind of perverted logic, it turns to the past of the people, and distorts, disfigures and destroys it" (p. 210).

Nearly 80 years before Fanon wrote these words, and before Freire described the process of alienation in the context of colonialism, Filipino insurgent and polymath Jose Rizal (1889/1972) described the Philippine predicament under Spain:

> Then began a new era for the Filipinos; little by little they lost their old traditions, the mementos of their past; they gave up their writing, their songs, their poems, their laws in order to learn by rote other doctrines which they did not understand, another morality, another aesthetics different from those inspired by their climate and their manner of thinking. Then they declined, degrading themselves in their own eyes; they became ashamed of what was their own; they began to admire and praise whatever was foreign and incomprehensible; their spirit was dismayed and it surrendered [to] . . . this disgust of themselves. (pp. 130-131)

Rizal (1890/1972) acknowledged that indolence—the infamous Spanish malediction of the Filipino—was a problem in his time. But he did not propose a "moral recovery program," as the Manila orthodoxy did nearly a century later in the aftermath of the People Power Revolution (Licuanan, 1994, p. 35), as the cure for the country's ills. That would have been too simplistic a solution for a problem so complex. Instead, he proposed cultivating a historical awareness, demonstrating it himself in all his work, so that "instead of regarding [indolence] as the cause of the backwardness and disorder, we should regard it as the effect of disorder and backwardness" (Rizal, 1890/1972, p. 259). He traced the so-called Filipino inferiority to the "daily and constant plucking of the soul so that it [will] not fly to the region of light, [which] drains the energies [and] paralyzes all tendency towards advancement, . . . [so that] at the least strife a man gives up without fighting" (p. 259).

Rizal had accurately described the sense of powerlessness rooted in victimization: the price Filipinos paid—and still pay—for the privilege of contact with Spain. Their compulsory transformation "from *indio* to

Filipino," misrepresented as their particular accomplishment (Abella, 1971; Joaquin, 1965), describes instead the process of their inferiorizing.

Filipinos were victims and did not know it. Too many were invested in their not knowing: the powerful Catholic Church, which stood a chance of being repudiated; the Americans, for obvious reasons; and, of course, themselves, or rather, the alien in them—Catholic, educated, English speaking—who viewed their Christianization and superficial Europeanization as the very gift of heaven. Source of their confusion ever since, the misrepresentation of their history has been used to subjugate them and keep them subjugated. It denies the enduring damage done to their culture. It endorses the essentialist myths that their problems are entirely due to who they are: that history has little to do with them and the problems they confront; that the only way for them to solve their problems is to change themselves; that if they have not changed themselves yet, it is because they are too lazy or too cheerful or too ignorant or too feckless or too sinful, having strayed from the prescribed Catholic path of righteousness.

To know would have required them to confront their alien and to question the Spanish version of Filipino reality. The 1896 Revolution had this for a major task, but it lay unfinished after the American armada inconveniently docked at Manila Bay. Acknowledging themselves as victims and understanding how they were victimized are today the most urgent challenges for Filipinos everywhere. Choosing what to do with this knowledge is the next. What they choose will determine if they can ever change the way they relate to themselves and, less important, to the West.

Notes

1. The Tagalog word *tao* simply means "person," "people," or "humans," which is what precontact Filipinos called themselves. I find this term, like the neutral term *indigene*, more appropriate than the Spanish-given *indio*, which, like *native*, has been encrusted with connotations of "inferior" and "primitive."

2. Historical narratives traditionally and uniformly refer to the precontact person as "he," as if women did not exist then. I feminize the precontact indigene because if women did not bear the brunt of colonial oppression, they shared it at least equally with men.

References

Abella, D. (1971). From indio to Filipino. In D. Abella, *From indio to Filipino and some historical works by Domingo Abella*. Manila: n.p.

Allport, G. (1958). *The nature of prejudice*. New York: Anchor.

Augustinian memoranda. (1965). In Filipiniana Book Guild (Ed.), *The colonization and conquest of the Philippines by Spain: Some contemporary source documents*. Manila: Filipiniana Book Guild.

Bernal, R. (1967). *Prologue to Philippine history*. Manila: Solidaridad.

Castro, A. (1970). The Spanish sense of nobility. In H. B. Johnson (Ed.), *From reconquest to empire* (pp. 189-208). New York: Knopf.

Constantino, R. (1974). *Identity and consciousness: The Philippine experience*. Quezon City, Philippines: R. C. Constantino.

Constantino, R. (1975). *The Philippines: A past revisited: Vol. 1. Pre-Spanish-1941*. Quezon City, Philippines: R. C. Constantino.

Cushner, N. (1971). *Spain in the Philippines: From conquest to revolution*. Quezon City, Philippines: Ateneo de Manila University Press.

DuBois, W. E. B. (1961). *The souls of black folk*. New York: Fawcett. (Original work published 1903)

Ellis, H. (1920). *The soul of Spain*. Boston: Houghton Mifflin.

Fallows, J. (1987, November). A damaged culture. *Atlantic Monthly*, pp. 49-58.

Fanon, F. (1965). *The wretched of the earth*. New York: Grove.

Farganis, S. (1986). *The social reconstruction of the feminine character*. Totowa, NJ: Rowman & Littlefield.

Fast, J., & Richardson, J. (1979). *Roots of dependency*. Quezon City, Philippines: Foundation for Nationalist Studies.

Freire, P. (1970). *Pedagogy of the oppressed*. New York: Continuum.

Gillen, J. (1948). *The ways of man*. New York: Knopf.

Graham, D., Rawlings, E., & Rimini, N. (1990). Survivors of terror: Battered women, hostages and the Stockholm syndrome. In K. Yllö & M. Bograd (Eds.), *Feminist perspectives on wife abuse*. Newbury Park, CA: Sage.

Instruction to Miguel Lopez de Legazpi from the Royal Audiencia of New Spain. (1965). In Filipiana Book Guild (Ed.), *The colonization and conquest of the Philippines by Spain: Some contemporary source documents*. Manila: Filipiniana Book Guild.

Joaquin, N. [Quijano de Manila, pseud.] (1965, May 1). Ikon, friar and conquistador. *Philippines Free Press*, pp. 7, 70, 72, 85-86.

Johnson, H. B. (1970). Introduction. In H. B. Johnson (Ed.), *From reconquest to empire*. New York: Knopf.

Lea, H. C. (1968). *The Moriscos of Spain: Their conversion and expulsion*. New York: Burt Franklin.

Legazpi, M. L. de. (1965). Relation of the voyage to the Philippines. In Filipiana Book Guild (Ed.), *The colonization and conquest of the Philippines by Spain: Some contemporary source documents*. Manila: Filipiniana Book Guild.

Licuanan, P. (1994). A moral recovery program: Building a people—building a nation. In M. B. Dy (Ed.), *Values in Philippine culture and education: Cultural heritage and contemporary change: Vol. 7. Asia*. Washington, DC: Council for Research in Values and Philosophy.

Memmi, A. (1965). *The colonizer and the colonized.* Boston: Beacon.

Nandy, A. (1983). *The intimate enemy.* New York: Oxford University Press.

Noone, M. (1986). *The discovery and conquest of the Philippines* (Vol. 1). Manila: Historical Conservation Society.

Phelan, J. L. (1959). *The Hispanization of the Philippines.* Madison: University of Wisconsin Press.

Philip II. (1965). Philip II to Luis de Velasco, 1559. In Filipiana Book Guild (Ed.), *The colonization and conquest of the Philippines by Spain: Some contemporary source documents.* Manila: Filipiniana Book Guild.

Redfield, R. (1953). *The primitive world and its transformations.* New York: Cornell.

Rimonte, N. (1989, June 1). Wounded by civilization. *Philippine-American News,* p. 24.

Rimonte, N. (1991). A question of culture: Cultural approval of violence against women in the Pacific Asian community and the cultural defense. *Stanford Law Review, 43,* 1311-1326.

Rizal, J. (1972). The Philippines a century hence. In National Historical Commission (Ed.), *Political and historical writings* (Vol. 7, pp. 130-163). Manila: National Historical Commission. (Original work published 1889)

Rizal, J. (1972). The indolence of the Filipino. In National Historical Commission (Ed.), *Political and historical writings* (Vol. 7, pp. 229-259). Manila: National Historical Commission. (Original work published 1890)

Rodriguez, E. (1965). Legazpi's voyage of discovery and conquest of the Philippines, 1564-1565. In Filipiana Book Guild (Ed.), *The colonization and conquest of the Philippines by Spain: Some contemporary source documents.* Manila: Filipiniana Book Guild.

Rosaldo, R. (1989). Imperialist nostalgia. In *Culture and truth: The remaking of social analysis.* Boston: Beacon.

Roth, C. (1974). *A history of the Marranos.* New York: Schocken.

Said, E. (1990). Yeats and decolonization. In T. Eagleton, F. Jameson, & E. Said, *Nationalism, colonialism and literature.* Minneapolis: University of Minnesota Press.

Sanchez-Albornoz, C. (1970). The continuing tradition of reconquest. In H. B. Johnson (Ed.), *From reconquest to empire.* New York: Knopf.

Sartre, J.-P. (1965). Introduction. In A. Memmi (Ed.), *The colonizer and the colonized.* Boston: Beacon.

Spurr, D. (1993). *The rhetoric of empire.* Durham, NC: Duke University Press.

Thomas, N. (1994). *Colonialism's culture.* Princeton, NJ: Princeton University Press.

Todorov, T. (1982). *The conquest of America.* New York: Harper Colophon.

Turnbull, C. (1962). *The lonely African.* New York: Touchstone.

Urdaneta, A. de. (1965a). To Philip II, 1560. In Filipiana Book Guild (Ed.), *The colonization and conquest of the Philippines by Spain: Some contemporary source documents.* Manila: Filipiniana Book Guild.

Urdaneta, A. de. (1965b). To Philip II, ca. 1560. In Filipiana Book Guild (Ed.), *The colonization and conquest of the Philippines by Spain: Some contemporary source documents.* Manila: Filipiniana Book Guild.

Weis, K., & Borges, S. (1973). Victimology and rape: The case of the legitimate victim. *Issues in Criminology, 9,* 71-115.

5

Coming Full Circle
Narratives of Decolonization Among Post-1965 Filipino Americans

Leny Mendoza Strobel

S tudies about the Filipino American community show that when
compared to the Chinese American, Japanese American, and lately
Korean American communities, it lags behind these groups in areas such
as economic mobility, representation in higher education, community
development, and political clout (Cabezas, Shinagawa, & Kawaguchi, 1987;
Chan, 1991; Kitano & Daniels, 1988; Waugh & Chin, 1989). However, these
findings must be contextualized to show that this perceived marginality is
the result of the interdependent relationships between variables such as
the structural and historical determinants of immigration, the consequences of the United States-Philippines colonial relationship, the global
capitalist system that influences the movement of peoples from poor to
affluent countries, and the political and historical events in the United
States that mark the timing of Filipino immigration to the United States.

AUTHOR'S NOTE: Material from the interviews and discussions with Ruth Constantino, Teresa Ejanda, Cheryl Elacio, Peter Golpeo, Laurie Quillopo, Michelle Bautista,
Marissa Felizardo, and Luz De Leon is used with their permission.

The location and situation of Filipino Americans within this larger context may lead to a broader, more accurate perspective. The Filipino American scholar E. San Juan Jr. (1992) wrote that the work that needs to be done is to articulate the silence and invisibility of the Filipino in the United States. This project requires a critical historical consciousness that challenges the master narratives that have externally defined the Filipino/Filipino American. I propose that the development of critical consciousness is facilitated by the process of decolonization.

Context of the Study

The study described in this chapter is about Filipino Americans coming full circle through a process of decolonization. Decolonization is a process of reconnecting with the past to understand the present and be able to envision the future. It is a process that makes the mythical and historical past available to the present. Decolonization strengthens the cultural connection to the Filipino indigenous culture as a source of grounding. Decolonization promotes the cultural and spiritual connection to one's *kapwa* (fellow beings), making it possible to identify with one's people and history despite personal, generational, educational, economic, class, and other forms of difference.

Decolonization studies span many centuries and many postcolonial countries. The seminal works of Freire (1970, 1985), Fanon (1963), and Memmi (1965) have shaped the theoretical foundations of decolonization and postcolonial movements. These works describe the consequences of colonization in both the colonizer and the colonized. Freire's work discussed the need for the colonized to develop critical consciousness whereby they come to understand the process of dehumanization that made their colonization possible. The violence wrought on the psyche of colonized peoples has been called internalized oppression: the learned self-hatred when they start to believe that they are not as good as their colonizers. The work of Filipino and Filipino American scholars today also contributes to the understanding of decolonization and postcoloniality (Alejo, 1990; Campomanes, 1995; Enriquez, 1990a, 1990b, 1992; Gonzalez, 1992, 1995; Ileto, 1979; Rafael, 1988; San Juan, 1995).

The Filipino writer N. V. M. Gonzalez (1992) described decolonization as a "confrontation with our many bankruptcies . . . spewed out of
the lahar of colonizations" (p. 55). Decolonization is a psychological and
physical process that enables the colonized to understand and overcome
the depths of alienation and marginalization caused by colonization. By
transforming consciousness through the reclamation of one's cultural
self and the recovery and healing of traumatic memory, the colonized can
become agents of their own destiny. Decolonization is a necessary phase in
the development of a healthy Filipino American cultural identity in the
United States. The critical consciousness that develops from the decolonization process is capable of grasping the political and social implications of one's position within the relationships of power in society.

Conscious decolonization is a source of courage and agency to
choose and act in ways that uplift the Filipino American community and
engage and contest the dominating aspects of white culture. To understand that culture is a site of ideological struggle is to develop the ability
to become a border crosser in order to build coalitions with other
oppressed groups and the ability to use one's position as a starting point
for dialogue with people similarly located.

This study begins to articulate the process of decolonization as it has
been observed in the experience of a segment of post-1965 Filipino
Americans, namely Filipino American college students and community
and cultural leaders in Northern California. I used the participatory
research method and its parallel, *pagtatanung-tanong:* an indigenous
Filipino research method grounded on the Filipino core values of *pakikiramdam* (shared perception) and *pakikipagkapwa-tao* (shared identity;
Enriquez, 1990a, 1990b; Pe-Pua, 1990).

Research Method

There were eight participants in this study. Over a period of more than
a year (spring 1995 to spring 1996), they engaged in in-depth dialogues,
interviews, and other related activities, such as casual visits, eating
together, and socializing together, to discuss and write about their decolonization experience. There were seven women and one man, ranging
in age from 19 to 48 years old; most of them are "1.5 generation"—that

is, they came to this country when they were children. The selection of participants was not gender based; it was based on their willingness to make the necessary commitment to the research project. With their permission, their real names are used in this study: Ruth Constantino (35), Teresa Ejanda (22), Cheryl Elacio (19), Peter Golpeo (24), Laurie Quillopo (21), Michelle Bautista (22), Marissa Felizardo (26), and Luz De Leon (48). The study required each participant to keep a journal for a year and to participate in structured interviews, informal dialogues, and a group discussion with all the participants. The researcher documented all aspects of the research project. Transcripts of the interviews, dialogues, and the group discussion were returned to each participant for further input and revisions. For a final product, the participants were asked to rewrite the transcripts in the form of personal narratives.

The final phase of the study was an all-day group discussion facilitated by the researcher. In the group, each participant generated the themes from his or her personal narrative, and further discussion followed. After the group discussion, the researcher reviewed all the materials from the study—the transcripts from the interviews and informal dialogues, the personal narratives, and the transcript from the group discussion—in order to weave all the various generative themes.

The research questions in this study were related to (a) the manifestations of decolonization; (b) the turning points in the participants' lives that created the need to reconnect or rediscover their ethnic roots as Filipinos; (c) what the participants did to meet the needs of decolonization; (d) the role of parents, the Filipino community, the educational system, and popular culture in decolonization; and (e) the patterns and commonalities in the participants' experiences.

Results of the Study

In this chapter,[1] I present five of the most important generative themes that emerged from the study: (a) the affective content of decolonization, (b) the power of naming and telling, (c) the need for Filipino cultural and historical knowledge, (d) the role of language and memory, and (e) the role of Filipino spirituality. Table 5.1 summarizes the framework for decolonization.

TABLE 5.1   Framework of Decolonization

Naming:

- To decolonize is to be able to name internalized oppression, shame, inferiority, confusion, anger.
- To decolonize is to acquire cognitive knowledge about Filipino culture and history.
- To decolonize is to understand the meaning of "loss of cultural memory" and its consequences.
- To decolonize is to understand how the loss of language affects Filipino identity.
- To decolonize is to heal the self, heal the culture.
- To decolonize is to name the oppressor and the oppressive social structures.
- To decolonize is to recognize the orality of Filipino culture.

Reflection:

- To decolonize is to develop the ability to question one's reality as constructed by colonial narratives.
- To decolonize is to develop critical consciousness that can understand the consequences of silence and invisibility.
- To decolonize is to understand the need to recover one's cultural and personal memory.
- To decolonize is to understand the generational gap as being constituted by historical realities that shape each generation's experiences.
- To decolonize is to understand ideological struggles within a multicultural context and the relationships of power within these struggles.
- To decolonize is to understand the need for connection with the parent culture.
- To decolonize is to ask: Where do I go from here?

Action:

- To decolonize is to decide to give back to the Filipino American community.
- To decolonize is to learn to question.
- To decolonize is to support and become involved in developing community institutions.
- To decolonize is to take leadership positions in moving the Filipino American community toward visibility and empowerment.
- To decolonize is to tell and write one's story, that in the telling and writing, others may be encouraged to tell their own.

The Generative Themes

The Affective Content of Decolonization

Decolonization is an emotional process. It stirs up feelings of anger, betrayal, confusion, doubt, and anxiety. Simultaneously, it feels empowering and inspiring to name a process that for some participants began years before this research project started.

Peter and Cheryl felt that they were in an angry stage because they were realizing, for the first time, the losses associated with colonization. Peter said, "I think I am going through an angry stage. I'm mad that so much of my history has been deprived of me. But I don't want this anger to completely take over me and blind me of what I need to do."

Michelle responded to Peter and Cheryl by identifying with their anger and went on to describe how she was able to overcome it:

> Once I got over the anger, it was a matter of building something out of that. I tried to figure out what I need. How do I look for the knowledge, what could I find, where to meet people? . . . It's hard being angry because life is so much nicer when you aren't. Life is less complicated and confusing, but once you pass that you have to keep going because you can't go back to the time when you didn't care.

Decolonization allowed participants to name and acknowledge their feelings of denial, shame, insecurity, loneliness, and inferiority about being Filipino. The participants gave examples of how these feelings manifest themselves both in themselves and in other Filipino Americans they have observed. As Marissa described it,

> My idea at that time of Filipino culture and identity was split into two forms: the FOB (fresh-off-the-boat) and the Filipino American. I didn't associate with FOBs. They were backward, had accents, and just acted weird. . . . Then there was me, the "non-FOB," who spoke perfect English, born and raised here, had only white friends. . . . I was "white" in every way except for the color of my skin, my nose and eyes. . . . I hate to admit it, but I have been an accomplice to the cruel acts that have been perpetrated against Filipinos. But I too have been a victim because I have lost a lot and have given up in my desire to fit in. I chose the easy way of living, never challenging the preconceptions set up by Western culture.

The awareness of losses under colonialism elicits powerful emotions. Ruth recalled that she felt angry and betrayed for not knowing about her father's past. Through the piecing together of his memorabilia, his unfinished stories, Ruth was able to understand the pain behind her father's silence. All the participants had similar feelings of loss and pain that they had begun to process. The acknowledgment of these emotions signifies the emergence from the culture of silence. As the participants shared these emotions with each other, there was also the recognition that these emotions were giving them a voice.

Luz, the director of Philippine Resource Center in San Francisco, reassured the participants that anger is a "common and legitimate reaction to the 'loss of memory' and not being able to access that memory." She encouraged students to acknowledge their strong emotions. She also said, "You should have some peace in your heart to nurture the culture that you know would be good for the community. Our community is segmented or parsed, so the work is difficult. So the pain you feel is legitimate, but it is the pain of childbirth; you are becoming."

The metaphor of decolonization as childbirth is powerful. It signals the transition from naive consciousness to critical consciousness. The knowledge that something good is being born enables the participant to bear the pain. As the positive and negative emotions were recognized and named, the participants were able to acknowledge that their feelings were legitimate and were related to other variables other than a sense of guilt or shame over being Filipino or Filipino American.

The participants also talked about feeling tired and exhausted because of the heightened awareness of the things that need to be done in the Filipino American community and trying to do as much as one can. Peter expressed frustration at having to explain himself constantly to friends who did not understand and therefore resented that everything Peter did was related to his Filipino culture. His friends perceived this as an attempt to separate himself that was therefore un-American. Laurie felt angry because she believed that the current conservative backlash demanded political participation from students but found that not very many students were interested in political activism.

It was discussed that the lack of a visible political movement is due not only to students' reluctance to participate in political activities but to a combination of political, social, and economic factors in the larger society that shape the lives of college students. The group also agreed that the culture of consumerism and materialism often distracts young people from what is important.

Although there is anger, a sense of loss, and frustration, there are also good and warm feelings that come from being connected to the Filipino people and culture. Ruth stated in her story that she had always been told that she was the black sheep in the family but that now she found herself in the midst of her family because of her "recovered devotion" as a result of decolonization. Michelle felt the same way; she stated:

> So, where am I now? Am I here? Am I there? Well, here and there are here within me. Filipino is who I am, along with my activism, writing, and sports. It is something that will never change and is intrinsic to who Michelle Bautista is. . . . The Philippines is not in the heart, nor is America. Being Filipino is in the heart. What is it that you cherish and love despite everything and that brings you both joy and sorrow? For me a part of that is Filipino.

The Power of Naming and Telling

According to Freire (1970), liberation begins with the naming of the social and political structures that dominate and silence. The word *decolonization* does not yet circulate in the Filipino American community. Many of the participants did not use the word prior to their participation in the study, but with its naming, they recognized that they had been decolonizing all along, through the intuition and thinking that led them to make certain kinds of choices that in turn led to their participation in this study. The word *decolonization* named their feelings and intuitions and the things they had done unconsciously and consciously in relation to their search for a Filipino connection or identity.

The process of decolonization includes the naming of indigenous cultural values that have been intuited but not articulated. Teresa expressed this well:

> It was not until 2 years ago that I learned the words *kapwa, magandang loob, pakiramdam, utang na loob*. I have to let you know that it was an immense feeling to be able to attach words to these emotions. For years I would try and attempt to explain my feelings, and never did I feel that I was able to relay them to my non-Filipino friends.

The ability to name one's experiences leads to telling—the telling of one's stories to family, friends, and the world. All the participants shared what they were learning with their family and friends, creating opportunities for dialogue. These dialogues led to remarkable transformations in the families of the participants. Cheryl, for example, stated:

> When I would talk about what I was learning in Asian American studies at home, my brother and sister would overhear my conversations, and I notice that my brother gets angry. . . . I notice that when he watches television and sees minorities getting attacked by racist white people, he gets pissed off. Then I feel bad. Then I laugh at it, too, because I think he knows what is happening. I try to tell him not to think bad thoughts about other people, but I am not sure if that is a good idea. He also has a right to feel angry.

Decolonization is the ability to tell one's story in a manner that makes sense and makes meaning out of all the experiences of the past. To locate one's personal history within the history of the community is to find the relationship between the self, the nation, and narration. The story of the self contains the narrative of the nation. To tell one's story is to allow the fragments of consciousness to be sutured and healed so that the Filipino story can be told in its wholeness.

The participants said they could hardly wait for this study to be published so they could give it to their parents and friends to read.

The Need for Filipino Cultural and Historical Knowledge

A critical aspect of decolonization is the integration of Filipino historical and cultural knowledge. Without this knowledge to provide the content for the Filipino story, the decolonization process would be empty. The invisibility of Philippine and Filipino American history in the participants' education in the United States was a common lament. The participants agreed that their confusion, ignorance, and sense of inferiority came in part from this invisibility. Marissa observed:

> Throughout my life, I have had experiences that have made me feel like I have no respect of pride for my culture or my heritage. That upsets me because I have always been proud of who I am and have never once wanted to be someone else. But now I realize that I really don't know why I am proud; I don't know what being Filipino is all

about. I want to be able to say that I am Filipino American and know what that means.

The lack of Filipino cultural knowledge can also sometimes result in negative interpretations of Filipino practices. One of these examples is Laurie's perception of her mother's "submissiveness":

> I always saw my Mom as submissive, being really obedient to my Dad before they got divorced, and I thought that was part of the Filipino culture to be that way, and I didn't want to be that way. . . . And then when I realized that in precolonial history the women were really strong, it made me feel like a new person. I wanted to be that kind of woman, and I thought it would be even stronger for me to say that I am a Filipino woman.

It was not until the participants went to college that they finally found some good resources through their Asian American classes or Filipino American classes. Teresa said that she had always understood the concept of colonization but just did not have the knowledge to pull it all together. But this found knowledge leads to more questions, such as Teresa's:

> If Filipinos are resilient, I also question it. How are we resilient? How many of us are aware of the controls of society? When will we stop looking for the ultimate consent from the oppressor? When are we going to look at ourselves for answers? When will I begin to do all this myself? When can I trust my own judgment without having to look at everyone for answers? When will Filipinos wake up and realize that we are and may be the only ones who can help ourselves succeed?

When participants learned that knowledge is constructed, they also learned to question the construction of the colonial and dominant narratives written in "authoritative" historical texts. The process allowed them to reflect on how sources of knowledge within their home cultures were either minimized or trivialized. Sources of knowledge and wisdom such as cultural practices, folk sayings, proverbs, stories, myths and folklore, songs, dances, and humor have not been considered legitimate sources of knowledge in the colonial culture. Decolonization reverses this negative regard for Filipino culture and practices. Today, these sources are being mined as sources of meaning and rerooting in the parent culture. As the participants became aware of how colonization demeans and represses the indigenous culture, they expressed their resolve to return to these sources by interviewing family members, asking them to recall both their personal and historical memories about life in the Philippines. Michelle stated:

> A side effect I didn't realize of this added knowledge would be a closer connection to my parents. As I returned home, telling them of all I had learned, it would help them remember as well. My mother had always told us stories of my great-grandfather, the one who could walk on hot coals, and that's all I or my siblings knew of him. When she found out I was taking Kali, she revealed something more about him, that he was an Arnis master. The news struck me. Why hasn't she ever told us this before? Why is she telling me this now? *It was if I had opened a new door into her memory* [italics added].

Another source of cultural connection is food. Filipino food serves a very important function in maintaining ties with the culture. Food was a major part of this research project; many dialogues took place while cooking and eating together. As a social event, eating together fosters a deep connection with Filipino culture, in much the same way that language does. As a nonverbal tool of communication, food is a powerful carrier of cultural meanings as well as the powerful feelings of belonging and being loved and nurtured. Marissa said that she got to know her mother during those times of wrapping *lumpia* together and watching her mother cook.

The Role of Language and Memory

In oral cultures, memory becomes the repository of a people's knowledge and wisdom. Myths, folktales, proverbs, folk beliefs, songs, poems, epics, rituals, and humor are teaching tools for how to live with nature, with other people, and with the spirit world. Filipinos are residually oral even with the reported high rates of literacy (Alaras, 1993; Strobel, 1994).

Decolonization must be grounded in a sense of history. The process of reclaiming Filipino history as a counternarrative to the history written by outsiders therefore becomes a process of reclaiming one's memory:

The recovery of Filipino language(s), of one's voice, of one's story, is re-created in the memory. There is a sense of turning in one's soul through the power of language and imagination.

To reclaim memory at the personal level is to engage in the process of creating a collective memory of a people's history. From their memory banks, the participants were able to connect their personal struggles to the struggles of the Filipino people in the Philippines, the United States, and all parts of the world. They recovered knowledge of a past in which people participated in resistance to colonization and did heroic deeds. In dialogues and in the writing of their personal narratives, the participants recovered some of their family histories and recognized the validity of the oral traditions of indigenous Filipino culture. As reconstructed memories, these were imbued with new meanings for the present. The recovery of memory became a part of the healing of painful past memories.

The participants' narratives chronicled many of those stories that had circulated in the family but had never been committed to text. Laurie spoke of her grandfather escaping the Bataan Death March during the Japanese occupation by hiding under a woman's skirt. Ruth told the long story of how a group of women from Borongan, Samar, married a group of Filipino merchant marines and later found themselves in San Francisco. These and other stories were all retold within a historical context.

The participants recognized that their oral consciousness, through its immersion in a literacy-based society in the United States, was slowly transforming this consciousness. They realized that their personal and family histories needed to be connected to those memories that had never been committed to texts. The decolonization process gave them the opportunity to create texts out of their recovered memories.

Michelle's story illustrated the process of reconstructing her identity from her past remembrances. In interrogating her Filipino identity at a younger age, she went through a period of depression that led to suicidal thoughts, because, she said, "Nothing that I could claim as my identity was defining who I was. So I had to begin reconstructing this identity and discovering and rediscovering who I wanted to be and who I was before." In her senior year in high school, she began to write for the student newspaper:

I had my own column—the Bautista Beat, where I ranted and raved about whatever I wished. Stuck for article ideas, I hit upon writing a three-part series on my observations of being Filipino, which included meeting Filipinos on the street and their disappointment in my lack of knowledge in speaking a Filipino language, my mother's incessant need to cook in surplus and freeze leftovers, and my feelings of feeling different and out of place. The articles took like wildfire.... People would stop me and talk about their own experiences or tell me that they sent copies to daughters or cousins or friends. I thought the articles were just a part of my babbling confusion over this unexplored part of my identity. But if anything, I knew I was no longer alone in being Filipino.

Memories are stored in language. The participants recognized that their Filipino language loss was also a historical consequence of colonization. Peter questioned how ties to the English language, as the language of colonization, could be symbolically severed. He asked whether decolonization required it. Ruth reminded the participants of Virgilio Enriquez's remark, at the 1993 Symposium on Filipino Values, that perhaps English should be considered a Filipino language because Filipinos have nativized it and made it their own. The issue of language has been associated with markers of assimilation. A newly arrived immigrant who speaks a variety of Filipino English can be discriminated against by other Filipinos who speak fluent "standard" English because the former's language is often associated with inferiority, lack of intelligence, and "otherness." This arrogant perception is based on the assumption that "standard" English is a universal norm and a universal marker of intelligence. The hierarchical status of "standard" English has long been refuted by postcolonial critique. When this knowledge was integrated by the participants, they came to realize that the cultural divide within the Filipino American community marked by language use was a false dichotomy.

The participants also discussed the Filipino indirect communication pattern of *pahiwatig:* the evocative ways of expressing the need or want of something. *Pahiwatig* is grounded on the value of *pakikiramdam*—keen sensitivity to a complex of verbal and nonverbal cues interacting within a given communication context—and *pakikipagkapwa-tao*—to feel one with the other (Maggay, 1995). This discussion with the participants served to contextualize the differences in communication patterns between themselves and their parents and more recent Filipino immigrants.

Luz talked about the need for a new language in which to theorize and conceptualize the Filipino American experience for the 1990s. She stated that the language must challenge, for example, the Filipino American community's use of the phrase "We lack unity." To insist on "unity" as if there were a homogeneous way of assimilating all things into a single entity is to miss the mark, she argued:

> We must ask who is imposing this concept on us; the imperial center always wants to define itself by defining the other in contrast to itself. Filipino Americans must resist those definitions by our ability to question what is being imposed. You need a new language to express that. We should look at coalition and alliance building as alternatives to the concept of unity.

The Role of Filipino Spirituality

Filipino religiosity and spirituality was a major theme in each dialogue with the participants. The participants expressed a need to understand their parents' religiosity, Catholicism in particular. They wanted to understand not only the images and symbols of the Catholic faith but also its theology and complicity with colonialism. They asked: How is it related to colonization? If the Spanish brought Catholicism to the Philippines, isn't it a colonizing tool? How then can we reconcile the acceptance, devotion of [our] parents to the Catholic religion, in particular, the worship of saints with Caucasian features? Cheryl stated:

> Religion is a big question mark for me. I know a friend who goes to confession even though she does not believe in it, but she does it for her Mom. When we talk about questioning Catholicism as being brought by the Spanish, she says it would be really to question something that has become a part of yourself, your family. So because her mother is religious—she believes in all the saints and about the predictions about the end of the world—she does not question it. . . . There is so much I do not understand. If I should question everything, I do not even know what questions to ask, how to ask. . . . But I also feel that the Catholic religion is also a part of the Filipino culture. So I still go to church because I feel if I don't go, then what religion would I follow? I know I don't have to have religion to believe in God, but the rituals are a part of my life and who I am.

The researcher discussed the indigenous religious consciousness of Filipinos and how it became possible to "contract with colonialism"; the works of Rafael (1988), Ileto (1979), and Maggay (1990) were introduced to discuss why Filipinos seem to accommodate Catholicism easily and still maintain their indigenous beliefs that are rooted in the shamanic and animist tradition.

The other questions raised by the participants were: To decolonize, do I have to leave the Catholic faith? What is Filipino indigenous spirituality? How can I know the deeper spiritual meaning of Filipino superstitions, folk beliefs, and folk sayings?

The Filipino indigenous consciousness was repressed by the imposition of a Western-formulated Christianity. Phelan's (1959) *The Hispanization of the Philippines* discussed the survival of a vague precolonial indigenous culture in the Philippines partly because of the refusal of the Spanish clergy to train Filipino clergy, which resulted in the poor quality of indoctrination. It would be more accurate to say that the coercive tactics of colonization pressured Filipinos to accommodate to the forms of Catholicism but did not transform the indigenous consciousness. Filipino indigenous consciousness is more animistic and polytheistic and at home in the spirit world and its multiple gods. Indigenous symbolisms are still expressed in the belief in *anting-antings* (amulets to ward off evil spirits), superstitions, miraculous healings, ghosts and spirits, and enchanted places and beings—all of which exist side by side with Catholic rituals and sacraments. Maggay (1990) stated that the Filipino has been impervious to alien worldviews even after 90 years of Protestantism and American education. Filipino Catholicism is an appeal to the gods for inner strength (*lakas ng loob*) rather than an appeal for salvation or release from guilt. Filipino religiosity is undergirded by a much more ancient faith that today appropriates Western symbols and rituals but whose meanings are indigenous. The Filipino concept of *loob* relates to equality, honor, human rights, truth, relatedness to others, and relatedness to God and all of creation. As the source and core of creativity, it embraces the body and the soul; it embraces the world (Alejo, 1990).

Teresa's narrative recalls her mother's superstitious beliefs and folk sayings as having had a tremendous impact on her because in understanding the foundation of these beliefs, she was able to understand why in the past she had not been able to articulate these beliefs and the feelings they engendered to her non-Filipino friends. She stated:

Being a white American meant almost always being so practical. I would hear others say to me, "Ghosts do not exist"; "Why do you leave your money around, people will take it!" Other Filipino homes I have visited I see a cross, a Jesus statue, a Santo Nino, and a Rosary. . . . I felt comfortable knowing that these were beliefs we shared. And yet while I believe in the concept of God and a higher being, I question: Is there a Jesus Christ? Why practice Catholicism?

The theme of spirituality in this study questions the complicity of Christianization with Spanish and American colonization. The participants raised this question in an attempt to clarify how the decolonization process would affect their religious life. Many of the participants admitted that they did not understand the meanings behind the Catholic symbols and rituals but that the Catholic religion had become part of their identity because it was an important part of their parents' identity. It was explained that it is necessary to understand both the Western-formulated theology of Christianity and the Filipino indigenous religious consciousness and that by studying the cultural meanings behind Catholic religious rituals, the participants would be able to interpret the form of Catholicism that came to the Philippines. The researcher also shared the growing body of literature in Filipino indigenous theology and the politics of conversion being written in the Philippines by such authors as Ileto (1979), Rafael (1988), and Alejo (1990). This literature explains how Filipinos resisted and negotiated the imposition of a religious view as an instrument of colonialism.

Summary and Conclusion

Naming the world, as participants said, changes a lot of things; it changes one's perception of reality. For the participants, this naming led to a process of reflection that was facilitated by their participation in this research project. The participants were able to have a longer, broader, and wider perspective so that they were able to understand how their present positionality was connected to the historical past. As the participants learned to fill the gaps in their knowledge about Filipino and Filipino American history and culture, they were also able to imagine a future, healing the cultural amnesia and sense of shame about being Filipino and Filipino American.

The feelings and emotions that accompany this process show the cultural force of emotions and how they can become a source of meaning and new creative energy. Most of the participants were able to move beyond anger. This did not mean that they were not angered by oppressive situations. But they found niches for activism and involvement within their families, schools, and community.

The Filipino oral consciousness is recognized through the remembering of stories told in childhood and stories that come from the collective memory of the Filipino people. Stories that used to be hidden or negated regain their capacity for myth making. We remember most that which is meaningful, so the oral consciousness's insistence on maintaining the deeply personal/communal quality of relationships, the need for dialogue, the sharing of a vision, comes from a deep and abiding love for one's fellow Filipinos. It is this depth and breadth that decolonization makes possible, creating cultural continuities and bridging generational and historical gaps in the consciousness of Filipino Americans.

This chapter is a very broad description of the decolonization process among selected post-1965 Filipino Americans. The generative themes that emerged from the study can be considered as markers or signposts of a movement that is being deeply embraced by those who seek to come home, to come full circle.

Note

1. The full documentation of this study is in my dissertation, "Coming Full Circle: The Process of Decolonization Among Post-1965 Filipino Americans" (University of San Francisco Ed. D. dissertation, 1996).

References

Alaras, C. (1993). The concept of English studies in the Philippines. In C. Pantoja-Hidalgo & P. Patajo-Legasto (Eds.), *Philippine postcolonial studies: Essays on language and literature* (pp. 16-25). Quezon City: University of the Philippines Press.

Alejo, A. (1990). *Tao po! Tuloy! Isang Landas ng pagunawa sa loob ng tao*. Quezon City, Philippines: Ateneo de Manila University Press.

Cabezas, A., Shinagawa, L., & Kawaguchi, G. (1987). New inquiries into the socio-economic status of Pilipino Americans in California. *Amerasia Journal, 13*(1), 1-21.

Campomanes, O. (1995). The new empire's forgetful and forgotten citizens: Unrepresentability and unassimilability in Filipino American postcolonialities. *Critical Mass: A Journal of Asian American Cultural Criticism, 2*, 145-200.

Chan, S. (1991). *Asian Americans: An interpretive history*. Boston: Twayne.

Enriquez, V. (1990a). Indigenous personality theory. In V. Enriquez (Ed.), *Indigenous psychology: A book of readings* (pp. 285-208). Quezon City, Philippines: Philippine Psychology Research and Training House.

Enriquez, V. (1990b). Towards a liberation psychology. In V. Enriquez (Ed.), *Indigenous psychology: A book of readings* (pp. 123-136). Quezon City, Philippines: Philippine Psychology Research and Training House.

Enriquez, V. (1992). *From colonial to liberation psychology*. Quezon City: University of the Philippines Press.

Fanon, F. (1963). *The wretched of the earth*. New York: Grove.

Freire, P. (1970). *Pedagogy of the oppressed* (M. B. Ramos, Trans.). New York: Seabury.

Freire, P. (1985). *The politics of education*. Boston: Bergin & Garvey.

Gonzalez, N. V. M. (1992). Even as the mountain speaks. *Amerasia Journal, 18*(3), 55-67.

Gonzalez, N. V. M. (1995). *Work on the mountain*. Quezon City: University of the Philippines Press.

Ileto, R. (1979). *Pasyon and revolution: Popular movements in the Philippines, 1840-1910*. Quezon City: Ateneo de Manila University Press.

Kitano, H., & Daniels, R. (1988). *Asian Americans: Emerging minorities*. Englewood Cliffs, NJ: Prentice Hall.

Maggay, M. (1990). The indigenous religious consciousness. *Patmos Magazine* [Manila, Institute for Studies in Asian Church and Culture], *6*(2), 1, 9-14.

Maggay, M. (1995). *Pahiwatig: Tuwiran and di tuwirang pagpapahayag sa konteksto ng kulturang Pilipino*. Unpublished doctoral dissertation, University of the Philippines.

Memmi, A. (1965). *The colonizer and the colonized*. Boston: Beacon.

Pe-Pua, R. (1990). *Pagtatanung-tanong:* A method for cross cultural research. In V. Enriquez (Ed.), *Indigenous psychology: A book of readings* (pp. 231-249). Quezon City, Philippines: Philippine Psychology Research and Training House.

Phelan, J. L. (1959). *The Hispanization of the Philippines*. Madison: University of Wisconsin Press.

Rafael, V. (1988). *Contracting colonialism: Translation and Christian conversion in Tagalog society under early Spanish rule*. Manila: Ateneo de Manila University Press.

San Juan, E., Jr. (1992). *Reading the West/writing the East: Studies in comparative literature and culture*. New York: Peter Lang.

San Juan, E., Jr. (1995). *Racial formations/critical transformations: Articulations of power in ethnic and racial studies in the United States*. Atlantic Highlands, NJ: Humanities.

Strobel, E. (1994). The cultural identity of third-wave Filipino Americans. *Journal of the American Association for Philippine Psychology, 1*(1), 37-54.

Strobel, L. M. (1996). *Coming full circle: The process of decolonization among post-1965 Filipino Americans*. Ann Arbor, MI: University Microfilms.

Waugh, D., & Chin, S. (1989, September 17). Sleeping giants ready to wake. *San Francisco Chronicle*, p. A-14.

6

Contemporary Mixed-Heritage Filipino Americans
Fighting Colonized Identities

Maria P. P. Root

Whether planful or accidental, centuries of invasion and visitation by traders, seafarers, missionaries, warfarers, and colonists guaranteed that Filipinos across the archipelago would fuse multiple ethnic influences and physical features. Across families, the family portrait defies neatly delineated boundaries; Filipinos belong to no race[1] and belong to all. Skin tones range from the strongest coffee color to the creamy color of banana flesh. Hair texture ranges from coarse to smooth, kinky to straight, light brown to blue-black. Short to tall, thin to large, and everything in between exists. Likewise, eye shapes and color and noses vary. In short, physical appearance cannot be the definitive marker defining or identifying Filipinos or Filipino Americans. This chapter outlines the evidence and impact of the colonizing tool of racialization on Filipino American ethnic identity through the experiences of contemporary mixed-heritage Filipinos.

Background

Four hundred years of combined colonization, first by Spain and then by the United States, widened the Filipino gene pool with the possibilities of lighter skin, hair, and eyes. The tools of colonization gave meaning to the variation in physical appearance among Filipinos. Spain introduced colorism; preferential treatment was clearly associated with lighter skin color. Centuries of this education primed the Filipino for vulnerability to internalize American rules of race. Colorism and then racism inculcated the notions "White is beautiful," "White is intelligent," and "White is powerful" in the psyches of many brown-hued Filipinos, thus inferiorizing the Filipino.

Countries colonized by light-skinned people of European origin (e.g., the United States, Puerto Rico, Brazil) have developed elaborate terms to denote color gradients or racial mixing (e.g., Comas-Diaz, 1996; Daniel, 1992). In the Philippines as in Mexico, the term *mestizo* or *mestiza* signified a cross between the indigenous people and the Spaniard. In the Philippines, its meaning was extended to refer to mixtures between Filipinos and white Americans. Its use in the United States continues to be extended, much as the term used in Hawai'i to describe mixture, *hapa*, has transcended its original meaning. Originally connoting a mixture between Hawaiian and foreigner, usually white, *hapa* now generically refers to all phenotypic mixes in Hawai'i, even if not of Hawaiian ancestry. Likewise, the term *mestizo* has been extended to almost all mixes of Filipino heritage. Contemporarily, it is a term that has a mixed reception in the United States. It carries unjustified connotations of superiority in the Philippines and, ironically, the connotation of imposterhood or inauthenticity in this country.

Unfortunately, Filipinos are acquiring the rules that guide domestic race relations. First, some Filipinos are accepting the notion of a racial hierarchy with white at the top and black at the bottom. If Filipinos had not accepted the concept of a racial hierarchy, the term *mestizo* would have been abandoned; pejorative terms would not exist for those Filipinos now of contemporary African ancestry (even though, as a Malayan people, we were recipients of the African diaspora). Second, lacking an appropriate road map to negotiate race relations in this country, Filipino

Americans are basing ethnic authenticity on fictional and toxic notions of racial purity. For example, in one of my classes, a student talked about how affronted she felt when people thought she was of "mixed" heritage rather than "full-blooded" Filipino.

Consider the confluence of two historical processes for further understanding Filipinos' susceptibility to a racialization process: the civil rights movements of the 1960s and 1970s and the post-1965 immigration wave of Filipinos. The largest number of Filipinos are immigrants; most Filipino Americans arrived after the change of immigration laws in 1965. Unlike previous Filipino immigrant cohorts, a large portion of the post-1965 cohort came from an educated and privileged class that had and often retains some status (Lott, Chapter 2 of this book; San Juan, 1992). They advocate for their children to become Americans—and to maintain or achieve status for the family. Furthermore, they enter this country as beneficiaries of the civil rights legislation that removes some obstacles to upward mobility for some people of color. The lessons around race are no longer as harsh, but they are nevertheless insidiously present (Pido, Chapter 3 of this book).

This period of time also coincides with the contemporary civil rights movements in this country, in which culture and ethnicity were largely reduced to race (Omi & Winant, 1994). Subsequently, Filipino American ethnic solidarity has been increasingly racially defined. In this transformation, ethnic solidarity has acquired and required the application of oppressive racial authenticity tests (Root, 1990, 1992), by which some Filipino Americans reject mixed-heritage Filipinos. At a time when Filipino Americans are continuing to try to define who and what is Filipino American (Gonzalves, Chapter 11 of this book; Revilla, Chapter 7 of this book), this narrow definition constructs a divisive reality inconsistent with the facts of Filipino history. Filipinos have forever been and forever will be undefinable by race. Contemporary mixed-heritage Filipino Americans are potential and unfortunate casualties in this transformation of ethnicity. Denying one's cultural relatedness testifies to the colonization of identity suffered by most visible ethnic oppressed groups in this country (Atkinson, Morten, & Sue, 1989; Cross, 1991). Self-protection results in rejecting all that is perceived as part of the colonizer; mixed-heritage Filipinos are the physical embodiment of the Filipino's contact with the colonizer. Thus, in the contemporary context, more so than in previous moments in history, the mixed-heritage Filipino is placed in a liminal position between two cultures (Hill, 1994), which are basically in tacit agreement that American is better than Filipino and which continue to define "American" as white.

This conceptual analysis also suggests a juxtaposition of positions on mixed-heritage Filipinos. On one hand, mixed-heritage Filipinos who inherit African, Latino, and/or Native American ancestry may be more easily welcomed as Filipinos by some because they inherit another legacy of oppression. On the other hand, when the racial hierarchy is invoked, these members of community are deemed even less valuable Filipinos. Those Filipinos of immediate European heritage may be regarded as less authentic by some, yet enviable by others.

Despite the diversity of physical appearance embodied in looking Filipino, many children of Filipino descent of cross-cultural and/or interracial marriages in the United States experience gatekeeping comments such as "But you don't look Filipino" or "You're American, not Filipino."[2] What are the costs of these comments to those persons who are the object of scrutiny for the moment? What might be the costs to the Filipino American community? Such statements suggest that an insidious process of translating ethnicity into race prevails with the assimilation of American values. Thus, the colonizing of the Filipino continues in the United States (Pido, Chapter 3 of this book; Rimonte, Chapter 4 of this book). A brief analysis and summary of Filipino intermarriage is essential to placing the emergence and experience of contemporary Filipinos of mixed heritage in context.

Filipino Intermarriage

The U.S. military presence in the Philippines from 1890 through the 1990s guaranteed continued racial and cultural mixing for Filipinos. In a patriarchal structure, the colonized is constructed as a female to be dominated by the superior colonizing male. Consider that the Philippines and all other colonized countries are referred to in the female gender. And consider that patriarchy constructs itself as heterosexual, possessive, and aggressive; it will possess the women (Young, 1995). It constructs men of color in the female gender to reduce their threat to the

colonizer (Lerner, 1986) and assumes that the colonizer is a more attractive mate to the colonized woman. In reality, she is property; thus, she
does not necessarily have free choice to refuse the colonizer as a lover or
partner.

Unlike the Chinese, Japanese, and Koreans before them, Filipino
men would be open to marriage with American women other than
Filipinos. Filipino male intermarriage in the United States, primarily
with white women, would have occurred because of uneven sex ratios
between Filipino men and women in the United States due to patterns
of sojourning and immigration, availability and proximity of white
women, and some familiarity with and positive regard for American
European-originated culture. More insidiously, primed to prize light
skin, and without Filipina women, Filipino men could be expected to
find white women particularly attractive. For example, in Chicago from
the early to mid 20th century, Filipino men mixed with daughters of other
recent immigrants of Polish, Irish, and German descent (Posadas, 1989).
However, Filipino men mixed with other racially visible ethnic groups
with whom they found some cultural affinity when there was proximity.
In the Northwest, Filipino men mixed with American Indian women; in
San Diego and Imperial counties of California, Filipino men mixed with
Mexican and Mexican American women.

The mixing of Filipino men with white women brought the wrath of
white citizens and politicians intent on keeping the line between white
and not-white well defined. Specific legislation was introduced to prevent Filipino men from marrying white women. For example, although
California had antimiscegenation laws that prevented whites and blacks
and whites and Asians from intermarrying, it was not clear if Filipinos
were Asians. However, in a landmark case, *Roldan v. Los Angeles County*
in 1933, Filipinos were classified as Malays and quickly added to the list
of persons prohibited from intermarriage with whites. Several states eventually added Filipinos (Malays) to their list of persons prohibited from
intermarriage with whites. Nevertheless, intermarriage continued in
states in which laws did not prohibit it. Furthermore, marriages between
U.S. servicemen stationed in the Philippines and Filipinas continued.

Several historical factors have sustained Filipino-American inter-
marriage since World War II. The presence of American military in the
Pacific, specifically with military bases in the Philippines during World
War II, the Korean War, the Vietnam War, and onward, guaranteed there

would be interracial mixing and, subsequently, children (Root, in press-b). The Immigration and Nationality Act of 1965 amended the previous immigration law and opened the door to increased immigration. The repeal of the remaining antimiscegenation laws in 1967 paved the road for an increase in interracial marriage in general. Since then, the numbers of Filipinos in the United States have multiplied, and their rates of intermarriage have increased.

The profile of contemporary children and young adults of mixed Filipino heritage has changed in the United States during the course of the century. Prior to World War II, the majority of mixed-heritage Filipinos had Filipino fathers and white American mothers. These men were primarily employed as laborers, though they might have initially come to this country as *pensionados* to study at universities. With the limitation imposed on Filipino migration with the Tydings-McDuffie Act of 1934, sex ratios remained imbalanced, and similar marriages continued where they were legal. However, following World War II, and particularly the Korean War, the Filipina war bride entered the United States exempted from immigration quotas through the Soldier Brides Act of 1947. During this period of time, a generation of Filipinos, many of whom were born in the Philippines of white American fathers, emerged. With the 1965 Immigration and Nationality Act and the consequent growth and transformation of Filipino communities in the United States, the majority of young people of mixed heritage under 20 may have either a Filipino mother or father who may indeed have been born, if not raised, most of his or her life in the United States.

International marriages still occur, largely through military contact and the mail-order bride business. Each year, thousands of women leave the Philippines in search of better economic opportunities than the local economy offers. Unfortunately, the bridal export business has changed cross-cultural and cross-national marriage from a romantic event to a suspect catalog business in which the Philippines is the largest supplier of international brides via this industry (Lin, 1991; Mochizuki, 1987; Ordoñez, Chapter 9 of this book) to Germans, Danes (Ravn & Trier, 1980), Australians (Boer, 1988), Japanese (Samonte, 1986), and Americans (Glodava & Onizuka, 1994) in the past decade. Denigrating stereotypes of Filipinas as exotic, childlike, subservient, and gold-digging maintain an attitude that dismisses the validity of a majority of these relationships (Ordoñez, Chapter 9 of this book) and the children from them. When these women have children and are unmarried, separated, or divorced, negative stereotypes are extended to their mixed-race children.

Though few contemporary studies of intermarriage in the United States for Filipinos exist compared to studies of intermarriage for Japanese and Chinese (Kitano, Yeung, Chai, & Hatanaka, 1984; Sung, 1990), two pilot studies suggest that rates of intermarriage for Filipinos will continue at a high rate. Revilla (1989) surveyed Filipino American college students in the Los Angeles area. In 1996, Bergano and Bergano-Kinney (Chapter 13 of this book) surveyed East Coast and Northwest Filipino college students involved in Filipino organizations. Despite some geographic and gender differences, the two studies share two findings. First, a considerable number of college students in these samples do not feel compelled to marry Filipinos. And second, although the rates vary by region, both young men and women are open to interracial dating and marriage. Agbayani-Siewert and Revilla's (1995) survey of studies on Filipino intermarriage underscores these findings.

Agbayani-Siewert and Revilla (1995) observed that although studies confirm the tendency of Filipinos to intermarry white partners as consistent with Asian American intermarriage patterns, there are two distinct differences for Filipinos as compared to other Asian Americans. First, the men intermarry as often as the women in California, where the second-largest population of Filipinos exists in the United States. On the basis of 1980 census data for California, Jiobu (1988) found that although Filipinas tend to marry non-Filipinos more frequently than the men do, when women married to U.S. military men are excluded from the figures, the rates for men and women are similar and high: 20% or greater. This rate of intermarriage places Filipinos as a group with the highest rate of intermarriage for the four groups that Jiobu examined (Japanese, Chinese, Korean, Filipino). Their second observation is that Filipinos intermarry with other Asian Americans (e.g., Japanese, Chinese, Vietnamese) less frequently than Japanese, Chinese, and Koreans who intermarry. Using Jiobu's analysis, Filipinos in California married persons of Latino or Hispanic descent next most frequently. This is an ethnic group that has some cultural similarity to Filipinos.

Several factors currently suggest that intermarriage for Filipinos will continue at a high rate, if not actually increase. First, the removal of legal barriers to intermarriage throughout the United States in 1967, in tandem with other civil rights legislation such as fair housing and equal employment practices, ensures the likelihood that most Filipinos will live, work, and play in neighborhoods where there are non-Filipinos. Furthermore, the educational level of many post-1965 immigrants will place them in neighborhoods and workplaces that are middle class and primarily white. Although there is concern for the cultural preservation that inmarriage more likely ensures, many Filipinos wanting success for their children encourage them to be as American as possible; this wish for their children may stem from vestiges of colonialism that increase the acceptability of intermarriage with white Americans. (The high rates of Japanese Americans' intermarriage with white Americans have in part been attributed to the push to become Americanized at a more accelerated pace after their incarceration during World War II.) Whereas not all Filipino intermarriage with whites is driven by these factors, this factor would certainly make the Filipino more willing to look on a white partner favorably over other non-Filipino partners. Simultaneously, affinity through oppression and class similarity opens the door for intermarriage with other ethnically oppressed groups who are not white.

Growth of the Filipino American Community

The high rates of intermarriage for Filipinos in the United States suggest that the physical diversity of appearance among Filipinos and those of Filipino descent in the United States will only increase. Although Filipinos are perhaps most similar in appearance to persons of Latino and Native American and Native Hawaiian heritage, defining and identifying who is Filipino cannot rest predominantly on physical appearance. However, without articulation of what is Filipino, without recognition of the injurious process of racialization, and without positive role models of Filipinos for some persons, young people are subject to using the template by which people struggle with racial identity in a limited, monoracial paradigm. Thus, they may deny their Filipino heritage to be accepted and fit in with their white peers. According to researchers, this rejection is common to persons who are members of devalued groups and have internalized a devalued sense of self and have internalized a white reference group (e.g., Atkinson et al., 1989; Cross, 1991). With

exposure to eye-opening experiences that suggest that there are structural and attitudinal barriers to being wholly accepted by white dominant culture, individuals are thrust back into examining their roots and
reacquainting themselves with and immersing themselves in what is
positive about their culture of origin. Eventually, they may appreciate
the positive attributes of different people and critically evaluate what is
negative or positive on an individual basis. At times, this is at the risk of
either rejecting being Filipino or absorbing some other identity that is
articulated more clearly for them.

Psychological and social alienation seems to be part of the experience associated with American adolescent individuation from family. Contemporary mixed-race Filipinos, particularly during adolescence and young
adulthood, may be unable to untangle their feelings of alienation from the
typical adolescent experience, marginality as a person of color in a
society in which race matters, and difference as an ambiguous Filipino.

With their parents' cross-cultural union, at least one parent is likely
to be indoctrinated into the racial system. Thus, their Filipino parent may
at times be viewed as racially distinctive from their non-Filipino parent
by the non-Filipino parent. Or the children may be constructed as superior or inferior because they are similar to one parent or the other;
ethnicity and race are likely to be confused. The subtlety of this process
constructs race and constructs the child as mixed race. In a society that
is racially diverse and stratified, one's race is a social address for many
contexts. Thus, individuals symbolically become the embodiment of
differences, often striving to make meaning out of their unique social
position as bicultural and biracial.

Ironically, centuries of colonization have left a multiracial people
without an appropriate road map in a system that subscribes to a
monoracial ideology that values pure race. The Filipino struggle with
identity bears much resemblance to the process of working out a mixed
racial identity, particularly when one group is oppressed or subjugated
by the other (Bradshaw, 1992; Chao, 1995; Hall, 1992; Root, 1992, 1996c).
We must reexamine the paradigms by which we seek our identity. If they
do not fit our history, we will be forever lost trying to find our way home
with a map that does not have our address. The dominant frameworks,
even within Asian America, do not fit Filipinos well. Contemporarily,
multiethnic and multiracial paradigms are emerging that fit the Filipino
American experience better.

Being contemporary mixed heritage of Filipino ancestry in the United States adds a complexity to the struggle with identity that is both similar to and different from being of mixed race of other Asian descent such as Japanese, Chinese, Vietnamese, or Korean. In general, there is not a defamation of physical appearance or assumed defect of character associated with mixing gene pools. As self-identified mixed-heritage people, to empower ourselves we must refuse to account for ourselves in fractions—one half Filipino, one half something else (Root, 1996a)—which is an act of colonizing identity; we must refuse to be gatekeepers of racial authenticity; we must refuse to participate in divisions originating in class, phenotype, education, dialect, and nativity. That we have not and may not attain a singular resolution of identity pathologizes Filipinos. We must redefine solidarity and resolution in light of our history as a people colonized, invaded, and spread out geographically in the archipelago and now internationally. We must respect the diversity in our community rather than strive to eliminate or ignore it.

Implications for the Filipino American Community

Given the high rates of intermarriage for Filipino American men and women, we are going to raise a large generation of people who are mixed race by the American definition of race. Furthermore, the Filipino American population will grow more rapidly through intermarriage if those of mixed heritage are welcomed and encouraged to identify as Filipino. Our community will be stronger if we do not require people to pass "blood quantum" tests such as those generated by the U.S. government for determining who is American Indian or Native Hawaiian. Our community will also be stronger if we can accommodate the distinct possibility that many of our young people will be multiethnic: that is, Filipino *and* something else, such as Japanese, Chicana/o, Indian, African, or Jewish. Historically, Filipinos have been able to do this. Researchers of multiethnic and multiracial identity note that a normal part of possessing multiple affiliations is that in some contexts one aspect of identity will be more prominent while others are background (Hall, 1992; Root, 1992, 1996a, 1996b; Stephan, 1992). Ramirez's (1983) work on Mexican American bicultural identity suggests that the ability to switch or be both increases flexibility of thinking and problem solving. Ultimately, this flexibility may be a survival skill in the twisted world of racial paradigms.

The lack of articulating and valuing what diversity means in the Filipino American community places the multiethnic or multiracial Filipino at risk of being alienated by and from the Filipino community. For those already likely to be misidentified as belonging to another ethnic group, such as Chicana/o, American Indian, or some more familiar Asian group, depending on the part of the country, rejection from the Filipino community is particularly meaningful, and therefore hurtful. Multiheritage Filipinos will frequently be asked the question asked of racially ambiguous people, "What are you?" The frequency with which some individuals receive these questions informs them about how race is conducted and confounded with ethnicity in the United States.

Young people react to ethnic inquisition differently. Some, very secure in their identity, may refuse to prove they are Filipino; they are likely to be living in a community of friends that recognize them as Filipino. Others will try to be more Filipino than Filipino, absorbing every aspect of Filipino and Filipino American knowledge that comes their way; they establish their belonging by their cultural expertise. Still others will interpret the inquisition as a rejection. They may turn their back on the community as a defense against repeated scrutiny and rejection. This latter response concerns me. With the first alternative, it is possible to be Filipino identified and proud and to accept that people are having a difficult time adjusting to the expanding diversity of the contemporary Filipino community. The second alternative is developmentally predictable; having to demonstrate cultural expertise eases up as one feels more secure in one's sense of who one is—even if others do not reflect one's identity accurately. Unfortunately, the third alternative is a worst-case scenario. The rejected one may invoke an equally oppressive attitude toward the inquisitor: The inquisitor is defective. Both parties are casualties of racial colonization.

There are some actions parents can take to help their children claim their Filipino heritage proudly. These recommendations are gathered from the literature on the empowerment of mixed-race persons and the current knowledge of factors affecting ethnic identity (Root, 1992, 1996c, in press-a). First, give your child a first or middle name that is connected with their Filipino heritage. Particularly for a female child who through marriage may relinquish her maiden name, a given name becomes that much more important. Although children may be embarrassed by this name at different times in their life, it also reassures them that they are Filipino; it may also be part of their passport into Filipino communities in which the family is unknown. Second, talk positively about what you value about being Filipino. Children may make fun of you for feeling or talking so positively about things that are Filipino, but they are likely to absorb some positive feeling from these reflections. An absence of comment may speak as strongly as negative comments about Filipinos. Third, connect them to the Filipino community through stories of relatives and family roots in the United States, the Philippines, and elsewhere. Creating a family tree may be a way to make this connection (Dearing, Chapter 20 of this book). Reading Filipino and Filipino American literature may be another avenue for connection (Bacho, Chapter 1 of this book). Being connected to the past is a foundation for knowing who you are in the present. Fourth, if you live in or near a community where there are Filipino community gatherings, go to some of these. Role models, sense of similarity, and exposure to the diversity of behavior, attitudes, accents, and physical appearance can help children subsequently counter stereotypes they may hear about Filipinos. It will also probably expose them to other young people who have contemporary multiethnic or multiracial origins. Fifth, do not make disparaging comments about Filipinos in general or other groups of people of color. A child may identify with those persons you denigrate. Last, inquire if your child has encountered any of the gatekeeping, curiosity questions. Some children will wonder if they are "real" Filipinos or "what" they are. Help them develop answers that maintain their sense of control over who they are. Such discussions can help them recognize and fight the racial colonizing of their identity.

Conclusion

The profile of the mixed-heritage Filipino in the United States has changed and diversified through this century. Predominantly fathered by Filipino American men prior to Philippine independence from the

United States, then subsequently and predominantly birthed by international brides of U.S. servicemen after World War II and particularly through the Korean and Vietnam war eras, the contemporary Filipino of mixed heritage emerges in a different historical context post civil rights and in a different class context post 1965. Subsequent to the 1965 Immigration and Nationality Act, contemporary mixed-race people may be fathered or mothered by a Filipino parent and, increasingly, American born.

The American social system is littered with dangerous interpretations of physical, behavioral, and social differences among people. Unfortunately, many Filipinos attempting to compete economically and be accepted as Americans uncritically accept the American rules of race. They are not aware of alternative road maps or frameworks for identity. Consequently, they relinquish the fight against the colonization of Filipino identity.

The Filipino of mixed heritage is positioned liminally and symbolically in the psychological space that confronts the larger community. What does it mean to be Filipino in America? What does it mean to be American of Filipino heritage? If Filipino Americans emphasize race-based markers in determining and defining who is Filipino, our community will suffer. We will use the colonizer's tool against each other.

With high rates of intermarriage for both genders, the phenotype of the Filipino American will continue to diversify. As our community works to define who is Filipino, it is incumbent to our viability, solidarity, and health to be as inclusive as possible and to embrace the growing cohort of contemporary Filipinos of mixed heritage. Many contemporary Filipinos of mixed heritage have resisted a colonized identity. They are evidence that the juxtaposition of Filipino and American is resolvable but requires a different road map. Ultimately, the health, viability, and resilience of the Filipino community will depend on our ability to resist becoming casualties of colonized racial identities. In Paulo Freire's (1970) words, "The solution . . . is not to become 'beings inside of,' but . . . [people] . . . freeing themselves: for, in reality, they are not marginal to the structure, but oppressed . . . within it" (pp. 10-11).

Notes

1. Race is used as a social construction throughout this chapter.

2. Some of this gatekeeping is experienced by American-born Filipinos from Philippine-born Filipinos.

References

Agbayani-Siewert, P., & Revilla, L. (1995). Filipino Americans. In P. G. Min (Ed.), *Asian Americans: Contemporary trends and issues* (pp. 134-168). Thousand Oaks, CA: Sage.

Atkinson, D. R., Morten, G., & Sue, D. W. (Eds.). (1989). *Counseling American minorities: A cross-cultural perspective.* Dubuque, IA: William C. Brown.

Boer, C. (1988). *Are you looking for a Filipino wife? A study of Filipina-Australian marriages.* Sydney, Australia: General Synod Office.

Bradshaw, C. K. (1992). Beauty and the beast: On racial ambiguity. In M. P. P. Root (Ed.), *Racially mixed people in America* (pp. 77-88). Newbury Park, CA: Sage.

Chao, C. M. (1995). A bridge over troubled waters: Being Eurasian in the U.S. of A. In J. Adleman & G. Enguidanos (Eds.), *Racism in the lives of women: Testimony, theory, and guides to antiracist practice* (pp. 33-44). New York: Harrington Park.

Comas-Diaz, L. (1996). LatiNegra: Mental health issues of African Latinas. In M. P. P. Root (Ed.), *The multiracial experience: Racial borders as the new frontier* (pp. 167-190). Thousand Oaks, CA: Sage.

Cross, W. E., Jr. (1991). *Shades of black: Diversity in African-American identity.* Philadelphia: Temple University Press.

Daniel, G. R. (1992). Passers and pluralists: Subverting the racial divide. In M. P. P. Root (Ed.), *Racially mixed people in America* (pp. 91-107). Newbury Park, CA: Sage.

Freire, P. (1970). *Cultural action for freedom.* Cambridge, MA: Harvard Educational Review Press.

Glodava, M., & Onizuka, R. (1994). *Mail order brides: Women for Sale.* Fort Collins, CO: Alaken.

Hall, C. I. I. (1992). Please choose one: Ethnic identity choices for biracial individuals. In M. P. P. Root (Ed.), *Racially mixed people in America* (pp. 250-264). Newbury Park, CA: Sage.

Hill, R. C. (1994). Liminal identity: Clinical observations. *Journal of the American Association for Philippine Psychology, 1,* 55-68.

Immigration and Nationality Act of 1965. 8 U.S.C. § 1101 *et seq.*

Jiobu, R. (1988). *Ethnicity and assimilation.* Albany: State University of New York Press.

Kitano, H. H., Yeung, W.-T., Chai, L., & Hatanaka, H. (1984). Asian American interracial marriage. *Journal of Marriage and the Family, 46,* 179-190.

Lerner, G. (1986). *The creation of patriarchy.* New York: Oxford University Press.

Lin, J. L. (1991). *Marital satisfaction and conflict in intercultural correspondence marriage.* Unpublished doctoral dissertation, University of Washington.

Mochizuki, K. (1987, May 7). I think Oriental women are just great. *International Examiner,* p. 13.

Omi, M., & Winant, H. (1994). *Racial formation in the United States from the 1960s to the 1990s* (2nd ed.). New York: Routledge.

Posadas, B. M. (1989). Mestiza girlhood: Interracial families in Chicago's Filipino American community since 1925. In Asian Women United of California (Ed.), *Making waves: An anthology of writings by and about Asian American women* (pp. 273-282). Boston: Beacon.

Ramirez, M., III. (1983). *Psychology of the Americas: Mestizo perspectives on personality and mental health*. New York: Pergamon.

Ravn, M., & Trier, B. (1980). *Asian heart*. New York: Filmmakers Library.

Revilla, L. (1989). Dating and marriage preferences among Filipino Americans. *Journal of the Asian American Psychological Association, 13*, 72-79.

Roldan v. Los Angeles County, 129 Cal. App. 267, 18 P2d 706 (1933).

Root, M, P. P. (1990). Resolving "other" status: Identity development of biracial individuals. In L. S. Brown & M. P. P. Root (Eds.), *Diversity and complexity in feminist therapy* (pp. 185-206). New York: Harrington.

Root, M. P. P. (1992). *Racially mixed people in America*. Newbury Park, CA: Sage.

Root, M. P. P. (1996a). A bill of rights for racially mixed people. In M. P. P. Root (Ed.), *The multiracial experience: Racial borders as the new frontier* (pp. 3-14). Thousand Oaks, CA: Sage.

Root, M. P. P. (1996b). The multiracial experience: Racial borders as a significant frontier in race relations. In M. P. P. Root (Ed.), *The multiracial experience: Racial borders as the new frontier* (pp. xiii-xxviii). Thousand Oaks, CA: Sage.

Root, M. P. P. (Ed.). (1996c). *The multiracial experience: Racial borders as the new frontier*. Thousand Oaks, CA: Sage.

Root, M. P. P. (in press-a). The biracial baby boom: Understanding ecological constructions of racial identity in the twenty-first century. In R. H. Sheets & E. Hollins (Eds.), *Race, ethnic and cultural identity formation*. New York: Lawrence Erlbaum.

Root, M. P. P. (in press-b). Multiracial Asian Americans: Changing the face of Asian America. In L. C. Lee & N. W. Zane (Eds.), *Handbook of Asian American psychology*. Thousand Oaks, CA: Sage.

Samonte, E. L. (1986). *Filipino wives with Japanese husbands: Communication variables and marital satisfaction*. Unpublished doctoral dissertation, University of the Philippines.

San Juan, E., Jr. (1992). *Racial formations/critical transformations: Articulations of power in ethnic and racial studies in the United States*. Atlantic Highlands, NJ: Humanities.

Soldier Brides Act of 1945. 59 Stat. 659.

Stephan, C. W. (1992). Mixed-heritage individuals: Ethnic identity and trait characteristics. In M. P. P. Root (Ed.), *Racially mixed people in America* (pp. 50-63). Newbury Park, CA: Sage.

Sung, B. L. (1990). *Chinese American intermarriage*. New York: Center for Migration Studies.

Tydings-McDuffie Act of 1934. 48 Stat. 456.

Young, R. J. C. (1995). *Colonial desire: Hybridity in theory, culture and race*. New York: Routledge.

7

Filipino American Identity
Transcending the Crisis

Linda A. Revilla

In the past, I was ashamed to admit I was Filipino. . . . I
never wanted to learn the language even though I was
brought up with my parents and grandparents speaking it.
Student paper, University of Hawai'i,
Ethnic Studies (1994)

You may put up a white shell, but deep inside your heart
you are a beautiful Filipino. You can't hide it, even if
your parents hid your native tongue to shut you off from
your Filipino-ness, it's still there.
De Castro, "Identity in Action"

What does it mean to be a Filipino in the United States? Who *are*
Filipino Americans? The question of Filipino American identity
has been significant since the large-scale immigration of Filipinos to the

United States began in the early 20th century. Spanish and American colonizations affected the Philippines in such a way that we are still dealing with their legacies. Filipinos in the United States have a variety of experiences as people of color in America. These two factors combine with other issues to make the question of "What is Filipino American identity?" complex. This chapter will discuss some of the elements that are connected to this question, with an emphasis on concerns for youth.

Identity is "a definition, an interpretation of the self" (Baumeister, 1986, p. 4). Ethnic identity is "the cognitive product of identification . . . defined as labeling oneself in ethnic terms" (Garcia, 1982, p. 298). For the purposes of this chapter, Filipino American ethnic identity is assumed to be the product of our historical and cultural backgrounds and the process of negotiating and constructing a life in the United States. Ethnic identity is important because it affects the maintenance and expression of traditional culture, helps individuals enhance their self-concept and self-esteem, and enables individuals to have a sense of belonging to an ethnic group. In addition, it is a necessary ingredient for ethnic consciousness and activism. I argue that part of the "identity crisis" of youth in the Filipino American community (and here I mean "community" in the broadest sense) is reconciling issues of self-love and self-respect as Filipinos. The other major category of issues concerns being accepted and included as Filipinos by the larger Filipino American community. Concurrent with issues of empowerment concerning politics and economics, Filipino Americans must grapple with these issues of self-definition and inclusion to define our community, outline our concerns, and determine our path for the 21st century.

The Past

> Do you know what a Filipino feels in America? . . . He is
> enchained, damnably to his race, his heritage.
> *Carlos Bulosan (1995),* On Becoming Filipino

Carlos Bulosan wrote of his life, and the lives of other immigrant Filipino men during the 1930s through 1950s, often illustrating the hardships that Filipinos faced as victims of American racism. The ethnic identity struggles of many of the men Bulosan and his contemporaries describe seem to be linked to the racism they faced and their desire for full status as Americans. The immigrant Filipinos fought to change America into the promised land that they had learned about as schoolboys in the Philippines. Their children, the "bridge" generation, attempted to bridge the traditional Filipino culture they learned at home with the American culture they learned at school (Filipino American National Historical Society Conference, 1994):

> As children of immigrants, we believed in the American dream and welcomed the opportunities which beckoned. Those aspects of my identity linked to Hawai'i and America were ones that I believed to offer future promise because they were my home. Filipino culture, on the other hand, I saw as the culture of my parents and their friends. While I participated in Filipino activities, I did so mechanically mainly to please my parents. It was not because of any conscious effort to reject my Filipino heritage, but it was only because it appeared to be so foreign and irrelevant compared to the vibrance and promise which characterized Hawai'i and America to the young. (Andaya, 1996, p. 6)

However, the Filipino American movement, which began in the 1960s and gained momentum in the early 1970s, changed the orientation of many Filipinos in the United States. The movement helped create and reinforce feelings of pride in being Filipino and in having a culture, language, and history worth preserving. Related to its social and political agendas, organizations within the movement encouraged youth to learn about the history, culture, and politics of the Philippines (Bello & Reyes, 1986-1987) and of Filipinos in the United States. Filipino Youth Activities (FYA) in Seattle, which began in the 1950s, taught children to be proud of their Filipino background by teaching them about Philippine and Filipino American history and culture and making it relevant to their lives. FYA's drill team, for example, merges indigenous Filipino music and costumes with the American drill team tradition. Katipunan ng mga Demokratikong Pilipino (KDP) focused on supporting the democratic revolution in the Philippines and fighting for social justice in the United States (Bello & Reyes, 1986-1987). The Philippine-American Collegiate Endeavor (PACE), part of San Francisco State's Third World Liberation Front, worked with the community in a variety of ways. One focus was working with youth, recruiting them for college and then helping them graduate. PACE also encouraged Filipino youth to organize and fight for their rights (Umemoto, 1989) and oppose racism and "internal colonialism" (Wei, 1993). According to Juanita Tamayo Lott (1980), "internal colonialism," the exploitation and oppression of a subordinate group by the dominant group, was one of the factors that prevented Filipinos from fully and equally participating in the United States. Lott identified another factor as a "colonial mentality."

In her controversial discussion of the colonial mentality existing within the Filipino American community, Lott (1980) wrote that among other things, cultural traditions such as *bayanihan, utang na loob,* and *hiya,* the lack of social organization, and regionalism and factionalism reinforced the inferior position of Filipinos in the United States. Others agreed in spirit with Lott, arguing that Filipinos are overshadowed by the Chinese and Japanese because the latter brought skills and traditions that enabled them to deal more effectively than Filipinos with American racism (Wagner, 1973). During this time period (early 1970s), Fred Cordova (1973) wrote an article about the ever-present "Filipino American identity crisis," echoing Lott's arguments of the colonial mentality and quoting Filipinos who grappled with issues of self-definition. More than two decades later, both the "Filipino American identity crisis" and "colonial mentality" are still widely discussed.

The Present

> No history, no self; know history, know self.
>
> *Seminar taught by Mel Orpilla,*
> *Filipino Americans for Affirmative Action*

The landmark *Puro Pinoy* issue of *Pacific Ties* had a major focus, described in the editorial as "identity. In one word, this is the direction that each of the articles attempts to take us in. Who are we as Pilipinos?" (Pulido, 1990, p. 2). Filipino community publications discuss identity issues on a regular basis (Castilla, 1993). A volume commemorating four significant historical anniversaries in Philippine and Filipino American history, including the 100th anniversary of the Philippine Revolution and the 90th anniversary of Filipino immigration to Hawai'i, was published in Hawai'i in 1996. Despite the historical nature of the events being celebrated, the publication focused on identity issues: 8 of the 10 articles in that publication mentioned Filipino identity issues, and 3 were entirely devoted to the topic of identity. Within descriptions of Filipino identity, in addition to the "colonial mentality," themes of social disorganization, factionalism, and inferiority are common.

> [In the Philippines,] I was taught to look outside the indigenous culture for inspiration, taught that the label "Made in the USA" meant automatic superiority; in other words, like most colonized individuals, I was taught a negative image of myself. (Hagedorn, 1994, p. 174)

> My images of the Philippines and of the local Filipino community were sources of shame and embarrassment. History classes had taught me that my ancestors were beaten up and colonized by Spaniards for 400 years, by Americans for another 50, and by the Japanese for a brief period during World War II. Newspapers had taught me that the Philippines was a Third World banana republic run by a corrupt dictator and his shoe-crazy wife. And that the Seattle Filipino community was a disjointed, ineffective bunch. (Tizon, 1990, p. 11)

In recognition of colonial influences and "social disorganization," Filipinos are choosing to "decolonize" their minds in different ways. Questioning white racism (De Castro, 1994) and engaging in political and cultural activism (Quemuel, 1996) are only a few strategies. A new movement emphasizes instead the primacy and robustness of Filipino culture:

> Far from being "damaged," Filipino culture held its own, body and soul wherever the Filipino might be, in identity and spirituality, in spite of all the incursions by foreign cultures notably Spanish and American. In fact, Filipino culture is better characterized as a culture of invulnerability. "*Marunong lang sumakay ang Pilipino*" (the Filipino can dance to the music). . . . That we have a damaged culture is a myth

which conveniently reassures people who are bent on denigrating the
Filipino soul. (Enriquez, 1994, p. 12)

Related to this is the strategy of focusing on what is indigenous to
Filipino culture. Virgilio Enriquez was a leader in the movement to
study indigenous Filipino psychology and its applications to modern
life. This movement to develop a formal Filipino psychology, *sikolohiyang Pilipino*, incorporates indigenous psychology and values and concepts relevant to Filipinos around the world. *Kapwa*, a core value, is the
unity of the "self" and "others," an awareness of shared identity. "The
ako (ego) and *iba sa ikin* (others) are one and the same in *kapwa* psychology" (Enriquez, 1994, p. 10). Although *hiya, utang na loob*, and *pakikisama*
are commonly called significant Filipino values, they are merely colo-
nial/accommodative values (Enriquez, 1990, as cited in Strobel, 1994).
Using the framework of *sikolohiyang Pilipino*, Leny Mendoza Strobel
(1993) articulated Filipino re-presentation incorporating indigenization
and multiculturality:

> Indigenization . . . requires the grasping of the process of psychologi-
> cal colonization/marginalization and the reconstruction of your own
> personal history. . . . For even though on the one hand, the colonization
> of Filipinos seems to be total, there remains an unarticulated/intuited
> sense of primordiality in their sense of self, something deeply rooted.
> (pp. 124-125)

Indigenization includes returning to oral traditions and folklore
and returning to the use of Filipino languages. Multiculturality includes
learning about Philippines and Filipino American history. Indigenization and multiculturality strategies to reclaim identity are growing in
popularity in the United States. The demand for Filipino American
studies is increasing across the country. For example, students at the
University of the Pacific were willing to fund a Filipino American
professor out of their own pockets until the university came through
with funding for a culture class (Magagnini, 1996). Pilipino Cultural
Night, held on college campuses across the West Coast, often including
traditional songs, dances, and folklore, is another way that Filipinos
learn about, affirm, and then transmit their culture and heritage (Benito
& Thornton, 1989).

For many young Filipinos today, the "identity crisis" revolves around the lack of self-respect and self-love as Filipinos. An illustration of some of the reasons beneath the lack of pride in being Filipino is contained in the following essay written for a class assignment by a university student. The student first talks about her father, describing his experience as a new immigrant:

> Being an immigrant was a source of shame for my dad. He remembers being in elementary school, speaking broken English, and having his classmates tease him for not speaking as everyone else did. Whenever he was accused of being from the Philippines, he would absolutely deny it, and say that he was born in Hawai'i. Because he was teased so often and stereotyped, things associated with the Philippines came to denote something degrading in my dad's opinion. Being Filipino and speaking Tagalog were sources of ridicule for him, and he came to resent these parts of him.

The student then described her own experiences in elementary school, more than 20 years after her father:

> Throughout my days at elementary school I had an acute fear that someone would discover that I was Filipino. It was open season on Filipinos. There were the "book book" [sic] jokes, other derisive nicknames created by students, and a large number of stereotypes expounded and attributed to Filipinos. They were labeled as being stupid, backwards, and capable of only the most menial jobs available. . . . In my own experiences, I knew that these generalizations were false, but still I feared association with them. These images and stereotypes persisted in the consciousness of the student body for so long that I began to look at being Filipino as a curse. It embarrassed me that I should be a part of a race so disregarded and dehumanized by society. (Revilla, 1996a, p. 10)

Both this student and her father experienced the same sort of denigration of Filipinos, more than two decades apart. They are not alone in their ambivalence at being Filipino (Nagtalon-Miller, 1993; Tizon, 1990). Would knowledge about Filipino history and culture help foster a sense of pride for young Filipinos who are ashamed of their ethnicity? Bearing in mind these complexities of the Filipino American experience, E. San Juan (1994) questioned the tactic of learning history as the key to learning about self:

> As for celebrating Filipino "firsts" in order to generate ethnic pride, what does it signify if we learn that Filipinos were the first this and that, to wit, the first Asians to cross the Pacific Ocean for the North American continent or that their descendants in New Orleans, Louisiana, fought with the pirate Jean Lafitte and the Americans during the War of 1812? (p. 214)

Nonetheless, San Juan is outnumbered, as historical and cultural knowledge are continually posited as a key to identity in contexts ranging from the university to the juvenile justice system (Altonn, 1996). The *Puro Pinoy* journal issue mentioned previously recommended solutions to community problems, beginning with "education. Rediscovering our own history is the first step in developing a stronger sense of pride and self-esteem that is being lost in the next generation of potential leaders" (Pulido, 1990, p. 2). Tania Azores's (1986-1987) study of Filipino educational levels recommended the use of culture, in the form of bilingual/bicultural educational materials, to encourage educational aspiration. Herminia Menez (1986-1987) stated that a curriculum that includes the Philippine folk epics can provide young Filipinos with an anchor to their past, reinforcing their ethnic identity as well as validating the Philippine literary tradition (p. 147). Dean Alegado's (1994) study of immigrant Filipino youth encouraged the development of self-respect as Filipino Americans, stating that it was critical for our "at-risk" youth to feel a part of the larger society:

> Ethnic awareness, in the view of youth workers, can impart a richness lacking in the emotional lives of young people, as well as a sense of personal history: links across time, generation, and place generally unavailable to immigrant youngsters raised in anonymous, turbulent inner-city environments. Youth leaders who make ethnic or cultural awareness a central part of their program philosophy and orientation note that this emphasis represents not "ethnic or racial chauvinism" but rather an effort to reconcile individual identity and larger social diversity. (pp. 17-18)

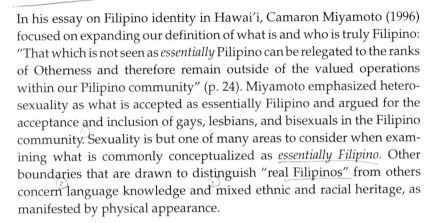

Who *Is* Filipino?

In his essay on Filipino identity in Hawai'i, Camaron Miyamoto (1996) focused on expanding our definition of what is and who is truly Filipino: "That which is not seen as *essentially* Pilipino can be relegated to the ranks of Otherness and therefore remain outside of the valued operations within our Pilipino community" (p. 24). Miyamoto emphasized heterosexuality as what is accepted as essentially Filipino and argued for the acceptance and inclusion of gays, lesbians, and bisexuals in the Filipino community. Sexuality is but one of many areas to consider when examining what is commonly conceptualized as *essentially Filipino*. Other boundaries that are drawn to distinguish "real Filipinos" from others concern language knowledge and mixed ethnic and racial heritage, as manifested by physical appearance.

Sexuality

> While I was discovering my Filipino-American identity and
> was immersed in the political struggle of social justice for
> Filipinos both in the United States and the Philippines, I was
> struggling with my sexual identity. I wanted to understand not
> only what it meant to be gay, but also to participate as an
> openly gay male in society. Initially, I felt that these two
> identities—Filipino and gay—were contradictory and
> irreconcilable.
>
> *Mangaoang, 1994, p. 39*

Gil Mangaoang's essay tells of how isolated he felt while searching for his gay identity as a Filipino. Mangaoang noted that today Filipino gay organizations do exist, unlike during the 1970s when he was grappling with his sexual identity. In Martin Manalansan's (1994) study, informants report varying levels of acceptance of homosexuality by Filipino families, ranging from rejection to acceptance, to acceptance without acknowledgment of sexual orientation. Family rejection or denial of homosexuality and bisexuality widens the distance between lesbian and gay Filipinos and their families and communities (Miyamoto, 1996).

"It's a bigger deal when a family of color disowns their gay son or daughter. Because of racism, it is an especially painful loss, to lose your connection to your family" (Ordona, 1994, p. 143). Including our gay and lesbian sons and daughters, brothers and sisters in our definition of "who is Filipino" can only strengthen our community.

> Keeping Pilipino gay-ness and lesbian-ness in the closet, hidden from the realm of public discussion and dialogue, masks the ability for segments of Pilipinos to articulate their passions. . . . I am arguing for the right of all Pilipinas and Pilipinos to express the pride and power that can be found in self-love and respect. Only then can our passions and pride for being Pilipino emanate outward into our communities. With this in mind, we can make the personal political and work together for social change. (Miyamoto, 1996, p. 26)

Language

> You need to know a Philippine language to have a strong identity.
>> *Comment at International Philippine Studies Conference,*
>> *Honolulu (1996)*

> If you don't know a Filipino language, then you're stupid.
>> *Comment at Association for Asian American Studies*
>> *Hawai'i Regional Conference, Honolulu (1996)*

Scientists know that thought and language affect each other, but the exact relationship between thought and language has yet to reveal its labyrinth dimensions. Research on language, culture, and thought attempts to answer the question, "To what extent does a particular culture and language system determine the nature of one's mode of thinking?" (Elkind, 1977, p. 356). Although the answer to this question may remain unsettled in research, some Filipinos have definitely answered this question for themselves, as evidenced by the comments above.

The issue of language and the Filipino identity evokes passionate arguments in the Filipino American community. Filipino American soldiers born and raised in Hawai'i recall being labeled as *desgracia* (a disgrace) while on duty in the Philippines because they could not speak a Filipino language (Revilla, 1996b). Filipinos born and raised in the United States who do not speak a Filipino language or who speak one with an American accent also report being denigrated. Despite the popular opinion that knowing a Filipino language is necessary to have a strong identity, research has indicated that this is not the case. It is possible for an individual to profess a strong Filipino ethnic identity without knowing how or desiring to speak a Filipino language (Lombos-Wlazlinski, 1996; Revilla, 1989). Nevertheless, this issue is an emotional one, explained in part by the politics behind language, identity, and cultural survival for Filipino Americans (Ramos, 1996). Leny Mendoza Strobel (1994) described how English was a tool used by Americans to colonize Filipinos and why it is so imperative that Filipinos learn their native tongue:

> More than a set of symbols, language integrates, makes complex patterns and relationships in the world, and creates meaning. How then can Filipinos, who have been educated in a foreign language, express indigenous meanings in the foreign tongue? While their think- ing structure and mental processes remained indigenous, they were made to express their ideas in a foreign language. As a neocolonial tool, this imposition of a foreign language implied the inferiority of the native language and of Filipinos in general. (p. 37)

Unfortunately, parents are not consciously teaching their children Filipino languages and culture (Morales, 1986-1987), and classes in Filipino languages are few and far between. Although Chinese Ameri- can and Japanese American communities have historically set up lan- guage and culture schools for their youth, Filipino American communities have not. The lack of community language schools, coupled with the virtual nonexistence of Filipino language classes in the secondary schools, makes learning a Filipino language outside the home impossi- ble for most Filipino American youth. It is only at a handful of colleges and universities around the country that Filipino language courses are part of the regular curriculum, and usually Tagalog is the only language taught. The majority of students taking beginning Ilokano or Tagalog courses at the University of Hawai'i say they are learning the languages to "learn more about my roots, appreciate my Filipino culture and communicate with my parents" (Ramos, 1996, p. 167). However, even the university's language professors realize that these students only "gain non-functional proficiency after two years" (Ramos, 1996, p. 168). The solution seems straightforward: Set up language schools in the community, advocate for Filipino languages to be included in the curricula at all levels of education, and accept the fact that there are some Filipinos who cannot speak a Filipino language.

To P or Not to P?

Another continuing debate within our community that is related to the arguments about language is the controversy about the labels *Pilipino* and *Filipino*. In academic articles on Filipinos, there is the inevitable note explaining the arguments for both spellings and the reasons behind the author's term of choice (Aguilar-San Juan, 1994; Manalansan, 1995). The debate seems to have taken regional dimensions. Many of those who prefer *Pilipino* reside in California. The term of choice in the Pacific Northwest and Hawai'i is *Filipino*. Scholars and writers from the East Coast use both terms in their writings. Community members in Virginia Beach, Virginia, report a movement to label themselves *Pinoy* (Filipino American National Historical Society, 1994), whereas in Hawai'i, many consider *Pinoy* and *Pinay* to be negative terms. In Hawai'i, *Fil-Am* is a common way to refer to Filipinos. A recent discussion on the Internet debated the political correctness or incorrectness of *Flip* (Labaz, 1996).

The divergent opinions on what should be the correct way to refer to ourselves can be interpreted as an example of the factionalism within our community. However, I argue that spelling and pronunciation are secondary to the inclusion of "Filipino-ness" in our self-definitions and that this debate is only an illustration of the diversity within our community. Instead of insisting on one label, which would provide the illusion for a homogeneous Filipino American community that does not exist, the diversity within the community is what should be recognized and encouraged. Jessica Hagedorn (1994) is one author who has argued for the positive aspects of Filipino American diversity:

> Most urban Filipinos and Filipino Americans probably suffer from cultural schizophrenia, like I do. Hopefully, we will use this affliction to our advantage, for this post-colonial condition has its positive

aspects. We need to turn the negative inside out, use it to enrich ourselves and our visions—for where would our extraordinary voices be without the outlaw rhythms of rock 'n roll, the fractured lyricisms of jazz, the joyous gravity of salsa, the perverse fantasies of Hollywood, and our own epic melodramas? (p. 176)

"Oh, You're Not Really Filipino"

Physical appearance, including manifestations of mixed racial or ethnic background, is another issue that affects identity, as others perceive and label Filipinos as "*really* Filipino" or "not *really* Filipino." There seems to be a prototypical Filipino physical appearance that many Filipinos do not meet. "You don't look Filipino!" or "Oh, I thought you were _____ [Chinese, Mexican, Japanese, Native American, etc.]" are commonly heard in Filipino gatherings. Writer Alex Tizon (1990) recalled his trip to the Philippines:

> During a tour of an elementary school in the heart of Manila, Andy and I peeked into one of the outdoor classrooms. Every head turned to look at us. The faces ran the gamut from the very light-skinned to the very dark, from the very Asian to the very European. Every classroom was the same.
>
> "So what are Filipinos supposed to look like?" Andy said later. His mother was Polish, and he had talked of incidents in Seattle when people told him that he didn't "look" Filipino. "I look in that classroom and I see the whole range. What were those people talking about?" (p. 18)

Mixed-heritage Filipinos also describe the feeling of not belonging to any of the ethnic groups that make up their heritage (Revilla, 1996a). Persons of mixed race or mixed ethnicity may have identity conflicts due to several factors (Mass, 1992), but all persons with Filipino ancestry, as products of the racially and ethnically diverse Philippines, should have the unquestioned option to identify as "Filipino." The irony of mixed-heritage Filipinos not being accepted as Filipinos is exposed when one considers the pains that Filipinos in the Philippines and abroad take to maintain a standard of appearance that has its roots in colonization: for example, keeping out of the sun so as not to get "too dark" or pinching the nose to make it less flat (Tizon, 1990). (See Root, Chapter 6 of this book, for a discussion on mixed-heritage Filipinos.)

Where Do We Go From Here?

The identity crisis and subsequent alienation of our youth is a serious problem in the Filipino American community (Alegado, 1994) and the larger community. Outside perceptions of the Filipino American community need to be shaped by us instead of for us. The following example from Honolulu provides evidence of the work that needs to be done.

A 16-year-old Filipino youth driving a stolen car was shot to death by police after he reportedly tried to ram their police cars during a traffic stop. The youth did not have an arrest record, and his family denied that he was involved in a gang (Pai, 1996; Witty & Barayuga, 1996). However, the media vilified the youth, reporting first that he had been a runaway ("Youth Killed in Car Chase," 1996), then that the youth's name was "familiar to auto theft investigators" (Witty, 1996, p. A3), and finally that he was a member of the "Little Pinoy Bad Boys" Ilocano gang ("Mayor Will Meet With Gang Members," 1996). The shooting received significant media attention and responses by the public in the form of letters to the editors of the major newspapers and listener call-in comments to radio stations. The police department opened an investigation into the shooting to determine if there was criminal misconduct by the officer who fired his weapon (Barayuga, 1996), but the television and print media converged with public opinion to blame the young man and his parents' inadequate supervision for the fatal shooting ("Letters to the Editor," 1996a, 1996b, 1996c, 1996d, 1996e, 1996f). One letter to the editor even suggested that the parents had "set up" the young man for his death by not providing him with good guidance. The youth's alleged gang membership was never proven. Also implied but never proven was the negative nature of the "Little Pinoy Bad Boys" gang that the youth was supposedly affiliated with. The dehumanization of the dead youth and other young Filipino males as "gang members," coupled with the blame placed on the dead youth's parents, illustrated to me how today in Hawai'i, as in California a few decades ago, it is still in many ways a crime to be a Filipino (Bulosan, 1943/1974). Despite the negative publicity that the youth's family and the "Little Pinoy Bad Boys" received, even more disappointing was the lack of any publicized response by the Filipino community. Although there are many Filipino organizations in Hawai'i, not one organization or community leader spoke out about the incident and the blatant stereotyping that was taking place. During the whole tragedy, Filipino voices were silent.

We must define who we are as Filipino Americans. The crime and the ambivalence of being Filipino must be more effectively addressed by the community. The primordial sense of being Filipino that Strobel (1993) described must be encouraged to blossom. Educating ourselves about our history and our culture is one way to confront our identity crisis. Narrow, essentialist assumptions of who is Filipino must be replaced with more inclusive conceptions to recognize the diversity and evolution within our community. It is not enough just to expand our definitions of who is Filipino to swell our ranks and play the numbers game for political and social empowerment; we must also recognize the psychological damage that neglect and conservatism inflict on our own people. We will only be truly empowered as Filipino Americans when we figure out who we are and what we want and work together toward those goals.

References

Aguilar-San Juan, K. (1994). A note about terms. In K. Aguilar-San Juan (Ed.), *The state of Asian America: Activism and resistance in the 1990s* (p. viii). Boston: South End.

Alegado, D. (1994, December). *Immigrant youths from the Philippines: Embedded identities in Hawai'i's urban community contexts.* Paper presented at the First World Congress on Indigenous Filipino Psychology and Culture, Quezon City, Philippines.

Altonn, H. (1996, April 16). How to win them over. *Honolulu Star-Bulletin*, p. A6.

Andaya, L. (1996). From *American*-Filipino to *Filipino*-American. In J. Okamura & R. Labrador (Eds.), *Pagdiriwang 1996: Legacy and vision of Hawai'i's Filipino Americans* (pp. 5-8). Honolulu: University of Hawai'i, Student Equity, Excellence, and Diversity (SEED) and Center for Southeast Asian Studies.

Azores, T. (1986-1987). Educational attainment and upward mobility: Prospects for Filipino Americans. *Amerasia, 13*, 39-52.

Barayuga, D. (1996, June 13). Officer shot teen in self-defense—attorney. *Honolulu Star-Bulletin*, p. A4.

Baumeister, R. (1986). *Identity: Cultural change and the struggle for self.* New York: Oxford University Press.

Bello, M., & Reyes, V. (1986-1987). Filipino Americans and the Marcos overthrow: The transformation of political consciousness. *Amerasia, 13*, 73-84.

Benito, T., & Thornton, M. (1989, Spring/Summer). Pilipino Cultural Night. *East Wind*, pp. 51-54.

Bulosan, C. (1974). *America is in the heart.* Seattle: University of Washington Press. (Original work published 1943)

Bulosan, C. (1995). *On becoming Filipino: Selected writings of Carlos Bulosan* (E. San Juan, Jr., Ed.). Philadelphia: Temple University Press.

Castilla, G. (1993, September 1-30). What a Filipino is: A personal reflection. *Filipino-American Bulletin,* pp. 3, 5.

Cordova, F. (1973). The Filipino-American: There's always an identity crisis. In S. Sue & N. W. Wagner (Eds.), *Asian-Americans: Psychological perspectives.* Palo Alto, CA: Science and Behavior Books.

De Castro, S. (1994). Identity in action: A Filipino American's perspective. In K. Aguilar-San Juan (Ed.), *The state of Asian America: Activism and resistance in the 1990s* (pp. 295-320). Boston: South End.

Elkind, D. (1977). Thought and language. In P. Mussen & M. Rosenzweig (Eds.), *Psychology: An introduction* (2nd ed., pp. 321-361). Lexington, MA: D. C. Heath.

Enriquez, V. (1994). Indigenous psychology: From traditional indigenous concepts to modern psychological practice. *Journal of the American Association for Philippine Psychology, 1*, 4-23.

Filipino American National Historical Society. (1994, August). "The Bridge Generation" Conference, San Francisco.

Garcia, J. (1982). Ethnicity and Chicanos: Measurement of ethnic identification, identity, and consciousness. *Hispanic Journal of Behavioral Sciences, 4*, 295-314.

Hagedorn, J. (1994). The exile within/The question of identity. In K. Aguilar-San Juan (Ed.), *The state of Asian America: Activism and resistance in the 1990s* (pp. 173-182). Boston: South End.

Labaz, Z. (1996, June 16). The virtual Filipino. *Hawai'i Filipino Chronicle*, pp. 4-5.

Letters to the editor. (1996a, June 21). *Honolulu Advertiser,* p. A23.

Letters to the editor. (1996b, June 10). *Honolulu Star-Bulletin,* p. A15.

Letters to the editor. (1996c, June 12). *Honolulu Star-Bulletin,* p. A19.

Letters to the editor. (1996d, June 14). *Honolulu Star-Bulletin,* p. A17.

Letters to the editor. (1996e, June 15). *Honolulu Star-Bulletin,* p. B3.

Letters to the editor. (1996f, June 18). *Honolulu Star-Bulletin,* p. A15.

Lombos-Wlazlinski, M. (1996, April). *Social and psychological determinants of language shift: The case of the Filipino community in the City of Virginia Beach, Virginia.* Paper presented at the International Philippine Studies Conference, Honolulu.

Lott, J. T. (1980). Migration of a mentality: The Pilipino community. In R. Endo, S. Sue, & N. Wagner (Eds.), *Asian Americans: Social and psychological perspectives* (Vol. 2, pp. 132-140). Palo Alto, CA: Science and Behavior Books.

Magagnini, S. (1996, May 19). Out from the shadows. *Sacramento Bee*, pp. A1, A10.

Manalansan, M. (1994). Dissecting desire: Symbolic domination and strategies of resistance among Filipino Gay men in New York City. *Amerasia, 20*, 59-73.

Manalansan, M. (1995). Searching for community: Gay Filipino men in New York City. In G. Okihiro, M. Alquizola, D. Fujita Rony, & K. S. Wong (Eds.), *Privileging positions* (pp. 291-300). Pullman: Washington State University Press.

Mangaoang, G. (1994). From the 1970s to the 1990s: Perspective of a gay Filipino American activist. *Amerasia, 20*, 33-44.

Mass, A. (1992). Interracial Japanese Americans: The best of both worlds or the end of the Japanese American community? In M. Root (Ed.), *Racially mixed people in America* (pp. 265-279). Newbury Park, CA: Sage.

Mayor will meet with gang members. (1996, July 11). *Honolulu Star-Bulletin*, p. A3.

Menez, H. (1986-1987). Agyu and the Skyworld: The Philippine folk epic and multicultural education. *Amerasia, 13*, 135-150.

Miyamoto, C. (1996). Personal identities, political identities: Pride, passion and power in our diverse Pilipino community. In J. Okamura & R. Labrador (Eds.), *Pagdiriwang 1996: Legacy and vision of Hawai'i's Filipino Americans* (pp. 23-26). Honolulu: University of Hawai'i, SEED and Center for Southeast Asian Studies.

Morales. R. (1986-1987). Pilipino American studies: A promise and an unfinished agenda. *Amerasia, 13*, 119-124.

Nagtalon-Miller, H. (1993). The Filipino plantation community in Hawai'i: Experiences of a second-generation Filipina. In B. Aquino & D. Alegado (Eds.), *The age of discovery: Impact on Philippine culture and society* (2nd ed., pp. 30-33). Honolulu: University of Hawai'i, Center for Philippine Studies.

Ordona, T. (1994). In our own way: A roundtable discussion. *Amerasia, 20*, 137-147.

Pai, D. (1996, June 10). Mother defends son shot by police. *Honolulu Star-Bulletin*, p. A3.

Pulido, M. (1990, June). The need for a Pilipino movement. *Pacific Ties, 1*, 2.

Quemuel, C. (1996). Filipino student apathy or activism? In J. Okamura & R. Labrador (Eds.), *Pagdiriwang 1996: Legacy and vision of Hawai'i's Filipino Americans* (pp. 17-19). Honolulu: University of Hawai'i, SEED and Center for Southeast Asian Studies.

Ramos, T. (1996). Philippine languages in Hawai'i: Vehicles of cultural survival. *Social Process in Hawai'i, 37*, 161-170.

Revilla, L. (1989). *Manifestations of ethnic identity: Pilipino Americans*. Unpublished doctoral dissertation, University of California, Los Angeles.

Revilla, L. (1996a). Filipino Americans: Issues of identity in Hawai'i. In J. Okamura & R. Labrador (Eds.), *Pagdiriwang 1996: Legacy and vision of Hawai'i's Filipino Americans* (pp. 9-12). Honolulu: University of Hawai'i, SEED and Center for Southeast Asian Studies.

Revilla, L. (1996b). "Pineapples," "Hawayanos," and "Loyal Americans": Local boys in the first Filipino infantry regiment, U.S. Army. *Social Process in Hawai'i, 37*, 57-73.

San Juan, Jr., E. (1994). The predicament of Filipinos in the United States: "Where are you from? When are you going back?" In K. Aguilar-San Juan (Ed.), *The state of Asian America: Activism and resistance in the 1990s* (pp. 205-218). Boston: South End.

Strobel, L. (1993). A personal story: Becoming a split Filipina subject. *Amerasia, 19*, 117-129.

Strobel, L. (1994). The cultural identity of third-wave Filipino Americans. *Journal of the American Association for Philippine Psychology, 1*, 37-54.

Tizon, A. (1990, November 18). Love and shame. *Seattle Times (Pacific Magazine)*, pp. 10-12, 14, 17-20, 39, 44-46.

Umemoto, K. (1989). "On strike!" San Francisco State College strike, 1968-69: The role of Asian American students. *Amerasia, 15*, 3-41.

Wagner, N. (1973). Filipinos: A minority within a minority. In S. Sue & N. Wagner (Eds.), *Asian Americans: Psychological perspectives* (pp. 295-298). Palo Alto, CA: Science and Behavior Books.

Wei, W. (1993). *The Asian American movement*. Philadelphia: Temple University Press.

Witty, J. (1996, July 2). Parents sued over Waimalu shooting. *Honolulu Star-Bulletin*, p. A3.

Witty, J., & Barayuga, D. (1996, June 8). Family angered by police shooting. *Honolulu Star-Bulletin*, pp. A1, A9.

Youth killed in car chase ran off from home. (1996, June 11). *Honolulu Star-Bulletin*, p. A3.

8

Living in the Shadows
The Undocumented Immigrant
Experience of Filipinos

Concepcion A. Montoya

There are subtle and insidious ways of dividing communities, especially communities of ethnic minorities. The strategy of "divide and conquer" is a well-used tool of those in power, making its way into constitutional and legislative agendas. Nowhere is it more evident than in the area of immigration. When the definition of who is legally acceptable and who is not is subject to the whims of those in power instead of being subject to the larger social, historical, economic, and political realities of the times, the promise of democracy and the promise of justice are both compromised. The current immigration bills passed in the 104th Congress reflect an anti-immigrant sentiment now embodied in law. The best hope of retaining some balance in the equation, however, is to begin listening to the stories of those marginalized, including those whom we consider illegal and/or undocumented. Perhaps, by listening to them, we who do belong inside the boundaries of legitimacy and who are able to effect political change can find the conviction to do so.

The government defines "undocumented persons" as persons who (a) enter the country without any type of legal visa, (b) enter the country with a legal visa but overstay, and/or (c) enter the country legally but violate the terms of their visa (e.g., become employed despite work restrictions on their visa; Bean, Edmonston, & Passel, 1990). Undocumented Filipinos, also known as *TNTs* (*tago ng tago*, translated as "to keep on hiding" from immigration authorities), typically fall into the two latter categories. Yet living in the United States as an "undocumented person" is rarely written about. For example, the unfortunate practice of Filipinos disclosing the illegal status of other Filipinos to Immigration and Naturalization Service (INS) authorities in exchange for monetary compensation makes the topic very difficult to broach even in the safest settings.

Essentially, one's immigration status defines the contours of an immigrant's life in the United States. Filipino American immigration in the late 20th century is better understood with the inclusion of the undocumented immigrant experience. The economic situation in the Philippines and the demand for a highly skilled but underpaid labor force in the United States have precipitated the continuing exodus of Filipino professionals, technicians, and skilled workers (Pido, Chapter 3, this volume). As we shall see from the following narratives of Filipino TNTs, whose names have been changed to protect their identities, their struggles in the United States illuminate the shadows behind the American dream. Ultimately, they raise important issues of identity, assimilation, and community responsibility.

From the Darkness, We Speak

> I left my wife and daughter in the Philippines. We were separated for 5 years. Somehow, they got a visa to Canada. My friends crossed the border and met them there. My wife and 6-year-old daughter hid in the trunk of their car. They were very lucky. I met them on the U.S. side. This happened 10 years ago. We are now citizens, and my daughter is graduating from high school. (Mario, 42 years old, laboratory technician)

I came to this country in 1985. There were very few jobs in the Philippines for college graduates. My brothers and sisters, who are U.S. citizens, paid for my ticket and helped me get settled. I was on a tourist visa. My brother asked a friend to marry me. While waiting for my papers, my father had a heart attack and died. I could not leave the country, as my papers were still being filed. When my green card came, it was too late—Papa was already dead. (Marissa, 30 years old, hotel executive)

I thought that being in San Francisco was like being back home in Manila. There were a lot of Filipinos, and I thought it would be a good place to start out. After all, Filipinos help each other. I was wrong. When I started getting promotions at work, it was even my co-Filipino workers who called INS to say that there is an illegal alien working at the company. I had to quit my job. I moved from state to state for fear of the INS. I could not send money to the Philippines. My wife eventually found work in Italy as a domestic worker. It was the only way we could keep our children in school. (Tony, 35 years old, computer programmer)

I am 46 years old, an artist. I arrived in 1986. I came on a tourist visa and overstayed. I first started working at fast food joints and moved on to hotels. I had friends who were managers at these places and did not ask for papers. I already got my Social Security number when I was on a student visa in the late '70s. It was very easy to get an SS number then. I got paid on the books, and paid my taxes. Finally, a friend said she knew somebody who will fix my papers: $5,000 and you got a working visa first and then a green card. Something about agricultural workers. Just show up at the INS. I even dressed up as a farmer, would you believe? I was nervous, but hey, I had no choice. Thank God, it was easy. The contact made good at the INS. I got my green card. That was in '89. I just became a citizen 2 months ago. (Laura, 46 years old, graphic artist)

I came to this country when I was 6 years old. My dad was a student taking up his master's degree, and we decided to stay. My dad got a working visa and eventually applied for permanent residency.

I could never really explain my immigration status while waiting for the petition. And this got harder when I applied for colleges. Many colleges were asking for green cards, and I did not have one. My parents told me to say that I was being petitioned—which was the truth. But what kind of papers could you show for that? The schools wanted something tangible such as a green card or a passport. I got accepted at an Ivy League college with a scholarship, but they withdrew the offer when I could not produce proper documentation.

Things got worse when I turned 21 because I was now over the age limit for family petitions. You work hard, pay your taxes, study well, and then something happens in your life, and all of a sudden, you fall out of the immigration categories. Go figure. . . . (Eric, 24 years old, customer representative)

Putting Illegal Immigration Into Perspective

The Facts

The presence of undocumented Filipinos or TNTs is a known fact in the Filipino immigrant community, which is considered one of the fastest-growing Asian populations. As of 1995, there were 2.1 million people of Filipino ancestry in the United States (Cruz, 1996). In a study done in 1988 (Warren, 1990), the Philippines was the number three provider of visa overstayers in the United States (Mexico was the first and Haiti the second). From 1985 to 1988, the Philippines averaged 14,800 visa overstayers per year, making it the top Asian country that supplied visa overstayers in the United States. Warren also found that the percentage of Filipino overstayers who intended to stay permanently in the United States was significantly high. Today, immigration from the Philippines—legal and illegal—is not abating. The reality, therefore, is that like their legal *kababayans* (countrymen), Filipino TNTs are here and are most likely here to stay.

The Myths and the Realities

It is important for the Filipino community to view the phenomenon of undocumented immigration as realistically as possible. In other words, we should not be easily swayed by the hysteria surrounding the anti-

immigrant sentiments sweeping this country. The search for better economic conditions for both themselves and the families they leave behind
drive Filipino TNTs to endure the hardships they encounter in the United
States. Unlike their legal *kababayans,* who often arrive in the United States
with their spouse and children, the majority of Filipino TNTs experience
separation from their families for prolonged periods of time.

As shown from the previous stories, Filipino TNTs arrive in the United
States with the intent to work. This disproves the popular claim of many
politicians that immigrants—legal or illegal—come to this country to
stay on welfare. Undocumented immigrants shun welfare primarily
because they fear getting caught. It is the very same fear that encourages
them to pay taxes and obey the laws, for one single mistake can reveal
their identities and status to the INS. In fact, undocumented immigrants
pay $7 billion per year in taxes. Moreover, because they are subject to
payroll deductions and income taxes, they help support Social Security
($2.7 billion in 1990) and unemployment insurance ($168 million in 1990;
Urban Institute, 1994). Furthermore, undocumented immigrants work
in jobs that legal immigrants and citizens often shun (e.g., garment
factories, tomato fields, restaurant kitchens; Kuttner, 1991).

It is also important to keep in mind that the immigration status of
Filipino TNTs is bound to change. Filipino TNTs do not remain undocumented throughout the entire time of their stay in the United States. Again,
as the stories above reflect, Filipino TNTs are constantly trying to find ways
to legalize themselves. Increasingly, it is becoming more common to
discover that some of those who are now green card holders or naturalized citizens have been "undocumented" at one time or another.

New Immigration Legislation

Despite the commitment and dedication of undocumented immigrants
to work hard and legalize themselves, Congress has passed the Immigration Control and Financial Responsibility Act of 1996, a bipartisan
immigration bill that drastically alters the lives of both undocumented
immigrants and legal immigrants. For example, legal immigrants are now
subjected to an affluence test when petitioning their families (140%

income above poverty level). Along with the Welfare Reform Bill (Personal Responsibility and Work Opportunity Act of 1996) passed in August 1996, which denies legal immigrants access to many public assistance programs, these laws create an unnecessary burden to immigrants.

Yet the outright intent of the new immigration laws is directed at illegal immigrants. Essentially, these laws are aimed not just to discourage undocumented migration to the United States but also to make life much more difficult for undocumented immigrants so that they will have no other choice left but to leave the country. For example, according to the National Immigration Forum (Forum Policy Team, 1996) and the *New York Times* (Gray, 1996), the new law will

- Bar undocumented immigrants from receiving Medicaid, food stamps, housing, unemployment, and financial aid for college
- Preclude payment of Social Securities benefits to undocumented immigrants
- Bar anyone unlawfully present for an aggregate of 12 months from adjusting his or her status to legal residency for 10 years
- Require states and higher education institutions to transmit to the INS copies of documents they accept from individuals verifying such individuals' citizenship or status
- Establish pilot programs in five states with high illegal populations so that employers can verify the legal status of prospective workers through a Justice Department program
- Raise the burden of proof for prospective employees who claim hiring discrimination on the basis of immigration status

Instead of making the transition from undocumented immigrant to legal immigrant easier and providing opportunities for undocumented immigrants to become bona fide contributing members to society, these laws condemn them to a slow death.

Nevertheless, the ramifications of these bills are not entirely confined to undocumented immigrants. These new laws will reduce the quality of life for us all. Despite their intent to drive undocumented immigrants out of the country, experience has proven the opposite result: That is, undocumented immigrants will be driven further underground. Withholding health care and education from undocumented immigrants poses numerous health and social risks. It will make treatment and prevention of communicable diseases all the more difficult. Restriction of educational opportunities is most likely to breed more discontent and violence. For those who experience psychological and sexual abuse from their employers, especially those Filipinas who work as domestic workers, the new laws leave them with almost no options at all.

Another difficulty with the new legislation is its tendency to sort immigrants into two categories—legal and illegal, documented and undocumented—and thus to simplify a complex reality. For instance, if an individual is waiting for a petition for residency in the United States, to what category would that person belong? What about those whose petitions were approved but who have now undergone a change in age or marital status that makes them ineligible for the petition they were approved for in the first place? My conversation with three immigration lawyers in New York City in October 1996 revealed that in these instances, the decision becomes discretionary on the part of the immigration judge. Furthermore, a new petition can be filed under a different category provided that the individual meets preexisting definitions and requirements of the category. Ultimately, the individual's legal limbo is then prolonged.

Finally, these bills have the effect of splitting the Filipino community apart. This is already evident in the lobbying and advocacy efforts of immigration activists. Already, the focus is on preserving the rights of legal immigrations while the needs and basic human rights of undocumented immigrants are neglected.

The increasing restrictiveness of U.S. immigration laws may indeed have the intended effect of discouraging Filipino illegal immigration, but it does not address the bigger problem of what to do with a large group of undocumented Filipinos who may have no intentions or means of leaving the United States. If the willingness to work and to assimilate is a condition for welcoming immigrants, then immigration laws should reflect this. But current immigration laws reflect otherwise.

Living as an undocumented immigrant is already fraught with danger. The new laws will increase such immigrants' vulnerability to all types of social and institutional abuse. Because massive migration of displaced workers from less developed to well-developed countries is already a global phenomenon, this reality must be considered in policy-making processes. The dilemma we are in is moral as well: When the powerless are systematically abused, where does our responsibility lie?

Conclusion

From the Chinese Exclusion Act of 1882 to the current immigration bills, anti-immigrant sentiment has ebbed and flowed with the politics of a given time. In the 1996 presidential election year, the issue of immigration was once again on the table, with the spotlight on undocumented immigrants. What has been touted as good policy, however, may simply be another political tool. And the effects on all immigrant communities, especially the Filipino immigrant community, are devastating.

Undocumented Filipinos seem to be the kind of immigrants that the United States is looking for: hardworking, averse to welfare, and English speaking. This observation was made by an immigration official who granted permanent residency to a Filipino undocumented family in December 1995. Yet the success story of this one Filipino family continues to be a rarity simply because immigration laws and procedures make it increasingly difficult and cumbersome to obtain legal residency even if a person has been living the United States for most of his or her life and has been a taxpayer.

Continuing the silence surrounding the realities of undocumented immigration is to remain tolerant of the injustices of our adopted country. The stories we have read in this chapter are real. Given the ebb and flow in immigration policy, these stories could well have been ours had we entered the United States at an inopportune time. Now that minority groups are asserting their political power, Filipino Americans have the opportunity to take the issue of undocumented immigration seriously. As undocumented Filipinos eventually acquire permanent residence and/or citizenship, they too face a greater responsibility to those they have left behind. In the words of one former undocumented immigrant, "Now that I'm a citizen, I will never vote for any politician who is against immigrants, legal and illegal. All the hardships I experienced could have been avoided if only the laws applied justice evenly."

References

Bean, F. D., Edmonston, B., & Passel, J. S. (Eds.). (1990). *Undocumented migration to the United States: IRCA and the experience of the 1980s*. Washington, DC: Urban Institute Press.

Cruz, N. (1996, August). *From individual to collective: Building a movement for Filipino American women*. Paper presented at the meeting of Filipino American Women's Network, Minneapolis.

Forum Policy Team. (1996). *Immigration bill, minus much of Title V, passes House and Senate* [Fax Memorandum]. Washington, DC: National Immigration Forum.

Gray, J. (1996, October). Senate approves a big budget bill beating deadline. *New York Times*, p. 1.

Immigration Control and Financial Responsibility Act of 1996, H.R. 2202, 104th Cong., 1st Sess. (1996).

Kuttner, R. (1991). Illegal immigration: Would a national ID card help? In N. Mills (Ed.), *Arguing immigration: Are new immigrants a wealth of diversity . . . or a crushing burden?* New York: Touchstone.

Personal Responsibility and Work Opportunity Act of 1996, H.R. 3734, 104th Cong., 1st Sess. (1996).

Urban Institute. (1994). *Immigration and the Filipino American community: Fact Sheet #1*. Washington, DC: Author.

Warren, R. (1990). Annual estimates of nonimmigrant overstays in the United States: 1985 to 1988. In F. D. Bean, B. Edmonston, & J. S. Passel (Eds.), *Undocumented migration to the United States: IRCA and the experience of the 1980s*. Washington, DC: Urban Institute Press.

9

Mail-Order Brides
An Emerging Community

Raquel Z. Ordoñez

Search for the American Traditional Wife and Blue-Eyed Babies

The practice of matchmaking between Americans and foreign women is not new in American culture. Obtaining wives through brokers played a great role in the early days of settlement of the United States. This is perhaps why American men assert that introductions and referrals through ads, letters, and fee-for-service businesses are perfectly legitimate ways of searching for their mates. What is new in the recent mail-order-bride phenomenon is that instead of looking for Europeans, American men have now turned their eyes toward Asians.

Although the practice of matchmaking or marriage brokering via letters has a long American tradition, it is something new among Filipinos. Marriage via correspondence and brokers did not play any role in the migration history of Filipino women as it did with the Japanese and Korean "picture brides" between 1907 and 1924 (Bradshaw, 1994). As an American colony, the early Filipino immigrants, who were mostly male farm laborers, were considered American nationals without citizenship privileges, and their wives and families were free to come with them to the United States. Not many women joined their husbands, for they had always thought that their husbands would return to the homeland. The biggest wave of migration of Filipino women was the military or war brides. They were wives of U.S. servicemen deployed in the Philippines during World War II and later during the Vietnam War when U.S. military installations in the Philippines expanded. Though Filipinos had a tradition of prearranged marriages negotiated by families to exchange, preserve, and expand family wealth and patronage, the practice of entering marriage by correspondence facilitated by commercial organizations was something unheard of—hence the social stigma. That this phenomenon is occurring simultaneously with the globalization of the world economy and the exodus of Filipino women as overseas contract workers evokes outrage among women advocates in the Philippines and in international forums. They protest the "wholesale commodification" of Filipino women in particular and of Third World women in general.

For both Filipino women and American men, stereotyped and idealized images influence the decision to seek each other. The testimonies of husbands manifest an idealization of the Filipino woman as possessing the virtues of a traditional wife that American women possessed in the past. What we are hearing from American men is a nostalgia that American women have now lost those qualities because of women's liberation.

Roberto,[1] 53, a doctor and a subscriber to an international matchmaking agency (IMA) called Asian Experience, laments the loss of the virtues of American women:

> I believe that more and more women in the United States have been conditioned into believing that only through a successful career can they be fulfilled, yet they would also like a happy marriage and a family although they don't seem to be as willing to sacrifice and work as hard for it as they do with their careers. As a result, they have downplayed the value of a successful and happy marriage. It is this conflict of confusing roles that they are grappling with that I believe has caused the unbelievably high divorce rates and infidelity in the U.S. (Asian Experience, n.d.)

In the same publication, David, 27, an electronic technician, describes the bride he seeks as "a homebody, a woman who is satisfied with the simple things in life: a loving husband and a nice home."

The American men imagine the Filipino woman as the epitome of the traditional wife: submissive, subservient, eager to please men and easy to please, erotic, exotic, a good housekeeper, contented with a nice home, faithful, loyal, and not inclined to divorce her husband. Promotional literature helps to reinforce and disseminate this stereotypic image. Imagine the expectations raised by the Asian Experience brochure with the following ecstatic testimonies:

> Congratulations! You have taken the first step towards discovering an eternal pleasure! This will happen when you find your number one Asian lady whose main objective is to please her husband. The enthusiasm shown and the pleasure they derive in accomplishing this goal is almost embarrassing! The beauty in this unique kind of treasure quest lies in the reality that somewhere on that vast Asian continent, a compatible lady is waiting to hear from you and we intend to do everything within our power to help you find her! As a matter of fact, we wouldn't be at all surprised if you entertained thoughts of polygamy before making your final selection! The happiest time of my life took place in 1982 when I met and married Victoria. In addition to being my wife and very best friend, she is also my nurse and my mother all rolled into one. However, don't be misled by rumors portraying Asian women as submissive and subservient as this is sheer nonsense! They are seeking a loving and permanent 50-50 relationship.

On the other hand, internalized colonization influences the Filipino women's preference for American men. Almost 400 years under two Western colonial powers, the ubiquitous presence of U.S. military men, and Hollywood have impressed on their consciousness a romanticized image of America and the American man. The most despicable evil that colonization has wrought is the longing to be the oppressor that remains in the enslaved consciousness of the colonized people long after the oppressor has gone. What is perceived as beautiful is fair skinned, high nosed, *mestiza*, and blue eyed. America is the land of milk and honey. Marrying a white American can lend Filipino women a sense of status and power, to the extent that when they look at their brown skin, they see white. It is interesting to note that in the catalogs, Filipino women always indicate their preference for Caucasians.

The newlyweds' visions of success and happiness are thwarted when reality does not confirm their idealized images and stereotyped expectations. Conflicts occur, and the new relationship is far from idyllic. Coming from a strong matriarchal culture, the Filipino wife demands more and more authority over family finances and decision making. Family obligations require her to send money back home, often without the agreement and knowledge of her husband. To have her own income, she works as a nanny or a domestic and learns new trade and skills at the same time, neglecting her housework. She is no longer submissive. Many Filipinas have survived the riskiest of situations as servants in Hong Kong, Japan, Singapore, and the Middle East. They have become empowered and have become confident that they could live without being dependent on a husband. They come to the United States determined to build a niche for themselves, equated with earning more money and having their own house. Interestingly, in this particular community that is the focus of the present study, the few women who demonstrated exceptional courage to leave abusive relationships and to seek help to redress the injustice done to them had all been overseas workers before coming to the United States. They also demonstrated extraordinary boldness in seeking and pursuing their own paths, independent of their husbands (Coalition for the Advancement for Filipino Women, 1994-1996; Ordoñez, 1996b).

On the other hand, as newcomers to the country, immigrant Filipino women encounter myriad problems exacerbated by language, misinformation about their legal rights, unemployment, and fear of deportation. They experience a level of racism permeating their husband's family, the workplace, and the community that will remain incomprehensible until they realize that marriage to a white American does not make one a white woman. On top of rejection by their white family, they suffer stigmatization by their own community, which could have provided them support in establishing their home and integrating them into the larger society.

Scope of the Study and Conceptual Framework

This chapter focuses on a mail-order-bride community in Long Island, New York City, and New York State that consists of some 40 families, and I refer to other such communities in other parts of the country as necessary. I am the president of the Coalition for the Advancement of

Filipino Women (CAFW), a New York-based network of organizations and individuals from all walks of life, cutting across class, gender, age, and professions, and dedicated to raising the status of women and their families and communities. Most of the husbands and wives cited in this chapter are members of CAFW. The information presented here was gathered through several years of living and working with them. Several cases discussed here were documented earlier by CAFW (1994-1996) for purposes of advocacy and legal assistance.

I will attempt to examine how psychosocial, economic, political, and cultural factors have influenced the growth of the mail-order-bride phenomenon in the United States. I will analyze the interplay of these factors with the historical issues of power, gender, class, and race—ubiquitous issues that amplify the injustice and stigma heaped on these women in both nations. In this context, I will describe the transformation of the mail-order bride into an immigrant Filipino woman and how these factors affect her capability and that of her American husband to integrate into the larger Filipino American society and American society.

Although this work is organized by transcultural and feminist frameworks, vast differences exist between the Third World and the developed world and between East and West. As we move back and forth in this study between the two worlds and worldviews, the same concepts may resonate in totally different ways. For instance, "racism" can never be existentially grasped by a Filipino woman until she comes to the United States. Although in her homeland she may be aware of the difference between the color of her Caucasian lover and her own brown skin, it is not until she experiences rejection by her white mother-in-law for being a brown-skinned Filipina that she will recognize the meaning of being a woman of color. In the same vein, the oppression caused by systemic poverty in the Third World is an experience alien to her American husband and family. Hence, her new family may never fully appreciate the nobility of the Filipino woman's act of taking the risks of marrying a stranger and leaving her homeland for a strange land in the hope of liberating herself and her family from poverty. If they do not reject her, they may patronize her and regard her as opportunistic.

An eclectic approach influences the development of the transcultural and feminist frameworks that inform this study. I draw from various schools that it is not possible to acknowledge adequately here. In trying to define the character of the emerging feminism among immigrant

Filipino women, I realize that it is not quite the same as the ideologies espoused by our white American sisters. First, feminism among Filipino women has its roots in an indigenous matriarchal culture. It was grounded in politics and the central role of women in the community. Women led the rebellions to overthrow the colonial power. Later, they became a force in the movement for national democracy, a movement that was strongly influenced by Leninist-Marxist ideology. However, Philippine laws (property, marriage, etc.) are based on Roman law (brought by Spain and the United States), which is patriarchal. Second, Filipino migration history has given feminism among Filipino American women a very different dimension. It has created a class society more rigid than the class system in the islands. In a way, the migration experience has suppressed the growth of feminism among Filipino American women. Their efforts have been concentrated on surviving in a strange land and overcoming migration stresses. Women came as the principal providers for families, here and in the homeland. Fear of losing their jobs is a very strong disincentive. They have tended to cooperate with the oppressive system and have generally not organized on a large scale, as black women and Latinas have, to fight discrimination, racism, or sexual harassment. On the other hand, they may show little interest in white feminist ideology because they are, in a way, more liberated. They are the breadwinners; they make major decisions on money and family matters. Issues such as abortion are not their major concern. Their concerns are how to keep their jobs, legalize their immigration status, petition their parents and children, buy a house, and keep their children in school.

The position of Filipino American women, like that described by Audre Lorde (1984) for African American "women of color," who have a parallel history of colonialism and slavery, is inextricably bound up with issues of class and race. Colonialism and slavery efficiently destroyed indigenous structures and replaced them by structures that breed oppression, injustice, and inequities dividing peoples by class, race, and gender. The immigrant woman of color is multiply oppressed— being a woman and being a woman who belongs to a racially discriminated class. The oppression suffered by the mail-order bride is even more intense and complex because she is also a woman stigmatized by her own class and by both women and men within her own community for the method by which she enters into marriage.

Definitions

Strictly, the term *mail-order brides* refers to women who are wives or fiancées of men who are U.S. citizens or permanent residents, whom they met through fee-for-service programs operated by international matchmaking agencies (IMAs). These agencies may offer dating, matrimonial, or social referral services, and they employ diverse schemes such as mail-order catalogs; recruitment of women; memberships; subscriptions; advertising; exchange of names, telephone numbers, addresses, or statistics; selection of photographs; bridal tours; parties; and introductions into various social environments in a foreign country. For higher fees, some IMAs offer additional services such as drafting letters, administering psychological tests to prospective wives, and planning wedding parties. Engagements or marriages occur after a period of correspondence. The immigration process begins when the U.S. citizen or permanent resident husband/fiancé petitions the Filipino bride/fiancée. On receiving the appropriate visa, she joins her American husband/fiancé in the United States.

The term *mail-order brides*, largely popularized by the media, is also widely used in government and United Nations documents; proposed legislation in the U.S. Congress uses this term. In their studies, Jedlicka (1991; personal communications, 1995, 1996) and Lin (1990) used the terms *intercultural correspondence wife* and *intercultural correspondence marriage* because they felt that the popular term unfairly stigmatizes the women involved. Nonetheless, replacing *mail-order bride* with a more neutral word runs the risk of losing the distinct contemporary meaning and connotations of this phenomenon.

The term *overseas contract workers* (OCWs) refers to men and women migrating to another country to perform services specified under a contract. Contract labor migration may be viewed within the context of the international division of labor, in which developing countries supply developed countries with cheap raw materials and cheap high- or low-skilled labor. A sexual division of labor has emerged in which women are recruited for low-skilled jobs traditionally performed by women: namely, as domestic helpers and entertainers.

The mail-order-bride phenomenon can be viewed from several perspectives. It can be seen as a tributary of the ever-widening stream of overseas migration—a flight from the depressed economic conditions, socioeconomic and natural upheavals, and extreme poverty that characterized the Philippines from the 1970s through the 1990s. It can be interpreted as a form of commodification and sexual exploitation of women. Here, industry, driven by supply and demand, and the Philippine government, driven by economic considerations, play a major role. The U.S. Immigration and Naturalization Service (INS) looks at it as a source of marriage fraud and a way for women to cheat the immigration restrictions. Still, it can be viewed as a natural way for people seeking friends and life partners to get together across national borders. Each and all of these perspectives demonstrate the interplay of a host of interrelated psychosocial, cultural, economic, political, and colonial factors both in the Philippines and in the United States.

Description of the Emerging Community

In the community I studied that originated from mail-order-bride unions, about 40 interracial families are closely bonded with each other. The community grows fast as children are born and as more women follow in the footsteps of those who came before them. An informal network exists, expanding across county and state boundaries. Considering the strong anti-immigrant sentiment sweeping the nation and the stringent legislative proposals that once passed would slash the Philippine quota by 85%, keep children over 21 years of age from being united with their parents, and make employer sponsorship virtually impossible, marriages with U.S. citizens might be the only door open for future Filipino immigration to the United States. Thus, Filipino arrivals under this arrangement may rightfully claim to be the last wave in the over 200 years of Filipino migration history until a time when the American society overcomes its fear of immigrants, and specifically Asian immigrants.

The duration of marital unions in the community that I studied ranged from 20 years to less than a year. Edith, an engineer at the New York City Transit Authority, and Joe, a teacher in Brooklyn, have been married for over 20 years. Mirriam and Jacques have been married 7 years and Joseph and Carla for 2 years, and Marissa, married to Gary, has just arrived from the Philippines. The wives, ages ranging from 23 to 35 at time of marriage, are usually younger than their husbands, with the age difference ranging from 5 to 30 years. The husbands are mostly middle class and highly educated; a few of them are not highly educated and work as bus drivers and salespersons. The majority have above-average income. The ethnicity of the husbands reflects that of the society: German-Jewish, German, French, Italian, and one African American from the Caribbean.[2]

A few of the women of this community are professionals—nurses, engineers, and teachers—and the majority have some college background. Except for a very few, most of the wives have worked for 5 or more years in Hong Kong, Japan, Singapore, and the Middle East before coming to the United States. This explains why they did not complete their college education and why they were older when they arrived in the United States. They must have left the Philippines as OCWs when they were 16 or 18 years old.[3] Without appropriate technical training, they find jobs as nannies and domestic helpers. These jobs are in high demand in New York, New Jersey, and Connecticut, where business executives and wealthy people reside. As former OCWs, sometimes in the houses of people of wealth such as princes and business executives and cosmopolites such as diplomats and socialites, some of them have acquired exceptional skills as international chefs and nannies with foreign language skills and social graces. Many are well traveled. These are qualifications that are very marketable and can command high fees.

The informal leader of the community is Diana. Diana herself is not a mail-order bride. She met Paul, a British engineer, while he was a U.S. corporation expatriate executive in the Philippines. They have been married for over 20 years. Paul returned to the United States with Diana 15 years ago. In the Philippines, she was a travel agency executive. In the United States, she had to work as a domestic to augment the family's income. After several years, she established her own job placement agency. Through this agency, even new arrivals are immediately placed in jobs. They are also trained and employed through the network of the Coalition for the Advancement of Filipino Women (CAFW).

Although this community originated from mail-order-bride relationships, it is growing with less use of the matchmaking organizations. Brides and grooms, husbands and wives now initiate and act as brokers and matchmakers by introducing relatives and friends to each other. American men and Filipino women in the Philippines correspond with each other and exchange photographs. Over a 2-year period, six more couples have been added to the community.

Carla, 33, and Joseph, 65, met through the Asian American Worldwide Services. They got married in Cebu after a year's correspondence. After 11 months, Carla arrived in the United States. Soon after, Carla's sister, Marissa, 29, requested that Joseph place her photo in a catalog. Joseph's friend, Gary, 52, was introduced through letters to Marissa. A few months later, Marissa arrived in the United States as Gary's fiancée.

Christenings of babies, birthdays, Thanksgiving, and Christmas are occasions when all of them get together and celebrate, sometimes in Suffolk County, Long Island, or New York City. In the summertime, they take a breather for several days in Matthew and Celine's sprawling estate in upstate New York. A perfect host, Matthew welcomes this occasion, accommodating as many as 60 families each time. It is a birthday party he gives Celine every year to lessen the homesickness she feels from being away from her friends.

The women also petition for their parents to come to the United States for the same reasons that other Filipino Americans do. They entrust the rearing of their children to their parents so that they can work outside of the home. Ten years ago, when Ruth was expecting her daughter, Dexter, her German American husband, thought it might be a good idea to petition her mother and father to help Ruth take care of the baby. Christine, their daughter, is now 9 years old. Ruth's father and mother, now U.S. citizens, still stay with them, an arrangement that allows the husband and wife to manage the family's jewelry shop.

They build their own support groups and network—find jobs, baby-sit, take care of the sick, and raise funds for each other. When Margie's husband and mother-in-law threw her and their baby out, Joseph and the other American husbands took up the cudgels for her. They accompanied her to the police to get an order of protection from her abusive husband and accompanied her to the court for the trial. Meanwhile, the group provided her a bed in their homes alternately and raised funds for her legal fees and the baby's milk. The case is still ongoing.

When CAFW did an advocacy for Carolina Consolacion, a 23-year-old Filipino woman who was accused of manslaughter for killing her abusive boyfriend, the group spontaneously responded. They sustained the support for almost 2 years, alternately visiting her in jail and attending the trials until Carolina was acquitted and released. Although Carolina is not a mail-order bride herself, it seems from the sincerity of their response that the group has more easily identified with her plight as a victim of injustice than other Filipinos in the community.

On another occasion, a women's shelter in northern New Jersey called the CAFW seeking help for Ceres. She had fled from her husband who was abusing and threatening to kill her. At the time, she had been in the United States barely 4 months. Her husband had sexually abused her and kept her virtually a prisoner. When she landed a job, her husband would take her to and from work. Her fear heightened when she discovered documents revealing that she was actually her husband's fourth wife. The two wives before her were both Filipinas and mail-order brides. From work, she fled to the shelter, which advocated for her. CAFW got legal assistance for Ceres, connecting with several agencies in New York and New Jersey, while the group raised money to relocate Ceres. A computer programmer, she now works in another state. It is not clear what fate befell the other wives.

In contrast to media reports, Lin (1990) found average to high levels of marital satisfaction among international correspondence couples, comparable to those of noninternational correspondence couples. There is evidence in the present study consistent with Lin's findings, except that the present study did not find a direct relationship between income and marital satisfaction. This might be due to the smallness of the group described in the present study. In Lin's study, 17% of those sampled reported incidents of violent behavior, a proportion higher than the national average of 11%. In my own study, in a group of some 40 families, there were two divorce cases and four documented cases of domestic violence over a period of 2 years (i.e., a rate of 10%). The relatively low prevalence of violence might be due, partially, to the support system and interventions provided by CAFW. This justifies the importance of early interventions. Yet contrary to the popular notion that the American husband is the perpetrator of violence, in one of the four cases, it was the Filipina wife who was the perpetrator and the American husband who was the victim. The psychological abuse suffered by the husband required him to be treated in a mental health facility. CAFW provided support systems for both husband and wife. The community members were understandably divided in their sympathy.

To all appearances, the mail-order-bride community that I studied is like any ordinary settlement, except that the group has kept to itself and does not reach out to or mingle with the larger Filipino American community, even in the same neighborhood. The stigma and shame are more keenly felt by the Filipino wives, and they discourage their husbands from participating in community activities. Not only the method by which the Filipino woman was able to "capture a Kano" but also the age difference between husband and wife is the subject of jokes in the larger Filipino American community. The husband is called "cradle snatcher," "seducer of a minor," and "sugar daddy." Filipinos talk openly about the young Filipina wife who married the old American husband only "to vacuum his wealth." They even tell her directly to spend as much of her husband's money as she can. When there are rumors of incidents of violence, divorce, and troubled marriage, they immediately conclude that this is because of the mail-order origin of the marriage, as if violence and turmoil never visited their marriages. They are outraged by stories of Filipino mail-order brides in the media and in cyberspace; it is "racially demeaning." They invite the couple to their parties, but behind their backs, they say that she is a disgrace to the Filipino race, that she is the cause of whites' racial slurs. At the same time, the Filipina wife suffers discrimination from her husband's family. In unprintable language, Margie's mother-in-law told her that she could not accept her as a daughter-in-law. Her mother-in-law's constant interfering with the couple's household, racial slurs, and the indecisiveness of Margie's husband and his inability to stand up for his wife caused the breakdown of the marriage. Margie sought help of CAFW only after she and her baby had been thrown out of their home. Margie left a Long Island house worth $225,000 and a husband who earns $80,000 a year as a physical therapist.

The history of migration of Filipinos to the United States has resulted in rigid class divisions. Responding to U.S. immigration policies, Filipinos came in several waves of migration, each wave bringing in a distinct class of people. This alienated them further from each other, fragmenting a community already divided by tribalism and regionalism in the homeland. The class issue is even more sharply delineated in the case of mail-order brides. Not only are they pariahs for the aberrant method by which they contracted marriage—a method that according to the National Economic and Development Authority (NEDA; 1989-1990) "erodes the values of marriage and family and the women's self-worth" (p. 125)—they also occupy the lowest rung of the totem pole: the ex-OCWs, the nannies, and domestics. The ambivalence with which Filipino Ameri-

cans regard mail-order-bride couples, manifesting simultaneous acceptance and rejection, patronizing and aversion, undermines the couple's
capability to integrate into the Filipino American community and American society.

Feminization of Poverty and Overseas Migration

Considering the motives that impel women to leave their country, the
mail-order-bride practice could be seen as an alternative to overseas contract work or becoming an "imported bride" for a Japanese man. Though
all these practices entail risks, marriage presents a much better alternative
to contract working because it implies a more permanent relationship
and the opportunity to work, and there is less problem in legitimizing
one's status in a foreign country. Furthermore, marrying an American is
a much better alternative than marrying a Japanese mainly because of
the possible involvement of the Japanese underworld in the brokering
that attends the recruitment of Filipino brides for Japanese men.

The massive migration of women, either as temporary contract
workers or as permanent migrants, could be attributed to the feminiza-
tion of poverty. Working abroad is perceived by these women to be
"their—and their families'—only hope of breaking away from the vicious cycle of prevailing poverty and unemployment besetting the country" (NEDA, 1989-1990, p. 125).

The patriarchal structures grafted by both the Spanish and American
colonizers onto the indigenous matriarchal culture of the colonized
people resulted in the ambiguous status of the Filipino woman and the
many roles she plays in the family and in the society. By statutes, she is
subservient to her husband. It is only now—with the pressures from the
home-grown feminist movement in the Philippines—that laws are being
examined and revised to give women more rights, including rights to
own property, to enter into contracts without their husband's consent,
and to initiate dissolution of marriage without being penalized. By
tradition, however, the woman possesses substantial authority in the
family, as well as equally enormous responsibilities. She manages the

family finances and makes major family decisions; she is the principal caregiver. Her husband gives her his income, and she is expected to meet all the needs of the family. When the income is not sufficient, or when her husband loses his job, she is still expected to meet all the needs by using her own wits.

Family obligation is a very strong tradition shared by men and women and parents and children alike. Contributing to the economic advancement of the family is a major obligation, and overseas contract working presents an opportunity to pursue this goal. Entering into marriage via the mail-order-bride scheme presents another opportunity. Obtaining material security for the family is such a compelling reason for both men and women that if there were an avenue for men such as the women have with the mail-order-bride business, I have no doubt that Filipino men would not hesitate to try their luck.

Glaring economic and social inequities and inequalities in the Philippines, especially in land ownership and access to resources and capital, are aggravated by a huge foreign debt. External debt servicing averaged 52.8% of the annual budget from 1986 to 1991, and structural adjustment imposed by creditors left almost nothing for economic and social services.[4] The cutbacks in basic services and in subsidies for food and commodities increased the obligation of women to work harder for less and less real income because of devaluation, inflation, and taxation.

In a country where 70% of the resources and capital in the Philippines is owned by the top 10% of the population, 50.5% of Filipinos live under the poverty level (1991). The United Nations Development Programme's (1994) *Human Development Report 1994* indicated that in 1992, 35.2 million Filipinos out of a total population of 65 million were in absolute poverty. *The Philippine Country Report on Women, 1986-1995* (National Commission on the Role of Filipino Women [NCRFW], 1994) underscores the highly unequal structure of wealth and income as the big stumbling block to alleviating poverty. The top 10% of families continue to receive more than one third of total family income, while the bottom 30% and 50% of families receive 9% and 20% of total family income, respectively. Only 15% of the 10 million Filipinos who make up the agricultural labor force own the land they till. When Cory Aquino took power in 1986, the poverty threshold per family of five was $749; it took $1,075 to support a family. In 1991, the poverty threshold per family was $1,470 when average family expenditure was $2,080.[5]

The Aquino administration (1986-1992) was wracked with seven coup attempts, natural disasters, and huge external debt servicing (more than 50% of the GDP). In the second quarter of 1991, the unemployment rate for women peaked at 18.3%, compared with the 11.9% for men during the same period. The situation appeared to have worsened: The lowest unemployment rate for women was reported in 1989 at 9.2; that for men was reported in the fourth quarter of 1987 at 6.6%.

Although women dominated the working-age population, their participation in the labor force was generally lower than that of men. Women's participation rate in 1985 was 47.3%, an increase of 5.3% from 42% in 1980; it remained steady at 47.5% in 1990. In comparison, men's participation in the labor force increased slightly, from 77.7% in 1980 to 79.9% in 1985 and remained at this level up to 1990. In 1990, only 9.1 million out of 19.5 million women of working age were economically active (NCRFW, 1994, pp. 75-78).

To alleviate the financially strapped, corruption-riddled, and labor surplus economy, the Philippine government not only sanctioned but even encouraged overseas employment as a strategy for development. Bilateral labor agreements were sought aggressively, especially with governments in the Middle East, Hong Kong, Japan, Singapore, and the United States, for nurses and health care professionals. From some $300 million in the 1970s, OCW foreign exchange remittances reached $6.8 billion in 1995 ("OCWs," 1996).[6] This is an enormously significant contribution to revitalizing the Philippine economy. It has also bled the country of skilled human resources, so much so that the Philippine Institute for Development Studies reported that out of four professionals, three go abroad (Dass, 1996; Orbeta & Sanchez, 1996). It is questionable whether the OCW dollars can adequately compensate for the human and social costs of overseas migration, including the breakdown of families, the exploitation of workers, and the sexual exploitation of women.

Whereas the earlier wave of overseas workers, mainly to the Persian Gulf, consisted predominantly of male construction workers, the OCW population has recently become increasingly female. The Philippine Overseas Employment Agency estimated that in 1991 there were 476,693 OCWs, increasing by 59% since 1984. The National Statistics Office's (1992) *October 1991 Survey on Overseas Workers* reported that in 1991 there were 721,100 OCWs in the United States, including both legal and illegal workers. In 1991, 52% of all OCWs were women. More than half, or almost 60% of these, were employed as domestic helpers in more than 175 countries. This trend is consistent with earlier years. In 1987, female contract workers were engaged in service (59.2%) and professional, technical, and related work (34.8%). Over three quarters (75.9%) of those in service were domestic helpers, and over half of those engaged in professional, technical, and related work were entertainers.

Entertainers going to Japan, which corners 97% of the market for entertainers, increased sevenfold in just 7 years, from 9,100 in 1979 to 77,275 in 1986. At the same time, Filipino women left for Japan as brides of Japanese men, averaging 1,500 a year. The Commission on Filipinos Overseas (CFO) reported that for the period August 15-31, 1989, alone, it had interviewed 389 Filipina would-be brides of Japanese men (NCRFW, 1994).

It is not by accident that during the same period the mail-order-bride practice has flourished. Migration figures from CFO reveal that female migration has increased considerably through the years, registering a 31.9% increase from 1984 (24,581) to 1987 (32,429). In just 1 year, women going to the United States as fiancées doubled; in 1987, 2,113 Filipino women were registered as fiancée-visa holders, an increase of 91% from the 1986 figure of 1,109. This does not include those who left the country as spouses of foreign nationals, tourists, and nonimmigrant visa holders who may permanently stay abroad. As of the first 7 months of 1988, there were already 2,317 registered fiancée-visa holders. Available statistics from CFO show that about 21% of all interracial marriages involving Filipino women are through the mail-order-bride practice. CFO confirms that the figure would increase significantly if unreported cases of mail-order-bride marriages were included. The United States is the number-one country of destination, absorbing 50% of those registered in 1987; next are Australia (40%) and Canada (6%; NCRFW, 1994).

U.S. Policies Reinforce Oppression of Immigrant Women

Congressional findings revealed that there are approximately 200 IMA companies operating in the United States, with an estimated 2,000 to

3,500 American men finding their wives through mail-order catalogs each year. It is interesting to note that several big organizations are owned by husband-and-wife teams who married through the mail-order-bride scheme. Tessie Florence founded the Asian American Worldwide Services (AAWS) in 1980 with her Caucasian husband, Lou, immediately after their marriage. George and Victoria Elkington got married in 1982 and have been operating the Asian Experience ever since. The businesses seem lucrative. AAWS was reported to gross $250,000 a year; Cherry Blossom grossed about half a million dollars.

In the Philippines, women's and Christian organizations protested the exploitation of women and were successful in persuading the Philippine government to take some steps to discourage the mail-order-bride industry. In 1990, legislation was passed to ban personal advertising and to penalize local recruiters and publishers with imprisonment and fines. But even if this policy were enforced, it would not be very effective because the business is a global network and many Filipino women have gone overseas as OCWs, where they get more contacts. Thus, Tessie Florence could truthfully claim that AAWS's "supply of Filipino women did not stop" despite this measure.

On March 2, 1995, in a Seattle courthouse, Timothy Craig Blackwell, 48, shot and killed his wife, Susana Remerata Blackwell, who would have been 26, and her two friends, Phoebe Paclibar Dizon and Veronica Laureta Johnson. Susana, a hotel and restaurant management graduate, and Blackwell, a computer technician, had met through the *Asian Encounters* magazine. They corresponded for 18 months and got married on March 31, 1993, in the Philippines. Susana finally arrived in the United States on February 5, 1994. The incidents of abuse were well documented by the police, when Timothy was jailed briefly for assault and released, and by the shelter where Susana sought refuge just 12 days after her arrival. Ten days after Susana had left him, Blackwell filed a petition for the annulment of the marriage, accusing her of being a fraudulent gold digger. He claimed that he had spent $10,000 in marrying her and wanted her to pay him back. Susana, in a countersuit seeking divorce, claimed that she had been a victim of physical and sexual brutality by Blackwell. It was during a court hearing on the annulment of their marriage that he shot his wife, her unborn baby, and her two friends in cold blood. Blackwell's lawyer argued that Blackwell suffered a "mental snap" after learning that Susana had become pregnant by a Filipino after she had left him (Beltran, 1996; Ordoñez, 1996a). This was after he had sought annulment of the marriage.

Although intimate violence affects all ethnic, socioeconomic, and age groups, the prevalence might even be higher among mail-order-bride unions (Lin, 1990). Fear of husbands and of deportation, social stigma, taboos, and ignorance prevent women from accessing services and, even if they do, from volunteering information about their real circumstances. Migration stresses, including economic pressures, social pressures, discrimination, rejection, alienation, and stigmatization within and outside of their own communities, are a burden to the interracial couples. These are exacerbated when differences in norms, values, and habits and thwarted expectations lead to conflicts and tensions. Incidents of domestic violence are largely unreported, and only the most diabolic ones get into the mainstream media.

Emelita Villa was only 18 when she married Jack Reeves, a retired master sergeant from Texas whom she met through a catalog service. She was Reeves' fourth wife. His first marriage was annulled. Both his second wife, Sharon, and his third wife, Myong, a 26-year South Korean mail-order bride, died under mysterious circumstances. On October 12, 1994, Emelita was reported missing. Exactly a year later, her skeletal remains were found in Lake Whitney, the same lake where Myong had drowned. Her death had been ruled accidental by the investigators. Emelita's death reopened Sharon's case, which had been ruled as suicide in 1978. Reeves was convicted for the murder of his two wives and was sentenced to 99 years' imprisonment, on top of the 35 years for killing Sharon. It was reported that within only weeks of Emelita's disappearance, Reeves was already searching for a new bride ("Texan Meted 99 Years," 1996).

These incidents called the attention of Washington State Representative Velma Veloria and Senator Herbert Kohl of Wisconsin to the evils of the mail-order-bride business. Senator Kohl (personal communications, April 22 and September 13, 1996) authored a bill requiring IMAs to disseminate immigration and naturalization information to recruits (Mail-Order Bride Business Amendment to the Immigration Control and Financial Responsibility Act of 1996). The bill also imposes a penalty of $20,000 for each violation. The bill, when passed, will give some measure of justice to women, as it prescribes that profit-making businesses assume a degree of responsibility. It also reinforces the protection provided for the abused wives under the Violence Against Women Act of 1994.

The primary intent of U.S. immigration laws and policies has been to control illegal immigration and marriage fraud by penalizing the women. The INS position has been that the women are frauds trying to cheat the INS and the American citizen; thus, American society and American men must be protected from these foreign women. In 1985, INS Commissioner Alan Nelson testified in Congress, asserting a 30% fraud rate in marriage arrangements between foreign nationals and U.S. citizens. This estimate was later adjusted to 8%. Under the Immigration Marriage Fraud Amendments of 1986 (IMFA) and the Immigration Act of 1990, the wife is granted a 2-year conditional resident status (which may be renewed for an indefinite number of years), during which time the couple must remain married. The good faith of the marriage must be demonstrated to adjust the wife's status. If the marriage is dissolved during this period, the wife becomes a deportable illegal alien because only the husband can petition her. In 1991, the INS published interim rules amending the conditional residence regulations. Under the new rules, battered spouses are required to prove abuse and extreme mental cruelty with expert testimonies.

The injustice that these laws inflict on immigrant women is very grave because the laws reinforce the husband's total control over the petition process, consequently giving him ample power over his newly arrived wife, who is already economically dependent on him. Considering the precarious situation of illegal aliens in the United States, this gives the husband total power over his wife's life and puts her at greater risk for abuse. It gives the wife no alternative but to remain in marriage, even if the relationship is abusive. The amended rules on conditional residence regulations are more onerous because of the high evidentiary requirements. A newcomer who is abused, without resources, rejected, ignorant of the bureaucratic maze, and without family or a support system is hardly the person who could satisfy the INS's "impossibly high standard of proof." In 1994, the Violent Crime Control and Law Enforcement Act amended the IMFA to allow married conditional permanent residents who could prove battery and extreme cruelty perpetrated by their spouse to self-petition for removal of the conditional status. It is landmark legislation that gives immigrant women a certain measure of justice, as well as power and control over the immigration process. It reduces their dependency on marriage to survive in this country and gives them more power and control over their own lives.

Conclusion

In this chapter, I have attempted to present the Filipina mail-order bride from several perspectives. I have also tried to humanize her so that she may be seen not simply as a poster girl denouncing sexual exploitation or a catalog girl courting consumers but as an immigrant Filipina woman. Given certain conditions and a support system in an accepting environment, tensions and violence may be reduced, and mail-order-bride unions can evolve into healthy families and communities. Another context that needs to be examined, but that the scope of this chapter did not allow, is the mail-order-bride migration wave in relation to the various waves of Filipino migration to America and the evolving Filipino American community. U.S. policies have always determined what kind of people could come, thus contributing to the fragmentation of the community and division along class lines. Yet the evolving community manifests diverse cultures that are beyond class definitions. In this context, we may better appreciate the meaning of the mail-order bride in the totality of the Filipino American experience.

Notes

1. All names, except those of public information, have been changed to protect the individuals' privacy.

2. The husbands' profiles are consistent with those from the samples of Jedlicka (1991) and Lin (1990). The profiles of wives reflect those of Lin's sample, except that Lin's sample reported 15.1 years of education compared to 12 years in the present study. This difference may be due to the fact that the women in Lin's study have an average of 3.9 years of marriage and might have continued their studies in the United States.

3. Minimum legal age for recruitment as an OCW is 18 years. However, in the desire to recruit more women, unscrupulous entrepreneurs fake the women's birth certificates. Some of the women are only 16 years old, or as young as 14, as in the case of Sarah Balabagan.

4. All figures cited in this and the next six paragraphs are Philippine government figures from NEDA (1989-1990) and the NCRFW (1994).

5. The Cory Aquino administration could be credited for establishing the poverty line. The Marcos regime during the military rule evaded establishing the poverty threshold.

6. The Central Bank's estimate of OCW remittances was $4.93 billion in 1995 ("OCWs," 1996). A study made by HG Asia Securities Co., a global stock investment firm, estimated $6.8 billion. The study argued that the Central Bank's estimate was based only on remittances handled by banks ("OCWs," 1996).

References

Asian Experience. (n.d.). *Membership newsletter*. Novato, CA: Author.

Beltran, M. (1996, March). When looking for Mr. Right goes wrong. *Filipinas*, pp. 42-44.

Bradshaw, C. K. (1994). Asian and Asian American women: Historical and political considerations in psychotherapy. In L. Comas-Diaz & B. Greene (Eds.), *Women of color: Integrating ethnic and gender identities in psychotherapy*. New York: Guilford.

Coalition for the Advancement of Filipino Women. (1994-1996). Unpublished records, New York office.

Dass, J. (1996, August 7-13). Three out of four professionals go abroad. *Manila Mail* [San Francisco], p. 12.

Immigration Act of 1990. 8 U.S.C. § 1186a(c)(4)(Supp. V 1993).

Immigration marriage fraud: Hearing of fraudulent marriage and fiancé arrangements to obtain permanent resident status before the Subcommittee on Immigration and Refugee Policy of the Senate Committee of the Judiciary, 99th Cong., 1st Sess. (1986).

Immigration Marriage Fraud Amendments of 1986. 8 U.S.C. § 1184(d), 1186(a) (1988 & Supp. V 1993).

Jedlicka, D. (1991). Modes of mate selection. In W. M. Kephart & D. Jedlicka (Eds.), *The family, society, and the individual* (7th ed.). New York: HarperCollins.

Lin, J. L. (1990). *Marital satisfaction and conflict in intercultural correspondence marriage.* Unpublished doctoral dissertation, University of Washington.

Lorde, A. (1984). *Sister outsider*. New York: Crossing.

Mail-Order Bride Business Amendment to the Immigration Control and Financial Responsibility Act of 1996, H.R. 2202, § 652, 104th Cong., 1st Sess. (1996).

National Commission on the Role of Filipino Women. (1994). *The Philippine country report on women, 1986-1995*. Manila: Author.

National Economic and Development Authority, Philippine Government. (1989-1990). *Philippine Development Plan for Women, 1989-1992*. Manila: National Commission on the Role of Filipino Women.

National Statistics Office. (1992).*Highlights of the October 1991 Survey on Overseas Workers*. Manila: Author.

OCWs add $6.8 billion to Philippine economy. (1996, June 28-July 4). *Filipino Reporter*, p. 14.

Orbeta, A., & Sanchez, M. T. (1996, January-June). The Philippines in the regional division of labor. *Philippine Labor Review* [Manila], pp. 5, 17, 46.

Ordoñez, R. (1996a, May 31-June 6). Mail marriage very risky. *Filipino Reporter*, pp. 19, 34.

Ordoñez, R. (1996b, January 5-11). Meet mail-order brides. *Filipino Reporter,* pp. 19, 35.
Texan meted 99 years in fourth wife's slaying. (1996, September 26). *Philippine News*, pp. 1, 11.
United Nations Development Programme. (1994). *Human development report 1994.* New York: Oxford University Press, p. 134.
Violence Against Women Act of 1994. 4 U.S.C. §§ 40701-40703.
Violent Crime Control and Law Enforcement Act of 1994. 8 U.S.C. § 1154(a)(i)(H).

10

Part of the Community
A Profile of Deaf Filipino Americans in Seattle

Cynthia C. Mejia-Giudici

Deaf people can do anything . . . except hear.
I. King Jordan, President of Gallaudet University

T his is the story of seven Deaf Filipino Americans living and working in the Seattle metropolitan area, their unique status within the Filipino American and Deaf communities, and their desire to be recognized as valuable members of their communities.

They will help us to understand deafness and Deaf Culture and, most important, to respect the deaf or hard-of-hearing Filipino Americans in our community. (Following current accepted practice, we use the terms *deaf* and *hard of hearing* rather than *hearing impaired*.)

AUTHOR'S NOTE: Material from the interviews with Robert La Torre, Ernesto and Lila Del Rosario, Giancarlo Gelicame, Maria Udarbe Lee, Evelyn Banez Jackson, and Ariele Belo Faulkner is used with permission.

143

Background: Deafness

There are some 22.5 million people in the United States with a hearing loss. Of that number, about 2 million are deaf. (Deafness is a medical condition, and the lower-case "d" in words such as *deafness* or *deaf* is used when discussing that condition. On the other hand, a capitalized "D," as in *the Deaf* or *Deaf community*, indicates a distinct group of people with an explicit sense of Deaf identity who are embraced by the larger Deaf community.)

The medical condition of deafness is a hearing impairment ranging from a mild to a profound loss. Speech sounds in the English language occur in the 5- to 35-decibel (db) range. A hard-of-hearing person (40 db to 69 db) has a mild or moderate loss that makes it difficult to understand speech through the auditory channel with or without the hearing aid. Therefore, a deaf person with a severe to profound loss (70+ db) cannot understand speech through the auditory channel with or without the use of a hearing aid (Moores, 1978).

American Sign Language (ASL), mistakenly confused with "broken English," has been identified after years of controversy as a true language with syntax and grammatical rules (Stokoe, 1978). Now the Deaf have attained a "new consciousness . . . with a special linguistic identity" (Sacks, 1989, p. 150). ASL, widely used among the Deaf, is an expression of Deaf Pride and Deaf Power in every part of the United States. Seattle, the home of our focus group, is a progressive and scenic city in the Pacific Northwest that attracts many Deaf people. One of the nation's five Regional Centers for the Deaf is in Seattle Central Community College. It has an Interpreter Training Program that works alongside the Community Service Center for the Deaf and Hard of Hearing; the Hearing, Speech and Language Center; Abused Deaf Women Advocacy Services; and schools offering ASL classes. The 130,519 deaf people living in the surrounding King County represent 8% of the county's total population (Colon, 1996). Seattle has proven to be an ideal place for deaf and hard-of-hearing people to find resources and support services and to network with other deaf people.

Background of the Interviews

These seven Deaf Filipino Americans were interviewed during the winter of 1995 and the spring of 1996. In each interview, I sought the basis of their sense of identity and pride as Deaf people and Filipino Americans and discussed several broad issues with them: Which took precedence, Filipino pride or Deaf pride? What factors encouraged or discouraged membership in either community? How could these two groups work together toward a better community? Were these seven individuals as uninterested in the Filipino American community as the community was in them?

The interviewees (who gave permission for their names to be used for this chapter) were Robert La Torre, Ernesto and Lila Del Rosario, Giancarlo Gelicame, Maria Udarbe Lee, Evelyn Banez Jackson, and Ariele Belo Faulkner. Of this group, only Ariele was American born. I already knew two of the participants; the others were introduced to me at typical Filipino social gatherings after word of our project spread in this small community.

Filipinos: Appearances and Citizenship

In general, Filipinos are obsessed with appearances and their sense of beauty. How many times have I heard, "She is beautiful! She must be a *mestiza* [lighter skin tone, a European nose, and tall—usually a mixture of native Filipino and European parentage]," "Too bad he has such a flat nose!" or "What a *potoot!* [shorty]." Physical appearances are easy to change, and some blemishes are easy to conceal. But how can you hide a disability? Should you try? Do Filipinos discriminate against the Deaf more than other groups do? Does an "invisible handicap" such as deafness make Deaf people unattractive?

Deafness is not "cured" because it is not a disease. A growing number of deaf individuals would not trade their hearing loss for the ability to hear after struggling with barriers in a nondeaf population that uses stereotypes of disabled people and pities the deaf. Such "Deaf Pride," like pride in any other heritage, can only advance society's efforts to eradicate fear and long-held prejudices.

Indeed, Deaf Filipino Americans are like citizens of a Philippine "province" who speak a distinct dialect (the language of signs) yet pledge allegiance to the Philippines and the United States.

This "minority within a minority" also incorporates those who received most of their education in the Philippines (Giancarlo Gelicame, Ernesto and Lila Del Rosario, and Robert La Torre) and those who came here at an early age—including one American born—and were educated in the United States (Maria Udarbe Lee, Ariele Belo Faulkner, and Evelyn Banez Jackson). Both groups communicate primarily in ASL or, with the "signing-impaired" general public, with a pad and pencil, body language, and gestures.

Like most Filipinos, all seven were taught that a good education guaranteed career opportunities. All attended high school, and some received bachelor of arts or bachelor of science degrees. One is considering graduate school.

Digression on Deafness: Deaf Education in the Philippines and the United States

The Philippine-educated group includes graduates of the Philippine School for the Deaf (PSD) and the Southeast Asian Institute for the Deaf (SAID), located on the campus of Maryknoll (now Merriam) College in Quezon City. PSD (until 1976 the School for the Deaf and Blind) was established in 1907 when Dr. David P. Barrows, Director of Education in the Philippines, invited a Miss Delia Rice from the United States to teach a group of deaf students. PSD, located in Pasay City, is the only governmental school for the deaf and the best model of public education for the deaf in the Philippines. PSD, which offers housing when needed, offers classes in kindergarten (for 3- to 6-year-olds) to high school levels, literacy, continuing education, and extracurricular activities. Sign language and

English are the mediums of instruction. Special services include speech, speech training, and rhythm and auditory training.

Deaf and hard-of-hearing students in the United States can attend state institutes of the Deaf, usually residential, that provide a strong sense of community and membership for their students and an emphasis on ASL and Deaf Culture. Other deaf students can also attend a public school with a "mainstream" program for the deaf and hard of hearing (Maria Lee, Evelyn Jackson, and Ariele Faulkner in our group, for example).

Public Law 94-142, the Education for All Handicapped Children Act (renamed the Individuals With Disabilities Education Act in 1990), was passed by the U.S. Congress in 1975 to guarantee every child an education in the least restrictive environment. It also supports a child's right to an individualized education program (IEP) agreed on by the parents and school, including services in his or her native language or the most comfortable means of communication. Deaf or hard-of-hearing students in mainstreamed classrooms receive support services such as speech therapy, audiological services, interpreters (manual or oral), and resource classes. Thanks to such services, deaf students can participate in classes alongside their nondeaf peers, as well as in self-contained classes with other deaf or hard-of-hearing students.

Heated debate among experts in education of the Deaf on the value of the prevailing educational philosophy ("inclusion") continues. This places all students regardless of learning capacity or disability in general-population classes, sometimes with minimal special services. Opponents say that regular class placements are not ideal for many deaf and hard-of-hearing students. And in many mainstreamed settings, there are very few, if any, deaf adults or Deaf role models on staff.

The Interviews

Interview settings varied: They were held one on one, at a birthday party, or over Filipino food; some were recorded. Follow-up interviews with all seven were done by the teletypewriter (TTY; see the following section, "A Digression on Deafness: Communication Devices").

The Ticket Out: Robert La Torre,
Born in Manila in 1965

> **Q:** Why are you proud of your deafness and your Filipino back-
> ground?
>
> **A:** I am not exactly proud of my deafness, but I am not ashamed of
> it. I accept it as God's plan for my life. True, it is not easy for me
> to communicate with hearing people, but there are many ways to
> communicate with them if they are patient and willing enough to
> communicate with us. I am proud of my Filipino background
> because of the value we place on friendship and neighborliness.

Robert La Torre had the parental and financial support he needed
for his school years. Marcelino, his father, always encouraged his deaf
sons, Robert and George, to do their best. Robert's deafness was detected when he was 3 years old. Marcelino wanted a second opinion on
his son's diagnosis and even considered corrective surgery. Of Robert's
hearing loss, he felt "hopeless" and worried about the future: "I thought
I would not be able to impart any of my idealism to them. They would
not be able to comprehend the abstract ideas about friendship, loyalty,
honesty, and other virtues to survive in this life."

Robert was enrolled in the PSD day program when he was 5 years
old. Throughout Robert's school years, Marcelino supported the local
Deaf population by telling neighbors and peers that his sons and their
friends were just like anyone else and that sign language was another
communication system. He also invited Robert's PSD classmates to the
La Torre home. Robert's special aptitude for computers led to a job as
data entry operator in Manila.

In 1985, when Robert was 19 years old, the La Torres moved to
Seattle. There Robert and George quickly learned ASL and about American Deaf culture while continuing their interest in computers. They work
as computer operators for the city of Seattle and Boeing.

Robert enjoys his life here in the United States after living in the
Philippines, where he was teased by insensitive or even rude people who
laughingly mimicked him with sloppy, made-up signs. But his tremendous self-confidence has enabled him to become a major link to various
members of the Filipino Deaf community; he introduced me to several

members of the community, such as Ernesto and Lila Del Rosario, at a
Philippine Independence Day celebration.

The Oldest Son: Ernesto Del Rosario,
Born in Manila in 1933

> Q: When you graduated from the Philippine School for the Deaf
> and Blind, what did your parents hope for you to do?
> A: I don't know . . . no goals.

Ernesto Del Rosario's mother liked to watch Tarzan movies, and her
favorite character was the chimpanzee who communicated with Tarzan
through gestures. As a result of her fondness for these movies, it was
no surprise to her that Ernesto was born deaf soon afterward. This
superstitious belief is accepted by his friends and family. Heredity,
illnesses, or accidents are major causes of deafness. Moores (1978, p. 67)
stated that about 30% of cases of deafness cannot be attributed to any
known cause.

Ernesto attended public school first but stayed home after being
ostracized by his classmates. He communicated with his family through
the use of "home signs": gestures for bathroom, eat, sleep, here, there,
you and I, and so forth. Toward the end of the war, a relative enrolled
him in PSD, and he jokes about standing out as a 13-year-old in the
primary school classes. He soon mastered sign language and when
graduating at age 22 was the class valedictorian.

Ernesto then worked at the Luneta Coffee Shop—well-known for
employing the deaf—as dishwasher, waiter, and then manager. He held
that position until retiring a few years ago.

He and Lila are perfect hosts today when Filipino American Deaf
friends visit their daughter's home to socialize. Ernesto obviously en-
joyed teaching me signs for various versions of the typical Filipino dish
pancit.

But Ernesto becomes very serious when he talks about the Philippines and its lack of young, strong leaders in the Deaf community back
home. He is still in awe of the events initiated by student leaders at
Gallaudet University[1] in Washington, D.C., in March 1988: a landmark
year for proud Deaf Americans. Students at Gallaudet, the premier

institution of higher learning for the Deaf, rejected the fourth university president because she was not deaf and not only did not know sign language but knew nothing about Deaf culture. The well-publicized "Deaf President Now" movement swept Gallaudet psychology professor I. King Jordan into office as Gallaudet's first Deaf president in its 124-year history. Deaf Americans taking such unabashed control of their own destiny impressed Ernesto, himself a leader of the Deaf community in the Philippines. He paints a bleak picture of deaf people's lot there. The lack of special services such as interpreters, communication devices such as closed captioning and teletypewriters (TTYs), good job opportunities, and counseling limits their social, emotional, and physical advancement. The government cannot afford to provide some of the "luxuries" available to the Deaf in the United States. Although he does not admit it, perhaps Ernesto Del Rosario dreams of returning to the Philippines to fill the critical role of inspirational leader or advisor for his countrymen and countrywomen.

A Homemaker: Lila Del Rosario,
Born in Manila in 1931

Maybe God didn't love me.

Ninety percent of deaf children have hearing parents. One can take preventive measures against deafness with German measles (rubella) immunization. Other common uninherited causes of deafness include uncontrolled fever, falls from high places, and inadequate medical attention for chronic ear infections. Once deafness is detected, parents often fall into the familiar cycle of guilt, blame, and hopelessness.

Lila's mother was taken by surprise. Lila was born hearing but became deaf at age 2 from an overdose of antibiotics. She was suddenly thrown into a silent world. Her mother, wanting Lila to grow up as "normal," told her daughter to use her voice in public instead of signing. Having invested a lot of time and money in Lila's education (even hiring a tutor when her school closed down during World War II), her mother had high expectations for acceptance by the public. Lila resumed classes at PSD after the war but was uncomfortable being a 14-year-old in elementary school. And her mother was suspicious of the boys in Lila's classes at PSD, so she transferred Lila to a high school program at Philippine Women's University.

In 1957, Lila's priest brother insisted that she come to Philadelphia to see him and live in the United States. She stayed until 1961, working as a catechism teacher for the mentally retarded. She hoped to become a nun until her Mother Superior, advising against it because of her deafness, sent Lila back to the Philippines for a home visit. During that visit, she met Ernesto Del Rosario and fell in love. She was a little embarrassed about not becoming a nun, reasoning that "maybe God didn't love me because I did not become a nun," and felt that her mother would be disappointed by her decision to marry a deaf man after all her mother's efforts to "normalize" her. So she eloped, further straining the relationship with her mother. The Del Rosarios then moved in with Ernesto's mother and gained the oral language model for their nondeaf children. (Occasionally Lila will use her voice when she signs to nondeaf people, but neither she nor Ernesto "voice" when they sign to each other or to other deaf people.)

Lila and Ernesto raised three successful children and, since Ernesto's retirement, have traveled extensively. Today they live with their daughter and her family in Seattle. They have transformed this home into a popular meeting place for the Philippine Deaf community—a vital resource for the preservation and diffusion of Philippine Sign Language, ASL, Philippine culture, and Filipino American Deaf culture.

A Digression on Deafness:
Speech Reading and Hearing Aids

Imagine learning how to speak a foreign language such as Urdu in a soundproof room, aided only by a mirror and your teacher's example for visual cues. The profoundly deaf learn to speak and comprehend the English language in such a vacuum. The deaf use speech reading (formerly "lip reading") to interpret our messages in a "highly complex process" (Moores, 1978, p. 237). In fact, even the most skilled speech readers catch only about 30% to 40% of what is being said. It involves distinguishing sounds by watching the speaker's lips, mouth, and facial movements. Try this experiment: Go to the mirror and say the words *Kate* and *gate* or *cap* and *cab*. Can you distinguish the two pairs of words solely on the basis of what you see in the reflected image? In particular, the phonemes /p/, /b/, and /m/ as well as the phonemes /t/,/d/, and /n/ are homophonous: That is, they are articulated in a similar way and look similar on the lips. Obviously, the speech reader will have to rely on the context of the message and closure. But a lot still comes down to good guesswork.

The use of hearing aids is also misunderstood. Although awareness of sounds is heightened with a hearing aid, the ability to decipher or discriminate between sounds is not improved by mechanical devices. Some people even say that hearing aids give them headaches and take them off. A profoundly deaf person may want to be aware of the presence of environmental sounds: a car honking, an airplane flying overhead, a fire alarm, and so forth. But hearing aids do not always provide enough auditory input for users to understand speech. Other factors such as family background and support (or rejection), age when deafness was detected, cause of deafness, early placement of services, and even the mode in which the particular person chooses to communicate (oral or manual) may be as important to communication as the use of hearing aids.

In recent years, cochlear implants have received wide media coverage. These sophisticated electronic instruments are surgically implanted in or behind the ear to sort out useful sounds and transform them into electrical impulses. Although they provide a sense of sound, they do not restore normal hearing (National Institutes of Health, 1995), and they can cost up to $25,000.

Straight From the Heart: Giancarlo Gelicame,
Born in Quezon City in 1970

INSULT!

Giancarlo's mother contracted rubella late in her pregnancy. Rubella (German measles) is a highly contagious viral disease. Some of its effects are mental retardation, deafness, and even death.

My first impression of Giancarlo was that he did not want to talk about his background. A question on the interview form obviously hit a nerve: "Can you be specific about some personal difficulties you have had with the Filipino American community?"

To show us how he had been insulted by this question, he signed "Pipi," and the other Deaf people nodded in agreement. (*Pipi* is a derogatory Filipino term comparable to "deafie" or "deaf and dumb" in the United States.) He mimicked nondeaf people play-acting at sign language, teasing him by laughing and mocking a deaf person's speech. Giancarlo revealed deep emotional scars with his reaction to the word *pipi* and its negative connotations. Everyone else's pained reaction emphasized how difficult dealing with such verbal abuse had been. I sensed that Giancarlo's natural ambition may have been stifled by such offensive social experiences in the Philippines.

Giancarlo came to the United States when he was 21, 5 years before our interview, after attending the Southeast Asian Institute for the Deaf (SAID) in Quezon City. American nuns had taught him Signing Exact English (SEE) instead of Tagalog. (SEE is a manually coded signing system based on strictly grammatical English language. These are signs to represent parts of the English language separate from meaning and concept. The SEE system, developed for use in an educational setting, is used primarily by hard-of-hearing people who voice their words in English word order.)

Giancarlo is a hard worker who considers himself a success and is eager to take advantage of all the opportunities the United States has to offer. He is glad that his nondeaf son can achieve important goals more easily than he can without the psychological, economic, social, and communication barriers that still exist for the Deaf. Giancarlo and his wife, Sheila (also Deaf), do not think being deaf or nondeaf is the underlying issue. They realize that being deaf in a nondeaf-oriented society would have posed a real challenge for their son. Both their families are relieved that he is nondeaf. "My son is hearing, and I wished that my children would be because it is easy for them to go to college and easy for them to find a job," says Giancarlo, but Sheila adds, "It doesn't matter to me, but my family really wanted my children to be hearing."

Enjoying Life in the United States:
Maria Udarbe Lee, Born in Cagayan in 1962

> Growing up deaf in the U.S., my life has been easy for
> me. My mother and sisters know sign language. It's easy

for us to communicate. My job provides interpreters for
staff meetings. . . . I think I enjoy my life here.

Maria's mother caught rubella when she was 7 months pregnant. Her
parents suspected that something was wrong with their baby's hearing
when she was slow to respond to her name. When Maria was 3 years old,
her deafness was confirmed. The Udarbes, financially stable and wanting
their daughter to receive the best services and education available,
moved to the United States and enrolled Maria in Chicago's Bell School
when she was 7 years old. She attended mainstream programs throughout high school and learned ASL from Deaf friends and teachers.

Maria is blessed with a winning personality. She is vivacious, intelligent, gracious, and helpful. She lives in a bustling suburb of Seattle with
malls and other creature comforts. She has been working for the city of
Seattle as a secretary for a number of years, and her husband, also Deaf,
works as an engineer at Boeing. Her two nondeaf daughters are constantly exposed to sign language. Their father does not use his voice
when communicating in sign language, but Maria "voices" when she
signs to her daughters—an optimal model for a bilingual home. She says,
"My children are hearing. I'm very happy to have hearing children
because they may help interpret when they get older."

Unfortunately, Maria cannot depend on this convenient signing and
voicing exchange outside the home. Communication barriers limit socialization within the larger Filipino American community. She would like
more people, in particular Filipino Americans, to learn ASL, and she
suggests that the Filipino American community distribute flyers about
special events and provide equal access to those events by hiring interpreters.

When I asked Maria to participate in this project, she was more than
happy to share names and numbers of other Deaf Filipino Americans in
the area. She agrees that it is important to teach nondeaf Filipino America
about the Filipino American Deaf community and that the Filipino
American Deaf group must find a forum to share some of its struggles
and triumphs, hopefully increasing the cohesiveness of the wider Filipino American community.

Her family, relatives, and some older students at school were role
models who encouraged her to get a good education. She eventually
graduated from the National Technology Institute for the Deaf in Ro-

chester, New York, with double AA degrees in office technology and accounting technology. She retains her Filipino identity and values by occasionally cooking and eating Filipino food, paying respect to elders, making the family her priority, and emphasizing the benefits of a good education. She admitted not knowing the term *pipi* or knowing what *mano* (a sign of respect given to elders) means; those terms are of little importance in her life.

A Digression on Deafness:
Communication Devices

If you visit a deaf person, you may notice some equipment strategically placed around the home. A teletypewriter (TTY or TDD) machine will often be hooked up to the telephone. This device converts the telephone's electronic impulses to letters that can be read on the digital display panel (resembling a large pager display) of the TTY. It also has a keyboard to type out messages to the other party. When the phone rings, a light on the TTY flashes to signal a call. Similar bell/light hookups connect to doorbells and fire alarms in many deaf homes as well.

Closed captioning is the transcription of dialogue and sounds onto television screens, similar to subtitles for foreign movies. Since July 1992, Congress has required all television sets with 13-inch or larger screens to be equipped with closed-captioning devices. They can show captioned television programs, identified in program listings with the symbol "CC." But most programs have yet to be closed captioned, with the exception of most prime time and a few daytime shows.

Maria's business card shows the usual information: address, TTY number, fax number. It also gives the 1-800 number for relay services so nondeaf people without TTYs may call her. A nondeaf person can phone the relay service number and give the relay operator the deaf person's TTY number. The operator connects with the deaf person's TTY and communicates via TTY. The relay operator then reads to the nondeaf caller from the relay TTY. "The Americans with Disabilities Act requires that all states set up statewide dual-party TDD (telecommunication device for the deaf) relay systems" (Metropolitan Washington Telecommunication, 1991, p. iv). Relay services provide a vital confidential communication link between Deaf and nondeaf communities.

Rights and Privileges: Evelyn Banez Jackson,
Born in Santa Maria, Ilocos Sur, in 1958

> In the U.S., there's a lot of sign language services and
> interpreters that motivate me to go any place. No
> discrimination here. People look and treat me as a
> normal person.

Evelyn's hometown, Santa Maria, is far from the hustle and bustle
of Manila. When her deafness was detected at the age of 2 years, her
parents knew nothing of services and education for their child. She
endured a fragmentary early education without supplementary services to accommodate her special academic needs. In the meantime, her
family's search for an ideal placement for Evelyn led to her attendance
at PSD in distant Manila. She studied there from 7 to 12 years of age,
then moved with her family to Seattle.

Evelyn recalls a rich social upbringing in the Philippines, including
visits to the beach, parties, and other pleasurable activities. She often
participated without understanding the purpose of these outings. Today
she appreciates never having been ostracized by her relatives or friends
because of her deafness and having a family as role models in a supportive and nurturing environment. They learned sign language, encouraged her to continue her studies until graduation, and were delighted
when she got a job. She has worked at the National Oceanic and Atmos-
pheric Administration (NOAA) for 15 years, recently completed accounting courses, and is confident of finding work in that area.

When the term *mixed marriage* is mentioned, a "mixed racial" marriage comes to mind. But in this case, Evelyn Banez, a Deaf woman,
married a nondeaf man, Anthony Jackson. Anthony has studied ASL and
is enrolled in the Interpreter Training Program at Seattle Central Community College. This program for the Deaf with a diverse group of Deaf
students, staff members, interpreters, and interpreter trainees is a stimu-
lating environment for socialization of Deaf and nondeaf populations.
Such "mixed" marriages are not unusual. Evelyn and Anthony's court-
ship and marriage, based not on sympathy or curiosity but on love,
provides a good example of how a "mixed" couple can socialize in Deaf
and nondeaf circles, feel comfortable in each other's environment, and
accommodate to each other's needs. "We are part of the community,"

says Evelyn. "No difference [between the Deaf Filipino Americans and hearing Filipino Americans] because I do the same activities, have the same rights and privileges like the hearing people. . . . They should look into the needs and concerns of deaf Filipinos so they will not be left out."

Evelyn is adamant. Long gone are those days in the Philippines when she meekly accompanied her family to events. She wants to attend more social functions where Filipino Americans congregate. Neither she nor other Deaf Filipino Americans should have to hope that when attending a function an interpreter will happen to be there. Deaf Filipino Americans have not taken the initiative to achieve equal access. Until that happens, Evelyn will have to rely on Anthony to interpret for her.

The One and Only: Ariele Belo Faulkner,
Born in Seattle, Washington, in 1971

We don't bite!

At age 3, Ariele underwent surgery to drain water from her ears after doctors detected neural damage. Her parents accepted her deafness and were undaunted at the prospect of raising their only daughter responsibly. Ariele is a product of mainstream programs for the Deaf in Seattle. In elementary school, she was introduced to SEE, then Pidgin Signed English (signs in English word order but with ASL concepts) in middle school and high school, then ASL in college. She "suffered" through speech therapy: "Yuck! Good for those who can talk, but don't force it on those who cannot talk." She recalls endless hours spent with speech therapists who helped her improve the tonal quality and enunciation in her speech. Ariele will confess the obvious benefits of speech therapy. She has no qualms about using her voice when communicating with nondeaf people who do not know sign language. (Some Deaf prefer to "turn off" their voice because of the grammatical differences of ASL; they may also realize that their voices are considered unintelligible by nondeaf listeners.)

Ariele set herself high educational goals and attended Gallaudet University for 1 year. Ariele's ASL skills and positive identity as a Deaf person flourished, but the East Coast lifestyle did not agree with her. She transferred to California State University at Northridge (CSUN), since

1962 the home of the National Center on Deafness and its extensive library. Each semester, over 200 Deaf students attend classes and extra-curricular activities there featuring interpreters and note-taking services.

Ariele thrived in this ideal environment: Interpreters were "every-where" and "at everything," even homecoming games. She bridged Deaf and nondeaf cultures and graduated from CSUN with a BS in leisure studies/recreation.

Ariele hails from a distinguished educated family, whose members hold important positions in their respective fields. Her mother is the first Filipino American ordained as a Presbyterian pastor; along with Max Atienza, she founded the Filipino Fellowship Church. But Ariele can now boast of her own accomplishments: She is the first Asian American to be president of a Deaf sorority at CSUN, and she will be the only Filipina American in a leadership position at the Asian American Deaf Conference in Los Angeles in 1997. (Asian Deaf college students are forming organizations such as the Asian Deaf Club at the National Technical Institute for the Deaf in New York and the Asian-Pacific Association at Gallaudet University in Washington, D.C.) She wants to go on to graduate school and teach or to return to community service work. Her dream is to open up her own Filipino restaurant to rave reviews from local food critics.

American born and well educated, married to a Deaf Caucasian man, Ariele prefers the company of the larger Deaf community to the few Deaf Filipino Americans she knows because of a gap in education and interests. Ariele has not met the other Deaf Filipino Americans featured in this chapter, but like them she takes pride in her deafness, her upbringing, and her ideals. She attributes her standards to her role models: her mother (who taught her to be proud of herself) and a Deaf woman teacher who exemplified an attainable goal. When Ariele met Leila Petersen, her high school teacher, she was deeply impressed by her teacher's intelligence and by the realization that a Deaf woman could succeed in her chosen profession.

While growing up, Ariele sometimes wished she were born nondeaf. Now she stands proud as a Deaf Filipina American. Her mother would like her to socialize more with the Filipino American community, but Ariele is uneasy about *chismis* (gossip) and condescending attitudes. She has little patience for those who do not take time to understand her or make her acquaintance: "I have to do all the work in a conversation! We Deaf don't bite!" She is frustrated with the nondeaf Filipino American community.

The Reality for Some

Each person in this group mentions his or her helpful, loving, and understanding family as being crucial for his or her self-image. Unfortunately, the families of Maria, Lila, Giancarlo, Evelyn, Ariele, Robert, and Ernesto are exceptions that do not represent the whole community of Deaf Filipinos. Most Deaf Filipinos' families offer love and some support, but many families cannot fully accept the truth and responsibility. They may also become hung up on stereotypical terms such as *handicapped* or *disabled* and forget about the child him- or herself.

"Carlos Prado," actually a composite of several people, is an example of this type. The Prados had an undying belief that their son would recover his sense of hearing again. As a result, they did not communicate with Carlos, a proficient user of ASL. They were embarrassed by his disability and virtually ignored their child's existence or tried to hide it from the community while praying for their son's "recovery." Carlos knew they were ashamed of his deafness and never considered himself part of the family. After attending mainstream programs for the Deaf and graduating from high school, he held menial jobs, had a string of romantic affairs, and encountered trouble with the law. He and his nondeaf siblings have no affinity with each other. His family members do not know sign language but use pad and pencil or shout at Carlos, hoping that he will capture the gist of their message. Whose responsibility is comprehension in this case—is it always Carlos's?

Carlos's pathetic tale is not surprising to some Deaf people. Hairston and Smith (1983), in their book *Black and Deaf in America*, contend that black Deaf Americans face three major problems: undereducation, underemployment, and, most important, an "unfavorable self-image" (p. 79). This black Deaf Americans' reality also applies to some Deaf Filipino Americans.

Conclusion

Because of the "drama" of life without hearing, a nondeaf person cannot help but be curious about how a deaf person functions every day. Nondeaf people tend to feel shame and pity for those with a hearing loss.

In the past, many thought that the Deaf not only had lost their hearing but also were mentally retarded. How many deaf children have been and still are misdiagnosed as mentally retarded and mistakenly sent to institutions by those who still refer to members of this important community as "deaf mute" or "deaf and dumb"?

The medical term *congenital, prelingual* signifies deafness at birth and before acquiring language. Consider the implications of the prelingually deaf: If you are not able to master the language of the majority, contact with people around you is severely limited. We are sociable beings who need social, physical, and emotional interaction and feel devastated when cut off from most meaningful communication.

Since beginning this project, I have learned that deafness has always been present in our Filipino American community. Several community members have revealed that they have relatives who are deaf. Nondeaf Filipino Americans may be curious about sign language and the communication devices that the Deaf use to access the larger society; curiosity and interest are not enough to keep these Deaf members from becoming outsiders in their own families and communities. On the whole, Deaf Filipino Americans have been "invisible" to the larger Filipino American community.

All seven Deaf Filipino Americans like it in the United States, feeling that in the Philippines they would be in low-paying jobs with severely limited chances for educational, social, and emotional growth. They would not have the opportunity to break out of the stereotype of a pitied or ignored disabled person. It would take a tremendous fighting spirit to overcome these barriers, based as they are on common ignorance and fear.

In *The Mask of Benevolence*, Harlan Lane (1992) wrote of Burundi in Africa and its Dutch colonizers who stated that "the Burundians were like children that showed traits of coarseness [and] cruelty" and were "incompetent socially, behaviorally, and emotionally" (p. 34). For Lane, this list of negative characteristics was "all too reminiscent of what hearing experts have so often claimed about deaf people" (p. 37). Such harmful attitudes toward disabled people reinforce negative stereotypes. We ignore the Deaf and try to hide them and other disabled people in our midst. But we cannot afford to lose many valuable people like these seven Deaf Filipino Americans who can enrich our lives and make our community stronger.

The United States is enlightened by the civil rights movements, is nurtured by the philosophy of multiculturalism, and is famous as a land of opportunity. Its ideal of "pulling oneself up by one's bootstraps" has served as a "gold mountain" for many seeking the "land of the free, home of the brave." Yet these seven Deaf Filipino Americans still face the same stereotypes and prejudices they tried to leave behind in the Philippines and are not given the same respect, rights, and opportunities as their fellow Filipino Americans. They feel frustrated, discouraged, and deeply disappointed with the Filipino American community. As a result, they feel more empathy with other groups. It is time to accept, welcome, and be tolerant of our differences. If we do not, our Filipino American community will remain close-minded, exclusive, and stagnant. We must bridge the gaps between the various subgroups within the Filipino American community and help each articulate its particular needs. In turn, we should learn about each other and find ways to cooperate with each other. It is my hope that this chapter can help begin that process.

Note

1. Since 1864, Gallaudet University in Washington, D.C., has been the world's only liberal arts insitution for the Deaf—the deaf community's "Ivy League" school, with an enrollment of about 1,000 students. Elementary and secondary model schools for the Deaf as well as a graduate school open to Deaf and nondeaf students share a beautiful campus with the large undergraduate program. Since then, programs for the deaf associated with other universities and technical colleges have been started.

References

Colon, A. (1996, February 18). A sense of connection. *Seattle Times*, pp. L1, L4-5.
Hairston, E., & Smith, L. (Eds.). (1983). *Black and deaf in America*. Silver Spring, MD: T. J. Publishers.
Individuals With Disabilities Education Act of 1990, 20 U.S.C. § 1400 *et seq.*
Lane, H. (1992). *The mask of benevolence*. New York: Vintage.
Metropolitan Washington Telecommunication Directory for the Deaf, Inc. (1991). *TDD directory*. Silver Spring, MD: Author.

Moores, D. (1978). *Educating the deaf: Psychology, principles, and practices.* Boston: Houghton Mifflin.

National Institutes of Health. (1995, May 17). *NIH panel recommends implant device to restore sound for children and adults* [News and Events press release]. Bethesda, MD: Author.

Public Law 94-142, The Education for All Handicapped Children Act (renamed the Individuals with Disabilities Education Act).

Sacks, O. (1989). *Seeing voices: A journey into the world of the deaf.* Berkeley: University of California Press.

Stokoe, W. (1978). *Sign language structure.* Silver Spring, MD: Linstock.

11

The Day the Dancers Stayed
On Pilipino Cultural Nights

Theodore S. Gonzalves

The foreign folk dance troupes that keep visiting the U.S.
seem set on convincing their American audiences that
life back home is just one big, happy, handsome hop.
Russian, Indian, African and Israeli companies have all
been over in the last two years and now a troupe of
Filipinos is on a cross-country tour showing that the
simple life moves with a joyous lilt on their islands. The
troupe is stocked with 20 lovely girls—all of them
unmarried, all in their late teens, most of them less than
five feet tall. All are given to flirtatious smiling while on
stage. The men are lively and graceful. Their dances
blend the islands' Muslim and Spanish cultures with a
lot of high-spirited Indo-Malayan doings. After a fast
tour through primitive war, funeral and victory rites, the
girls and their male partners concentrate on harem
ceremonials, fire dances and a harvest festival celebrating
the riches of the rice crop. Before each show they gather to
pray that the performance will go well. If it does go
well—and it delighted viewers in New York—they end the
show singing love songs to the audience.

"Philippine Dancers," Life Magazine (1959)

Of all our arts, the dance has gone fastest and closest to
achieving a native identity; our music, painting, and
literature still have a hybrid look.

                    Nick Joaquin (quoted in UNESCO, 1973)

Any study of the colonial world should take into
consideration the phenomena of the dance and of
possession. . . . The circle of the dance is a permissive
circle: it protects and permits.

                    Frantz Fanon (1965), The Wretched of the Earth

                    Only in dance
                    is there union
                    Only in dance
                Do spirit, soul, and self
                        Unite
                That is why we like it
    Juan Gomez-Quiñones, "The Ballad of Billy Rivera"[1]

Culture Is For-Getting and For-Giving

In the past generation, something remarkable has been happening
on stages on college campuses. We could talk of surfaces, of the theatri-
cality of the event itself, of the visceral reactions generated when one is
experiencing the show in a large dark room, seated patiently among
others. Think of those times, and of those surfaces. Thousands of college-
age students have taken the stage and have developed a sophisticated
cultural form known as the Pilipino Cultural Night (PCN).

Think in terms of condensation or pressure points, in terms of the
ways in which families are held together or the ways in which memories
are kept alive. For the veterans of the event, think of the first time you
saw the show. What was it like? What do you remember of the show?
The costumes? Your friends and family members? Who was next to you?
How have the shows changed? Think of the distances friends and
relatives have had to traverse to get to the shows. How hard it was to

find parking, to find the gig itself, to find tickets, to find a good seat. To find something to drink during the intermission.

What this chapter takes up is a phenomenon that is still under construction. Think, also, of making associations across categories including, but certainly not limited to, constitution, entertainment, performance, democracy, narration, nationalism, culture, editing, authenticity, and articulation. Ultimately, this kind of show marks the immediate past of Filipino Americans in the United States. What, exactly, is it? Is it an art form, a political movement, a political statement, a form of entertainment? Why are so many people deeply interested in it? What are some of the consequences? Do some students actually suffer in their academic work? Are Filipinos *really* the best dancers from Asia? Are Filipinos Asians?

To develop a cultural history of the PCN is to launch a line of inquiry that is at the crossroads of many disciplines: American history, Southeast Asian studies, performance studies, cultural studies, ethnic and Asian American studies, American studies, sociology, and anthropology. Some of the other disciplines that would have relevance here would be political science and political economy. The questions that the show raises for me are numerous. In a rather clumsy way, we could simply start by asking: How does culture work? How does it change? Who is involved? What is being said? What are the investments and consequences? The idea of "culture" "at work" is highlighted here. The PCN affords us a chance to examine an analytic of culture—to found theoretical discussions and intellectual spaces for the kinds of cultural practices that many young people have chosen to undertake. Getting close to the PCN allows us a chance to ask some questions about what we do with our time, to attempt to piece together larger stories of ourselves in the United States—about the time and place around us, about some of the consequences for what is edited and constructed as Filipino and Filipino American culture.

Some other dimensions of these discussions will be aspects of the debate on subjectivities and the writing of histories. Concerning subjectivities, I mean, first, that we have an opportunity to examine how we come to shape meanings, bend stories or narrations, and assume stances, poses, and styles—and thus effect a type of active subjectivity. Second, a serious aspect of the study has to deal with the notion of the PCN as a "straitjacket"—as something that has been not only instrumental in the enabling of Filipino American identities in the United States but also constricting. These critical reflections suggest that the PCN raises questions about how culture, politics, and history are related for this young immigrant community—how the stories we tell about ourselves are often managed, disciplined, monopolized, hoarded, dictated, maybe even railroaded.

Concerning the writing of history, the PCN affords us the chance to bear witness to the narration of a community's history as it takes place with some regularity on stages every year. Certain versions of Filipino and Filipino American histories are being authored, passed around, passed down, and (mis)handled each year. To inquire into the writing of history (and here I am using the term *writing* rather loosely) is to examine how histories are being generated, sustained, maintained, and circulated. One amazing aspect of this dimension of history writing is that such a historiographical intervention takes place amid thousands of learned academic writings that have constructed images, paradigms, and notions about Filipinos and Filipino Americans as lazy natives, little brown brothers, fawning tutees of American democracy, and so on.

Furthermore, the historical narration of the PCN takes place largely without the community's benefit of institutions that sustain memory as well as individuals who would determine the shapes of such lines of inquiry. Institutions such as the Japanese American National Museum or the Chinese Museum of the Americas are quite a distant prospect for the Filipino community in the United States. As for faculty, we would be hard pressed in the present moment to name more than a handful of full-time, fully tenured professors who focus specifically on the Filipino or Filipino American experience (we need not concern ourselves with better "token" counts). The number is practically nonexistent for those who hold critical positions such as department chairs, administrators, development officers, or even advisors in graduate programs.

Would such a change in personnel and infrastructure really make that much of a difference in our communities? This has yet to be studied in great detail. What is certain for now, at least, is that the PCN is one of the most dynamic history lessons that thousands of Filipino and Filipino American youth have chosen to create during their college careers since the 1980s.

Finally, as I write this, the PCN is intriguing because it comes at a time in American history precisely when "historically challenged" voices in the culture (even in our own community) are attempting to take America "back" (as exemplified by the Buchanan Republican convention address in 1992). Studies on the PCN are part of that larger labor to recover parts of ourselves: Foucault (1980) suggested a labor of heeding "insurrectionist knowledges"; Yuji Ichioka (1974) turns our attentions to "buried pasts."

Stepping Into It

This essay grew out of some experiences I have had in planning PCNs in northern California. Of course, one of the primary aims of a serious study of the PCN would be to return to the earlier shows—to examine continuities as well as breaks in themes and concerns over the years.

Let us turn initially to reasons that it is important to study. First, the show is a *mass* form. Second, the PCN is a Filipino American-centered event, providing another way to develop methodologically an aspect of Asian American and ethnic studies scholarship—to explore how expressive forms are vital areas of shared life experiences. And third, attention to the show allows us to embrace some political dimensions of the world around us. The show is a symptom of the political climate as much as it is a response to it—that climate being one of mass mobilizations of college students during the Reagan/Dukemeijian era, an era of Asian and Pacific/Islander Student Union (APSU) chapters on college campuses attempting to hold onto the gains wrought by a previous generation of Asian American youth through ethnic studies curricula as well as minority student services.

But first, I would like to go back to one of my first eye-openers concerning these shows. Actually, it was not even one of the PCNs itself, but a Christmas show produced by San Francisco State University's Pilipino American Collegiate Endeavor (PACE) and entitled *I'm Dreaming of a Brown Pasko*. After having taken in that show, I threw myself into the planning for next spring's show. It was a bit of a leap for me; up until then, my performing credits were largely musical, accompanying singers or other soloists in some jazz combo or lounge act format. This was different: I read for one of the "skit" parts. That year, the director insisted on calling it a "play," and in truth, the script amounted to much more than a skit. This year's theme for the play was the founding of PACE in 1967. We got a large dose of history there, rehearsing in people's garages, classrooms, and student union conference areas. Our scriptwriter researched PACE's founding and San Francisco State's strike in the late 1960s. We were stepping into a history not only of the group that would later be PACE but of Filipina/os' participation in the Third World Liberation Front's historic genesis of the 1968 strike that put ethnic studies on the map. Paris had its barricades of students, philosophers, and workers; we had San Francisco State College. I came to learn as well some of the positive contributions that groups such as PACE make to the academic and social life of Filipino Americans on campuses by building leadership and organizational skills, developing valuable cross-cultural friendships, and enabling one to learn to be part of something larger than oneself.

Working on that show encouraged me to continue working with the (PACE) organization. I decided to run as internship coordinator. That stint later offered a useful model for managing relations between the student organization, the Asian American Studies Department, and local on- and off-campus projects. My goal that year was to make explicit the linkages between communities, classrooms, and the organizational mission. One of the directives was to support the educational life of Filipina/os on that campus. I am sure that many people were more interested in the social aspects of getting people together; I was interested in that as well. But there was nothing preventing us from framing the need for social activity within a larger understanding. At the time, young people were getting started working on issues that affected many of our lives—for example, violence, substance abuse, and the health threat of AIDS. For Filipina/os to get together at all *meant* to get together under those conditions of death, dying, and survival. That is the level of importance I assigned to the work of PACE during those years. Those concerns were also tempered by dropout rates, shaky academic performances, and the rising costs of higher education in the state of California.

What I found as we turned our attention to the planning of the PCN in 1993 was the beginning of what would eventually develop into a criticism of the shows. Because of their commitment to the shows, students were taking incompletes in the spring semesters from their courses. This was the opening to other criticisms, namely, of how the show was becoming counterproductive to the success of Filipina/os on campus. A small group of members on the coordinating committee began to question the organization's role in promoting the value of education for Filipina/o youth. During this time as well, tuition was being driven up throughout California's institutions of higher education. Although major campuses of the University of California garnered much television and print media attention, it was the California State University system (of which San Francisco State is a part) that was especially hard hit. Many students did not return, and this only heightened the commitment of many around the organization to reassess the value of what we were doing with our time and energies.

When the summer came, planning for the upcoming year's PCN began to take shape. We met wherever we could—living rooms, porches, and coffee joints—for the committee meetings. This is where we first began to raise questions about this process. At first, those criticisms were unfocused, framed hastily around a cost-benefit analysis: For the time, energy, and money invested, we were not getting much on a return. My indices for success meant active recruitment, retention, and graduation of Filipina/o students at San Francisco State. If our group could not keep track of that larger goal, then everything else had to be reworked. Those first debates were contentious and concerned with just about every aspect of the production. As debate unfolded, it became clear that many of us had much more to say about the specifics of the show as well as about the more general statements surrounding notions of "culture" for Filipina/o Americans in the United States.

The terrain of the debate soon centered on the show's format. The question of the "one-night" performance drew major criticisms. Why was "culture" represented on one night? For many, the format seemed to be too constraining, as if what we could say about ourselves could be summarized neatly in 3 or 4 hours (if you were lucky) on a stage. Larger questions quickly surfaced: What was meant by "culture"? When we began to ask this question, we took on a larger set of problems. Questions of representation and ideology were now being addressed. Why did we choose these symbols—these dances, musics, costumes, formats? What was at stake in the theatrical narrations used to organize the show—that is, the play's plot lines? What did the show say about ourselves?

What was clear at this stage was that many of us in the organization were simply *not* asking these questions. For the most part, our coordinating body was busy preparing next year's show, albeit mechanically. This dimension of the production of "culture" was evident: We *expected* another PCN; we did not plan it. The show disciplined us; it told us about the meanings of "Filipino"-ness rather than encouraging young people to actively engage their experiences. It was "culture"—or our varied yet consolidated notions of it—that acted on us, rather than our interacting with each other. By the end of the debates, I felt even more distant from the notion of PCN and even the term *culture*. It did not take much at that point to propose that we abandon the whole affair.

Two sides of the question had emerged. A small group attempted to raise the issue of reformatting and reprogramming, adopting an approach that placed the show within the group's larger commitments to students. However, the majority were frustrated by the change that was proposed. The conflict certainly was not as bad as it could have been. PCN lore contains many stories of how, on many campuses, people have lost friendships, groups have devolved into competing and at times unworkable factions, and some groups have never quite recovered. But for those in our own group, proposals of changes to the show were received, as in the case of any other serious changes that people often have to face, with considerable skepticism. What both sides shared was the problem of how to negotiate an immediate future. This was new ground, and we were learning how to walk again. By including these anecdotal comments on PCNs at San Francisco State, I am suggesting that criticisms about cultural practices can and should come from the very things that take up our time.

On With the Show

Producing Culture

The PCN is vulnerable to the charge of *essentialism*, or the presentation of a static, singular conception of Filipinos *in* America. In addition, I will highlight an alternative format to the PCN, one deploying a "strategic essentialism" that aims to present one view of Filipinos *of* America. This distinction and the movement from "*in* America" to "*of* America" highlight a political moment, when students—who have engaged the strategically essentialist format—take hold of the means of cultural production: that is, "the political production of culture" (Spivak, 1994). My intention in making this distinction is also to provide a contingent rhetorical device for denoting a decentered notion of "America" (that is, decentered from Europe as its sole author) and for highlighting the development of culture *from within* the specific site of America, the rooting of expressive forms.

The case study used as an alternative to the traditional PCN model suggests a return to the political question of such activity. These meditations are based on analyses of nine PCNs spanning a period from 1986 to 1996. All the shows analyzed were directed and executed by Filipino American student organizations at 4-year colleges in northern and southern California. The shows are University of California, Berkeley (UCB), Pilipino American Alliance (PAA), 1986; San Francisco State University (SFSU), Pilipino American Collegiate Endeavor (PACE), 1986; SFSU, PACE, 1988; Santa Clara University, Barkada, 1992; SFSU, PACE, 1992; SFSU, PACE, 1993; University of California, Los Angeles (UCLA), Samahang Pilipino, 1994; and University of California, Irvine (UCI), Kababayan, 1995-1996.

Life's Essentials

Before proceeding directly to the PCN, I take up a definitional matter by asking, What is essentialism? Although no strict definition to the term exists (if there were such a thing, it would be itself "essentialist"), E. San Juan (1992) took it to be "a fixed, ontological essence or a unitary, transcendental category predicated on the epistemological reasoning supplied by anthropology, biology, and other physical sciences" (p. 7). For Diana Fuss (1989), essentialism is "commonly understood as a belief in the real, true essence of things, the invariable and fixed properties which define the 'whatness' of a given entity" (p. xi). What both definitions are pointing to is this lack of flexibility—the foreclosure of multiple, even contingent, meanings concerning the "whatness" of culture—that is my concern. Similarly, the PCN categorizes what we know, or *should* know, about Filipino and Filipino American culture.

The PCN is not mandated from above; nor is it legislated by institutions or governmental bodies. It is *of Filipinos:* that is, produced by us. However, I want to stress here that the show tells us little about ourselves, how we practice, see, do, and live—rather, the show performs us. Take the planning of the event, in a rough sketch. Planning nearly 1 year

in advance, a committee of students gathers. The committee chair delegates one task per person: costume acquisition/design, venue rental,
choreography, script writing, program design, set design, rehearsal coordination, bookkeeping, marketing and ticket sales, music rehearsal
coordination, (don't forget!) deciding where the alumni will be seated in
the audience, and so on. Culture—as a dynamic, lived set of experiences,
as a catalog of pains, appetites, anticipations, and joys—is bracketed.
Rather, "culture," as the committee's center of attention, is commodified,
staged, packaged, and, most important, through the PCN, implied. The
committee is a witness not to a dialogue on what culture is (or could be)
but to the division of its labor.

In coming to terms with the essentialist logic of the PCN, I examine
what serves as a static definition of Filipino and Filipino American
culture. In defining what *is*, the PCN also defines what is *not* Filipino
culture. Here is where the PCN falters as a durable vehicle for a dynamic
discourse on culture and for participation and as a venue for creativity.

"I Left My Heart on Ifugao Mountain":
The PCN Today

The PCN is a sophisticated expressive form. Part of its complicated
nature derives from its ability to narrate histories in creative ways. I
begin this next discussion with a simultaneous reference to two senti-
mentalized "returns": The first is Al Robles' (1977) short story "Looking
for Ifugao Mountain," and the second is the popular U.S. American jazz
standard, "I Left My Heart in San Francisco." Robles is considered the
"dean" of the "Flip" poets (as they called themselves), a cohort of
Filipina/o American writers located primarily in the San Francisco Bay
Area who were instrumental in developing needed community arts and
cultural expression (Campomanes, 1992; Peñaranda, Syquia, & Tagatac,
1975; Syquia, 1974). His poetry speaks from another generation of youth
who, during the 1960s and 1970s, wrestled with questions of power,
resources, and the definition of the Filipina/o experience in America.
"Looking for Ifugao Mountain" is a children's story that begins with an
urban Filipino youth sitting in San Francisco's Portsmouth Square. He
is spirited away on a journey to the Philippines, searching for a mythic
figure who lives on Ifugao mountain. Along the way, he is beset by

obstacles and warnings: The mountain is dangerous, go back. He presses on; as he nears the mountain, he is told by a guide that he will find what he searches for, not on the mountain, but in the knowledge of the *manongs* who sit with him at Portsmouth Square. He returns to San Francisco and begins listening.

The show cannot be considered without an understanding of the Filipino American student organizations that direct and execute this annual activity. Since the influx of Filipino students at college campuses in the 1980s, the PCN has become the central organizing activity for many student groups. During spring academic terms, officers for the upcoming academic years are elected by the organizational membership; usually certain positions are reserved exclusively for coordinating PCN logistics. Beginning in the fall, students are delegated various tasks—set design, costume making, catering, dancing, music, and so forth—toward the final production. Many hours of rehearsal time and planning are sacrificed by several (hundred, in some cases) students.

In addition, obtaining funding for the show is a long-term task. Although private donations and community sponsorships are encouraged and (at times) secured, the show's funding emanates from special accounts within the campus's funding structure. Particular sources may be sought in student government grants, from student activities offices, from the office of the university president, and so forth. Also, the amounts granted for such shows have wildly varied: from a student organization's budget at a small campus, $300, to nearly $20,000 for one evening's worth of entertainment. Justifying such expenditures involves detailed records kept by the organization for every aspect of production: securing a venue (the bigger the better), buying new costumes (last year's simply won't do), paying professional choreographers, catering receptions, mounting publicity and outreach campaigns, and so forth. I point to these two elements—namely, time and money—to emphasize that the PCN is a serious enterprise. The students organizing the show do not take their obligations lightly, and nor should we, the audience, take the production lightly.

Turning from preproduction to the production itself, I notice five (although not exhaustive) consistent elements in the show's format and program—that is, indispensable characteristics in the essentialist logic of the PCN. These are (a) the opening of the show with both the Philippine and the U.S. American national anthems, (b) the use of Tagalog in the programs, (c) the marking of bodies through Philippine costumes, (d) the standard (required) inventory of Philippine dance styles, and (e) the narrative within the show as a vehicle for historicizing the Filipino American experience.

The traditional PCN opens with the Philippine and U.S. American national anthems. Written by A. C. Montenegro, the Philippine national anthem ("Pambansang Awit") is written in a standard march style reminiscent of European and U.S. American band music. The lyrics speak to strong nationalistic strains that are commensurate with imagery found in Francis Scott Key's "Star Spangled Banner." In some productions, the choir deftly merges the tunes in a continuous medley. The effect here is of continuity—between two nations singing of prideful traditions of liberty, battle, and democratic "friendship."

Second, Tagalog occupies a central role in these productions. The following partial list bears out importance of framing the shows around what has become a nationalized dialect: SFSU, PACE, 1986, *Fiesta Sa Ating Bayan* (Celebration at Our Town); SCU, Barkada, 1992, *Pagsasama Sa Pamamagitan Ng Cultura* (Unity Through Culture); UCLA, Samahang Pilipino, 1994, *Ang Nawalang Kayamanan* (The Lost Treasure). Also, many of the shows feature a translation of the entire production, rendered in English and Tagalog. The issue of language here is central to the project of the PCN, in that as the Filipino community in the United States quickly develops into the largest Asian American ethnic group, the retention of language becomes a symbol of cultural unity, a reminder that Filipino culture has roots elsewhere and in other tongues besides English. More significantly, though, this use of Tagalog reflects the demographic shift from the dominance of Ilocano immigration in the pre-World War II era to the Tagalog-dominated post-1965 immigration. The net *political* effects locate the specificity of Filipino culture by laying claim to an indigenous language and, therefore, to pre-European influences.

As members of the indigenous psychology movement in the Philippines point out, the deployment of indigenous languages as a transnational cultural expression has a tremendous impact for the theorization of "citizenship"—that is, those concepts specifying who belongs and who does not (Enriquez, 1992). Indeed, as Enriquez asserted, if Tagalog or Pilipino is one of the languages spoken by Americans (it is one of the top 10), then it too becomes an American language. Those, however, who would recognize Tagalog as the *only* language of the Philippines and as the dialect most often spoken by Filipinos in the United States need to be mindful of the homogenization of the culture's linguistic plurality, of which Tagalog is only one (albeit a major) part.

Third, the Filipinos presented on stage are culturally marked through "indigenized" costume. I say "indigenized" rather than "indigenous" to point out that there is a question as to the authenticity of the presentations: Do they really wear those costumes in the Philippines, anyway (Gaerlan, 1994)? To say that something is *indigenized* is to point to an active and complicated process of editing. This is the process in which a vision of Philippine life is manufactured whose immediate origins may be located within Ferdinand and Imelda Marcos's management of cultural images through major exponents: the Cultural Center of the Philippines and the national dance troupes that have played to world acclaim since the 1950s. Those highly successful dance presentations have translated as a model for younger PCN organizers eager to demonstrate the authenticity of Philippine cultural symbols. In the current period of PCNs, every aspect of physicality is rendered in its Philippine equivalent: headdresses, fingernails, clothing, weaponry, sashes, and so forth. In addition, indigenized music is coupled with costuming to stage what Barbara Gaerlan (1994) noted as the "orientalizing" of Filipino culture (p. 6). Careful observers such as Gaerlan and Edward Said (1978) point out how this process of "orientalizing" is part of a larger historical process of robbing people of their history, of making them objects of study rather than participants in a discussion, of ensuring that the "Oriental" is "exotic," "alluring," and "mysterious"—a perspective that is supposedly rational, Western, and "progressive."

Fourth, and crucial to the show, is the standard inventory of dances arranged in suites. Four suites of indigenized Philippine dance dominate the programs. Particular dances chosen for each suite vary at the discretion of program coordinators; however, the suites remain strikingly consistent throughout this examination. They include the Spanish (or "Maria Clara"), the tribal or mountain, the Muslim, and the barrio or rural suites. A major addition by Filipino American students is the squeezing in of a "modern" routine that lets loose a contemporary choreographed sequence. The routine is "modern" not as in the European understanding of modern (jazz, for example) dance, but *in contrast to the indigenized forms*—actually more reminiscent of the Janet Jackson armies of hip-hop street dance.

The effect here is to draw attention to the rich and eclectic inventory of dances emanating from the Philippines. This inventory throughout the late 1980s and early 1990s has remained *static* as it has also dehistoricized the groups that are being (re)presented through the dances. Often, historical periods shift unevenly in the presentation of the program and are depicted with little attention to chronology. Also, regions are (re)presented contiguously, without reference to linguistic, religious, or other forms of localized difference.

Fifth, the shows employ a narrative that aims to connect the various dance sequences for the purpose of historicizing the Filipino American experience. Often, characters in a skit or play are presented at the beginning of the show in need of historical help: They do not know their history. In a familiar turn of the "quest" motif, the characters meet guides—elders, spirits, parent figures—who "transport" them to the Philippines. During their journey, the characters come in contact with a host of sounds and visions in the form of the dance suites. By the end of the evening, the characters reach an epiphanic state of cultural awareness and pride that they take back with them to the United States. This motif—of the quest and the "reverse exile"—is the most familiar one deployed throughout the shows. Literary critic Oscar Campomanes (1992) referred to it as an exilic motif, used by Philippine-born and Filipina/o American writers who turn their attention to the Philippines. Yet for many of the young people who put on the show, we will have to consider the problematic of American-born Filipina/os who do not "go back" to a place where they have never been. For our young characters, "something" is missing that is replaced by an imagined "return" to the Philippines where the "crisis" of Filipino American identity is "solved." The tacit assertion being made here is that the Philippines is a sturdy repository of "knowledge," a repository of authentic representations of Philippine life that can be accessed and brought back. The exercising of the "reverse exile" motif refuses to acknowledge the fact of cultural change, indeterminacy, and reconstruction at work in *both* the Philippines and the United States.

Thus, the traditional PCN possesses elements that demonstrate that Filipinos *do* have a culture, that they are visible despite the persistent, institutional erasure from U.S. American "official" history. Although the *intent* of the show varies according to the organizing group (perhaps to demonstrate the cultural significance of the Filipino in America), the *effect* of the show is to leave viewers with a static notion of "culture." In this sense, the political aspects of subversion, defiant cultural assertion, and a vibrant rearticulation of the racial order are left behind, in favor of increased technical mastery of performance and concomitant symptoms of spectacle and extravagance à la Cecil B. DeMille. The show has become predictable, repetitious, and increasingly problematic in justifying its expenditure of thousands of dollars for one evening's worth of *entertainment*. Consider when we are being "entertained"—that is, "occupied" or kept busy. For months at a time, students tax themselves, their studies, and their parents in preparation for the show. The audience is held in thrall for an evening. In the matter of a few hours, it is over. Indeed, we have come a long way from a "dime a dance." Throughout the early part of the 20th century, dancing in taxi dances temporarily satisfied Filipino Americans' need for companionship and eased the sting of loneliness, while depleting their hard-earned depressed wages (Catapusan, 1940; Cressey, 1932; Vedder, 1947). These histories allow us an opportunity to link aspects of popular culture with the social conditions of Filipina/o American communities in the United States.

Strangers From a ~~Different~~ (Strategically Essentialist) Shore

Not all shows are alike. And by applying more critical energies to this expressive form of cultural production, a "strategically essentialist" approach suggests some possibilities for a resituating of the "political" dimension of these cultural productions. By *strategic essentialism*, I mean the application of Lisa Lowe's (1991) "model for the ongoing construction of ethnic identity" (p. 39). In this model, Lowe views "the making and practice of Asian American culture as nomadic, unsettled, taking place in the travel between cultural sites and in the multi-vocality of heterogeneous and conflicting positions" (p. 39). What this offers for those of us who are observing the show is a way of understanding culture as being changeable, actively built up from our discussion and labor. This is quite a distance away from the static confines of the present PCN model, in which "culture" is replicated through familiar Philippine dance suites from the year before and Filipino culture is presented as a seamless tapestry of sounds and visions that are internally consistent. Borrowing from Spivak, Lowe highlighted the "strategic use of a positive essentialism in a scrupulously visible *political interest* [italics added]" (p. 39). Often, "culture" is something that belongs to the past—the best of what has gone before and what continues unchanged today.

I highlight "political interest" here because the terms of the shows are framed by fundamental questions: Why put on the show? Who is listening? What is being said? Lowe's model is further textured by Elaine H. Kim's (1993) claim that Asian American identities are "fluid and migratory" (p. 4) and Radhakrishnan's (1987) view of "contingent" identities (p. 211), both of which challenge the program of the traditional PCN model. Both Kim and Radhakrishnan point to a view of culture that is open to the possibilities of change and editing. Culture—more specifically, cultural practices—is not simply an item to preserve in a box, to be shown with reverence, or to be stored in its pristine state. Rather, the PCN offers students a chance to think of "culture" as a messy process, loaded with contradictory meaning, subject to human error as well as collective realization as part of the social struggle for the good life.

I offer as a case study and as a response to the above challenges an alternative program: SFSU Pilipino American Collegiate Endeavor's 1993 production of *Cultural Evidence*. Note also that the discussion of this show is not meant to be definitive, merely suggestive. The format of *Cultural Evidence* differed sharply from the traditional PCN model. Lasting over 3 days, the series of shows attempted to spend less than the previous years' one-night galas. The overall emphasis of *Cultural Evidence* was to provide a "venue" for the creativity of its members and its surrounding community (Belale, 1993, p. 2).

Throughout the 3-day event, *Cultural Evidence* aimed to showcase original works: alternative expressive forms of Filipino Americans. The first evening was devoted to film and spoken word/musical improvisation. The film screening featured works written, directed, and produced by Filipino Americans. The "Spoken Word" event featured poetry and prose written by students and former members. A musical (jazz) dialogue was also offered. Some of the evening's works were also presented at the National Asian American and Telecommunication Association's 1993 International Film Showcase as well as the Asian American Jazz Festival.

The second evening presented the "Hip-Hop Experience." Again, emphasis was lent to artists actively performing within the reach of the campus. This approach featured all aspects of hip-hop culture, of which Filipino Americans continue to be a major creative force. The range of forms included scratching/mixing, dance, rap, and graffiti styles. The unexpectedly large attendance of the event drew Filipino American hip-hop artists from throughout the Bay Area: Q-Bert, Bubala Tribe, Urban Soul, and Lani Luv, to name a few. Not merely a miming of African American style, Filipino American hip-hop demonstrates how younger segments of the community are accessing, struggling with, and coming to terms with the most vital cultural forms of late 20th-century America. It is not surprising that we find Filipino Americans engaged in hip-hop. Filipinos have taken part in aesthetically innovative moments in American culture. Consider the zoot-suiters and beboppers of another generation; Filipino American hip-hoppers of today not only participate in but rearticulate the form through a distinctive and improvisatory soulful style.

The third night saw a return to the traditional model, albeit with many alterations. This "finale" was the venue for what remained of the large-audience traditional model, although indigenous dance from the Philippines was not the centerpiece of the show. With only the "mountain" and "tribal" suites representing indigenous dance forms, the finale featured a pastiche of sounds and visions not found in the traditional PCN model. A series of pieces written, directed, and performed by students covered much ground in experimentally theatrical forms: a reading of a poem featured in a Filipino American literary journal; a meditation on Pinay adolescence and personal maturation; a lengthy "epic-documentary" of Filipino history, with the narrator (*Lapu Lapu*) as prophet; a play raising the problem of interdiasporic conflict; and a dialogue set to the rhythm of two Pinoys talking about how Filipinos created jazz. With the attention to the dance forms displaced, *Cultural Evidence* organizers left open the problematic of their editorial decision to highlight certain suites. Left out of the program were the "barrio" suite (which features the show-stopping "Tinikling") and the Muslim suite's "Singkil" (one of the most dazzlingly overproduced numbers in many repertoires).

This eclectic, sometimes unfocused, and largely uneven finale lacked the presentational unity or clarity of other PCNs. However, *Cultural*

Evidence accomplished much in taking to task larger theoretical and political concerns with definitions and expressions of "culture" and with the articulation of what Lowe (1991) referred to as "multiple-vocality." In strategizing with essentialisms rather than receiving them uncritically, *Cultural Evidence* organizers set the static inventory of dances aside (note that the dances were not wholly jettisoned) and opened the creative spaces for members to engage actively in a conversation over what they felt was important, over how they viewed their "culture." They highlighted the *process* of identity as an unfolding set of contradictions and possibilities, rather than the fixed *structure of identity to be (re)presented. Thus, as Filipinos of* "America," participants in *Cultural Evidence* reached deep into the Philippine tradition while stretching wide the range of constructive sources for engaging the U.S. American terrain through film, improvisational music, poetry, and so forth. From shore to shore, the nomads press on.

Coda: Dancing Matters

This critical review of the PCN has had two aims: not only to reveal multiple meanings of Filipina/o American cultural production as it unfolds on the stage but to cast an eye to the creativity of Filipina/o American expressive forms in general, which have been sorely neglected by the traditional PCN model. *Cultural Evidence* organizers did not edit any more than their previous cohorts. Instead, the major contribution of those organizers was their recognition that they were editing in the first place.

The stakes involve not simply fighting over what to include in or dismiss from the show. The PCN affords an opportunity to found discussions on what we do with our time and our labor, to question how we carry ourselves, to pose questions whose answers may not seem readily available. The PCN may be a venue opened for the experimentation with contingency, transgression, testimony, and even *entertainment.* In another sense of the term, *entertainment* means *reception*—welcoming and harboring, as in "entertaining an idea." For Filipino Americans seeking such "entertainment," the PCN can do more than simply keep one busy; rather, it can set aside some time for laughter, tragedy, surprise, and wonder—for entertaining ourselves.

Note

1. The poem by Juan Gomez-Quiñones, "The Ballad of Billy Rivera," appears in *5th and Grande Vista: Poems, 1960-1973*. Staten Island, NY: Editorial Mensaje, copyright 1974. Used with permission.

References

Belale, D. (1993). *Cultural Evidence* [program]. San Francisco State University, Pilipino American Collegiate Endeavor.

Campomanes, O. (1992). Filipinos in the United States and their literature of exile. In S. Geok-lin & A. Ling (Eds.), *Reading the literatures of Asian America*. Philadelphia: Temple University Press.

Catapusan, B. T. (1940). Leisure time problems of Filipino immigrants. *Sociology and Social Research, 24*, 541-549.

Cressey, P. G. (1932). *The taxi dance hall: A sociological study in commercialized recreation and city life*. Chicago: University of Chicago Press.

Enriquez, V. G. (1992). *From colonial to liberation psychology: The Philippine experience*. Quezon City: University of the Philippines Press.

Fanon, F. (1965). *The wretched of the earth*. New York: Grove.

Foucault, M. (1980). *Power/knowledge: Selected interviews and other writings, 1972-1977*. New York: Pantheon.

Fuss, D. (1989). *Essentially speaking: Feminism, nature and difference*. New York: Routledge.

Gaerlan, B. (1994, March). *"In the court of the sultan": Filipino American students encounter Orientalism and nationalism in Philippine dance*. Paper presented at the meeting of the Comparative and International Education Society, San Diego.

Gomez-Quiñones, J. (1974). *5th and Grande Vista: Poems, 1960-1973*. New York: Coliccion.

Ichioka, Y. (1974). *A buried past*. Berkeley: University of California Press.

Kim, E. H. (1993). Beyond railroads and internment: Comments on the past and future of Asian American studies. *Association for Asian American Studies Newsletter, 10*(4), 3-7.

Lowe, L. (1991). Heterogeneity, hybridity, multiplicity: Marking Asian American differences. *Diaspora, 1*, 24-44.

Peñaranda, O., Syquia, S., & Tagatac, S. (1975). An introduction to Filipino-American literature. In F. Chin, J. Chan, S. Wong, & L. Inada (Eds.), *Aiiieeeee!* New York: Anchor.

Philippine dancers delight the U.S. (1959, November 9). *Life Magazine*, pp. 47-50.

Radhakrishnan, R. (1987). Ethnic identity and post-structuralist difference. *Cultural Critique, 6*, 199-220.

Robles, A. (1977). *Looking for Ifugao Mountain—Paghahanap sa bundok ng ifugao* (A. Cariagma, Trans.; J. Dong, Illus.). San Francisco: Children's Book Press.

Said, E. (1978). *Orientalism*. New York: Vintage.

San Juan, E., Jr. (1992). *Racial formations/critical transformations: Articulations of power in ethnic and racial studies in the United States*. Atlantic Highlands, NJ: Humanities.

Spivak, G. C. (1994, April 5). Center for Ideas and Society Lecture, University of California at Riverside.

Syquia, S. (1974). *Flips: A Filipino-American anthology*. San Francisco: San Francisco State University.

UNESCO National Commission of the Philippines. (1973). *Cultural policy in the Philippines: A study prepared under the auspices of the UNESCO National Commission of the Philippines*. Paris: Author.

Vedder, C. B. (1947). *An analysis of the taxi-dance hall as a social institution*. Unpublished doctoral dissertation, University of Southern California.

12

Pamantasan

Filipino American Higher Education

Jonathan Y. Okamura
Amefil R. Agbayani

It is a long-established cultural tradition in both Philippine and Filipino American society to bestow recognition on the "scholar" as an honored member of the community. Filipino American newspapers commonly feature articles about "topnotcher" students who have been awarded scholarships, selected class valedictorian, or otherwise distinguished themselves through their academic achievements. In these articles, the names and background of the student's parents also are prominently noted because it is understood that their child's accomplishments are the direct result of the family's support and encouragement over the years.

AUTHORS' NOTE: We would like to say *maraming salamat* to Michelle Macaraeg Bautista, Emily Lawsin, Darlene Rodrigues, John Rosa, and James Sobredo for providing us with current information on admissions and enrollment in the University of California system and to James for discussing these and other issues regarding Filipino American students and studies with us.

Accordingly, parents who have raised more than the usual number of college graduates are themselves honored by the community. There is no question concerning the Filipino value placed on education, particularly higher education, which parents view as the best legacy they can bestow on their children for the latter's future socioeconomic security. Unfortunately, Filipino Americans have encountered considerable resistance, as well as much disappointment, in their efforts to realize this highly cherished value.

This chapter discusses Filipino American achievement, access, and advocacy in higher education, including the misleading nature of their apparently high educational attainment, the institutional barriers that limit their access to higher education, recent declining trends in their college admission, and the status of Filipino American studies, especially as a result of student activism.

Educational Attainment and Socioeconomic Returns

Filipino Americans appear to have a relatively high level of educational achievement, according to 1990 U.S. census data. Filipino women (25 years and older) have an especially high percentage with a bachelor's degree or higher (42%) and rank second after Asian Indian women (49%), who very likely have the highest rate of college completion or higher among women in the United States (U.S. Bureau of the Census, 1993, p. 8). Filipino American men (36%) also have an above-average proportion of recipients of bachelor's degree or higher .

But it appears that these high levels of educational attainment are due primarily to the arrival of college-educated, post-1965 immigrants, a process that has been referred to as Philippine "foreign aid" to the United States. A sample survey of almost 2,100 adult Filipinos who had been issued immigrant visas to the United States in 1986 found that almost one half (47%) had attended or graduated from college and that another 10% had enrolled in or completed graduate school (Carino, Fawcett, Gardner, & Arnold, 1990, p. 28). In contrast, second- and third-generation Filipino Americans continue to be underrepresented in colleges and universities and are not achieving the same high educational status as their Philippine-educated counterparts (Azores, 1986-1987; Okamura, 1991; University of Hawai'i Pamantasan Council, 1996). Thus, the apparent gains that have been made in higher education can be attributed primarily to post-1965 immigration rather than to progressive advancement over the generations, as with Chinese and Japanese Americans.

The relatively high educational attainment of Filipino Americans obscures another problematic issue. Compared to other racial/ethnic groups, the socioeconomic returns they receive in income and occupational status are not commensurate with their educational qualifications. This situation is very likely the result of discriminatory employment practices (Barringer, Takeuchi, & Xenos, 1990, p. 90; Cabezas, Shinagawa, & Kawaguchi, 1986-1987, p. 40). Multiple-classification analysis of 1990 U.S. census data on personal income indicates that when other factors (e.g., occupation, number of weeks worked, age, gender) are controlled, Filipino Americans receive less compensation for education in comparison to whites and Japanese Americans (the only other group compared was Native Hawaiians; Barringer & Liu, 1994, p. 90). Among males, Filipinos gain $5,500 in personal income for completing college, compared to much greater increases for whites ($10,100) and Japanese Americans ($15,600; Barringer & Liu, 1994, p. 79). Filipino females fare better than their male counterparts, with a marginal increase in income of $5,900 for college graduation, which is higher than that for white ($4,400) or Japanese ($4,600) women. The larger proportion of Filipino women employed as professionals compared to Filipino men (see below) may account for these differences in income gains.

At the upper levels of the occupational scale among executives, administrators, and managers, Filipino American men receive substantially less personal income ($31,200) than their white ($44,400) and Japanese American ($53,000) counterparts, despite having comparable mean years of education (13.0 years). Female Filipino executives/managers ($24,500) also earn less than similarly employed Japanese women ($26,300), although they have more mean years of education (13.1 years) than the latter (Barringer & Liu, 1994, pp. 82-83).

Filipino Americans also do not have an overall occupational status commensurate with their relatively high educational qualifications. Despite the common perception that college-educated professionals predominate among post-1965 immigrants, service work continues to be the

largest occupational category for Filipino men (17%) and the second largest
for Filipino women (18%; Barringer & Liu, 1994, p. 56). A higher percentage
of Filipino Americans is employed as service workers than is the case among
Asian Americans (15%) and the total American population (13%; U.S.
Bureau of the Census, 1993, p. 9). Service-work employment is especially
prevalent among Filipinos in Hawai'i, with its tourism-based economy in
which nearly one of every three working Filipino women and one of four
Filipino men are service workers (Okamura, in press).

At the higher levels of the occupational scale, the proportion of
Filipino Americans who hold managerial and professional positions
(27%) is comparable to that for whites (26%) but less than that for Asian
Americans (31%), particularly Chinese (36%) and Japanese (37%) Americans (U.S. Bureau of the Census, 1993, p. 9). One reason for this lower
percentage of managers and professionals, despite their higher educational attainment, is the occupational downgrading to lower-status jobs
that professional immigrants commonly experience in the employment
arena (East-West Population Institute, 1990, pp. 12-14; Okamura, 1983).

Female Filipinos (18%) are employed to a greater extent as professionals
than their male counterparts (11%; Barringer & Liu, 1994, p. 56), perhaps
due to the substantial number of women working as nurses and other health
professionals. However, as many as 28,000 nurses from the Philippines
hold temporary H1-A visas that allow them to work only for 1 to 3 years in
the United States, and 5,000 of them may have to return to the Philippines
as a result of the expiration of the U.S. Immigration Nursing Relief Act in
August 1995 ("5,000 Nurses," 1996, p. A1). Thus, the relatively high
educational status of Filipino Americans ultimately is misleading insofar
as it does not reflect their historical and contemporary experiences in the
American educational system and may give the false impression that
their personal income and occupational status are similarly high.

Cultural Values and Institutional
Barriers to Higher Education

There is a troubling paradox in Filipino American educational attainment: Although immigrants come with relatively high levels of college

education, their children and other American-born Filipinos generally are unable to replicate these same high levels (Okamura, 1996, p. 68). The reasons for this situation are complex and varied, but a useful starting point toward an explanation is to avoid blaming Filipino American students for their educational status. Rather than focusing on their supposed academic deficiencies as evident in comparatively lower Scholastic Assessment Test verbal scores and in the high incidence of nonnative speakers of English, one should first consider their attitude toward and desire for education.

As noted above, a strong cultural value placed on higher education among Filipino Americans is evident in the encouragement and financial support that children receive from their parents, even if the latter are not college graduates and do not hold professional positions. A survey of first-time freshmen who entered the University of Hawai'i at Manoa (UH Manoa) in fall 1990 reported that a considerable majority of Filipino Americans (60%) indicated that their parents' desire for them to attend college was a "very important" reason in their decision to do so. This percentage was substantially higher than those for white (32%), Japanese (41%), and Chinese (42%) American freshmen, even though the latter two groups also are thought to value education highly. The same survey found that an extremely high proportion of Filipino freshmen (92%) were receiving financial assistance for their college studies from parents or family, which was again a higher figure than for students from the other groups (Institutional Research Office, 1991). Studies also have established the high level of college aspiration among Filipino American high school students—a variable that tends to correlate with high occupational aspiration (Azores, 1986-1987, p. 46; Young, 1985, p. 18). Thus, the primary explanation for the underrepresentation and underachievement of Filipino Americans in higher education pertains to factors other than a lack of appropriate cultural values or attitudes on their part.

Institutional barriers restrict Filipino American access to and persistence in college. These structural constraints are evident in the substantial decrease in Filipino American school enrollment following high school, and for some youth this nonstudent status begins in high school. In California, Filipinos have a significant high school dropout and noncompletion rate that is considerably above that for Asian Americans (Almirol, 1988, p. 60; Azores, 1986-1987, p. 41). According to 1990 U.S. census data, Filipino American school enrollment averages about 95% from elementary through high school age groupings, a figure that is quite comparable to the average percentage for other groups (Barringer & Liu, 1994, p. 46). However, only 77% of Filipinos in the 18- to 19-year-old post-high school age category are enrolled in school, and Filipino American school enrollment continues to decline in the 20-to-21 (61%) and 22-to-24 (36%) college-age categories. Though considerably higher than those of whites, these percentages for Filipino Americans are substantially lower than those of Japanese Americans (77% and 52%, respectively). Thus, Filipino students apparently are withdrawing from the educational pipeline to college. As a relevant example, in Hawai'i, which at 170,000 has the second-largest Filipino American population in the nation, Filipinos are the second-largest group (18%) in the public schools (K-12), but they make up less than 10% of students at the main UH Manoa campus (Institutional Research Office, 1995, p. 13). Thus, a significant factor in Filipino underrepresentation in postsecondary education is their not continuing after high school in sufficient numbers. This in turn can be attributed, at least in part, to their not being actively recruited and encouraged to pursue college study by their teachers and counselors and by university recruitment and admission offices because of stereotypic beliefs and attitudes about their educational abilities and aspirations.

Another institutional barrier to persistence in college is the limited number of Filipino American faculty who otherwise could serve as role models and informal academic advisors to students. Fewer faculty also means fewer courses and less research and publication on Filipino American topics that students have available for their education and knowledge. The relatively lower number of Filipino college students itself limits their persistence because they may experience feelings of alienation and of not belonging on predominantly white campuses— feelings that may contribute to the above-average attrition rate of Filipino American students (see below).

Affirmative Inaction in Higher Education

Although Filipinos are categorized as Asian American, their experiences and achievement in higher education are not comparable to those of other Asian American groups, particularly Chinese and Japanese Americans. As a result, Filipino Americans have been victimized by the model minority stereotype of Asian Americans that essentializes the latter as academically gifted, overrepresented in higher education, having relatively high occupational and income status, and able to succeed through their own individual and family efforts and sacrifices. Because they are classified as Asian American, Filipinos have been presumed not to be an underrepresented minority, so beginning in 1986 they were no longer considered a special target group for recruitment and admission under educational opportunity and student affirmative action programs in the University of California system (Almirol, 1988, p. 61). Critics of new admission policies instituted at the University of California at Los Angeles (UCLA) in 1989 maintained that these policies do not serve the specific recruitment, admission, and retention needs of Filipino American students ("Asian Frosh Admissions," 1991, p. 1). They pointed to the lower retention rate of Filipinos compared to other Asian American students as a need not addressed by admission policies.

Recent data on Filipino admissions to the University of California, in a state that has 52% of the 1.4-million Filipino American population (Barringer, Gardner, & Levin, 1993, p. 112) indicate a disturbing declining acceptance rate despite an increasing number of applicants. At UCLA for fall 1991, the 902 Filipino applicants had an admission rate of 39% ("Asian Frosh Admissions," 1991, p. 1). Other Asian American groups had much higher rates of acceptance at UCLA for that year: Chinese (55%), Korean (46%), and Japanese (46%) Americans. For fall 1996, of the 1,377 Filipino American applicants, only 26% were admitted—the lowest admission percentage of any ethnic/racial group. At the University of California (UC) Berkeley for fall 1996, although the 979 Filipino American applicants were the most numerous ever, the acceptance rate (16%) was the lowest in recent years and also was the lowest of all ethnic/racial groups and well below the overall admission rate of 25% to 30% (D. Rodrigues, personal communication, May 8, 1996). Filipinos may have the lowest acceptance rate because other disadvantaged minorities such as African Americans and Latinos are still eligible for soon-to-be-eliminated affirmative action admission programs.

Besides admissions, Filipino American enrollment at UCLA and UC Berkeley also has been decreasing in recent years. At UCLA between 1984 and 1988, Filipino freshmen enrollment averaged nearly 200 students each fall, with a high of 231 in 1985 ("The Cutting Edge," 1989, p. 9). Between 1991 and 1993, this figure declined to about 150 freshmen. The situation is far worse at UC Berkeley, where admission policies were changed in 1991 to give priority in affirmative action admissions to family socioeconomic status and to remove race-based affirmative action (Takagi, 1990, p. 589). For the past 4 years, entering Filipino American freshmen have averaged only about 50 each fall (M. M. Bautista, personal communication, May 13, 1996), about the same number as enrolled over 20 years ago in 1975 (Almirol, 1988, p. 61). Ten years ago, there were over 700 Filipino American undergraduates at UC Berkeley, but they have been reduced to about 500. The reasons for this dwindling representation of Filipino students include their removal from affirmative action recruitment and admissions programs, their being adversely affected by the above-noted changes in admission policies in 1991, and their lower retention rate compared to that of other students. In response to this troubling trend, two Filipino student organizations at UC Berkeley, Pilipino Academic Student Services and the Filipino Studies Working Group (1996), issued a "Statement of Concern" that argued:

> While the withdrawal of support from Affirmative Action has been undoubtedly a major factor in our gradual exclusion from the University, our invisibility on the institutional and academic levels has only fueled our growing conviction that UC Berkeley has no interest in providing Filipinos with the support and encouragement necessary for our survival here as an underrepresented minority. (p. 1)

As a notable contrast to the above cases of declining enrollment, Filipino Americans at UC Irvine, which has the highest proportion of Asian American students (53%) in the UC system and in the continental United States, have steadily increased to more than 900 undergraduates and to 6.5% of the undergraduate enrollment (J. Rosa, personal communication, September 20, 1996). San Francisco State University, which offers a minor degree in Filipino American studies, has more than 1,400 Filipino undergraduates, who represent almost 9% of its enrollment. UH Manoa very likely has the highest percentage (12%) and number (1,600) of Filipino American undergraduates at any university, and Filipinos are the largest ethnic/racial group in the seven UH community colleges (20%), although they still are very much underrepresented as graduate students (Institutional Research Office, 1995, p. 13). These gains can be attributed in part to the establishment of the Operation Manong recruitment and retention program in 1972 through the initial voluntary efforts of students and community leaders (Agbayani, 1996, p. 155).

What is especially troubling is that the declining trend in Filipino American admissions and enrollment at UC Berkeley and UCLA has been occurring during a period of unprecedented gains in Asian American representation in the UC system and in higher education in general. These increases followed changes in admission policies that resulted from formal charges that quota limitations had been imposed against Asian American applicants in the mid-1980s at some of the most prestigious universities in the nation (Takagi, 1993). In fall 1991, both at UCLA (39%) and UC Berkeley (33%), Asian Americans constituted the largest group of entering freshmen for the first time ever at both institutions. Given such increasing admissions, in fall 1994 Asian Americans (31%) constituted nearly one third of the domestic student enrollment in the nine-campus UC system, particularly at the Berkeley (35%), Los Angeles (35%), and Irvine (46%) campuses ("End Race-Based Admissions," 1995, p. A1). These percentages are remarkable for a group that makes up only 10% of the state population and very likely indicate an ongoing trend for the foreseeable future.

In July 1995, the University of California Board of Regents voted to eliminate affirmative action programs based on race and gender preference in admissions, hiring, and contracting in the UC system beginning in fall 1997. Should it pass, which appears likely, the so-called California Civil Rights Initiative on the ballot in November 1996 would go even further and prohibit such affirmative action programs throughout the entire state government system, including the state university and community college systems. A May 16, 1995, article in the *Wall Street Journal* estimated that elimination of race-based affirmative action programs in admissions in the UC system would result in substantial increases of Asian American and white freshmen, whereas African American and Latino admissions would considerably decline. For example, at UC Berkeley, if applicants are reviewed using socioeconomic status as an affirmative action admission criterion, Asian Americans may constitute a majority of enrolled freshmen in 1997. Unfortunately, these projected Asian American gains do not necessarily mean that Filipino Americans will similarly increase their admissions because their experiences and status in higher education have not been comparable to those of other Asian American groups. Given the recent declining admission rate of Filipino American applicants, the elimination of affirmative action programs may result in their being even more excluded from public higher education.

Filipino American Studies: Curriculum and Student Activism

Filipino American studies traces its more recent historical origins to the turbulent late 1960s as part of the emergence of ethnic studies and Asian American studies programs on college campuses on the West Coast. The first Filipino American studies program was started at San Francisco State University (then College) in 1969 when the Ethnic Studies Program (now College) was founded. Through the Philippine-American Collegiate Endeavor (PACE), Filipinos had a leading role in the student and faculty strikes at San Francisco State led by the Third World Liberation Front in 1968 and 1969 that resulted in the establishment of ethnic studies (Gonzales, 1994, p. 50). There also is a Center for Philippine and Filipino American Studies at California State University at Hayward, the only such center on a college campus, although the Center for Philippine Studies at UH sponsors activities focused on Filipino Americans, such as colloquia, publications, and cultural events, because of the sizable community in Hawai'i. Despite its relatively long history, Royal Morales's (1986-1987, p. 124) argument expressed 10 years ago that "Pilipino" American studies is a "promise and an unfinished agenda" still holds. In particular, the need to "institutionalize" the offering of its courses remains. As an indication of this unfulfilled agenda, Morales's edited work *Makibaka: The Pilipino American Struggle* (1974) remains, more than 20 years after its publication, the only major anthology in Filipino American studies. But the new *Journal for Filipino American Studies*, published by San Francisco State University, should contribute to curriculum development and further scholarship.

At most universities, courses on Filipino American history, culture, and community are offered through ethnic studies or Asian American studies departments or programs. A growing number of colleges and universities are offering such classes, although much more prevalently on the West Coast than in other parts of the country. However, these courses often are taught by part-time lecturers rather than by permanent faculty on a regular basis—an arrangement that is symptomatic of the continuing marginalization of Filipino American studies in Asian American and ethnic studies as academic disciplines and in American colleges and universities in general. Insofar as courses on Filipino Americans provide a culturally relevant curriculum that is generally lacking at the high school level, they can contribute to the recruitment and retention of Filipino students; therefore, more of these classes should be offered as part of the regular curriculum. However, the relative absence of Filipino American faculty on most campuses severely limits the development and teaching of courses with a Filipino American focus or content. UH Manoa has the largest number of Filipino American faculty (16, although they make up slightly more than 1% of the tenured and tenurable faculty), but the numbers are far fewer at most universities—for example, there is only one Filipino American faculty member at UC Berkeley. Furthermore, on many campuses, most Filipino faculty are from the Philippines rather than being American born; this indicates the need to recruit more of the latter into graduate education for academic careers. Particularly in Asian American studies as an academic discipline, greater voice and action should be given to the specific concerns and issues of importance to Filipino Americans through a more equitable sharing of power, representation, and resources (Okamura, 1995, p. 398).

Philippine language courses, primarily Tagalog (or Pilipino), are being offered at an increasing number of colleges and universities across the United States, often as a result of student demands. These institutions include San Francisco State University, UC Berkeley, UCLA, University of Michigan, University of Wisconsin, Cornell University, and University of Pennsylvania. UH Manoa has the largest (in terms of enrollment and faculty) and most comprehensive Philippine language program. It includes four levels of both Tagalog and Ilokano, as well as courses on Philippine literature, film, and folklore. The 400 students enrolled in these courses each semester commonly give as their reason "to learn more about my roots, appreciate my Filipino culture and communicate with my parents" (Ramos, 1996, p. 167). Language courses thus provide an important means for the maintenance and expression of Filipino

American cultural values and identity and therefore also should be viewed as a way to recruit and retain students.

Filipino American students have taken an active advocacy position in fostering, if not creating, Filipino American studies on their campuses. Students in the Asian Pacific Languages and Cultures Committee at UCLA led the effort to have Tagalog (along with Hindi, Thai, and Vietnamese) offered on a regular basis in the early 1990s, as Berkeley students also did. Graduate students in the Filipino Studies Working Group at UC Berkeley have convened a symposium the past 2 years at which they presented papers on their ongoing research. A recent student-led campaign at UCLA sought to have a Pilipino American Studies Program established within the Asian American Studies Center that would offer classes, publish scholarly materials, and sponsor conferences and lectures on Filipino American issues.

Filipino campus organizations are offering recruitment and retention services that universities are not providing specifically for Filipino American students. At UC Berkeley, Pilipino Academic Student Services (PASS) is a student group that makes outreach visits to high schools throughout California to encourage Filipinos to attend college, and the Pilipino American Alliance sponsors a *kuya/ate* (older brother/older sister) mentoring program that pairs incoming freshmen with upperclass students. The Filipino American Student Association at Washington State University hosts an annual conference for high school and college-age students. These various student organizations and activities are indicative of a significant Filipino American academic and political presence on college campuses across the nation. Moreover, this presence is expressed as specifically Filipino American, rather than as Asian American in coalition with other student groups, because of the desire to address Filipino Americans' particular educational and community concerns and problems that may not be shared by other groups.

Conclusion

Daryl Smith (1989) identified three types of campus responses to the goals of diversity, equity, and quality. The first focuses on "student assistance": Universities recruit minority students and provide them with tutorial services and financial aid. Smith noted that "fundamentally it is a 'deficit' approach to diversity in that it attempts to improve success by providing the student with support and resources" (p. 25). The second type of response is "institutional accommodation": It still focuses on the "special needs" of students but adds programs and makes modest changes to remove barriers to success—for example, establishing ethnic support centers. The third response is to build on the institution's capacity to organize for diversity. This means fundamental changes that result in diversity among faculty, staff, and students and in mission and values, quality of interaction on campus, commitment to educate students for living in a pluralistic campus and world, and broadening the concept of quality so that it does not conflict with diversity and equity.

Universities across the United States can be placed in any one of these categories. It is not easy to make generalizations because of the variety of institutions in terms of size, prestige, and public or private control as well as the wide range of percentages of Filipino and other Asian Americans on campus or in the community. Our informal assessment is that most institutions are best described as being Type 1 or 2.

Although the experiences of Filipino Americans in Hawai'i and at UH may not be typical (e.g., the 90-year history of Filipinos, the large size of the Filipino population—15%—in a state where no ethnic/racial group is a numerical majority), it is useful to look at their experiences to describe the advancement and future challenges that face the Filipino American community in higher education. It is our view that UH is in an early phase of the third type of response.

Prior to the 1970s, UH did not respond to the specific academic needs and concerns of Filipino American students. Even as late as 1977, only 3% of the student body was Filipino, although Filipinos were 12% of the state population. The first institutional response of UH was the establishment of outreach and support programs for socioeconomically disadvantaged communities as part of the federal "War on Poverty" Model Cities Program of the early 1970s. In 1972, a group of Filipino students, faculty, and community leaders applied for and received private and federal funds to establish "Operation Manong" so that UH students could provide tutoring and other educational support to Filipino and other immigrant children in the public schools. At the major campus, UH Manoa, courses in Philippine language and culture, Filipino American studies, and Philippine studies were established in the 1970s. During the 1980s, Operation Manong, ethnic studies, and Philippine studies worked hard to obtain more stable funding and institutionalization. Filipino American students have increased to 10% at Manoa and 20% at the various UH community colleges, although Filipino graduate students (4%) and faculty (1%) continue to be severely underrepresented. In the 1990s, UH has made strong public statements in its Strategic Plan, as well as its establishment of a Commission on Diversity, that it will address issues of campus climate, curriculum diversity, affirmative action, and student access and success for Filipinos and other groups traditionally underserved by the university.

Clearly, much more has to be done to reach parity and equity for Filipino Americans in higher education. The socioeconomic advancement of the Filipino community and scholarship and research on Filipino Americans by Filipino Americans cannot be accomplished without continuing to increase the representation and success of Filipinos in higher education. This task is the responsibility not only of Filipino Americans but of allies from other ethnic/racial groups and public policymakers.

References

Agbayani, A. R. (1996). The education of Filipinos in Hawai'i. *Social Process in Hawaii, 37,* 147-159.

Almirol, E. B. (1988). Exclusion and institutional barriers in the university system: The Filipino experience. In G. Okihiro, S. Hune, A. Hansen, & J. Liu (Eds.), *Reflections on shattered windows: Promises and prospects for Asian American studies* (pp. 59-67). Pullman: Washington State University.

Asian frosh admissions at 39%. (1991, Fall/Winter). *Crosscurrents,* pp. 1, 7.

Azores, T. (1986-1987). Educational attainment and upward mobility: Prospects for Filipino Americans. *Amerasia Journal, 13*(1), 39-52.

Barringer, H. R., Gardner, R. W., & Levin, M. J. (1993). *Asians and Pacific Islanders in the United States.* New York: Russell Sage.

Barringer, H. R., & Liu, N. (1994). *The demographic, social and economic status of native Hawaiians.* Unpublished report prepared for Alu Like, Inc.

Barringer, H. R., Takeuchi, D. T., & Xenos, P. (1990). Education, occupational prestige, and income of Asian Americans. *Sociology of Education, 63*(1), 27-43.

Cabezas, A., Shinagawa, L. H., & Kawaguchi, G. (1986-1987). New inquiries into the socioeconomic status of Pilipino Americans in California. *Amerasia Journal, 13*(1), 1-21.

Carino, B. V., Fawcett, J. T., Gardner, R. W., & Arnold, F. (1990). *The new Filipino immigrants to the United States: Increasing diversity and change* (Papers of the East-West Population Institute No. 115). Honolulu: East-West Population Institute.

The cutting edge: Redefining affirmative action, a case study on Pilipinos. (1989, Summer/Fall). *Crosscurrents,* pp. 3, 9.

East-West Population Institute. (1990). *Recent Filipino immigration to the United States: A profile*. Honolulu: Author.

End race-based admissions, UC Regent suggests. (1995, January 20). *Los Angeles Times*, pp. A1, A24.

5,000 nurses going home as immigration program ends. (1996, April 10-16). *Philippine News*, pp. A1, A12.

Gonzales, D. P. (1994, October). In troubled waters: Filipino American studies. *Pilipinas*, pp. 50-51.

Institutional Research Office, University of Hawai'i. (1991). *Freshman survey institutional summary for 1990* [Database Printout].

Institutional Research Office, University of Hawai'i. (1995). *Enrollment report University of Hawai'i, fall 1995*. Unpublished report.

Morales, R. F. (Ed.). (1974). *Makibaka: The Pilipino American struggle*. Los Angeles: Mountainview.

Morales, R. F. (1986-1987). Pilipino American studies: A promise and an unfinished agenda. *Amerasia Journal, 13*(1), 119-124.

Okamura, J. Y. (1983). *Immigrant Filipino ethnicity in Honolulu, Hawai'i*. Unpublished doctoral dissertation, University of London.

Okamura, J. Y. (1991). Filipino educational status and achievement at the University of Hawai'i. *Social Process in Hawaii, 33*, 107-129.

Okamura, J. Y. (1995). The Filipino American diaspora: Sites of space, time and ethnicity. In G. Y. Okihiro, M. Alquizola, D. Fujita Rony, & K. S. Wong (Eds.), *Privileging positions: The sites of Asian American studies* (pp. 387-400). Pullman: Washington State University Press.

Okamura, J. Y. (1996). Cultural factors in the instruction of Filipino American college students. In S. Benally, J. J. Mock, & M. Odell (Eds.), *Pathways to the multicultural community: Leadership, belonging and involvement* (pp. 67-74). Boulder, CO: Western Interstate Commission for Higher Education.

Okamura, J. Y. (in press). Institutionalized inequality: Racial and ethnic stratification in Hawai'i. In M. Haas (Ed.), *Multicultural Hawai'i: The fabric of a multiethnic society*. New York: Garland.

Pilipino Academic Student Services and Filipino Studies Working Group. (1996). *Statement of concern on the enforced invisibility of Filipinos at UC Berkeley*. Unpublished document.

Ramos, T. V. (1996). Philippine languages in Hawai'i: Vehicles of cultural survival. *Social Process in Hawaii, 37*, 161-170.

Smith, D. (1989). *The challenge of diversity*. Washington, DC: George Washington University, School of Education and Human Development.

Takagi, D. Y. (1990). From discrimination to affirmative action: Facts in the Asian American admissions controversy. *Social Problems, 37*, 578-592.

Takagi, D. Y. (1993). *Retreat from race: Asian American admissions and racial politics*. New Brunswick, NJ: Rutgers University Press.

U.S. Bureau of the Census. (1993). *We, the American Asians*. Washington, DC: Author.

University of Hawai'i Pamantasan Council. (1996). *Pamantasan: Filipino Americans in the University of Hawai'i*. Honolulu: University of Hawai'i, Student Equity, Excellence and Diversity.

Young, V. C. (1985). *Cultural and communication influences on Hawai'i Filipino students' educational aspirations*. Unpublished master's thesis, University of Hawai'i.

13

Images, Roles, and Expectations of Filipino Americans by Filipino Americans

Allan L. Bergano
Barbara L. Bergano-Kinney

Although Filipino Americans are one of the largest and oldest Asian Pacific American ethnic groups in the United States, information on them is scarce. This information is predominately confined to America's West Coast and Hawaii. In light of the assumed differences between East and West Coast Filipino Americans in their available frames of references, the following hypothesis was formulated: that young East Coast Filipino Americans, of whom a larger proportion are products of

AUTHORS' NOTE: We wish to acknowledge the support of the following people: Paula Angeles, Ann Boquiren, Damian Cordova, Maria Salientes, Meg Thorton, Bernadette Miranda, Andrea Yangus, Marlon Manralit, Jose Montano, Ray Obispo, Fred Cordova, Dorothy Cordova, Kristine Carranceja, Edwina Lapa-Bergano, Michelle Bautista, Annalissa Herbert, Filipino American National Historical Society, Filipino American Cultural Society of Salem High School, Filipino Intercollegiate Network Dialogue, Filipino American Student Association of the University of Washington. This chapter is offered in honor of Fabian C. and Aurora L. Bergano, for giving us the opportunity to be Filipino Americans.

post-1965 Filipino immigration, are more likely than West Coast Filipino Americans, who are products of Filipino immigration from the 1920s to 1930s, to have grown up in an environment where it is assumed that they will be able to assimilate easily into Anglo American society and strong ties to the Filipino American community are consequently not expected of them.

According to the 1990 U.S. census, nearly 70% of East Coast Filipino Americans are first-generation Americans who arrived after 1965. Post-1965 Filipino immigration to the East Coast was characterized by individuals who possessed professional degrees (doctors, nurses, accountants, and engineers) or were employed by the U.S. Navy (Pido, 1984). Because of favorable social, economic, and historical conditions, they were able to root themselves in terms of income, achievement, and command of Anglo ways (Broom & Kitsuse, 1955). Therefore, their acceptance by Anglo Americans was easier, resulting in more assimilationist attitudes.

West Coast Filipino immigration between the 1920s and 1930s was characterized mostly by young males with no college degrees who were leaving impoverished provinces. Most of them became migratory menial laborers for survival's sake because of the Great Depression of the 1930s (Filipino Oral History Project, 1984). Their attitudes and beliefs about Anglo American society were influenced historically by racism and discriminatory practices imposed by law, such as denial of American citizenship, antimiscegenation laws, and legislation outlawing ownership of real estate. Therefore, their expectations of and attitudes toward Anglo American society were less assimilationist. Consequently, they became more oriented toward the establishment and preservation of the Filipino American community. These attitudes have prevailed among their descendants.

Literature on Filipino American perspectives is sparse. This chapter serves more as an exploratory study and a catalyst calling for future research than as a crucial experiment that would solve a theoretical problem. In this chapter, perspectives from Filipino Americans living on the East and West Coasts were based on results from an opinion poll administered to Filipino American high school and college students involved in venues promoting Filipino American community awareness. We specifically polled high school and college-aged students because (a) they constitute the largest segment of Filipino Americans by age, (b) they represent the first significant generation to enroll in and graduate from college, and (c) they all possess an interest to discover who they and what they can become as Filipino Americans.

▨

Methodology

The 150 high school and college students participating in the present investigation were obtained from three samples:

1. 40 East Coast high school students attending a monthly meeting of the Filipino American Cultural Society of Salem High School in Virginia Beach, Virginia (20 women, 20 men; Salem High School has one of the largest Filipino American student populations on the East Coast, with over 400 students, constituting 20% of the total student population)

2. 60 East Coast college students attending a workshop during the Filipino Intercollegiate Network Dialogue (FIND) Conference in Philadelphia (30 women, 30 men; FIND is recognized as the largest college-student-based organization on the East Coast, with over 85 East Coast colleges and universities represented)

3. 26 West Coast college students attending a class on Filipino American history at the University of Washington in Seattle and 24 students attending a Filipino American Student Association meeting (28 women and 22 men, total) at the same university

Follow-up individual interviews were conducted with approximately 20 students and working professionals, randomly selected to provide data interpretation based on their personal experiences. Their comments are captured in the discussions below. The issues raised were based on high and low frequency of responses to the following statements: (a) "I am expected to marry a Filipino/a," (b) "I am expected to experience racism and discrimination," and (c) "I am expected to become a community leader."

▨

Results

Tables 13.1, 13.2, and 13.3 show the significant findings on students' responses about others' expectations of their marrying a Filipino/a, experiencing racism and discrimination, and becoming a community leader.

TABLE 13.1   Percentage of Respondents Agreeing to the Statement "I Am
Expected to Marry a Filipino/a"

	East Coast		West Coast	
	Female	*Male*	*Female*	*Male*
College	20	83	74	60
High School	20	95	NA	NA

Marrying a Filipino/a

Students were asked if they agreed or disagreed with the statement
"I am expected to marry a Filipino/a." Table 13.1 clearly demonstrates
a significant low perceived expectation of East Coast high school and
college women to marry a Filipino man. This low expectation suggests
that among East Coast Filipinos, no high value is placed on finding a
Filipino husband specifically. In contrast, among West Coast Filipinos
(specifically Seattle Filipinos), Filipino husbands are highly valued, as
74% of the women surveyed say that they are expected to marry a
Filipino.

Filipinos possess a colonial mentality after being colonized by Spain
for over 300 years and the United States for 50 years. As a result, they
perceive themselves as inferior to their colonizers, the Anglo Americans
and the Spaniards (Pido, Chapter 3 of this book; Rimonte, Chapter 4 of
this book; Schirmer, 1987, pp. 38-43; Strobel, Chapter 5 of this book). This
mentality also perpetuates the belief that all people of color are inferior.

At the end of the Philippine-American War in 1902, American political and educational systems were immediately established throughout
the Philippines. English became the common language at all institutions.
Filipinos adopted many aspects of the American lifestyles from tennis
shoes and Levi jeans to hamburgers and French fries. They believed that
they were Americans and that the United States was their motherland
(Ubalde, 1996). It is only logical that many of the post-1965 immigrants
who came to this country were already assimilated to some aspects of
the American system. The people implementing those cultural changes
were all Anglo Americans, and as a result, Filipinos began perceiving
themselves or anything Filipino as inferior (Schirmer, 1987, pp. 45-51).
This inferiority complex was covertly fostered through images and
beliefs controlled by the Anglo American mass media. Filipinos aspired
to be like those who set the standards, made up the rules, and had access

to power. Unlike the early Filipino immigrants, who came to this country to make enough money to return home, post-1965 Filipino immigrants, who were primarily professionals, came to this country to stay and to become American; many believed they were almost already Americans. With this belief, and with the strong identification with Americans, there was no need for them to create or re-create their own educational, political, and economic institutions. The American institutions were familiar, so they accepted the American way and made it their way of life (Ubalde, 1996).

The colonial mentality is a reality confronting young East Coast second-generation Filipino Americans. We believe that it encourages the assimilation process and distorts the roles, images, and expectations of Filipino Americans. The following comments from a young East Coast woman confirm its existence and demonstrate its effects on choosing a marriage partner:

> Because of the American colonization process, Filipinas are being taught that "marrying up" means "marrying white." The Filipina's standard for beauty has changed so that they see white men as desirable and "bearers of the ideal beauty," . . . not the Filipino man. The "white-oriented" mass media has blinded and brainwashed to-day's Filipina at the expense of the Filipino male.

Another young East Coast woman, now living in Manila, adds:

> Over here [in the Philippines], white skin is considered better. I cannot tell you how many products are advertised and sold here to "whiten" our skin. Marrying a white man for Filipinas is a step up . . . socially and economically. Mixed children by white men here are thought of as more valuable, precious, and better prepared for modern society. This mentality isn't new. Many of the elders here believe "White is right." All white boyfriends, husbands, and mixed children are shown off here as trophies . . . and not always at the doing of the girl-friend/wife. My mother "shows off" my white husband more than I ever would.

We believe that the colonial mentality causes many East Coast Filipino Americans to possess favorable images of Anglo American men at the expense of Filipino American men. As a result, marrying a

TABLE 13.2 Percentage of Respondents Agreeing to the Statement "I Am Expected to Experience Racism and Discrimination"

	East Coast	West Coast
Total College	57	70
Females	44	60
Males	80	80

Filipino/a may be perceived by some as a "lateral" move and by others as a step "backwards." Marrying an Anglo-American is perceived as an "upward" move.

Racism and Discrimination

Prior to 1965, most West Coast Filipino American communities were made up of distinct, marginalized neighborhoods defined by segregation (Cordova, 1983). Because of segregation, the Filipino American community of Seattle was made up of the easily identified neighborhoods of Beacon Hill, Central District, and Rainier Valley. Like many other ethnic groups, Filipinos have chosen to remain separate by choice as well as by necessity. For the most part, they have often found this the easier course because immigrants need not strain to change their ways and manners or eliminate their accents. Staying within the Filipino American community was part of survival. The community provided a relative "safe place" where new cultural acquisitions could be tried out and where, at the same time, traditional practices could be maintained and passed on to the next generation.

On the East Coast, segregation was not a factor. Most East Coast Filipino Americans, particularly professionals, possessed financial resources to live in neighborhoods where racism and discrimination were less frequent due to more positive images of this largely educated and professional group. Table 13.2 supports that notion by its reporting of students' responses to the statement "I am expected to experience racism and discrimination."

Compared to all other groups of men and women, a lower percentage of East Coast female college students says they are expected to experience racism and discrimination (44%). One reason may be the subtle or covert nature of racism and discrimination today, which this group in particular may find it difficult to recognize. The following comment by a West Coast man, suggesting differences in how Filipino American women and men are treated by white employers, adds some perspective on the above findings:

> Most employers are white men. White men are attracted to the beautiful "exotic" Filipina. They hire them partly for their skills, but also to uplift their white fragile egos. Once hired, they showcase their "China dolls" or "geisha girls" as symbols that their company promotes diversity. This is blatant, covert discrimination and racism at its best. The Filipino male applicant is viewed as a threat. Not only does he have access to white females in the company, but also to the prized Filipina. Therefore, if he is employed, he is hired mainly for his skills (usually overqualified) in making the company more production efficient and would work for cheaper wages, making the company more economically efficient. This is another example of covert racism and discrimination.

In another interview, a West Coast woman elaborates:

> In addition to being viewed as a "prized trophy," the Filipina may also be viewed as an easy target for sexual harassment. Sexual overtones, jokes, and other inappropriate behavior would seem permissible to demonstrate in front of the Filipina, who may be perceived as a "shy, quiet one" or emulate the image of the perfect "mail-order bride." However, if the female does not play the game by refusing to comply to do certain prized-trophy duties . . . like going out for a drink after work, tolerating racial comments or sexist jokes, she is then viewed differently. If she becomes assertive and outspoken, she is then labeled as a "troublemaker" or an "uppity one," thereby jeopardizing her "prized-trophy" status. As a consequence, she becomes a victim of a hostile work environment. Her contributions are ignored, her access to vital information is curtailed particularly to information where developmental and career advancement opportunities exist.

We believe that East Coast Filipino American female college students' low likelihood of reporting that they are expected to experience racism and discrimination may be due to racism's subtle and covert nature. It is due in part to an overall lack of understanding of racism and discrimination, the denial of their existence, and the inability of this group to admit, identify, and recognize racial and discriminatory acts and behaviors.

Becoming a Community Leader

We believe that developing and mobilizing a Filipino American community around civic issues, such as immigration restrictions, is critical to preserve, unify, and establish dialogue among Filipino Americans. However, it has been our experience that social activities, such as induction balls, queen pageants, and picnics, are placed higher on the community agenda by most community leaders. On the basis of the results of our survey, the following top three problem areas were identified by Filipino Americans between the ages of 18 and 30: (a) identity, (b) gang violence, and (c) immigration restrictions. Filipino American community leaders attend to these problems minimally or not at all. Perhaps some community leaders do not know what to do or perceive the issues as unimportant. Therefore, issues remain unresolved, and more focus is directed on social events. As a result, apathy and frustration exist. In fact, 75% of all respondents agreed that "apathy" is a problem confronting Filipino Americans. One East Coast woman shares her comments on apathy deriving from an assimilationist mentality:

> Many Filipinos believe that if they are individually "doing well" and prospering in America, there is no obligation to be involved in the upliftment of our community. If I could "do well," why can't they? Besides, who wants more frustration in their lives, championing causes for an ungrateful people.

Apathy includes skepticism about the value of the Filipino American community. If the community is devalued, then expectations of becoming a community leader would be low. Table 13.3 clearly demonstrates our findings.

The low rate of endorsement by East Coast college students, particularly women, of the statement "I am expected to become a community leader" reflects a low value placed on the Filipino American community. One explanation may be the colonial mentality, which, in this case, discounts the existence of the problem within a community. However, if

TABLE 13.3   Percentage of Respondents Agreeing to the Statement "I Am
Expected to Become a Community Leader"

	East Coast	West Coast
Female college students	32	52
Male college students	50	35

an issue is identified by the properly recognized American social institution as a "problem," then it becomes a "real problem" for the Filipino
American community. Another reason is offered by a West Coast woman:

> In working with youth and young adults, I have observed that there
> are not enough vehicles or processes instituted in Filipino organiza-
> tions for them [young adults] to be validated for their ideas and
> actions. Because of this, community politics can be demoralizing—a
> definite turnoff for young bright minds. For example, I was not
> validated for my ideas or actions because I was too young, female, not
> being from the area, not having parents who were active in the
> community, and being perceived as "*mestiza* American" even though
> both my parents are Filipino. I think it's pathetic that ideas or actions
> for the betterment of our community are completely disregarded if
> one happens to be too young, female, not a doctor, not possessing a
> college degree, doesn't look "Filipino," or doesn't have a big house,
> fancy clothes, or a nice car.

Interestingly enough, West Coast men also had a low endorsement
rate for this statement. One explanation is offered by this West Coast man:

> Because of colonial mentality, a Filipino community leader lacks credi-
> bility unless he is a rich, white, *mestizo* male and has no accent. The
> more he is perceived to be assimilated into white America, the more
> powerful he would be as a leader. What the community fails to realize
> is if such a person exists, he wouldn't be wasting his time on the Filipino
> American people unless he is an opportunist for a non-Filipino politi-
> cal organization—their messenger boy!

There are many possible explanations for the low endorsement rate
by young Filipino Americans of the statement about expectations of
becoming a community leader. We believe the main reason is apathy
derived from the colonial mentality.

Summary

Our hypothesis was that young East Coast Filipino Americans, who are products of post-1965 Filipino immigration, would be more likely than West Coast Filipino Americans, who are products of Filipino immigration from the 1920s to 1930s, to be expected to assimilate into Anglo American society and less likely to be expected to maintain and value strong ties to the Filipino American community. We assumed that these differences between East and West Coast Filipino Americans are based on historical differences in how these two groups have been treated by whites and the extent to which their integration into Anglo American society has been tolerated. The three significant findings that support our hypothesis are (a) East Coast women's report of a low expectation of their marrying a Filipino American male, (b) East Coast college women's report of a low expectation of their experiencing racism and discrimination, and (c) all respondents' report of a low expectation of their becoming a Filipino American community leader.

East Coast Filipino Americans have developed positive images of Anglo Americans by assimilation through personal socioeconomic success. Upward social mobility may mean detachment from ethnicity, community ownership, and participation. Are we, as Filipino Americans, willing to pay this price?

References

Broom, L., & Kitsuse, J. I. (1955). The validation of acculturation: A condition to ethnic assimilation. *American Anthropologist, 57,* 44-48.

Cordova, F. (1983). *Filipinos: Forgotten Asian-Americans. A pictorial essay, 1763–circa 1963* (D. L. Cordova, Ed.). Dubuque, IA: Kendall/Hunt.

Filipino Oral History Project. (1984). *Voices: A Filipino American oral history.* Stockton, CA: Author.

Pido, A. J. A. (1984). *The Pilipinos in America: Macro-micro dimensions of immigration and integration.* Staten Island, NY: Center for Migration Studies.

Schirmer, D. B. (1987). *The Philippine reader.* Boston: South End.

Ubalde, A. (Ed.). (1996). *Filipino planning issues, design, and architecture.* Flipside.

14

Homeland Memories and Media
Filipino Images and
Imaginations in America

Rick Bonus

In many Filipino American commercial establishments in southern California, one rarely misses the presence of a wide selection of community newspapers on display and usually free for the taking. The same may be said, although in varying degrees and intensities, about other Filipino communities elsewhere in the United States and other countries. But with the exception of the Bay Area, as my informants tell me, no one set of communities matches the considerable number of local papers circulated in the counties and peripheries of Los Angeles and San Diego, owing primarily to the geographical distribution of Filipino immigrant settlements in North America.

Such ubiquitous newspapers occupy significant places not only in the sites where Filipino Americans meet but also, as I wish to emphasize here, in the contexts in which the narratives and dynamic formations of Filipino American identities are constantly imaged and imagined. Community newspapers constitute only one node in the vast array of apparatuses that link individuals together, from families and kinship systems to religious ties and other social organizations. They are also one among the many forms of media, such as radio, television, and film, that operate as communication systems within and between societies.

In this chapter, I focus on Filipino American community newspapers in southern California as illustrations of a historically specific and localized tenor of community formation and expression. I intend to situate these communicative channels within the larger contexts of both immigration history and cultural citizenship to understand better the local politics of ethnicity that Filipino Americans deploy to make sense of their lives here. I suggest that these print channels operate as alternative spaces for Filipino Americans who see themselves as active agents in the remembering, reconstruction, and representation of their collective identities.

This chapter is informed by an ethnography of Filipino American communities in southern California that I conducted between 1992 and 1995. I interviewed at length mainly first-generation Filipino immigrants, who constituted the bulk of the Filipino American population in this area. Historians refer to these Filipinos as part of the third wave of mostly professional immigrants who came to the United States from the 1960s to the present. In this part of the United States, many of them arrived as naval employees, recruited initially for manual and skilled labor (even before the 1960s as well), and a significant number (mostly women) worked as practitioners in the medical and allied health professions. Later, facilitated in large part by the family reunification provisions of the Immigration and Nationality Act of 1965, they also brought in other members of their families, including parents, children, and siblings.[1] Many of those with whom I talked had lived in southern California for at least 10 years and either were in the process of gaining formal citizenship status or had been naturalized already. I also spoke with a few earlier generation and second-generation nationals who self-identified as Filipino Americans. I found their responses to be especially significant as well in this project, and I have identified their status with their remarks accordingly.

For this study, I interacted with producers and readers of about nine community papers circulated in and around Los Angeles and San Diego counties. I say "about" because many publications appear, last for a few months, die out, then reappear once publishers regain control over resources. This situation is obviously created by the political economy of publishing in which these papers operate. As local undertakings, community newspapers are generally susceptible to the workings of investor pressures, fluctuating market size, dependence on advertising, intemperate competition, availability of humanpower, and increasing costs of paper, supplies, and printing. Nevertheless, most of the papers I looked at appeared weekly, with a combined circulation that served an estimated 350,000 Filipino Americans in southern California—the largest group of Filipinos outside the Philippines (U.S. Bureau of the Census, 1992). I also examined the kinds of media content that appeared with regularity, the distribution and reception of such papers, and the significance of such media activities in processes of identity construction.

Like most other ethnic newspapers in the United States, Filipino American community newspapers exist in communities where there is a great demand or need to serve the interests of people of the same group. Of course, the differences from mainstream papers are readily apparent. Ethnic presses are comparatively small scale, are run with a minimal number of journalists, and, especially with Filipino American papers, are usually free of charge, with the costs of production and distribution met by advertising revenues. Such a demand by members of an ethnic group to read a newspaper "of their own" is not entirely a new phenomenon. As early as 1922, sociologist Robert E. Park conducted a survey of American immigrant presses to highlight their significant roles in easing the transition of new arrivals into permanent settlements both by preserving languages, traditions, and values of their home countries and by "assisting [their orientation] . . . in the American environment" (p. 86). To some degree, Filipino American newspapers share this ground with immigrant presses of the past and present. Geared toward immigrant Filipinos as primary readers, these newspapers oscillate between the retention of values that are "dear to Filipino hearts," as one editor told me, and the encouragement to acquire "things American, like [formal] citizenship," as an advertisement of an immigrant law firm regularly asserted in the papers.

But to stop at merely locating commonalities of Filipino American presses with their counterparts in other ethnic communities is tantamount to masking the historical specificities of the conditions in which these newspapers exist and thrive—specificities that reveal unique experiences of racialization different from those faced by whites and other groups of color in the United States. Editors, journalists, and readers consistently reminded me of how "different" their papers were from the others "because others don't know how it is to be a Filipino in America." One reporter told me, "Other newspapers cover us . . . if at all, . . . but they really miss [out] on what we really are. We're called this and that . . . like blacks or Asians or Hispanics. Maybe we're all the same, but we're also different." Here we see how Park's assessments, in the long run, obliterate important differences across immigrant presses that have mattered significantly in determining not only their survival but, to a great extent, their nature and emphasis.

To understand the impact that such differences have had, one can refer to the vibrant press that Filipino American communities of the 1900s to the 1950s built and sustained against the climate of exclusion and the brutalities of nativism,[2] something that Park's survey almost completely overlooks (save for one entry). Unlike most immigrant presses of their time, these Filipino American papers sought to expose the bigotry and hatred especially directed at Filipino farmworkers and laborers. They informed their readers of a critical and creative mass of Filipinos fighting for equality, dignity, and access to civil society. They determined to clarify what "special" relationships the Philippines had with the United States when the designation of U.S. territory/colony did not match with Filipinos in America being ineligible for citizenship. This is a history that contemporary Filipino Americans inherit once they settle in their new country, a ground they find in common, not with other ethnic groups, but with Filipinos of previous generations (Flores-Meiser, 1987).

Outside of their group, the Filipino American press also shares a lineage of resistance with black, Latino/Chicano, and other Asian media against racial subordination. The connections between racial domination of groups over others and the dissemination of this ideology in media and popular culture in all sectors of society are difficult to overemphasize in this context. Media historian Jane Rhodes (1993) contended that in America, "racial identity has been and continues to be . . . a crucial factor in determining who can produce popular culture and what messages are created" (p. 185). To those groups who are relegated to the margins and lower rungs of the racial hierarchy, this has meant a sustained struggle to gain a foothold in mainstream and corporate-controlled media channels, to oppose and challenge dehumanizing stereotypes, and to seek alternative avenues for self-determination and counter-representation.

Cast against such historical and contemporary settings, it is undeniable how the impetus for publishing and reading a paper "of one's own" from a Filipino American perspective encompasses more than a mere fulfillment of a need for communicating with each other. Readers of the *Los Angeles Asian Journal*, *TM Weekly Herald* (Los Angeles), *Mabuhay Times* (San Diego), and *Filipino Press* (San Diego, Orange, and Los Angeles counties), among others, take pride in the abundance and regularity of these papers despite the perceived marginality of their ethnic group. "It's amazing to see that we can do it even though many others think that we are nobodies," said one Filipino American. Among editors and publishers, some of whom had previously worked in mainstream newspaper offices, such pride is most articulated in being able to do something worthwhile for the community beyond what the larger publishing system compels them to do: regard their audience as discrete interest groups and treat them merely as potential consumers. A Filipino American journalist told me:

> Of course, my publisher wants to make money, too. But, really, there are no viable information media at the moment for Filipinos. Our newspaper wants to do that service. Think about it, there's nothing much about Filipinos or, much less, even the Philippines, in the big papers. In the *San Diego Union-Tribune*, I found three clippings about Filipinos, two of them about Filipino youth gangs in San Diego. If it's not too little reporting, it's distorted reporting. What else can you trust to read about your own other than someone who wrote it for you?

The alternative appeal of such community newspapers among Filipino Americans also goes farther than simply providing a separate space for gathering information not covered by the mainstream press. Many readers inform me of how much it means to them to feel "at home" in a place they have already considered their new home but where they are also still regarded as guests by most people around them. "I am a citizen of this country now, supposed to be not a foreigner anymore, even though many think I am," one earlier generation Filipino American reader told me, "but that doesn't mean I've forgotten where I came from." Reading about Filipinos, whether from California, other parts of the States, the Philippines, or elsewhere, for these respondents, points to some fundamental ways of dealing with a strong sense of disconnectedness or displacement brought about by immigration and separation. In a world of heightened movements and impersonal arrangements, these Filipinos use the community press to reconnect with each other, not so much to bring the pieces back to their original whole as to reconstruct what used to be and still are discrete aspects of their lives into different forms and products. At the same time, the newspapers also serve as vehicles for the collective sense making of their conditions and experiences here.

It is no surprise, then, that what front pages of these papers cover are events and issues that emanate both from the former homeland and the new settlements. At the time I was doing my fieldwork, news about national and regional elections as well as calamities in the Philippines shared headlines with local political races and community organizational activities in which Filipinos in southern California participated. Knowing what is happening in at least two worlds vitally brings into public discourse traces of attachments here and elsewhere. "I've traveled far already," mused another Filipino reader, "but I always want to be reminded about my former home. It matters in understanding myself here." Many others said that this refusal to forget ties to one's former home is at odds with the pressures to conform to what they see as American-style values and interests. In the same breath, however, these people were also quick to alert me of the false promises of the "melting pot" ideology. Conformity, to them, has not resulted in their full acceptance as Americans and their true equality with others, and it is precisely their reluctance to assimilate fully that animates their media activities.

The papers' orientation to the Philippines serves as both a source and a sign of ethnic rootedness central to Filipino American identities, particularly those held by immigrants. This is apparent not only in the frequency of references to events in the Philippines but also in the regular coverage of activities of Filipino movie celebrities. Editors told me that their audience always looks forward to reading about gossip in the movie industry back home. These bits of information connect readers to popular culture they are familiar with, constantly reminding them of personalities they identify with and keeping them abreast of movies that might end up in the local Filipino video stores. "They like to know what's happening to their movie idols, . . . their latest films, . . . who got married to whom, and who has passed on," one reporter said. Many feature articles of popular tourist spots in the Philippines are also routinely written. She continued, "We also write pieces on our scenic spots, with photos. They're all beautiful. . . . It's nice to show them."

Like movie news, the persistence of memory about places and people left behind mitigates anxieties of distance and displacement. In reference to picture-perfect locales, there is a strong sense in which memories of the homeland are rendered pure, natural, and paradisiacal. Most readers delighted in such depictions. "That's how we want to remember the Philippines," intoned one. Against the harsh conditions of settling on foreign soil and encountering unexpected circumstances, these remembrances act as coping mechanisms—yet another way of momentarily suspending the ordeals of immigrant life. Such nostalgic retreats, however, cannot all be romantic. These same readers are also cognizant of the other faces of their changing home revealed alongside its picturesque representations. Said one, "But of course, we know that it's very different now too, . . . what with pollution, poverty, volcanic eruption, and all that."

These gestures aimed toward the Philippines mirror to a large extent Filipino Americans' understanding of their lives in the United States. As articulated in the newspapers, orientations to America-based activities and issues open up multiple and sometimes competing narratives of life here. Many of those I interviewed spoke of fantasizing about this "land of milk and honey" prior to coming over. Fueled by Hollywood movies and American-style education, they dreamed of starting better lives in places they assumed would afford them greater opportunities. Only on coming over did many of them realize the false promises of democracy and equality, for even those who were able to "make it" saw themselves relegated to "second-class citizenship." In many letters to the editor, commentaries, and news articles, accounts of racism, marginality, exclusion, and misunderstandings between Filipinos and the larger society reveal the contradictions of American ideals perpetuated within and outside of the country. During this period, much space in the papers was given to exposing and challenging the blatant forms of racism and sexism expressed, among others, by talk-radio announcer Howard Stern ("They eat their young over there"), a character in the television sitcom *Frasier* (November 29, 1994, episode; "For that amount of money, I could get myself a mail-order bride from the Philippines"), and superintendents of Filipina nurses (who ordered them not to speak Tagalog at work). Opinion pieces tried to make sense of these unexpected and unfamiliar situations, at times exposing painful individual experiences at work and in social settings to measure the extent of the dark sides of the American dream. Said one journalist: "It can get to be insane here. We have to bring [these incidents] out in the open. Our newspapers make us talk about these dirty things. We don't have to hide them. It's our right to bring them out."

Narratives of Filipino life in America also extend inward into more local affairs. On most of these pages, a great deal of coverage is reserved for reporting and announcing activities of the myriad social organizations that Filipinos in southern California have established. From hometown and provincial associations to alumni, trade, and religious clubs, these Filipino American groups find in their community papers the channels to convey their multilevel alliances with each other. These conduits of collective belonging aid in reconstructing identities and redefining agendas. A reporter told me how valuable the papers are for the associations in making their members regard themselves not merely as Filipinos who hail from the Philippines but as Filipinos who are also Caviteños, Pampangos, Ateneans, lawyers, and Methodists. These are the Filipinos who have also become American at the same time, and Filipinos who care about each other. Articles regularly reported meetings and fund-raisers aimed at benefiting common causes, including donations to calamity victims in the Philippines, scholarships to those in need on both coasts, and financial as well as volunteer assistance to local community projects for senior citizens and for the granting of free medical aid, voter registration, and cultural events.

It would be erroneous, however, to portray these community newspapers as sites of smooth and easy consensus. Like other ethnic groups, Filipino American communities do not speak with one voice all the time, and their interests and agendas occasionally run into conflict with each other. A Filipino American reader who used to be a reporter said:

> Oh yes, we have our own quarrels too. But I think these newspapers make us talk to each other so that we have dialogue . . . instead of not talking at all. We learn many things when we give each other a chance. And also, we make our own ideas known to others who are far away and those who never participate, but may want to.

On the editorial and opinion pages, various viewpoints on issues that affect Filipino Americans are explored and challenged. Analyses of local political activities identify intergroup cleavages and campaign errors, and the working out of such differences. Some of these even seep into comparisons and connections with politics in the Philippines, yet another remnant of Filipino American journalism of the 1900s and, especially, of the 1960s, 1970s, and 1980s (the histories of which have yet to be written), when numerous Filipino exiles were writing in their papers against the Marcos dictatorship.

The reach of these community newspapers goes beyond political, generational, and ethnic lines. Profiles of community leaders and achievers provide models of a variety of ways in which people can participate in political and social activities in their conventional or alternative forms. Articles on community activists and activities offer insights on running for public office, pursuing different causes, and managing small-scale events. Many write-ups also tackle issues that include and affect second- and third-generation Filipino Americans. From stories about political/cultural awareness and achievements of the youth to the adverse effects of gang involvement and troubling suicide rates, these papers also attempt to reach younger Filipino Americans in the communities they serve. Said one second-generation reader:

> At first, I was not really interested in reading these newspapers. But as I got older and more conscious of my roots, I gradually came to see them as important . . . and necessary in understanding who I am, where my parents came from, . . . our many cultures, the things we share, and where we are going too. These newspapers are also important to us, so I read them often now.

Some of these younger members of the population have already made their mark in their communities as active supporters and organizers of various endeavors. A few of them have been staff members or regular contributors in the papers and recently have also established their own San Diego monthly, called *Kalayaan*. Several Filipino American newspaper publishers have also attempted to broaden their readership across other Asian and Pacific American communities in their areas. Papers such as *Pacific Asian Times* and *Asian World* in San Diego County alone attest to the increasing importance among members of these groups to expand their efforts at combining energies toward common goals, perhaps realizing the opportunities that may be seized in forming pan-ethnic coalitions working for common interests. Subsections and advertisements in Thai, Chinese, and Vietnamese reveal more and stronger communication links among what used to be disparate minority-population groups.

On the whole, many Filipino Americans see these channels as rich and vibrant sources of empowerment. They use these newspapers to communicate with themselves and with others, offering a multitude of ways to define who they are, where they are from, and what interests and positions they could share in their present community (Anderson, 1983). These are the kinds of conduits that open up possibilities of agency despite exclusion. "What is most important to remember here," as a Filipino American reporter remarked, "is that we can call this paper ours. We hire our own, we print the stories we want to print, we make our own rules. We can't count on others to do this for us. Here, at the least, we are able to speak." This is a kind of activity that many would brush off as separatist or isolationist, given southern California's history and present conditions regarding interethnic and interracial relations. But in the minds of Filipino Americans who write and read about themselves and their larger world in their newspapers, it is a kind of self-determination that could potentially change the world around them—a kind of participation that for now will not be allowed space in mainstream press but later may be emulated by a more multivocal local and even national press.

What matters to these groups in a most fundamental way is the question of who can belong to this nation, and on what terms. Tensions about limited resources and employment spaces are usually expressed in arguments about citizenship and belonging, about who has rights and who does not. For these people, it is not a matter of merely coexisting or having a space relegated to a few of them, but on having voices and being heard. It is a matter of understanding their histories and realities, how they are different from others and what they have in common with others. Ultimately, it is a matter of having a sense of belonging and participating as full citizens in the nation that is America. In view of mainstream media exclusion, these newspapers serve as alternative sites for meaningful and empowering constructions of Filipino American communities.

Notes

1. I am abbreviating here a much more complicated history of Filipino immigration to the United States in order to outline the basic historical parameters of this chapter. For

example, not accounted for by this "wave" rubric were those who came in as students, political exiles, and visitors who later decided to stay. Parts of my larger project on Filipino American ethnicity discuss their histories in greater length. For further inquiry on Filipino immigration to the United States, see, for example, Cordova (1983), Espiritu (1995, esp. pp. 1-36), and Pido (1986).

2. Research and retrieval of these newspapers are currently and principally being undertaken by the staff of the Filipino American Experience Research Project under the directorship of Alex Fabros. I am referencing here from a working draft edition of their manuscript (Fabros & Herbert, 1994). Also see Flores-Meiser (1987) and Cordova (1983) for a more nuanced treatment of the role of Filipino newspapers in earlier communities.

References

Anderson, B. (1983). *Imagined communities: Reflections on the origin and spread of nationalism.* London: Verso.

Cordova, F. (1983). *Filipinos: Forgotten Asian Americans. A pictorial essay, 1763–circa 1963* (D. L. Cordova, Ed.). Dubuque, IA: Kendall/Hunt.

Espiritu, Y. L. (1995). *Filipino American lives.* Philadelphia: Temple University Press.

Fabros, A., & Herbert, A. (Eds.). (1994). *The Filipino American Newspaper Collection: Extracts from 1906 to 1953.* Fresno, CA: Filipino American Experience Research Project.

Flores-Meiser, E. P. (1987). The Filipino-American press. In S. M. Miller (Ed.), *The ethnic press in the United States: A historical analysis and handbook.* New York: Greenwood.

Immigration and Nationality Act of 1965. 8 U.S.C. § 1101 *et seq.*

Park, R. E. (1922). *The immigrant press and its control.* New York: Harper.

Pido, A. J. A. (1986). *The Pilipinos in America: Macro-micro dimensions of immigration and integration.* New York: Center for Migration Studies.

Rhodes, J. (1993). The visibility of race and media history. *Critical Studies in Mass Communication, 10,* 184-190.

U.S. Bureau of the Census. (1992). *1990 census of population and housing summary.* Washington, DC: Government Printing Office.

15

Deflowering the Sampaguita

M. Evelina Galang

First Holy Communion

First. Like never before. Like when you know everyone but you is doing it. Teenage girls wearing hose instead of anklets, sitting at the back of the bus among the boys; your older cousins with flip-teased dos and painted toenails, false lashes, and padded bras; the neighborhood sitter who reeks of nicotine, bubble gum lip gloss, and cheap eau de toilette; your beautiful auntie who flies from Russia to China to Norway to you, planting big red kisses all over your face, ripe and luscious as strawberries in late August; your mommy sleek and steady, smart and calm; and even your very old and shaky *lola*. They are doing it. Every week. Every Sunday. Some, even, every day. And up until now, on this, the first weekend in May, you have always been too young. Too innocent. Too irresponsible.

The priest has told you and an entire classroom of girls just like you: "When you are old enough. When you have matured. When you are able to understand and appreciate, you will have your turn. A chance. An opportunity to receive the body. To hold the body. To feel its texture on the tip of the tongue where you will hold Him there, gently, carefully, making sure you don't bite down. You will someday bond with Him. The first time is always the most special," Father tells you. "I still remember my First Holy Communion years and years ago, and you will too."

Until today, you were not part of the club. You watched the women, older than you, more sophisticated than you, painted and coiffed and powdered like beautiful angels, floating down the aisle, arms held up in prayer, eyes lowered. For years, you have imagined yourself in line with them. Painted up. Cloaked in white. Until today, you were not worthy, and neither are they, but they have been given permission. At last, it's your turn.

For the last month, you have spent your Sunday mornings preparing yourself. Locked up in the safety of your girl bathroom, you practiced walking down the narrow aisle—you lined your toes up and marched down the skinny row of tiles between the bathtub and the sink and toilet. Hands folded, eyes lowered, you walked right up to the edge of the full-length mirror. Stared yourself down, brown eye to brown eye. Studied the dark flecks in the center of your pupil. Looked for the light. The mystery. The glow you knew you'd possess once you received. "Body of Christ," you imagined Father saying.

"Amen," you answered loudly, proudly. Because as young as you are, you know you believe. You know with all your heart because Mary, your Mother of God, the woman whose name you bear, would never lie to you. This first time, this moment, the First Holy Communion is something blessed and real and meant only for good girls. For women like the ones you dream of growing up to be and you will—God damn it—be one of them. You stuck out your tongue, pressed it to the cold hard reflection in the glass, closed your eyes the way you'd seen Theresa, Carmen, and Tita Ana close their eyes—lashes fluttering—and you imagined some magic, some wave of holiness coursing through your body. Your soul, light and winged, soared to places you had never known. Took you up to heaven and back, to the outer limits of the universe, maybe as far away as Mars, or Saturn, or Jupiter. You left your body, and for a moment, you were one with God. You communed with Him and the saints and all the angels, tangible cherubs amid white gauze, luminous skies, and the clouds.

You know, today you will know this. This is what you've been told. Here is how we come to learn of Jesus, Our Savior. Here is what they tell us. First Holy Communion. Like the first time you are with the man you love—but they don't say that part. Even though they dress you up in white lace and pearls and satin and white veils—like the Bride you practice becoming. The nuns, the fathers, even your older brothers and sisters will tell you—First Holy Communion is just like that.

Such attention to detail. Such lessons. Such accuracy in the Divine. Such parallels to love and lovemaking. But no one ever tells you that part. Mothers never speak of it, and even when they suspect you know, you want, you do, there is silence. Silence, as if you are still too young, too innocent, too immature to understand this, the complexity of human relationships, the depth of desire, the transcending of spirit and the holiness of bodies. Love, desire, sex. Taboo.

As girls, we are taught the way. Given all the tools. The equipment. The desire. In our quest to be true, to have faith, to love, we seek love. Love of God and love of family and love, true love. But nobody ever tells you that part.

How You Learn About It

Slumber party. Sometime during fifth grade—the Michaels' basement. You don't even know what they told you. Who knows? All those seedy details cloaked in giggles and whispers:

"Uh-huh."

"No way."

"Gross."

What you remember is the damp of wet cement. The gray bricks, steel poles cold as ice in the bottom of a Mac's Coca-Cola. What you see is the pitch of midnight when all good 10-year-olds clustered together like moths wrapped tightly in their sleeping bag cocoons should be sleeping, should never know this hour of night, not even when they grow to be young women. Who knows what they said exactly, but that's when you first heard about it. And it was as true then as it is now. Yuck. Gross. No way my momma and daddy would ever do that. Why? It sounded so disgusting. And then the picture of it, the very image, awkward and misshapen—entirely inaccurate—of the two of them doing *that*. No way.

What for? To make a baby. To make you and Danny and Tony. Unbelievable. Disgusting.

No talk that night of love and desire. No connections between wanting, needing, giving. No understanding of the body and how it can be this gift—like springtime in February, or recess all day long, or chocolate for breakfast, lunch, *and* dinner. It was just something grown-ups did to make a baby. You imagined they closed their eyes when they did it. You imagined they must have turned their faces away in embarrassment—like when someone has farted and you pretend not to notice, or when your crazy cousin pretends she's a nun and blesses strangers on the street.

Shouldn't someone older than you, more knowledgeable and more caring, someone experienced in these matters and close to you—shouldn't someone like that have explained sex to you? Made connections for you? Told you, this is what happens, here is what to expect, here is what to do. Shouldn't you have been trained for this?

Of course, the one you kiss is the one who teaches you how to. Together, you explore, experiment, nudge your way around a lip, slip the tongue just so, across a row of teeth, smooth and white as a chorus line of shiny pearls. Together you learn when to swallow, when to breathe, when to open your eyes. Together, you learn about dancing your body around his, how to slide an arm, a leg, a finger just so. You learn to alter breath, to initiate a whisper and make it grow, loud like a cry that fills you up so full it bursts. You learn about timing, how it is everything. It is when you are out in that proverbial field that you learn the difference between love, lust, and the thing both share—desire.

But who tells you what it means? Why you do it? How come when the breathing falls and rises and rises and falls, your hands want to move around? A kiss becomes a fondle, the fondle initiates the undressing. The hook unhooked makes zippers slide, buttons snap right off. Why is it when he rolls his hips over yours, dances his way into you, teasing you like this, you ache? Grow full? Something blossoms wild and uncontrollable, peals open petal on petal like morning dew into hot noonday sun. You can hardly stand it, and you don't know why. And what about that moment—you know the one—the no-turning-back moment where it doesn't matter if you love him or know him? What do you do then? What happens that moment you let go?

And what has that to do with love? When one body slides over another, and he slips part of him into you, and you find yourself floating to some distant planet—is that love? Does it have anything at all to do with companionship or friendship—and why is it more fun with some than others, and is it about making babies after all?

Your mother should tell you. But your mother is silent. Babies are a gift from God, she says (not a lie at all), she and your father love each other (also true), and they had to fuck each other to make you (no word on this).

So what's a girl to do? What's she to think? How's she to find a life partner, the right one, without guidance?

Figure out sex on your own. Search and practice and watch. You may or may not, may never make the connections on your own. You may even come to think there are no ties between love, lust, and baby making.

Silence

With silence comes disapproval. What is not spoken of is not happening. Not to men and women, not to married couples, and never to single ones. And don't even dare think a boy and girl would ever—not even when no one's watching—not even when their parents have discreetly left the lesson out of all their never-ending lectures.

From littlehood, you have been taught how to speak, how to listen, how to behave in every circumstance imaginable—to your *lolas* and *lolos*, to the uncles and aunties you are not related to, to your teachers, priests, nuns, and even to the strangers in the grocery store. You've gone over this ground with Mommy and Daddy, and you will always come out gracious and elegant. Polite. You know how to make *mano*, offer anyone in a 5-mile radius of your house something to drink, something to eat, a place to take a nap. Even now you hear your Tito Boy saying to the plumber whose car has broken down, "Wanna eat? Want some rice? How 'bout beer?" You know how to behave at baptisms, weddings, and even you, at 5 or 6, have been briefed on the etiquette of funeral masses. You have been taught to respect people and their feelings, to be giving—so what's this? Why hasn't your mother, your father, your Tita Baby, Tito Butch, your *ates* and *kuyas*, why hasn't anyone told you how to act around him?

When the two of you are sitting so close that you feel him breathing, soft and low; when the whisper of his breath into your ear and the heat of him, the tiny wind that soars from the words he speaks, "I think of you always," spirals through you like some kind of strange monsoon, runs rampant round your ribs, circles the heart, flushes whatever it is you ate for lunch right out of you—BOOM, BOOM, BOOM—you are at a loss. Suddenly you feel faint, your body melting like mozzarella on pepperoni and black olives—and what you want and how you act and what you say conflict with everything Father, Son, and Holy Ghost have not said, scream out to all your mother refuses to acknowledge, your father will not see. Your body has taken a turn—and from the way your family acts, you believe it might be for the worst.

At night, you shift the shade from your lamp, cast a giant shadow of your body across the naked wall of your teenage bedroom. You lift your arms up, and with your eyes you trace your body—outline your breasts, tiny shells, cupped like oyster beds. Circle the space in your chest where you imagine a heart. Slide your fingers down the length of you— zing—in and out where the hips, not yet planted, not yet settled, but hopeful and anxious, will someday be. Brush the soft hairs, growing, silky like milkweed, hiding what? Covering who? Protecting some buried treasure, or is it a curse? Is something wrong with your body? Why is it you like him so and still, you don't know how to say it and how to act when the heat of his body affects your skin, your muscles, you, like this.

Once your mother stood up high against the windowpane of the living room and watched you sitting on a tree stump, hand and hand with the boy next door. When he leaned into you, put his arm around you, she pounded on the glass. She shook her head at you. Later, she forbade you to see him. Speak to him. Hung the phone up on him when he called. Your father took to ignoring him, looked right through him when he stood on the threshold of the door, called him some other boy's name, referred to him as "that guy." They never told you why.

What your mother didn't know is that while you sat there with him, listening to your transistor radio blurt "All you need is love," you were conducting a storm inside your belly. A hurricane spun in the hut of your chest. A host of discrepancies inhabited your body like demons taking possession of your soul. You wanted to kiss him. You didn't. You liked him, but you knew you shouldn't. You wanted nothing more than to lie with him, naked, wrapped only in his flesh, his embrace. You felt guilty thinking this was not a dirty image at all, it was beautiful. You didn't know why. And before your mother knocked on that glass, before you ever heard her, you were pushing him away from you, slapping him for touching you. Today because he did, tomorrow because he wouldn't.

Years later, you and your college boyfriend, home for the weekend, fall asleep on the couch, watching *The Way We Were*. Your parents, coming home from a Saturday night of poker and mah-jongg, suspect there must be something amiss when they enter a dark house at midnight, his car out in the driveway.

BOOM. Your father's voice calls your name, your mother bangs the den door wide open, and streaks of light reveal their silhouettes large, luminous, and angry. Their bodies merge, one gigantic torso. There are two heads. Arms flail in the night like giant birds swooping down on the two of you. "How could you do this to us?" your mother cries. "How could you?"

How could you do what? They never tell you. They never bring it up again. After your boyfriend leaves, the only thing your daddy says is "Behave."

Here, the silence, unbearable, tense, and fraught with disapproval, leaves you confused. So you stop watching old movies. Refrain from references to Robert Redford, Barbra Streisand, and that ridiculous song. You stop holding your boyfriend's hand in public. Pull away from him when your mother calls you. Move out of his embrace at the very mention of your family. Stop speaking all together. Behave.

Say prayers instead. Read books. Go to theaters where it is impossible to fall asleep. Years later, avoid those questions, the ones aunties and uncles throw at you. "So when are you going to get married?" and "Do you have a boyfriend yet?" Don't tell them, "Of course I do, have, will, but you will never know." Keep your love life to yourself. Like them, remain silent. Pretend your silence is tantamount to abstinence, virginity, and holiness.

Deflowering the Sampaguita

With a group of your best Pinay friends, and their boyfriends, pile into a van and take over a local dance club. Dance less than a breath apart.

Crowd the floor like a cluster of rich red grapes, threaded together by a single vine. You have colored your mouth burgundy, teased your hair, and decorated your neck, your ears, your skinny brown arms with gold and copper bangles. You have stretched a cotton shirt, scoop necked and slightly swollen at the breast, around your body. Your pants hang low, slide across your hips, just about reveal your belly. You and your friends are beautiful flowers, fragrant, sweet, ripe. You draw your boyfriends close. They hover just above you. Gaze into your eyes. Run their strong hands along your waist, torso, and thigh. Dance holding hands. Move together. To the beat. Closer and closer. Close your eyes, and he wraps his arms around you. Taken.

It is as though you move to that drum, that tribal gong. Your hips and legs move and sway, knees bend and pose, like a mountain princess crossing the river—head up, eye to eye. The drumming brings you closer, the bells chiming in the distance dispel reality. It is the Kulintang, dense rhythmic drumming. And even though you were never a Mindanao Princess, even if you never took a folk dance lesson in your life, the pressure of the heels, down on the linoleum floor; the way you hold your back up straight, tall and proud; the way you cast your spell, hypnotic and full as the golden moon; the way you float right out of consciousness is something that comes easy, part of your blood, indeed, part of your human condition.

Amid the confusion, of what to say, to think, to feel, you lose yourself someplace in the middle of a kiss. Feel stars bursting inside you, oceans washing up against your hips, water welling and brimming just below your pelvis, and before you can swim your way back to your senses, he is deep inside you. You not only let him in, you invite him. "Right this way," you whisper. Become part of this wave, this delightful tumult. Know nothing, only that you hope this feeling never stops. This is right. This is natural. This is your intuitive self, honest and true. You let go.

In the aftermath gloom sets in, chaos begins. Picture your mother and father, sitting in a pew before God and all the heavens. Think, better to die than ever let them know. Better to keep things a secret. Wonder how something this beautiful can be that wicked? Are you going to hell?

The very first time, when you knew little of love, when hormones controlled the sky and moon, he came and you said to yourself, "Is that all?" Like a tailor with a needle, he slipped in and out and in and out of you and you thought, so? And still, you couldn't help yourself, you opened up. Again and again. For years, you switched boys, lovers, men. You learned about give and take and generosity. Sewing turned into surfing, riding a wave high, wild, free, and dangerous. Instead of "Is that all," you thought, "Please, let's don't ever stop." You learned the difference between fucking and making love. You preferred the latter and saved your body for men you loved. The act became a gift you shared with lovers.

And when a baby grows, ripe and free, fills your baby fat belly with baby. You confess. Are sent away. You have a baby. You do one of two things: You give her away, like a door prize on Philippine Independence Day, or you bring her home and she becomes your baby sister. Your baby is not your baby. Your mommy no longer looks at you as if she were your mommy. Your daddy stops speaking. Be grateful, they tell you, you are lucky this is all.

Other girls from your First Holy Communion didn't get this far. Never got to see their babies. Sleeping was easier for them, dying was less disgraceful than bearing a child. There was no stopping the chaos in their bodies, no one to talk to, and there the fight died. And who could blame them, really? All that confusion bottled up inside, all that and a child smaller than each teenage girl, just as sweet and innocent as the child mother, in search of someone to love, to talk to, to cry to—all that bursting out of their still boylike bodies. Who could blame them for silencing the conflict of their hearts?

Or maybe you are one of the many who marry after all. Three months pregnant, 20 years young, loving your high school sweetheart. Nobody knows, just you and your boyfriend, your parents and his. No one tells. You bear your child, you bear many, and nobody is wiser. Not a word spoken. When your daughter and son grow, when their bodies change and their voices drift away from childhood, you begin the practice of silent disapproval, you continue the cycle. You insist on impossible chastity. You attempt to keep the Sampaguita in bloom, fresh, young, never acknowledging the nature of things.

You live your life like a spy. Secret agent 99, complete with double life. Another you. The doctor daughter, the lawyer daughter, the wife daughter, the well-behaved and decent daughter. You cook, you serve, you lead the family prayers. And when you leave your parents, you slow your walk. You sway. Smile out of the corner of your eye. Whisper. Charmer you, you seduce unknowingly. Walk into your cousin's office and kiss her boss on top of his balding head. Do it without thinking twice. Do it because you are young and you know that everyone will think it's cute. Do it because you know this and a thousand other traditionally unacceptable gestures are things you and only you can get away with. When your *ate* tells you to stop it, cut it out, and "Don't go kissing my boss on the crest of his balding head, " say, "But he's so delicious." Your mother, who knows you better than you think, who secretly knows, maybe even remembers what it's like to be this young, this beautiful, this brimming with sex appeal and truly powerful, says, "You've got to learn to control yourself, *hija*, even if he is delicious."

Sex stimulates you like a drug. Empowers you in new ways. Teaches you about walking around slinky and smooth, as if in constant dance, constant seduction. Teaches you that men want to do your bidding when you smile just so, or look away just when. Sex and being sexy charms you, and you like it. You can't help it. And when you try, when you let your two selves battle out right and wrong, marry love and lust, there is nothing but turmoil, and your lover wonders why he can never do anything right. "You are a walking contradiction," he tells you.

Because there is the family. Think. What if they found out. This prospect haunts you like ghosts in an old hotel. Pops up when you least expect, in the breath you take just after you've been together. Taps you on the shoulder as you answer the telephone. Think if on top of defiling your body, you made a baby too. Run away, first choice. Suicide, second. No, suicide first, run away after the failed suicide. You would rather die. You would rather float away in a stream, clear and fresh and cold. Take me away, you think. Take me far away, where Mom and Dad will never have to see me. Never have to be embarrassed because of me. Ultimately, you worry their worry is what others will say, will think.

Wild and fresh, little white star with fragrant petals, once planted, once in bloom, you are left clinging to the vine that is the family you were born to. Face up to the sun, stretching out, reaching, but never breaking free, you are tangled in two worlds—wanting and not wanting. Speaking and silent at once. Filipina girl, American born and of two cultures, Western like MTV, tropical as the Sampaguita, you are left alone to figure out the rest. Because no one dares to tell you that when you make love to your lover, your husband, your boyfriend; when you date one another and flirt; and when he leans over for that first kiss, first moment of intimacy, sinking into you long and slow; it is your first holy communion all over again. Spirit floating high in the sky and then, for an instant, for one breath, you are one.

References for "Deflowering the Sampaguita"

The "you" in this creative nonfiction essay represents the collective "you." The experience in this essay is neither biographical nor autobiographical to any particular woman but is a conglomeration of various *anonymous* interviews with young women from New York, Illinois, Wisconsin, Ohio, and Virginia. (Yes, these are your daughters speaking.)

16

Tomboy, Dyke, Lezzie, and Bi
Filipina Lesbian and Bisexual Women Speak Out

Christine T. Lipat
Trinity A. Ordona
Cianna Pamintuan Stewart
Mary Ann Ubaldo

This chapter is excerpted from a 2-hour telephone dialogue conducted in July 1996 between Filipina lesbian and bisexual women organizers in New York (Christine Lipat, Ann Ubaldo) and San Francisco (Trinity Ordona, Cianna Stewart). Invited to submit an article on Filipina lesbians for this anthology, Trinity instead gathered three other women to share their experiences as Pinays, gay women, and queer organizers. Their lives and opinions represent a range of different geographical, cultural, social, and political locations in the United States and the Philippines and reflect some of the diversity among Filipino lesbian and bisexual women.

Christine, 25 years old, born and raised in New Jersey, is the eldest daughter of two medical professional immigrants from the Philippines. She is an activist in Asian American arts, women's, and lesbian communities and is currently a board member of the Astraea National Lesbian Action Foundation and the acting executive director of the Asian American Arts Alliance in New York City. Ann, 44 years old, from a middle-class professional family, was born and raised in Manila and graduated from the University of the Philippines. She immigrated to New York City in 1985, where she lives as an artist, musician, photographer, and self-employed jeweler creating her designs in Filipino motifs using the *alibata* script. Christine and Ann are cofounders of Kilawin Kolektibo, a Pinay lesbian collective based in New York. Cianna, 29 years old, is a *mestiza* white-Filipina woman who lived in Davao City until she was 6, when her family returned to the United States following Marcos's declaration of martial law. Cianna studied theater and divides her time between theater directing and organizing around Asian/Pacific Islander sexual and gender diversity through the Visibility Campaign, Living Well Project: Asian and Pacific Islander AIDS Services in San Francisco. Trinity, 45 years old, was born and raised in San Diego, California, in a post-World War II immigrant family of 13 children. She has participated in the Filipino, Asian American, women's, and gay liberation movements over the past 25 years. Trinity is a community organizer and graduate student in history of consciousness at the University of California, Santa Cruz, conducting research on the social history of the Asian/Pacific lesbian and bisexual women's movement in the United States.

Coming Out—Finding Self, Finding Others

Coming out—accepting one's homosexual/bisexual identity—is a life-long process of revelation and disclosure. Sharing one's "coming out" story is a familiar ritual in the queer community and often establishes a common bond among people across race, nationality, age, class, and cultural differences. Christine and Ann knew each other through building Kilawin, a Pinay lesbian collective in New York City. Trinity and Cianna worked together in San Francisco in the Asian/Pacific Islander Parents and Friends of Lesbians and Gays (A/PI-PFLAG) Family Project to provide support to families of A/PI gay people. To build a friendship bridge between them, they first shared their "coming out" stories with each other.

Trinity: In the 1970s, I got involved in the Filipino movement and radical politics in the San Francisco Bay Area. I was editor of a radical Filipino newspaper, *Ang Katipunan*, and blacklisted by the Marcos government. I also fell in love with a woman in the '70s, but I could not come out in the Filipino movement. Open homosexuality was not acceptable in the community or movement. In 1986, I attended a lesbians of color conference. Soon, I sought out other Asian lesbians and organized the first A/PI lesbian retreat in 1987. I have been here in the Asian and Pacific Islander lesbian and bisexual women's (APLB) community ever since. Organizing Asian lesbians has been the easiest political work I have ever done. It is fulfilling, and it fits me. And it helps that I am married. (Everyone laughs.) My mother likes Desiree, and we had a big wedding ceremony in 1988. Now we are planning to have a baby next year. I do not feel very radical anymore. (Everyone bursts out laughing.)

Ann: Domesticated!

Trinity: I know. I feel very settled down.

Ann: It is about time, Trinity.

Christine: You do not have that edge anymore! (laughing)

Trinity: I am glad that I met Desiree when I did; I was ready. A year later, marriage came up when we decided to have children. Suddenly, the Filipino voice inside me said, "Des, we have to get married." When I tell this story to other Filipinos, they know what I am talking about. Do you?

Cianna: Yes, definitely. And when you get married, you stay married. You are not supposed to break away from that marriage.

Ann: Back home, we do not have divorce, so marriage is "forever." My parents never forced me to get married; it was never an issue. My mom asked me, "Do you have a boyfriend?" I said no. "It is okay," Mom said. Then I said to her, "Mom, I have a girlfriend."

Trinity: So you told your parents?

Ann: I told my parents, and they did not approve. They said I did not have a future. They care for me but do not think a long-term relationship will work with a woman.

Trinity: What about you, Christine? What is your story?

Christine: Let us see. I have been attracted to women since I was a kid. In junior high, I had dreams, but I knew it was not something to be talked about. In college, I finally came out, but it was not easy.

Trinity: What do you mean?

Christine: Oberlin College [Ohio] was a liberal place where students wore pink ribbons on their backpacks. It was okay to talk about sexuality, but finding people who I could personally relate to was difficult. Finally in my junior year, I heard of a people of color lesbian/gay/bisexual group, and I went to one of their meetings. Because I had a steady boyfriend then, they said, "Oh my gosh, Christine! What are you doing here?" (Everyone laughs.) So I met all these cool women and was able to come out. My first girlfriend was in that group. After graduation in 1992, I returned to New Jersey and started looking around, hoping for an Asian lesbian group. I had just returned from San Francisco for my first Pride March.[1] I was in Chinatown, New York City, wearing my San Francisco Gay Pride T-shirt, when two Asian women came up, gave me an ALOEC [Asian Lesbians of the East Coast] business card. One of them said, "I think you need this." "Great, I have been looking for you," I replied. "Come on, come to a meeting," they said. (Everyone laughs.)

Cianna: That is great!

Christine: I also met people from the Asian American Writers Workshop. They had a coffeehouse, and I told myself, "This is a place where I feel comfortable, in New York City." Then I joined Youth for Philippine Action,[2] and they told me about Kambal sa Lusog,[3] the Filipino lesbian and gay group in New York City. I had seen Kambal march in the New York City Philippine Independence Day Parade, which was the only way I knew about them. It was through networking, though, that I met some Kambal people.

Trinity: What about you, Ann?

Ann: Well, I will tell you my love story with the girls (laughing). When I first transferred to this new school in Manila, I knew there were girls looking. I was a guitarist and a player at that time. . . .

Trinity: Wait a minute. You were a "player"?

Ann: Yes, a softball player.

Trinity: Oh, I see. I thought you were a different kind of "player."
(Everyone laughs.)

Ann: I was 11 years old, Grade 5, and a softball player when I
learned there were some girls who had crushes on me. "Oh my
God," I said. I did not do anything until college, but I just felt it.
I met this classmate of mine 25 years later in the States, and she
said, "I knew you were a 'boy' when you went to our school."
Even all my classmates said they knew I was one. My first
girlfriend was when I was 19 in college. After that, I never left the
women. Twenty-five years later, I have "furthered my resume." I
have been pretty adventurous! (Laughing)

Trinity: You came out as a lesbian in college in the Philippines, then
came to the U.S.?

Ann: My girlfriend wanted to try it out in the States, so I said,
"Yeah, I want to." So I wrapped up my business in the Philippines
and told her to look for a place for me in New York and I will be
there. And I did. I came. But it did not work out with that
girlfriend I followed. After 2 months, she married a guy.

Trinity: Oh.

Ann: So I hung out with a few lesbian friends from back home. I
was a lost soul for a while. I only met the Kilawin girls after 10
years here in New York, after searching and searching for these
beautiful Filipina dykes.

Trinity: Let us talk about Kilawin.[4] It is the first Pinay lesbian group
in the U.S. How did it get started?

Christine: Everybody was involved in different movements and
learning different skills. Then we met each other and created our
own informal friendships. Some of us were involved in Kambal
sa Lusog, but by 1993 its membership was waning. Then a few of
us started going to Gabriela Network[5] meetings. They opened the
door for us and invited us to participate. . . .

Ann: What helped convince us to organize ourselves was meeting
many of the other Filipina lesbians who were organizing in San
Francisco, Toronto, and the Philippines during the Stonewall
March in New York City in 1995. During the next 6 months, about

15 of us met and created Kilawin Kolektibo, a sociopolitical collective working to create a cultural space for Filipina lesbians.

Christine: Our first political action, via letter and E-mail, protested the degrading, stereotypical portrayal of a Filipina mail-order bride[6] in the Australian drag queen road movie, *The Adventures of Priscilla, Queen of the Desert*. Our unique cultural viewpoint—as women, lesbians, and Filipinos—gave us the vantage point to critique this mainstream crossover movie.

Ann: But we were the lone voice of protest in the gay community! Many just did not "see" the problem, while others wanted to overlook it, saying, "The rest of it was so good." This is a good example of the gay community "advancing" at the expense of people of color!

Christine: After the "Priscilla" protest came the Philippine Independence Day March, the Gay Pride March, Asian American student conferences and community forums, benefits, fund-raisers, and potluck parties and a visit to our Pinay sisters in Toronto. It is amazing that we did so much in so little time!

Ann: There are about 30 Pinays on our mailing list, with at least 12 or so coming to the monthly meetings. We try and blend our personal friendship with our politics, and it's been exciting to have Kilawin around.

Trinity: Cianna, what about you? How did you come out and find community?

Cianna: For me, it was bisexuality. I came out at Wesleyan University [Connecticut], where I first met other lesbians. I went to the meeting of the "Lesbian, Bisexual and Questioning Women's Group." I walked in, and they all looked at me and said, "We have been waiting for you to show up. We knew you were coming." Then I said, "I am glad I am here. Finally I figured it out, I am bisexual, so that is why I came." They said that they would wait a little time longer.

Christine: You mean, until you turned lesbian?

Cianna: Yeah, until I turned lesbian. So I got really angry. I have been doing political activism since I was 9 years old. I started out as an environmentalist, then became an antinuclear protester and abortion rights activist. When I went to college, it was queer activism. I started a campus bisexual group with another bi woman. Everybody who went to school received our flyer: "If you are bisexual and want to talk about it, come to a meeting on Thursday." Forty people showed up.

Everyone: Wow!

Cianna: And everybody had told us there were no other bisexuals! It was support group with a political tone. We wanted the campus gay, lesbian, and bisexual organization to acknowledge that "bisexual" meant something. After college, here in San Francisco, I was later involved at the national level with the bisexual community and ran the national bisexual network[7] for 2 years. In 1992, I got to know individuals in the community through my safer sex work with the dykes in San Francisco. I was a founding member of the Safer Sex Slut Team,[8] so. . . .

Christine: I heard about them! (Laughing)

Cianna: Yep, yep (laughing). I got pulled into the community through dating an Asian dyke. Then I got this job here at the Living Well Project and have been working with the Asian/Pacific Islander community for the last several years. My primary community, however, are gay and bisexual men. I also have a lot of dyke friends, including A/PI dykes.

Coming Out Queer—Youth, Family, and Community

In this section, the women share their knowledge and opinions about differences among Filipino queers in the United States, especially between older and younger generations of Filipina queers. The section ends with a discussion of gays and lesbians in the Philippines, citing the greater social acknowledgment of gay men, counterposed by the invisibility of lesbian women in the Philippine society.

Trinity: Cianna, tell us what you know about gay youth.

Cianna: Through my own interest, and just being here at this agency, I am familiar with one of two A/PI queer youth groups in the country. AQU[25]A—Asian and Pacific Islander Queer and Questioning Under 25 Altogether—is really, really active. They have a combination of socials-plus-support, HIV/AIDS information, leadership training, and political activism. They lobbied in Sacramento, our state capital, to persuade state senators to include queer issues in the public school system during California Queer Youth Lobby Day. They use *queer* more than *gay* or *bi* or *lesbian*. Some people actually refuse to use any other word but *queer*.

Christine: Why?

Cianna: They have a more fluid conception of sexuality. They are still figuring their identity yet acknowledge there no single identity, no fixed qualities. They also have a stronger conception of the movement as a cogendered movement/multigendered movement. I think that is why they have embraced the term *queer*. Sometimes people from the older gay and lesbian movement think of *queer, lesbian, gay* as the same thing—and also eliminate the bisexual from their rubric. The youth, however, make a very clear, concerted effort to include bisexual and transgender folks. In fact, there is a member of AQU[25]A who is straight. She is kind of "queer" in that she does not align herself entirely with the straight, more homophobic straight community. She feels very comfortable in AQU[25]A, and everyone feels very comfortable with her because she fits in. She feels it is a group she can socialize with, even though she is not there to get social support around her own "queerness" because she is straight. She is part of AQU[25]A. Nobody has a problem with it.

Trinity: What about their parents? What do they think?

Cianna: Some of the youth are out, some of them are not. In AQU[25]A, they learn ways to talk about their sexuality. They get support for coming out and share coming out stories with each other. They are more prepared and have ways to support each other, regardless of the outcome of their coming out. There has been quite a range of reactions among their parents. Most parents have generally been okay—not openly excited or anything. Parents just say, "Do not talk about it." But no one has been kicked out of their house.

I have met more kids who have not come out, and their fears are really intense—fear of getting disowned, fear of parents not supporting them. Some of them do not want to come out until they have finished high school. Up until you are 18 or in college, you are so completely dependent on your parents. It is also hard to come out when you are living at home with your parents (everyone laughs), where you get monitored more closely.

Trinity: Have you noticed anything particular about the Filipino youth?

Cianna: Not specifically. Some Filipino families seem to have no real problem with it; other Filipino families have been very hostile. It does not really seem to matter whether they are immigrant or American born, or whether they self-identify very strongly as Catholic or not. There are both very devout Catholic parents who are really supportive, others do not really care, and some are really hostile. I have not seen anything that I can really put down as a "truism."

Trinity: What about in Kilawin?

Ann: Are they accepted in the family? The parents of some of the younger ones are pretty cool. But the older ones—like my parents' age—are conservative, and it's still not accepted. "Don't ask, Don't tell."[9] It is like that back home. But for the younger ones, I think it is more accepted.

Cianna: Younger parents or younger kids?

Ann: For parents who are in their 40s, it's not such a problem. Marisol is 18 years old and pretty new in our group; her dad joined us in the Independence Day Parade. We all said, "I wish my dad was like yours!"

Trinity: He marched with your contingent!

Ann: Yes. It was really cool, you know. Most of them, it is really cool with their parents.

Cianna: I've also seen the story that Sasha Mobley tells in *Coming Out, Coming Home*.[10] It is something I've heard before—parents are afraid there's something really, really bad going on in their kid's life. They're worried that their kid is going to be thrown in jail or becoming a social dropout. When the kid finally says, "I am queer," the parents say, "Oh. That is not as bad as I had imagined."

If anything, I have found it harder to generalize about the Filipinos than East Asians; it is that there is a wider range of reaction.

Ann: We have our Philippine Independence Day Parade, but the Irish lesbians and gays cannot march [in the St. Patrick's Day Parade].[11] But with the Filipinos, it is fine. I asked Ninotchka Rosca[12] why. She said that we have a very strong women's movement. When issues about gay/lesbian rights or children's rights or any other minority rights come up, the women hold up an umbrella. When lesbians are being discriminated, it is always the women that support us. That is how it is in the Filipino community here.

Christine: The first time we marched in the New York City Philippine Independence Day Parade, the parade marshals kept delaying us. Both Kilawin and Gabriela Network were moved from place to place to await our turn to march.

Ann: We had been waiting for 2 hours in the sun. We were the only all-female group in the parade, so there was instant discrimination. When Ninotchka finally said, "It is time for us to march," we started marching, and the parade organizers did not say anything.

Trinity: So the women's group and the lesbian group marched together?

Ann: Yes. We always march together.

Cianna: Cool.

Trinity: Christine, when Kilawin marched in the Independence Day Parade, what did it mean for you?

Christine: It was fun, and for the small number of people who do see the parade—there are never that many people—they were pretty supportive. The Filipino radio show *Radyo Pinoy* interviewed us too.

Ann: There was a good article on us in *Filipino Express*,[13] and we marched side by side with Gabriela. . . .

Christine: Not only because we support each other's causes but also so that the people in the closet could march with Gabriela.

Trinity: That means that you are really "out" in the Filipino community?

Christine: Yes, a lot of people would say that it is a lot easier to march in the Gay Pride than in your own back yard! (Laugh)

Trinity: That is for sure.

Ann: Half of us are Gabriela members. It is not hush-hush. We can be up front. Gay men, however, are more accepted than gay women, but we are trying to deal with it.

Trinity: Are gay men more accepted in the Philippines?

Ann: Yes, in Philippine society, gay men are more accepted. It has always been like that. But now the gay women are coming out. We are making a stand and saying we are more than the stereotype. It has been improving for the last 10 years.

Cianna: But it is a particular kind of gay men. The *bakla*.[14]

Christine: Yes, I was recently visiting Chicago, and they had a videotape of some Filipino comedy shows. They always have the drag queen character.

Ann: It is very popular.

Christine: I know I have seen a sitcom or two with a lesbian, but somehow they always end up with men. (Everyone laughs.)

Cianna: When I went back to Davao 3 years ago, my family told me, "Oh, the *bakla* boys are having a volleyball game. You might want to go down there." We own a hotel, and there is a disco in the hotel where a whole group of them hang out. One of my aunts is a clothing designer, and many of her designer friends are *bakla* boys too. They are always at the hotel or in the coffee shop—it was fine. [As for lesbians,] my aunt, whispering about a woman in this band, said, "I think she is a tomboy, so you'd better watch out."

Trinity: "Better watch out"—meaning what?

Cianna: Meaning, she might get "crushed out" on me (laughing). She was cute, too. But it was a real contrast from the States. My family, who are a very public family in the southern Philippines, have gay men all over our social engagements, everywhere.

Trinity: Openly gay?

Cianna: Yes, very open. You talk about it, and you laugh about it in public, too. The *bakla* boys were flirting openly with my brother—who is straight. And the whole family was kidding him about it without being derogatory to the guys flirting with him. But when it comes to any visibility of lesbians, the first time I met a lesbian woman from Davao was at Stonewall in New York City. ▦

Empowerment and Visibility

Citing a link between activism and the Filipino lesbian/bi women's community and organizing, this section probes the connections between gender and sexuality, oppression of women, and future prospects for organizing Filipina queer women in the United States and the Philippines.

▦   ▦   ▦

Cianna: Is there a strong *Mars* and *Pars*[15] presence in the Filipino women's community in New York?

Ann: Yes, they are mostly *Fil-Fils.*[16] They stick together; many came from the same schools and have common friends. Whatever their situation back home was, they bring to New York or wherever they go.

Trinity: But they are involved in the activist groups?

Ann: No, but with Kilawin coming out as well as other Asian lesbian groups, I think it will make everyone's situation better. Visibility is very important.

Cianna: I also think it is better. Hopefully, people can come out without the stereotypes getting in the way.

Ann: And being political and making people more aware of what we are doing will really improve the situation. Educating them too.

Trinity: Why do you think there is this connection between activism and Filipina lesbianism? To be visible, we also need some political consciousness just to put ourselves out there. The *bakla* are already known and accepted in Philippine society—I do not know about accepted, but at least known. But lesbians are invisible. They do not exist.

Ann: I was also wondering why we must have politics to be visible. With the gay men, they are the hairstylists, the artists, and it is okay. It is harder for us.

Christine: People do not talk about Filipino lesbians or even say the word *lesbian*. You have to educate yourself, learn the words for what you are and what you are feeling, but they are not common, everyday words. Even then, it's hard to talk about it!

Cianna: There have always been some women who have been dressing and living as men, blending into mainstream society there. If you are a flamboyant cross-dressing male, it is hard to hide. At the same time, he is not threatening to the power structure because he is "downgrading" his status by acting more feminine. He is not a threat; he is a joke. But a lesbian woman is actually threatening to the power structure because she is taking her own power. This is political because it is a power struggle.

Trinity: We cannot overlook the gender issues underlying sexuality. For example, women going up the corporate ladder are often criticized for being "bitchy" and "unladylike." In the same regard, when lesbians and bisexual women assert their sexuality preferences in their social and personal lives, then it too becomes threatening. The political edge to a lesbian or bisexual identity for Filipino women is a necessary path. Otherwise, we never get taken seriously.

Cianna: Yes. It becomes so completely tied into the role of women overall in society; we cannot escape that political correlation.

Trinity: It is one thing to put down a tomboy and say, "Oh, she is just trying to be a boy, but she does not have the equipment." But it is another thing to understand that also means that "she does not need men." Women who live that way, however they dress, are much more threatening.

Cianna: A straight butch is never going to come under fire as much as a tomboy. That is just the way it has always been.

Trinity: Right.

Cianna: There are athletic or butch women who may get harassed on the street, but in their social circles where it is known that they are *not* queer, they do not face the harassment that we do.

Trinity: It is also good to mention the case of Beth and Vangie in the Philippines and the emergence of several activist-oriented lesbian groups in the Philippines. Beth and Vangie worked in a social service NGO when they fell in love. Once everybody found out, half of the office got homophobic about it.[17]

Christine: Especially the guys.

Trinity: The presence of gay liberation groups in the Philippines is an expression of a growing political consciousness among Filipino gays and lesbian and bisexual people. The Philippines is no longer a country that people left behind. That was my father's experience. Since the 1965 immigration wave began, Filipinos continue to go back and forth to the Philippines all the time. So too with the gay connection. Linking up with gay groups in the Philippines is very helpful to our own visibility and coming out process here in the U.S. It also proves that homosexuality is not just a white thing or an American thing. It happens in all countries.

Christine: Being out and visible also has its problems. When you first start, there is excitement from organizing around the issues— like the *Miss Saigon* protest[18] with Kambal or joining the Stonewall March[19]—you meet a lot of people and get to know each other. But then division and factionalism start, breaking trust, breaking expectations. I think the real challenge is trying to get past those problems and find out our commonalties, what we are building for the future.

Ann: It is really hard to work together for a common cause. We have a common struggle, and we should work together wherever we are, whether we are here or in the Philippines. That is the hard part. But if we keep trying and communicating, we can work on projects together.

Cianna: My concern for the future is to get past the problem that I have encountered, not only with a queer Filipino movement but through several different Filipino groups—who is really Filipino and who is really queer? Proving yourself has been something that I personally live as a *mestiza* and bi. I hope we are going to stop "proving ourselves" and "questioning each other" and focus instead on the work that has to be done.

Trinity: Let us remember that up until the overthrow of the Marcos government, the Philippines has been in a colonial relationship to the world and within itself. It has never really had the chance to be its own country. This has had colonizing effects on people's thinking and how the whole country has developed or, rather, underdeveloped. We would not be able to talk about this subject if Marcos was still alive and running the country.

Everyone: Right, right.

Trinity: We have to appreciate our progress as Filipino gays just in the last 10 years.

Ann: The coming out of lesbianism in Philippine society is also part of the women's movement.

Cianna, Trinity: Yes.

Trinity: And lesbian rights was also advanced in Beijing U.N. Women's Conference.[20] It was a controversial issue among feminists in the international women's movement if lesbian issues would remain in the closet. Even though mention of lesbian rights and issues was eventually withheld from the official document, the struggle over its inclusion unfolded in front of the eyes and ears of the international women's movement. These were significant first steps. By the next decade's U.N. Women's Conference, our progress will be even greater. ▓

In conclusion, the lives of Filipina lesbian and bisexual women—as attested by the women's stories above—have changed radically over the past 20 years. For the two older lesbians, Ann and Trinity, family and community acceptance in the 1970s was minimal, if forthcoming at all. On the other hand, Cianna's and Christine's "coming out" experiences in college in the 1990s were positive and supportive. Although both generations of Pinays faced the same difficulties—coming out, negative stereotypes, societal homophobia, family rejection—new opportunities exist today for a greater degree of acceptance in the family, community, and overall society. Through the efforts of many gay liberationists before them, today's queers are surrounded by a community of friends and organizations and provide the context for this emergent Filipina queer empowerment and visibility movement. Filipina lesbian and bisexual women in the United States and the Philippines are part of a global pan-Asian queer movement and have been both agents and beneficiaries of this international mass liberation movement for gay, lesbian, bisexual, and transgender rights for the past 25 years.

▓

Notes

1. The Stonewall Rebellion, June 29, 1969, which launched the gay liberation movement, has been commemorated yearly in June with a Pride March in major gay communities across the United States. New York and San Francisco parades gather at least 300,000 celebrants.

2. A Filipino American youth activist group in New York City, 1990 to 1993.

3. Kambal sa Lusog, translated, means "Twins in Health," a name chosen to include both Filipino male and female homosexual and bisexual people. The organization was formed in 1992.

4. Kilawin, a hot and spicy Filipino dish; Kilawin Kolektibo, formed in 1995, is a "hot and spicy" Pinay lesbian collective based in New York City.

5. Gabriela Network, based in the United States, works with Gabriela-Philippines to organize, educate, and network on issues that affect the women and children of the Philippines but that have their roots in decisions made in the United States.

6. A sex-starved, half-crazed, Tagalog-speaking Filipina wife of an older Australian white man in the outback performs a gross dance routine popping ping pong balls from her anus (shown offscreen). Besides Kilawin, Filipina women's groups in Australia and Manila lodged complaints about this movie.

7. BiNet (Bisexual Network), founded in 1989 in San Francisco, is a national coalition of groups and individuals of bisexual-identified people.

8. A multiracial bisexual and lesbian health education outreach team that gave safer sex demonstrations in dyke bars in San Francisco, 1990 to 1993; sponsored by the Lyon-Martin Women's Health Services and organized by the prominent bisexual community organizer Lani Ka'ahumanu.

9. U.S. military policy, initiated under the Clinton administration in 1992, permits homosexual soldiers to serve but not to engage in homosexual activities while in the service.

10. A video interview of four families of Asian lesbian and gay children (A/PI-PFLAG Family Project, 1996). Filipina *mestiza* lesbian Sasha Mobley and her lover, brother, and mother share their experience with Sasha's "coming out" to the family.

11. Following street demonstrations and court litigation, the Massachusetts State Supreme Court ruled in 1994 that the Irish lesbian and gay contingent could be prohibited from participating in the Boston St. Patrick's Day Parade.

12. A well-known journalist, feminist organizer, and leading member of the Gabriela Network.

13. "New Filipina Lesbian Group" (1995).

14. Slang Tagalog term for homosexual men; connotes a soft, "swishy" man; like the English term *faggot*, it can be positive or negative, depending on the context and intent.

15. Tagalog slang for *Kumadre* and *Kumpadre* (close friend, female and male) used among Filipina lesbian tomboy and fem couples.

16. Philippine nationals.

17. Beth Castronuevo and Vangie Lim were fired on September 6, 1994, from their jobs at Balay Rehabilitation Center after news of their lesbian relationship polarized the office. Balay is a nongovernmental organization dedicated to aid families of Philippine political prisoners. Beth and Vangie's dismissal was met with public protests by lesbian and women's groups in Manila. A lawsuit is currently under litigation.

18. *Miss Saigon*, a musical update of *Madame Butterfly* by Alain Boublil and Claude-Michel Schönberg, opened in New York City in April 1991 after months of criticism for its sexist and racist content and casting practices. Lambda Legal Defense Fund, a leading national lesbian and gay organization, came under fire from Asian lesbian and gay groups for using *Miss Saigon* for its annual fund-raiser. A highly publicized protest led by a coalition of Asian and gay groups disrupted the April 6 and 11 performances during opening week. For details, see Yoshikawa (1994). Furthermore, according to Christine Lipat, the *Miss Saigon* controversy was the first activist campaign that brought Filipino gay men and women together, setting the stage for the later formation of Kambal sa Lusog, which in turn led to the formation of Kilawin Kolektibo, a Pinay lesbian group (see Note 4).

19. Celebrating 25 years of struggle since the Stonewall riots launched the gay liberation movement, over 1.5 million gay, lesbian, bisexual, and transgender people and their supporters gathered for a week-long celebration in New York City, culminating in an international march and rally in Central Park on June 25, 1994.

20. The 4th U.N. World Conference on Women, Beijing, People's Republic of China, August 30 to September 9, 1996, gathered over 200,000 international delegates. Controversy over lesbianism emerged before the conference when China wanted to deny access to lesbians, Tibetans, Taiwanese, Asian women's rights groups, and some organizations militantly opposed to abortion. In addition, the Non-Governmental Organizations (NGO) Forum, which preceded the U.N. gathering, was moved to Huairou, 30 miles outside the capital, making it nearly impossible for NGO groups to observe the Beijing event. At the U.N. conference, controversy focused on the specific inclusion of lesbian issues in the U.N. Platform for Action document. Before Beijing, prolesbian recommendations were submitted by NGOs at the Latin American and Caribbean preparatory meeting. The Europe and North American Regional Platform for Action mentioned sexual orientation in its preamble and directed governments to include lesbian groups in the design, development, and implementation of strategies for change. This was the first time that a document adopted by U.N. member states had included any mention of sexual orientation.

References

A/PI-PFLAG Family Project (Prod.). (1996). *Coming out, coming home* [Videotape].

New Filipina lesbian group joins Philippine Independence Day Parade. (1995, June 12-18). *Filipino Express*, p. 13.

Yoshikawa, Y. (1994). The heat is on "Miss Saigon" coalition: Organizing across race and sexuality. In K. Aguilar-San Juan (Ed.), *The state of Asian America: Activism and resistance in the 1990s* (pp. 275-294). Boston: South End.

17

At the Frontiers of Narrative

The Mapping of Filipino Gay Men's Lives in the United States

Martin F. Manalansan IV

> Personal [life] narratives allow us . . . to see lives as
> simultaneously individual and social creations, and to
> see individuals as simultaneously the changers and the
> changed.
> *Personal Narratives Group (1989),* Interpreting Women's Lives

L ife narratives or histories are compelling social and personal texts that have been used by social scientists and humanities scholars for decades.[1] The process of eliciting these narratives is itself a source of useful insights. In this chapter, I explore the ways in which narrative elicitation and telling render interesting performances of identities and experiences. From 1990 to 1993, I interviewed Filipino gay men living in New York City. Fifty of them consented to be involved in intensive life history elicitation, which lasted anywhere from 2 to 8 hours (sometimes split into several sessions).[2] I suggest that reflections on field experiences and life narrative methodology provide powerful sources of understanding about being Filipino and gay in America.

> Interview? What is this interview for? Who will even be interested in my life? Why do you want to know about my life? I am not a celebrity. Okay, I could be a celebrity [giggles], but I am just an ordinary *bakla*.[3]

These were the words of Mario, a 40-year-old Filipino gay man. He was quite jocular and somewhat uncomfortable about the prospect of being interviewed when I first approached him. Indeed, the practice of the interview is popularly constructed as somewhat removed from the mundane struggles of immigrant lives. For many informants who were immigrants, the interview is something that stands out as a bureaucratic and sometimes intimidating procedure such as the green card (permanent residence) or citizenship interviews with the Immigration and Naturalization Service. Therefore, the practice of eliciting life histories initially suggests a forbidding domain in which to navigate and redraw the inevitable axes of ethnicity, race, class, sexuality, and gender.

Mario's attitude was in fact shared by many of my informants. When I approached Filipino gay men about my project, many of them expressed some reservation about the whole process. Confidentiality was foremost in their minds. As one potential informant said, "*Baka maging front page news ang buhay ko* [My life might become front-page news]." Part of their trepidation may be due to what is perceived to be the very active rumor mill in the Filipino community. I had to present myself as another member of the community yet set apart by my academic credentials and professional project. Some potential informants' fear may stem from their various legal or citizenship statuses. Some were undocumented aliens, others did not want to be publicly identified as gay, and a few were diagnosed with AIDS. The hazards that surrounded each situation were real, and I tried to persuade them about the completely confidential nature of the interview and the eventual report. Therefore, all informants' names that I use in this chapter and in all of my work on the project are pseudonyms.

In contrast to worries about confidentiality, there was the allure of the "interview." Mario explicitly connects the practice of the interview and life narrative elicitation with something that celebrities do. In addition, many potential informants likened the life history interview to those in many TV talk shows, in which lives were continuously put on display. For some gay Filipinos, the interview was one brief moment to at least see themselves as movie stars or TV celebrities whose lives were necessarily part of public scrutiny. Despite their initial awkwardness, Filipino gay men who chose to participate in the life history interview provided compelling stories about themselves both in the content of their narratives and in the manner and situation in which these were told.

Language and the
Performance of Identities

The philosopher J. L. Austin (1962) argued that people's use of language in different situations betrays and portrays individual and group interests and backgrounds. In the negotiation and elicitation of the life narratives, the deployment of various linguistic strategies is a way of negotiating status, establishing roles, and confirming and performing identities.

Consider the first few minutes of my interview with Oscar, a 30-year-old Filipino immigrant who has been in the United States for 4 years. The initial interaction started with my asking the question "Do you speak Tagalog?" When he said yes, I asked whether he wanted the interview to be conducted in Tagalog or English. He said that it was okay either way. I started the interview in Tagalog and asked him mostly about general information such as his date of birth and ethnolinguistic group. However, when I started to ask him more personal questions about such topics as childhood experiences, he started to answer me in English. After an hour of stories about his childhood, he started to become comfortable and began to talk in Taglish. By the time he was answering my questions about his sexual and social experiences in gay life, he was freely using idioms and words from swardspeak,[4] the Filipino gay argot.

Here the relationship between Oscar as the narrator and myself as researcher was configured and negotiated with the particular uses of language. English was a way for him to ease the tension while he was getting used to the interview process. Then, as he settled into the situation, he began to use Tagalog. By the time the more sensitive issues about sexuality were being discussed, he was using swardspeak.

Social distance and proximity are particularly evident in the ways class, ethnicity and immigration status are implicitly articulated in linguistic situations during the interview process. The informant Paulo, for example, insisted on speaking English throughout the interview, although his command of the language was quite poor. During the interview, he was often unable to grasp the meaning of the questions. In his heavily accented English, he would often tell his stories in a very abbreviated, almost cryptic manner. At one point during the interview, he then revealed to me that he had only very recently become an American citizen. He had spent several years as an undocumented person. Through the amnesty program of the federal government, he had been able to legalize his status. He said, "I know that my English is not good, but I am an American now. I will try to talk like all Americans—in English."

In complete contrast, Rommel, who was born and raised in the United States, peppered his story with accented Tagalog words. He admitted that although he cannot hold a complete conversation in any Philippine language, he nevertheless attempts to punctuate his conversations with other Filipinos with a sprinkling of Tagalog. He does this to create a sense of affinity between himself and other Filipinos. In addition, this gesture is his attempt to show immigrant Filipinos that although he may not speak the "mother tongue" fluently, he is not arrogant or *mayabang* (arrogant).

Another informant who was a scion of a prominent family in the Philippines used a particular form of Taglish that is commonly seen as an elite form of code switching. During the interview, he was trying to find out if we knew certain people in common. Once we had established some common friends and acquaintances, he began to talk about his family's wealth and how easy his childhood had been and how all that had changed when he came to America. He said that unlike the Philippines, where people knew their "place," America brings Filipinos from different backgrounds together. He added that he tries to keep away from Filipinos who are "low class" or *bakya*, and he boasted he mingles only with his "own kind" as much as possible. His language behavior was meant to signal his upper-class status and crucial difference from other

Filipinos. It was also his way of finding out about my own class background. My ability to converse with him in his class-marked language code and our having a set of common friends and acquaintances enabled me to continue the interview.

In many ways, not only is language a tool or the means to tell a story, as these examples suggest, but its use in specific situations is part of the story itself. In sum, language locates the individual user within the social context as he weaves his life story. Filipino gay men's deployment of language forms and practices in their narratives and within the narrative elicitation process reflects the multiple positions and situations they occupy.

Kiyeme and *Etsing:*
Beyond What Is Said

In recounting their lives, Filipino gay men, particularly those who immigrated as adults, use specific idioms and hand and facial signals and codes to signify irony, exasperation, or dissimulation in certain parts of the narrative. These idioms and gestures are ways in which Filipino gay men read between the lines and go beyond the literal meanings of what is said.

The swardspeak idioms that capture these verbal and nonverbal cues and codes are *kiyeme* and *etsing*. *Kiyeme* and *etsing* can be used interchangeably and can mean artfulness, artifice, inauthenticity, untruth, and playful manipulation of social situations. Sometimes, after saying something, the speaker feigns a sneezing attack and says, *"Etsing!"* More often than not, these words are not said and instead are signaled by particular actions such as running one's finger over a hard surface such as a tabletop or a wall with a quick flick of the finger at the end. Another nonverbal signal is the raising of one's eyebrow or using a finger to push up an eyebrow.

The concepts of *kiyeme* and *etsing* permeated several interview situations. One particularly lively interview involved Carlo, who had been a migrant/overseas contract worker in the Middle East before immigrating to the United States. He suggested that the rules around sexuality and moral conduct in Saudi Arabia were so strict and forbidding that he had had to play it safe, so that many times he had acted very masculine. After saying that, he did the finger signal. During the interview, Carlo consistently used the signal, and when I asked him if everything he had told me was *kiyeme* and none of it was true, he said that it wasn't really important to know the truth or not, only to be able to "play" with the situation. When I asked him further about this concept, he said that Filipino gay men like to think of themselves as being in control of the situation, so the best way to think about any situation is to treat it as if it were all artifice (or, as he said, "fake"). The artifice of life in general allows Filipino gay men to cope, survive, and in some way control social situations. For example, he mentioned the lack of working papers that he and many of his friends were confronted with when they moved to the United States. When he applied for a job, he not only produced the required documents, such as a social security card, but also tried to act like an American, so, as he said, he made *kiyeme* to survive.

When I asked him if he thought the life history interview was the same thing as those situations of survival, he answered that it was a different kind of *kiyeme*. There is no attempt at dissimulation or trickery. It was his way of connecting with me and to show his view of the world.

Other informants talked about the importance of the idioms, particularly in the pleasure of speaking. As Exotica, one of the more eloquent informants, noted, "It isn't about what is said, but how it is said." *Kiyeme* and *etsing* provide a way of adding some excitement to what may turn out to be a boring activity such as the interview. Exotica further added, "Things are not what they seem." For Exotica and for many Filipino gay men, the use of idioms for pleasure and/or survival shows how things can have hidden or veiled meanings and how one needs to be aware at all times—otherwise one may not survive or make the most of any situation.

In the life history interviews, the narratives and their elicitation become part of this play for survival and pleasure. The idioms *kiyeme* and *etsing* suggest layers, dimensions, and regimes of truth that exist in the narratives. Indeed, one cannot rely solely on the spoken or the literal; there are meanings and truths that are partially covert and not so apparent. Some of the pleasure and value that the narratives afford the researcher, the narrator, and the readers of these texts lies in uncovering these meanings.

AIDS and Narratives From the Trenches

How does AIDS figure in the elicitation of life histories? In the pandemic, lives of people with AIDS become the grist of gossip, scientific inquiry, and journalistic and visual art renditions. For many of my informants, the AIDS pandemic is the implicit context within which the elicitation of life histories occur.

There was trepidation specifically among those who had AIDS to talk about the topic. Six months after he participated in a life history interview, an informant called and asked me out for dinner. During dinner, he admitted that he had intentionally omitted very important information about himself but that some events in the past few months had made him reconsider this deliberate oversight on his part. He then said that he had just been diagnosed with Kaposi's sarcoma, a type of skin cancer that many people with AIDS acquire and that is marked by purple lesions. He said that he had known he was HIV positive since 1986 and had been diagnosed with AIDS in 1989 but that during the interview, he felt that he could not, even with the confidential nature of the interview, disclose his condition to me. He said, " I was not ready to tell you [about the diagnosis]. A few close friends and family members know, but revealing this to you during the interview was something else. It was too public." With the visible signs of the cancer on his face, he said that his life had entered what he called a more "terminal" state and that he was ready to be more public about his condition.

For those who have seen the horrors of the epidemic, many perceived the recounting of their life stories as part of the fight against AIDS. In fact, some of my informants who were living with AIDS talked about their lives as if they were recounting a moral fable. Jesse, who died a few months after the interview, perceived the life narrative as a way of "helping others." In providing the public with an account of his life trajectory, he was then giving the people a kind of example and giving the disease a Filipino and an Asian face. Jesse was well aware that at that time, the representations and images of AIDS in America never included anybody who looked like him, who did not look white, black, or Latino. Jesse was worried about his other Filipino friends and other Filipino gay men who were not aware of how AIDS is transmitted and of how vulnerable they could be. Because of his Catholic background, he had first laid the blame on himself. After receiving some counseling, he eased his burden and accepted the diagnosis. He said, "Blaming myself was a waste of time. I got over that real quick." What he did not get over was his overwhelming need to make some sense of his predicament. He said that he had readily consented to participate in the interview because he knew that many Filipino gay men would be reading about it. He insisted that I use his real name. He saw his very public avowal of the disease as a kind of intervention into the silence and denial that permeated the Filipino American community at that time.

Those who did not have AIDS and were not HIV positive saw the whole interview process as being related to the epidemic, even if only a section of the interview was devoted to the subject. AIDS provided a kind of signpost or a historical marker for their own narratives. "Before" or "pre" AIDS and "after" AIDS are periods that mark many of the narratives. For many of the informants, AIDS was a way to differentiate the way their lives were lived before the pandemic and the way their lives were lived now. Many had witnessed people, including friends and lovers, die. These deaths and illnesses had been turning points in their lives. AIDS permeated the ways in which they viewed their sexuality, particularly in the kinds of caution and trepidation that many of them expressed about sexual practices. As many of them said, one needs to be careful "these days." Finally, the presence of AIDS was apparent in informants' perception of the necessity of the narratives. With many people dying, informants were worried that the stories of Filipino gay men would never be told. As one of my informants said in mocking jest, "You better take down our lives, we may not be here tomorrow—you never know."

Narratives and the Mapping of Identities

I have not exhausted the many connections between the production of life narratives of Filipino gay men and the arenas in which identities and experiences are performed and articulated. The three examples that I have very briefly presented extend what is simply seen as a tool for data gathering into a dynamic social activity like other rituals, routines, and practices in everyday life, fraught with the tensions and ambivalence created by racial, class, sexual, or gender issues.

Life narratives and their elicitation, then, are like the frontier, an eminently rich space for exploring and locating selves and groups. However, unlike the popular conception of the frontier, in which that supposedly virginal space is seen as detached from and existing independently of the larger social world, the production of life narratives is intrinsically linked to arenas in which identities and experiences are contested. In gathering Filipino gay men's life narratives, I amassed not only the richness of the actual life experiences themselves but also the valuable understanding of a myriad of issues brought about by the process. Whether it involves negotiating with the language of the interview, deciphering the "real" and the "dissimulated," or conversing in the shadows of the pandemic, the production of life narratives is a dynamic event in which people position themselves continuously within history and social life.

Notes

1. For critical discussions of life histories/narratives, see Personal Narratives Group (1989), Langness and Frank (1981), and Watson and Watson-Franke (1985).

2. These 50 Filipino informants live in the greater New York area. Most lived in Manhattan, Brooklyn, Queens, and Jersey City (New Jersey). They ranged in age from 22 to 60+ (two older informants were vague about their age). All but one of these informants worked in jobs, which ranged from fashion designer to computer programmer to bank executive. The lone nonworker was an undergraduate student. The informants can be divided into three groups. The majority included 37 "immigrants" or those who were born and raised in the Philippines until they were 18 or over. The next group were five informants who are popularly called "one point fivers," or those who came to the United States from the Philippines when they were less than 10 years old. Seven were born in the United States or U.S. territories (one was born on a U.S. military base in Europe). All those born in the United States were from California. All informants had lived in New York City for more than 2 years.

3. *Bakla* is a Tagalog word whose meaning encompasses homosexuality, transvestitism, hermaphroditism, and effeminacy. Though most of my informants identified as gay, they used *bakla* in specific situations, particularly in defining or differentiating themselves from American gay men.

4. Swardspeak is a popular way of connecting with other Filipino gay men living in America. Though some refuse to speak it because they see it as an anachronous practice, many informants report that it was one way of creating affinity between two or more Filipino gay men. Although there were a couple of U.S.-born Filipino gay men who understood and even used swardspeak, the argot was seen as part of an immigrant's cultural baggage. See my essay (Manalansan, 1994) for a more extensive discussion of the subject matter.

References

Austin, J. L. (1962). *How to do things with words.* Cambridge, MA: Harvard University Press.

Langness, L. L., & Frank, G. (1981). *Lives: An anthropological approach to biography.* Novato, CA: Chandler & Sharpe.

Manalansan, M. (1994). Talking about AIDS: Language and the Filipino "gay" experience in America. In V. Rafael (Ed.), *Discrepant histories: Translocal essays on Philippine cultures.* Philadelphia: Temple University Press.

Personal Narratives Group. (1989). *Interpreting women's lives: Feminist theory and personal narratives.* Bloomington: Indiana University Press.

Watson, L. C., & Watson-Franke, M. B. (1985). *Interpreting life histories: An anthropological inquiry.* New Brunswick, NJ: Rutgers University Press.

18

Throwing the Baby Out With the Bath Water
Situating Young Filipino Mothers and Fathers Beyond the Dominant Discourse on Adolescent Pregnancy

Antonio T. Tiongson Jr.

The "Problem"

According to the latest health assessment report of Filipinos in San Francisco (Pilipino Health Mini-Forums Committee, 1993), Filipino teens have the highest pregnancy rates among Asians (6.7%) and, in 1991, had the highest rate of increase in the number of births (65%) compared to African Americans, Latinas, whites, and other Asian groups (see Table 18.1).

In 1992, all ethnic groups exhibited a decline in total number of births to resident teens. Filipino teens, however, had the smallest percentage of

TABLE 18.1 Number of Births to Filipinas Who Are San Francisco
Residents, by Age Group

Year	Age			
	12-15	16-17	18-19	Total
1990	0	5	29	34
1991	7	17	32	56
1992	5	15	32	52

SOURCE: Birth records of the San Francisco Department of Public Health, 1990-1992.

decrease in total number of births among all ethnic groups. As a result,
Filipinos accounted for 7% of all teen births in San Francisco compared
to 6.7% in 1991 (see Table 18.2).

▓

Resetting the Stage

The data on San Francisco teen births seem straightforward. The numbers on Filipino adolescents indicate that there is a problem and that
something ought to be done. But how should we define and describe the
problem? Is it attributable to a decay in traditional family and moral
values? Or is lack of access to contraceptive and abortion services to
blame? Numbers do not speak for themselves; they are interpreted.
Describing the problem as a moral or economic one lies in the interpretation of the data and is not inherent in the data themselves.

How the problem of adolescent childbearing is posed and framed is
no small matter; it often corresponds to how it will be addressed. In other

TABLE 18.2 Percentage of Teen Births to San Francisco Resident Teens,
by Race/Ethnicity

Year	African American	Hispanic	White	Filipino	Chinese
1991	38	33.5	8.5	6.7	2.0
1992	33	28.7	9.0	7.0	2.0

SOURCE: Birth records of the San Francisco Department of Public Health, 1991-1992.

words, the interventions would look very different if the problem was defined as a matter of better managing sexual activity as opposed to rampant teen promiscuity. How do we go about addressing pregnancy among adolescent Filipinas/os?

The Dominant Discourses on Adolescent Childbearing

According to Nathanson (1991), there are three prevailing and competing discourses on adolescent pregnancy. The medical construction of teen pregnancy focuses on the negative health consequences of unprotected sex. The emphasis is on the adolescent's contraceptive behavior to prevent pregnancy and the adverse effects associated with it. Sex is inevitable, and, therefore, the focus is on how to best manage it by providing adolescents with facts and information on contraception and decision making. Adolescent pregnancy is categorized with other adolescent health problems such as acne and menstrual cramps.

For moral conservatives, the focus shifts from the consequence of sex to sexual intercourse itself. Moral conservatives question the inevitability of the sex. Sex poses a threat to the young mother's health and leads to other problematic behaviors such as abortion. Safe sex refers to abstinence, not the use of contraception. The use of contraception undermines and removes sanctions that one faces (or rather, that females face) when engaging in sex—namely, pregnancy and childbirth. Moreover, adolescent sex and pregnancy are immoral, symbols of moral and social decay of this country, and they undermine traditional family and gender norms.

The economic construction links adolescent pregnancy with public assistance and welfare spending; welfare payments actually encourage adolescent pregnancy. In this scenario, single parenthood is problematic because it costs the state and encourages teens to opt for public funds instead of looking for work. Moreover, early pregnancy compromises a young mother's future and is a direct path to poverty. Pregnant teens are more likely to drop out of school and are likely to end up in low-paying, low-prestige jobs. The economic construction equates teen pregnancy with teen mothers on welfare (perceived to be predominantly African American).

Limitations of the Prevailing Discourses

Many people subscribe to the foregoing arguments. They have intuitive appeal in that they seem to take into account much of what is wrong with America today and do so in a parsimonious way. Moreover, childbearing does make life more difficult for young mothers and their children, even though research indicates these adverse effects may not be as devastating and pervasive as once thought (Furstenberg, Brooks-Gunn, & Chase-Lansdale, 1989). But just how well do these stories capture the realities, experiences, and struggles of young parents? Also, are the difficulties that young mothers and their children confront attributable to the premature timing of childbirth, or are other factors involved?

The public knows only a distorted picture of teen pregnancy. If there was an epidemic of teen pregnancy, it would have been during the 1950s, when adolescents were having twice as many babies compared to previous decades. Since the 1950s, young adolescent females have been bearing children at about the same rate for most of the century (Vinovskis, 1988). Moreover, contrary to the image that the phrase "children having children" evokes, a majority (about 60%) of teenage mothers are 18 or 19 when they have babies, ages considered legal adulthood in most states (cited in Luker, 1996). Also, 70% of children born to unmarried parents are born to mothers 20 years and older (Hollander, 1996). Furthermore, the partners of young mothers are often adults, not boys. For example, in 1988, 65% of women ages 15 to 19 who became parents had male partners who were 20 years of age and older (Landry & Forrest, 1995; Males, 1996). In addition, though African American teens account for a large proportion of young mothers, 57% of all babies born to unmarried teens are born to white adolescents (cited in Luker, 1996).

The term *teenage* or *adolescent pregnancy* is problematic because it implies that adolescent pregnancy is just as problematic to a 12-year-old as it is to a 19-year-old. It also implies that the problem is that of a female alone because only females get pregnant. The term itself is a misnomer and misleading because "negative consequences of adolescent pregnancy described in policy and programmatic literature are, literally, the consequences of parenthood (childbirth), not pregnancy" (Nathanson, 1991, p. 163).

Furthermore, the assumption that early childbearing results in poverty and its corollary, that young women can avoid difficult lives by postponing childbearing, are both incorrect. About 80% of adolescents are already poor even before they give birth (Alan Guttmacher Institute, 1994). A disproportionate number of young mothers grow up in dilapidated neighborhoods and abusive homes, often having to attend run-down schools and lacking access to health care. Young mothers often have lower aspirations and are not as motivated to succeed in school and at a career even before pregnancy (Luker, 1996). In other words, young mothers are different from individuals who delay childbearing on many variables, not just on the timing of their child's birth, and in most cases, these differences predate the pregnancy.

Moreover, delaying conception is unlikely to enhance the lives of young mothers. They still wake up to a health system that does not address their needs, a school system that does not prepare them to compete in a global economy, and a job market in which the only jobs available pay minimum wage and do not provide child care regardless of whether these women delay childbirth or not.

For many, there will never be an appropriate age to bear a child if this is measured in terms of obtaining the financial means to support themselves and their children adequately. As Luker (1996) put it, "Although it is true young mothers tend to be poor women, it is much more meaningful to say that poor women tend to become young mothers" (p. 12).

Moreover, a large proportion of health risks associated with early childbearing for the mother and her child are significantly reduced if both have access to routine medical and prenatal care. When socioeconomic status is taken into account, differences between children of young mothers (over 15) and those of older mothers are negligible (Hayes, 1987; Makinson, 1985).

The purported link between early childbearing and dropping out of school is suspect as well. For example, Upchurch and McCarthy (1990) found in their study that childbearing among high school students did not lead to dropping out of school. Instead, the effects of childbirth were seen among high school dropouts: Childbirth made it less likely for these students to return to school and graduate.

The link between welfare and teen pregnancy is also untenable. Contrary to popular belief, welfare rolls are not saturated with young mothers. Teens made up fewer than 1 in 10 of mothers receiving Aid to Families with Dependent Children (AFDC) in the United States (Hollander, 1996). Does welfare dependency fuel teen pregnancy? Absolutely not. If it did, then why does the United States have one of the highest proportions of teen mothers, despite providing less support for single mothers than any other industrialized nation (Sorrentino, 1990)? Why, in states in which welfare spending is more generous, do we not see a higher rate of childbearing (Males, 1996)?

The dominant discourses themselves are problematic as well. Their focus on the individual precludes focusing on structural factors, such as inadequate pre/postnatal care and lack of meaningful jobs, that account for many of the problems attributed to teen pregnancy. As Rhode (1993) observed:

> Insufficient attention has focused on the societal level, on structures that offer female (and male) adolescents "too little too late": too little reason to stay in school, too little assistance in birth control, too little opportunity for child care, health services, vocational training or decent jobs, and too little understanding of the responsibilities of single parenthood. (p. 302)

Living in abject circumstances makes motherhood and fatherhood an attractive and positive choice for many adolescents.

Focusing on the individual also precludes deconstructing conventional ideas of masculinity and femininity, constructions that problematize the sexuality of females while accepting that of males as natural and inevitable. It fails to question a double standard. Why has society been preoccupied historically and currently with controlling the sexual behavior of females but not that of males (Nathanson, 1991)? It fails to question the assumption that equates a female's reproductive capacities with her destiny. It fails to ask why males are omitted from the discourse on adolescent pregnancy as if "pregnancy occur[red] via the stork" (Rhode, 1993, p. 318). It precludes focusing on images and practices that stigmatize adolescent mothers as promiscuous and as whores bearing children at the expense of public money; it implies that these young women assume the identity of welfare recipient as a badge of honor. It fails to take into account how these women are bombarded by images and messages that encourage female teens to dress and behave seductively but chastise them for engaging in sex or even preparing for sex (Rhode, 1993).

Finally, the dominant discourses fail to take into account sexual and reproductive changes affecting all of us in profound and significant ways across class, ethnicity, and age and tend instead to portray teens as the only population affected by these changes. Gender roles have changed. Women are increasingly becoming part of the workforce and are giving birth later and to fewer children. Sex is increasingly occurring outside the context of procreation and marriage. Childbearing is increasingly occurring outside of marriage. More and more people are living together not as a prelude to marriage but as a lifestyle instead of marriage, and fewer of us are part of "traditional" nuclear families (Wetzel, 1990).

Sex and Filipino Culture

A strong moral undercurrent informs Filipino cultural practices related to sex because of the influence of Catholicism in the Philippines. Sex is seldom discussed within the family (see Chapter 15, this volume). Abstaining from sex until marriage is encouraged, especially among young Filipinas. Maintaining a "good" reputation is emphasized among young Filipinas, and young Filipinos are strongly encouraged to complete their education and embark on a career before marriage. Dating, sex, and childbearing are to occur within the context of marriage. Contraception use and abortion are immoral. Filipino parents often struggle raising their children in a culture with more permissive sexual mores, and Filipino children often have to negotiate between conflicting sexual values at home and those from the larger society.

I do caution against making simplistic and causal links between Filipino cultural practices and sexual behavior of young Filipinas/os. The relationship between the two is complex and indirect, mediated by variables such as socioeconomic status and reproductive changes affecting all of us. For example, according to Rosaly Ferrer, a health educator in San Francisco who works predominantly with Filipino American teens, many of the Filipino teens she works with opt to have an abortion, a trend one would not expect in a predominantly Catholic community (Almendrala, 1993).

Where to Begin

What does this mean for young Filipino mothers and fathers? It is clear that we must go beyond the dominant discourses to address truly and humanely the needs of young Filipino mothers and fathers. Conspicuously absent from the dominant discourses on teen pregnancy are the voices and experiences of those whose needs and welfare are purportedly addressed by the dominant discourses. This is where I believe we need to begin. We must go beyond and behind the data and discourses on teen pregnancy and listen to the stories young Filipino mothers and fathers have to tell rather than only attending to how society portrays them. I conducted interviews with Filipinas/os who became young mothers and fathers. Following are their stories, a glimpse into their worlds and experiences.

Rearticulations

Janette was 17 when she found out she was pregnant. The news came as a complete surprise to her: "No, it could not be because we were using something." Another teenager, Joey, was also stunned at the news he was going to be a father at 16 years of age. "I was surprised. I should not have been because basically we had unprotected sex."

April, 17 years old at the time, suspected she might be pregnant because she had been sick and tired. When she did find out, April knew she was not going to have the baby and opted for abortion instead. She says, "I was antiabortion early on in high school but found out my older sister got pregnant when she was young and had an abortion. Until you are in that position, you can't tell whether you are antiabortion or prochoice." Janette initially decided to have an abortion. While waiting for the doctor, she started feeling guilty and had second thoughts. When she saw a bus coming, she took it home.

Although for some teens, such as Joey, abortion "is like murder, killing an unborn child," the choice was not difficult for April: "There was so much I wanted to do, and I know I could not have done it if I had a baby." April did not feel guilty after the abortion. She did want to feel guilty and sad because she felt it was inhumane not to do so. April feels that the absence of guilty feelings may be due to the fact that she was put to sleep during the process. She does not condemn herself for the decision and believes she is a good person notwithstanding the abortion.

When Janette did have her child, she took it on herself to take care of the child on her own: "When I was pregnant, I did not expect him [the father] to tell me what to do, like you know, I did not run to him saying what are we going to do now. It was all on me. I felt it was my problem." Janette feels that the father should have made more of an effort to raise their child: "Not once did the guy offer, I'll take care of the baby while you go to school, or I'll babysit him for the weekend." On the other hand, Janette feels she could have been more open with the father and made more of an effort to get him involved.

As for the prevalent image of irresponsible young fathers, Joey believes that "there are people out there like that. But then there are people who are pretty much responsible and geared toward raising a family at that age." Fatherhood made Joey more responsible. The most satisfying aspect of fatherhood is "watching my daughter grow up and be what she is now, real smart." Joey sees himself as a dedicated father:

> I'm 100% supportive to my daughter's needs. I can't see how a person could not. They are the biological father, they need to be there. When the child grows up they are going to wonder, have a lot of things cross their minds, where is my father, why didn't you support me? I don't want my daughter to grow up to be that way.

Sex for April, Janette, and Joey occurred within serious relationships. Joey and his partner had been together for a year. She was actually his first girlfriend. For April, it was the first time she had ever been in love. Janette had been with the father of her child for 3 years, and sex just seemed like the next logical step in the relationship.

All three found it difficult to tell their parents. Joey did not tell his parents he was a father until his daughter was born. They were initially angry but became supportive afterward. They did not pressure Joey to marry the mother and let him make the decision himself. Joey did not know "what they would accomplish by being mad, or holding a grudge, or disowning me."

Janette's parents did not know she was going to be a mother until 6 months into pregnancy. An aunt who had had a child out of wedlock gathered the family together and made the announcement. Janette's mother was furious. She considered kicking her out of the house. Janette wished her mother had been more understanding and had more faith in her.

April did not intend to tell her parents she was pregnant or reveal her decision to have an abortion. She did tell her older sister, whom she considered her mentor. Her sister was disappointed that April had not learned from her experience. When she did finally tell her parents, they, too, were disappointed that she had gotten pregnant but did support her decision to have an abortion. April wished her parents and sister had talked to her about possible alternatives. She also appreciated them for letting her make the decision herself.

Both April and Janette believe that males have it easier. April says,

> It's easier for males to think about having a child; it's not them that's directly affected. Nobody made a big deal if a guy got a girl pregnant. It's not their bodies. Women get affected more. It's her experience, her life. He can just walk out and they won't give up their lifestyle.

Janette believes males "get away with everything." Janette's parents blamed her for the pregnancy more than the father. Janette describes men as "complicated": That is, "They would just pull women down 'cause my mom, she never worked when she was together with my dad 'cause my dad said that's not the way or your place is in the house." Janette feels that the only way she is going to work and raise a child at the same time is outside marriage—in other words, by being a single mother. She "never really thought of marriage ever. I never pictured a house with my husband and I'm home comforting him after he comes from a job. I never thought of that." Ultimately, "Guys who don't get involved with their kid's life lose out the most because they miss out on their child's upbringing."

Janette, Joey, and April all scoff at politicians who tell teens to abstain from sex. Joey thinks the whole idea is "farfetched." He not only admonishes politicians for "prying into people's lives" but believes that

> they should really look because there are families who are actually doing their jobs, being able to raise a child like myself. Look at the positive side, not just the negative side 'cause I'm sure they are just

looking at the negative side, irresponsible parents. On the positive side, there are parents who raise their child. We don't smoke in front of our kids, we don't do drugs in front of our kids, we pay for our kid's education.

April thinks politicians who put all the blame on the girl are "naive" and "sexist." "It's as if girls should have all the willpower, but not guys. Politicians probably had sex early themselves." For both females, being pregnant at a young age was stigmatizing. April "did not want to be looked at as a girl who got pregnant before graduation who ruined her life." Janette was encouraged by her counselor to drop out of school and transfer to another school that did not even have the classes she needed to graduate when she told her she was pregnant. The counselor said, "Oh dear, you are so popular in school you can't stay here. We might have an epidemic."

Janette also experienced employment discrimination. Her employer would not give her time off for doctor's or dentist's appointments for her child or for certain school activities.

Joey believes that potential young fathers should really think about the responsibilities of raising a family, what it takes, before becoming one. April believes that young women "should think of themselves, how their decisions are going to affect their lives, over their parents' perceptions because they are the ones who are going to live with the decisions." Janette believes that it is foolish for young mothers to think they can do it on their own and that they also should not expect the father of their child to hang around. For Janette, "Once your child is born, best they'll do is give your child a birthday card. They are too young to know what they want."

Certain themes emerge from the foregoing stories. Young fathers and mothers negotiate with sex and issues related to it, such as pregnancy, childrearing, and abortion, in a variety of ways, just as adults do. And like adults, their coping ranges along the continuum of maturity. April, Janette, and Joey engaged in sex within the context of serious relationships, not casual relationships as many are apt to believe. Both April and Janette had to deal with sexism. Their families expected them to "have all the willpower" not to get pregnant. Societal institutions such as school and work reinforced and perpetuated the stigma associated with teen pregnancy, making it difficult if not impossible to go to school or work and raise a child at the same time. Joey, Janette, and April all expected their parents to be angry and disappointed in their decisions. Blaming them for decisions already made, moralizing on the ills of premarital sex, and talking down to them just alienated them further and exacerbated the situation they were in. What they wanted and needed was understanding, an opportunity to talk to their parents about alternatives and choices, and support for whatever decision they ultimately made. Finally, these stories demonstrate the "illegitimacy" of politicians in the lives of these young fathers and mothers. Political rhetoric is clearly not reaching them. Slogans invoked by these politicians ("just say no") fall on deaf ears and are irrelevant to the lives they are leading.

Prospects and Possibilities

These stories are not meant to provide answers or solutions to adolescent pregnancy, nor are they meant to be representative of the experiences of young Filipino mothers and fathers. By listening to these narratives, however, we can begin to pose and address questions relevant to the realities and needs of these individuals and thus expand and change the nature of the discourse on adolescent childbearing.

How do we deal with the fact that for many teens, as was the case for Joey, Janette, and April, abstinence is not a tenable option? How do we begin acknowledging that for many adolescents, motherhood and fatherhood are perceived as positive choices, or as the best option out of a number of limited and more negative choices? In Janette's case, how do we deal with the fact that single parenthood was empowering in that it enabled her to work and raise a kid at the same time? Where do we situate and how do we make room, within a discourse on adolescent pregnancy, for young fathers such as Joey who support their child? How do we go about broadening our analysis of adolescent pregnancy and attributing responsibility beyond the individual to institutions? How do we link the discourse on adolescent pregnancy with a critique of patriarchy, which renders a woman's body and sexuality problematic and an object of regulation and control (e.g., by withholding abortion funds; Rhode, 1993)? April's strong belief that decisions regarding pregnancy and abortion should be primarily the woman's may very well be an act of resistance, agency, and ownership of the body against regulation, control, and oppression. How do we go about acknowledging that marriage may not be the panacea that moral conservatives (mostly men) purport it to be? It can often be an oppressive institution for women and can exacerbate difficulties they face.

As a community, how should we respond? Should we, like moral and economic conservatives, be quick to judge and blame young fathers and mothers? Or are we going to realize that "it is neither just nor effective to condemn teenage mothers (and fathers) who make tragic choices while ignoring the constraints on choices that are available" (Rhode & Lawson, 1993, p. 24)? Do we honestly believe we can effectively address paternity and make fathers more accountable for their actions without ensuring that they are able to fulfill these responsibilities? It is easy to blame fathers or their inability and/or unwillingness to fulfill their responsibilities, but we should not forget that "our society's irresponsible behavior toward teenage parents and their children is no less critical than the irresponsibility of the fathers we are so quick to condemn" (Adams, Pitman, & O'Brien, 1993, p. 235). When are we going to realize that teens are "unlikely 'to just say no' to early sex and childbirth unless they have more opportunities for saying yes to something else" (Rhode & Lawson, 1993, p. 12)? Should we look to the national debate and agenda on adolescent pregnancy, even though it lacks a coherent policy and is "ahistorical, uninformed, and more attentive to political pressures than to adolescent needs" (Rhode, 1993, p. 317)?

What does this mean for young Filipino mothers and fathers? It means we cannot talk about adolescent pregnancy without talking about poverty. It is no accident that a disproportionate number of poor women are also young mothers. Instead of talking about "ending welfare as we know it," we should talk about ending the distribution of wealth and power in this country as we know it. We cannot address adolescent pregnancy without addressing the status of women in this society, as well as media and cultural practices that objectify and oppress women. We must determine how Filipino cultural practices bear on the sexual and reproductive behaviors and decisions of young Filipino men and women. We must ensure that societal institutions are responsive to our youth's needs.

Teen pregnancy cannot be reduced to economics, breakdown of family values, lack of contraceptive knowledge, or conflict between

Filipino and American values. If it is, we end up with failed and flawed policies inevitably resulting in more social regulation and control of women's bodies. These factors interact and bear on the sexual behaviors and decisions of young Filipino mothers and fathers in complex and indirect ways.

The easy way is to situate our responses within the dominant discourses on adolescent pregnancy. The more difficult but empowering and humane route is to begin building a discourse and praxis that encompass poverty and patriarchy, that reflect our vision of what constitutes a just world, that are informed by the voices and experiences of young fathers and mothers, and that enable them to move in directions other than the downward path on which society seems determined to place them.

References

Adams, G., Pitman, K., & O'Brien, R. (1993). Adolescent and young adult fathers: Problems and solutions. In D. L. Rhode & A. Lawson (Eds.), *The politics of pregnancy* (pp. 216-237). New Haven, CT: Yale University Press.

Alan Guttmacher Institute. (1994). *Sex and America's teenagers.* New York: Author.

Almendrala, L. C. (1993). Children who have children. *Filipinas, 12,* 8-10, 50-51.

Furstenberg, F. F., Jr., Brooks-Gunn, J., & Chase-Lansdale, L. (1989). Teenaged pregnancy and childbearing. *American Psychologist, 44,* 313-320.

Hayes, C. D. (1987). *Risking the future: Adolescent sexuality, pregnancy, and childbearing.* Washington, DC: National Academy Press.

Hollander, D. (1996). Nonmarital childbearing in the U.S.: A government report. *Family Planning Perspectives, 28*(1), 29-32.

Landry, D. J., & Forrest, J. D. (1995). How old are U.S. fathers? *Family Planning Perspectives, 27,* 159-161, 165.

Luker, K. (1996). *Dubious conceptions: The politics of teenage pregnancy.* Cambridge, MA: Harvard University Press.

Makinson, C. (1985). The health consequences of teenage fertility. *Family Planning Perspectives, 17,* 132-139.

Males, M. A. (1996). *The scapegoat generation: America's war on adolescents.* Monroe, ME: Common Courage.

Nathanson, C. A. (1991). *Dangerous passage: The social control of sexuality in women's adolescence.* Philadelphia: Temple University Press.

Pilipino Health Mini-Forums Committee. (1993). *Executive report: Pilipino health assessment report 1993.* San Francisco: Author.

Rhode, D. L. (1993). Adolescent pregnancy and public policy. In D. L. Rhode & A. Lawson (Eds.), *The politics of pregnancy* (pp. 301-335). New Haven, CT: Yale University Press.

Rhode, D. L., & Lawson, A. (Eds.). (1993). *The politics of pregnancy*. New Haven, CT: Yale University Press.

Sorrentino, C. (1990). The changing family in international perspective. *Monthly Labor Review, 113*(3), 41-58.

Upchurch, D. M., & McCarthy, J. (1990). The timing of first birth and high school completion. *American Sociological Review, 55,* 224-234.

Vinovskis, M. (1988). *An "epidemic" of adolescent pregnancy? Some historical and policy considerations.* New York: Oxford University Press.

Wetzel, J. R. (1990). American families: 75 years of change. *Monthly Labor Review, 113*(3), 4-13.

19

The Prevalence and Impact of Alcohol, Tobacco, and Other Drugs on Filipino American Communities

Jacqueline T. Jamero Berganio
Leonardo A. Tacata Jr.
Peter M. Jamero

There once was an elephant in the living room, but no one said anything about it. Family members walked around it, carried on their normal household activities in the cramped quarters, and pretended the elephant never existed despite its enormous mass.

An Elephant in the Living Room (Hastings & Typpo, 1983), a book often used in the substance abuse field, provides the analogy that living in a family in which there is alcoholism is a lot like living with an elephant in the living room. It illustrates how we tend to ignore or deny alcoholism in our midst. Alcoholism and other forms of chemical dependency are issues that often are not talked about. In the Filipino American communities, in particular, the "elephant" may remain hidden from sight and memory.

272

Within this chapter, we may use the terms *alcoholism, chemical dependency, substance dependency,* and *substance abuse* interchangeably. According to the criteria of the fourth edition of the *Diagnostic and Statistical Manual of Mental Disorders* (American Psychiatric Association [APA], 1994), substance abuse is defined as manifesting one (or more) of the following occurring within a 12-month period: (a) recurrent substance use leading to failure in meeting major responsibilities/obligations at work, school, and/or home; (b) recurrent substance use in situations in which there are physical hazards/dangers; (c) recurrent legal problems related to the substance use; and/or (d) continued substance use despite negative consequences—that is, chronic or recurrent social or interpersonal problems caused by or exacerbated by the effects of the substance. Furthermore, the substance abuse symptoms must not have met criteria for substance dependency for the specific class of substance.

Substance dependency may be considered a severe form of substance use that is often marked by tolerance or withdrawal. Specifically, substance dependency is defined as

> a maladaptive pattern of substance use, leading to clinically significant impairment or distress, as manifested by three (or more) of the following: (1) tolerance; (2) withdrawal; (3) the substance is often taken in larger amounts or over a longer period than was intended; (4) there is a persistent desire or unsuccessful efforts to cut down or control substance use; (5) a great deal of time is spent in activities necessary to obtain the substance, use the substance, or recover from its effects; (6) important social, occupational or recreational activities are given up or reduced because of substance use; and (7) the substance use is continued despite having knowledge of having a persistent or recurrent physical or psychological problem that is likely to have been caused or exacerbated by the substance. (APA, 1994, p. 181)

In addition, alcohol and tobacco are specific types of drugs, but we will use, when applicable, the phrase *alcohol, tobacco, and other drugs (ATOD)* to provide clarity instead of using the general term *drugs.*

This chapter will explore the extent of alcohol, tobacco, and other drug problems among Filipino Americans. It will summarize the existing research and data and look at consequences and correlates of ATOD use. Furthermore, we will discuss cultural considerations, such as the part that shame and denial play in preventing or delaying an individual and his or her family from seeking help. We will also focus on the aspects of Filipino American culture that build resiliency and help to prevent ATOD problems. The chapter will conclude with recommendations for future directions and efforts to deal with the elephant in the living room.

Extent of ATOD Use

A review of the literature shows that scant attention has been paid to the issue of alcohol use among Filipino Americans (Lubben, Chi, & Kitano, 1988). Even fewer studies have focused on Filipino Americans and their use of other drugs.

Most of the substance abuse research to date has included Filipino Americans as part of larger Asian Pacific American studies. Even the body of knowledge on Asian Pacific Americans is limited, although growing. Overall, there has been a lack of support for research on substance abuse among Asian Pacific Americans (Trimble, Padilla, & Bell, 1987, cited in Austin, Prendergast, & Lee, 1989). Trimble et al. attributed the lack of such research to the unfounded belief that Asian Pacific Americans are the "model minority"—a stereotype that implies that Asian Pacific Americans do not have problems and therefore do not need targeted research and services.

The few studies and surveys that do involve Filipino Americans are summarized below. The research has been conducted primarily on the West Coast of the U.S. mainland and in Hawaii, areas that contain large populations and high densities of Filipino Americans. According to the 1990 U.S. census (U.S. Bureau of the Census, 1993, pp. 153, 159), a total of 1,419,711 Filipinos were found to reside in the United States, with more than half located in California (733,941) and Hawaii (168,282). The preponderance of studies have looked at alcohol use and, minimally, the use of other drugs. The study samples have involved adult or in-school student populations. The findings are mixed and point to the need for further research in this area, especially given the diversity among Filipino Americans.

Alcohol Use and Drinking Patterns

From 1975 to 1980, the Epidemiology Program of the Cancer Research Center of Hawaii issued an annual health survey that included specific questions about adult alcohol use (Le Marchand, Kolonel, & Yoshizawa, 1989, cited in Austin et al., 1989). Whites and Native Hawaiians had the highest proportions of drinkers, and alcohol consumption was more frequent among Japanese than Filipinos. However, Filipinos drank more per occasion than Japanese.

A study sample of 59,766 California medical reports from 1978 to 1980 revealed that racial patterns differed in terms of alcohol use (Klatsky, Siegelaub, Landy, & Friedman, 1983). Patients self-classified their racial group and reported drinking alcoholic beverages as follows: white, 89.5%; Latin, 84.8%; Japanese, 81.9%; black, 79.8%; Chinese, 68.1%; and Filipino, 63.9%.

A 1984 survey by Hawaii's Department of Health reported the highest alcohol use and heaviest drinking among Native Hawaiians, followed by Filipinos and then Japanese (Murakami, 1989, cited in Austin et al., 1989).

A survey of male college students reported the highest proportion of alcohol users among whites, then Hawaiians, with the lowest proportion of drinkers among Chinese and Filipinos, and with Japanese falling in the midrange (Danko et al., 1988, cited in Austin et al., 1989). A similar pattern was found for the female college students except that the highest proportion of alcohol users was among the Hawaiian/part-Hawaiian group.

In a study of 3,712 adult (ages 20 and over) residents of Oahu, six different racial-ethnic groups were assessed in regard to their reasons for using alcohol, abstaining from alcohol, or ceasing to use alcohol (Johnson, Schwitters, Wilson, Nagoshi, & McClearn, 1985). The groups were persons of Caucasian, Chinese, Filipino, Hawaiian (including part-Hawaiian), Hapa-Haole (having both Asian and Caucasian ancestry), and Japanese descent. There were approximately twice as many male respondents as female respondents in each group except for the Hapa-Haole group, which had nearly an equal number of men and women. The number of Filipinos sampled was 654.

A higher proportion of Filipinos was abstainers (31.0%) compared with the other groups: Chinese (17.7%), Japanese (16.7%), Hawaiian/ part-Hawaiian (11.1), Hapa-Haole (7.0%), and Caucasian (4.3%). However, the Filipinos who did drink did so more often for relatively pathological reasons (e.g., drinking when tense, when worried, when wishing one was a different person, when one's conscience is bothering one, when shy, when angry, when sad). The authors stated, "There may be historical reasons for this anomaly; for example, Filipinos were the last major wave of plantation workers imported to Hawaii" (Johnson et al., 1985, p. 287).

Further analysis of the same data set as above (involving more than 3,700 residents of Oahu) provided support for the notion that cultural norms are important determinants of the level of alcohol use and probably the risk of alcoholism (Johnson, Nagoshi, Ahern, Wilson, & Yuen, 1987). Current use of alcohol was lower among foreign-born Filipinos (41.1%) than among Filipinos born in the United States (64.8% for Hawaii and 50.0% for the mainland or territories). Conversely, a greater proportion of abstainers was among the foreign-born Filipino group (39.6%) compared with those born on the U.S. mainland or in U.S. territories (20.0%) and in Hawaii (15.1%).

One study in Los Angeles focused solely on drinking behavior among Filipino American adults (Lubben et al. 1988). A total of 230 adults was included in the sample (145 men and 85 women). A nonprobability sample was drawn from a listing of Filipino American clients that was provided by local community organizations. The majority of the Filipino Americans was highly educated (some college education), born in the Philippines (97%), predominantly Catholic, and regular churchgoers.

The results revealed that approximately 50% of the Filipino women (Filipinas) were abstainers, whereas 80% of the Filipino men were drinkers. One third of the men were heavy drinkers. Only regular attendance at religious services significantly predicted both male and female drinking behavior (i.e., frequent participation in religious services distinguished Filipino men who were not heavy drinkers from men who were and distinguished Filipina abstainers from drinkers). The authors suggested further research to determine why Filipino male drinking conforms more to a Western pattern, whereas Filipina drinking fits the Asian pattern.

A final study that involved Filipinos looked at adult male patterns of drinking among four different Asian groups (Chi, Lubben, & Kitano,

1988). The study sample included 335 adult Asian males of Los Angeles who were between the ages of 19 and 39 years old. A random sampling technique that extracted names from a Los Angeles telephone directory was used to identify the Chinese, Japanese, and Korean groups. The Filipino sample was identified as discussed in the above study by Lubben et al. (1988). The sample included 81 Filipinos (average age of 29), who were most likely to be foreign born, married, college educated, and relatively well paid (median income of $27,000) and not to have English as their primary language.

One third of the Filipino young adult males were heavy drinkers, and only a small percentage (9.9%) was abstainers. Japanese made up the highest proportions of heavy drinkers at 44%, followed by Filipinos (33%), Koreans (26%), and Chinese (17%). Among Filipinos, income was negatively related to heavy drinking. Filipino heavy drinkers were more likely to go to bars or nightclubs and have friends who also drank alcohol.

Other Drug Use

A 1987 survey conducted in schools throughout Hawaii provided specific substance use data among six ethnic groups in Hawaii: Filipino, Japanese, Hawaiian/part-Hawaiian, white, "mixed," and "other." Among 12th graders, Filipinos and those who identified as "other" both showed the lowest prevalence of alcohol and other drug use (81%) compared with Japanese and mixed (86%), and whites and Hawaiians/part-Hawaiians (91%) (Anderson & Deck, 1987, cited in Austin et al., 1989). Filipino and Japanese seniors also had the largest percentages of low-level substance users. This survey also showed a similar pattern for lifetime use of illicit drugs, except that Japanese reported the lowest drug usage at 39%, followed by Filipinos at 41%.

A household study of 1,406 residents (43.1% male, 56.4% female) of the island of Oahu in Hawaii showed that the Filipino American group (*n* = 128) appeared to reflect the lowest overall lifetime prevalence of drug use (barbiturates, tranquilizers, marijuana/hashish, LSD, PCP, amphetamines, cocaine, methadone, pain drugs) as compared to the other four ethnic groups (Chinese, Japanese, Native Hawaiian, Caucasian; McLaughlin,

Raymond, Murakami, & Goebert, 1987). Lower rates were reported among Chinese only for the use of inhalants, methadone, and heroin (each 0%), compared with the Filipino rates of 0.8%, 0.4%, and 0.4%, respectively). The rates for alcohol use were Caucasian (13.6%), Native Hawaiian (11.0%), Filipino (6.7%), and Japanese and Chinese (both 5.2%).

Recent smoking rates among Asian Pacific Americans have been reported as follows: 24% for Filipinos and 35.8% for Koreans in California (Burns & Peirce, 1992).

Another study of Asian Americans reported the highest prevalence of smoking among Filipino American men (32.9%), compared with "other Asians" (30.9%), Japanese (22.7%), and Chinese (16.2%; Klatsky & Armstrong, 1991). The research was conducted in northern California during the years 1978 to 1985 with 13,031 adults 18 years old and above.

This study also showed a different pattern for Filipino American women. The Filipina American group constituted the second-to-lowest percentage of smokers among the Asian American groups. The prevalence rates for female smokers were Chinese (7.3%), Filipinos (11.4%), other Asians (12.6%), and Japanese (18.6%).

Similar results in terms of gender differences were demonstrated in a 1991 telephone survey of 1,312 Filipinos in California who were 12 years old and older (Asian American Health Forum, 1991). Filipino American males had higher rates of smoking (20%) than the females (6.7%). The prevalence rates were lower in the latter study, a finding that may be due to the younger population sampled and the methodology used.

The study also showed that Filipino Americans were more likely to smoke (a) if they tended to speak or think in a Filipino dialect rather than in English and (b) if they were in the presence of friends who smoked.

Consequences and Correlates of ATOD Use

We have established that Filipino Americans do use substances, although the precise patterns are not clear. This ambiguity is further compounded by our reliance on data that are 10 years old. However, despite these

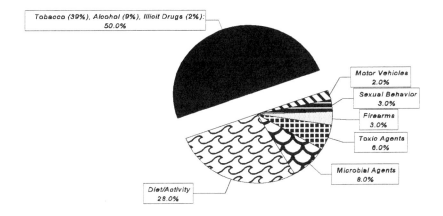

Tobacco (39%), Alcohol (9%), Illicit Drugs (2%): 50.0%

Motor Vehicles 2.0%

Sexual Behavior 3.0%

Firearms 3.0%

Toxic Agents 6.0%

Microbial Agents 8.0%

Diet/Activity 28.0%

Figure 19.1. Causes of Preventable Deaths in 1990
SOURCE: Center for Substance Abuse Prevention (1995).

shortcomings, the question we will address next is, What are the consequences and correlates of ATOD use or abuse?

ATOD use/abuse is a serious problem that has personal, social, and economic costs. Annually, about 120,000 deaths in the United States are attributed to alcohol and the use of illicit drugs (Center for Substance Abuse Prevention [CSAP], 1995). In addition, more than 400,000 deaths are due to tobacco use. Combined, the death toll from alcohol, tobacco, and other drugs represents 50% of all preventable deaths. Figure 19.1 shows the major causes of the 1,060,000 preventable deaths in 1990.

Alcohol and other drug use has been implicated as a factor in a host of other problems, including violence, injury, child abuse and neglect, HIV/AIDS, sexually transmitted diseases, teen pregnancy, school failure, car crashes, escalating health care costs, low worker productivity, and homelessness (CSAP, 1993). Among the alarming statistics:

- Alcohol and other drugs are a factor in 45.1% of all fatal automobile crashes and 20% of all injury accidents (FARS, National Highway Traffic Safety Administration, 1993, 1994, cited in CSAP, 1996d).
- Between 20% and 35% of suicide victims had a history of alcohol abuse or were drinking shortly before their suicide completion (Seventh Special

Report to the U.S. Congress on Alcohol and Health, January 1990, cited in CSAP, 1996b).

- Heavy alcohol use by women during pregnancy can result in Fetal Alcohol Syndrome, the leading known environmental cause of mental retardation (U.S. Department of Health and Human Services, 1993, cited in CSAP, 1996c).

Statistics alone, however, cannot convey the personal tragedies that may affect an individual, family, or community affected by substance use. It is difficult to depict the pain and suffering due to ATODs. The scenarios may be different, such as the death of a loved one due to an alcohol-related automobile crash or the loss and devastation following a family member's drug overdose; however, substance use remains a common denominator.

Cultural Considerations

Given the devastating negative effects of ATOD use, we need to look at the barriers that keep Filipino American individuals and families from seeking help for alcoholism and addictions. This does not mean to imply that Filipino Americans do not enter chemical dependency treatment or seek help through other means, including self-help groups such as Alcoholics Anonymous and Narcotics Anonymous. Many individuals are recovering from alcoholism and addiction and are leading clean and sober lives. However, there are cultural values that may hinder Filipino Americans from taking that first step toward recovery.

One of the cultural barriers is shame. Alcoholism and substance abuse may be viewed as a moral problem and a sign of weakness. The Filipino word *hiya* has several meanings, including bringing of shame on oneself or one's family (Paguio, 1991). The word is part of the larger phrase *walang hiya*, which means ungratefulness to the family circle or to society as a whole. Individuals may deny that a problem exists for fear of dishonoring their family name. In addition, disclosure of substance abuse may lead to sanctions such as losing a job or being ostracized. An overwhelming sense of *hiya* (as shame or guilt) may lead to suicide.

An example of *hiya* has been found in the article "A Life Maternal" (Babst-Vokey, 1996) in *Filipinas* (a monthly magazine for the Filipino American community). The author heaped praise on certain "worthy" mothers, then wrote:

> There are other mothers who have no right to be mothers; pregnant women on drugs and alcohol, who care more for their addiction than for the life growing in their abused bodies; still they bring children into the world whose lives will be an endless playing out of pain and defeat. (p. 67)

These mothers are blamed, in a voice of indignation. Nowhere can be found a sense of compassion for the pregnant woman who may be caught up in her addiction. She may not understand the consequences of substance use on her child—and might benefit immensely from an intervention by a health professional or chemical dependency counselor. She may want desperately to get clean and sober for herself and her child but lack the resources or support for treatment. Furthermore, the author of the article conveys the fatalistic attitude that her children will be doomed to this legacy of "pain and defeat."

As illustrated above, guilt and shame are often used as a form of social control in Filipino American communities (Anderson, 1983). This is not to suggest that *hiya* does not have its positive aspects, but when applied to substance abuse, *hiya* may interfere with an individual's ability to deal constructively with his or her problem.

Other aspects of Filipino American culture are also important to acknowledge. Similar to *hiya*, these cultural values have both positive and negative implications. Filipino Americans tend to have a strong family orientation. A *pakikisama* system (translated to mean "smooth personal relationships") was developed to ensure harmony (Paguio, 1991). In a healthy family system, *pakikisama* may be reflected in sociability, acceptance, and agreeability. To strengthen and maintain family bonds, individuals may refrain from "speaking their minds" because they do not want to hurt another person's feelings. Within a family system that is dysfunctional due to chemical abuse or dependency, *pakikisama* may take the form of noncommunication and codependency. Individuals living in this situation are likely to avoid a confrontation with the substance abuser and probably will not discuss how they are affected by the substance use. In typical codependent behavior, the individual learns key messages: Don't talk, don't trust, don't feel. The codependent family member may also take on additional responsibilities to cover for the chemically dependent person and circumvent the core issue. In the name of *pakikisama*, family members may also become alienated or isolated.

Paguio also defines the term *bayanihan* (literally meaning "moving a house") to signify the spirit of cooperation or unity among individuals of a group. In addition, *utang ng loob* (literally meaning "internal debt of gratitude") has its roots in mutual support and interdependence. The *utang ng loob* norm contains the element of reciprocity: If I do you a favor, you will owe me one in return. Again, these terms may mean different things depending on the situation. For example, an individual may be bonded to a "positive" group, such as his or her family, the church, or a community organization. Alternatively, as applied to substance abuse, an individual may be aligned with a "negative" group, such as drug-using peers, a "gang," or an alcoholic/addicted family.

It is not clear what exact role these values play in terms of substance abuse. However, the current research in resiliency does emphasize that key protective factors, such as caring and supportive relationships, high expectations, and opportunities to participate and contribute, may help prevent individuals from developing later problems, such as substance abuse (Bernard, 1991). Bernard advocates: "We must work within our families, schools, and community environments to build social bonds by providing all individuals with caring and support, relating to them with high expectations, and giving them opportunities to be active participants in their family, school, and community life" (p. 8).

Future Directions and Efforts

This chapter has attempted to address the issue of ATOD use among Filipino Americans. We believe that the mixed findings raise more questions and point to the need for further research focused on Filipino Americans. We would especially encourage expanding the knowledge base in regard to the prevalence of ATOD use and the factors that may increase or decrease the risk for alcoholism and substance abuse. Specifically, additional research is needed to determine why Filipino male drinking conforms more to a Western pattern of heavy drinking, whereas Filipino female drinking fits the Asian pattern. Is this due to the influence of religion—that is, are more Filipino American women than men involved in religious services? Perhaps the answer lies in gender role differences that allow Filipino American men more freedom to frequent bars and lounges but sanction women who engage in similar behaviors, so that their substance abuse is "underground" and hidden from public view. Another hypothesis is that Filipino American women are more adaptable and have more protective factors that build resiliency. Finally, the research to date may simply be inadequate in terms of including sufficient numbers of Filipino American women in studies that allow us to draw any conclusions.

We need to look at *hiya* and other Filipino cultural values and determine how they contribute to substance abuse or help prevent ATOD problems. We need to explore the meaning of *hiya, pakikisama, bayanihan,* and *utang ng loob* so that we can better understand how they are applied in our society and what their exact relationship to substance abuse is.

A 4-year landmark study is now under way that promises to add to the baseline knowledge of research on alcohol-related problems among Filipino Americans (Asian American Recovery Services, Inc., 1996). The Filipino American Community Epidemiological Study (FACES) is the first large-scale study of its kind. It will focus on the San Francisco Bay Area and the city and county of Honolulu, two areas with large populations and densities of Filipino Americans. A total of 3,200 respondents will be interviewed in regard to alcohol-related issues, as well as other underresearched areas such as acculturation, family and gender roles, and domestic violence. The research project of Asian American Recovery Services, Inc., is funded by the National Institute of Alcoholism and Alcohol Abuse (NIAAA) and the National Institutes of Health's Office of Minority Health.

There is a need to continue research with Filipino Americans in California and Hawaii—regions that account for more than half of the entire Filipino American population (U.S. Bureau of the Census, 1993)—but we also need to move beyond these geographic areas. Prevalence and patterns of alcohol and other drug consumption are likely to be different with populations in California and Hawaii, as compared to the rest of the country.

We also need to advocate for more appropriate data gathering in surveys so that the data are disaggregated by specific Asian and Pacific Islander ethnicity. Too few surveys report specific findings for Filipino Americans; most include them under the broader category of Asian Pacific Americans.

Finally, despite the bleak outlook in terms of federal and local funding for the chemical dependency field, more culturally competent programs are required to educate our communities about ATOD and prevent and treat alcoholism and substance abuse among Filipino Americans. It is our hope that FACES and other projects and studies will bring more visibility and answers to the problem of substance abuse in Filipino American communities.

References

American Psychiatric Association. (1994). *Diagnostic and statistical manual of mental disorders* (4th ed.). Washington, DC: Author.

Anderson, J. N. (1983). Health and illness in Pilipino immigrants. *Western Journal of Medicine, 139,* 811-819.

Anderson, P. S., & Deck, D. (1987). *Student substance use and abuse in Hawaii: Analytic report.* Portland, OR: Northwest Regional Educational Laboratory.

Asian American Health Forum. (1991). *Filipino smoking prevalence survey.* Unpublished manuscript.

Asian American Recovery Services, Inc. (1996). *Filipino American Community Epidemiological Study (FACES) project description materials.* Unpublished document, San Francisco.

Austin, G. A., Prendergast, M. L., & Lee, H. (1989). *Substance abuse among Asian American youth* (Prevention Research Update 5). Portland, OR: Western Regional Center Drug-Free Schools and Communities, Northwest Regional Educational Laboratory.

Babst-Vokey, A. (1996, May). A life maternal. *Filipinas,* p. 67.

Bernard, B. (1991). Fostering resiliency in kids: Protective factors in the family, school, and community. In Western Regional Center for Drug-Free Schools and Communities (Comp.), *Turning the corner from risk to resiliency: A compilation of articles from the Western Center News.* Portland, OR: Northwest Regional Educational Laboratory.

Burns, D., & Peirce, J. P. (1992). *Tobacco use in California 1990-91.* Sacramento: California Department of Health Services.

Center for Substance Abuse Prevention. (1993). *Discussion paper on preventing alcohol, tobacco and other drug problems.* Rockville, MD: U.S. Department of Health and Human Services.

Center for Substance Abuse Prevention. (1995). *Drug-free for a new century: A chart book.* Rockville, MD: U.S. Department of Health and Human Services. [Included in media kit referenced in Center for Substance Abuse Prevention, 1996]

Center for Substance Abuse Prevention. (Comp.). (1996a). *Making prevention work: Media kit.* Rockville, MD: U.S. Department of Health and Human Services.

Center for Substance Abuse Prevention. (1996b). *Making the link: Alcohol and other drugs and suicide* [Fact sheet]. In Center for Substance Abuse Prevention (Comp.), *Making prevention work: Media kit.* Rockville, MD: U.S. Department of Health and Human Services.

Center for Substance Abuse Prevention. (1996c). *Making the link: Alcohol, tobacco, and other drugs and pregnancy and parenthood* [Fact sheet]. In Center for Substance Abuse Prevention (Comp.), *Making prevention work: Media kit.* Rockville, MD: U.S. Department of Health and Human Services.

Center for Substance Abuse Prevention. (1996d). *Making the link: Impaired driving, injury, and trauma and alcohol and other drugs* [Fact sheet]. In Center for Substance Abuse Prevention (Comp.), *Making prevention work: Media kit.* Rockville, MD: U.S. Department of Health and Human Services.

Chi, I., Lubben, J. E., & Kitano, H. H. L. (1988). Heavy drinking among young adult Asian males. *International Social Work, 31,* 219-229.

Danko, G. P., Johnson, R. C., Nagoshi, C. T., Yuen, S. H. L., Gidley, J. E., & Anh, M. (1988). Judgments of "normal" and "problem" alcohol use as related to reported alcohol consumption. *Alcoholism: Clinical and Experimental Research, 12,* 760-768.

Hastings, J. M., & Typpo, M. T. (1983). *An elephant in the living room: A guide for working with children of alcoholics.* Minneapolis: CompCare.

Johnson, R. C., Nagoshi, C. T., Ahern, F. M., Wilson, J. R., & Yuen, S. H. L. (1987). Cultural factors as explanations for ethnic group differences in alcohol use in Hawaii. *Journal of Psychoactive Drugs, 19*(1), 67-75.

Johnson, R. C., Schwitters, S. Y., Wilson, J. R., Nagoshi, C. T., & McClearn, G. E. (1985). A cross-ethnic comparison of reasons given for using alcohol, not using alcohol or ceasing to use alcohol. *Journal of Studies on Alcohol, 46,* 283-288.

Klatsky, A. L., & Armstrong, M. A. (1991). Cardiovascular risk factors among Asian Americans living in northern California. *American Journal of Public Health, 81,* 1423-1428.

Klatsky, A. L., Siegelaub, A. B., Landy, C., & Friedman, G. D. (1983). Racial patterns of alcoholic beverage use. *Alcoholism: Clinical and Experimental Research, 7,* 372-377.

Le Marchand, L., Kolonel, L. N., & Yoshizawa, C. N. (1989). Alcohol consumption patterns among five major ethnic groups in Hawaii: Correlations with incidence of esophageal and oropharyngeal cancer. In National Institute on Alcohol Abuse and Alcoholism (Ed.), *Alcohol use among U.S. ethnic minorities* (NIAAA Research Monograph 18, DHHS Pub. No. ADM 89-1435, pp. 355-371). Rockville, MD: National Institute on Alcohol Abuse and Alcoholism.

Lubben, J. E., Chi, I., & Kitano, H. (1988). Exploring Filipino American drinking behavior. *Journal of Studies on Alcohol, 49*(1), 26-29.

McLaughlin, D. G., Raymond, J. S., Murakami, S. R., & Goebert, D. (1987). Drug use among Asian Americans in Hawaii. *Journal of Psychoactive Drugs, 19*(1), 85-94.

Murakami, S. R. (1989). An epidemiological survey of alcohol, drug, and mental health problems in Hawaii: A comparison of four ethnic groups. In National Institute on Alcohol Abuse and Alcoholism (Ed.), *Alcohol use among U.S. ethnic minorities* (NIAAA Research Monograph 18, DHHS Pub. No. ADM 89-1435, pp. 343-353). Rockville, MD: National Institute on Alcohol Abuse and Alcoholism.

Paguio, W. C. (1991). *Filipino cultural values for the Apostolate.* Makati, Philippines: St. Paul.

Trimble, J. E., Padilla, A., & Bell, C. S. (Eds.). (1987). *Drug abuse among ethnic minorities* (DHHS Pub. No. ADM 87-1474). Rockville, MD: National Institute on Drug Abuse.

U.S. Bureau of the Census. (1990). *United States census of population: 1990* (CP-2-1). Washington, DC: Government Printing Office.

U.S. Bureau of the Census. (1993). *United States census of population: 1990* (CP-2-1). Washington, DC: Government Printing Office.

20

The Family Tree
Discovering Oneself

Emilie Gaborne Dearing

In 1972, I was working as a psychiatric nurse practitioner in the Department of Psychiatry at a training hospital in Baltimore, Maryland. I was very fortunate and blessed to have worked for many years with a family consultant who, by using family systems theory (Bowen, 1978), guided me through the process of my family research, discovering myself in the context of my family system and within the many forces operating in my family. My consultant worked closely with Dr. Murray Bowen, who developed family systems theory. My consultant and mentor was also one of the forward thinkers in the field of family therapy at that time. The theories of Salvador Minuchin (1974), Virginia Satir (1976), and Walter Toman (1969) were also integrated in my family research and were illustrated in my understanding of my growing family tree. The writing of this chapter has been greatly influenced by my life experiences and clinical practice in the field of family therapy and mental health.

Our identity as Filipino Americans is a historical process of formation and development from birth to the present. It is a legacy of every Filipino American to the future generation. This process has been influenced and shaped by many different factors. I will discuss the myriad factors and forces by using the family tree as a graphic tool.

Definition of *Family*

Definitions of *family* vary according to one's point of view. The family as the basic unit of society has been accepted by many individuals in different cultures. The following definitions are offered for reflection and consideration. According to E. M. Berman,

> The family is a small social system made up of individuals related to each other by reason of strong reciprocal affections and loyalties, and comprised of a permanent household or cluster of households that persists over years and decades. Members enter through birth, adoption or marriages and leave only by death. (qtd. in Carter & McGoldrick, 1980, p. 23)

Bowen (1978, pp. 154-155) defined family as an emotional and relationship system in that the level of functioning of any member of the family is dependent on the functioning of other family members or the family as a whole. The behavior of one family member affects the functioning of other members.

In Western, European-derived cultures, the family is composed of the father, the mother, and their children. This is often referred to as the *nuclear family system*. The nuclear family system has changed significantly within the past three decades in the United States, so that a stepparent or stepsibling or half-sibling who lives in the home is considered part of the nuclear family. In other cultures, the family includes the grandparents, aunts, uncles, and/or cousins. In yet other cultures, the tribal system is the foundation of the family life, and the whole tribe or community is the family. Specifically, in many Filipino American families, distant relatives, godparents (or *ninong/ninang*), very close friends, and maids (or *yayas*) who take care of the children also are regarded as extended family. At present, there are individuals in the United States who consider friends and significant others as part of their family due to the caring, loving, and nurturing relationship.

Definition of the Family Tree

The family tree is a creative and visual tool for family members to learn about each other, members of the extended family, and significant others. It is a graphic representation of meaningful information, dates, and events of the family in a three-generation span. The family historian who generates this tree gathers factual information by asking the "who," "what," "where," and "when" questions. For example, some important information to include are the dates and reasons for leaving the Philippines, traveling companions on this journey, and arrival location in the United States. The family structure, patterns of communication and transactions, roles and relationships, and rituals are identified. The family resources and support systems are identified. Significant individuals who have influenced and shaped the personal identities of family members are recorded. Strengths and limitations of the family are recognized so that strengths can be enhanced and limitations or weaknesses may be corrected and compensated. Patterns of behavior between individuals or among family members across the generations can be recognized.

The family tree also marks significant events in the family. These events may include a variety of happy and joyful occasions and sad events: immigration, illness, traumatic situations, and deaths. Awareness of these events may alert the family to acknowledge the situation and prepare for anniversary dates that may trigger different and emotional images, thoughts, feelings, and behaviors among members and significant others. Illnesses, diagnoses of diseases, and hospitalizations are important factors to keep on record so that prevention efforts and health promotion activities can be maintained. In families in which there is positive genetic predisposition for addiction, diabetes, heart diseases, and other problems, the knowledge of the ages of onset is critical in managing one's health as well as the health of the family and the next generation.

This information provides personal opportunities for awareness and growth and may help establish a more meaningful personal relationship with others, both living and deceased. Ultimately, one's personal identity is also strengthened and enriched through connections with individuals who are part of one's family history.

▓

Construction of a Family Tree

To understand the structure of the family, constructing the family diagram or family tree is a basic step (Bradt, 1980; Carter & McGoldrick, 1980; Guerin, 1976; Stine, 1989). You can start your family tree by using a newsprint or sketch paper or any paper that can accommodate three generations. Symbols are used when diagramming the family tree, such as a circle for female, a square for male, a triangle for a miscarriage or abortion, and an "X" mark for death (see Figure 20.1).

The individual members are connected to each other by lines indicating their family relationships, such as husband and wife, parents and children, brothers and sisters, and other significant individuals. A horizontal line (with a short vertical line extending upward at each end) connecting a husband (square) and wife (circle) connotes a marriage. A vertical line extending downward from the horizontal line symbolizes the presence of children; persons of the same generation are on the same horizontal level. The oldest child is placed furthest left on the horizontal line, and the youngest child is located furthest right, with the middle children in between. An adopted child is indicated with the letter "A." Fraternal twins are indicated by having the vertical lines for their symbols originate from the same point on the horizontal family line. Fraternal twins may be of the same sex or different sex. Identical twins must be the same sex and are indicated by a line connecting the two symbols. This configuration of parents and children is the beginning of the family chart. A dotted line between two individuals illustrates a living-together or common-law relationship (see Figure 20.1). These are important pieces of information to be recorded in the family tree.

You are now familiar with the basic symbols used in doing the family tree. There are slight variations in the manner in which different individuals construct a family tree or family diagram. The first step is to lay down your paper with the widest side horizontally. Draw a square to

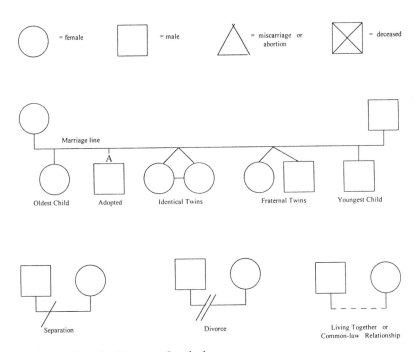

Figure 20.1. Family Diagram Symbols

designate your father at the left side of the middle of the paper. Estimate the length of where you are going to draw a circle for your mother to provide appropriate space for your siblings in between the symbols of your parents. Connect your father and mother with the short vertical and horizontal lines. Put your father's name and nickname, if any, inside the square. Add his birth date, place of birth, and date of death (if deceased) and its cause. Write down the same information for your mother.

The birth order of your siblings is next. For example, suppose you are the oldest and you have two younger sisters and a younger brother. Distribute all four siblings horizontally below the horizontal line of your father and mother. Draw your siblings using the appropriate symbols. Write down the same information noted for your father and mother. You have the basic beginning sketch of your family.

The next step is to identify the membership of your mother's family. Draw a vertical line upward from your mother's symbol, then draw a horizontal line that links your grandfather (square) and grandmother (circle). Next, draw the siblings of your mother. Once you have their rank order or birth order, you can add them to your mother's family side located on the right side of the paper. Suppose your mother is the youngest of four children with three older brothers. Draw three squares (uncles) to the left of your mother's symbol and connect each square vertically to the horizontal line. You have just finished drafting your maternal side of the family.

You are now ready to tackle your father's side of the family. Follow the same procedure of connecting an upward vertical line on the middle part of the square designating your father and draw a horizontal line connecting your paternal grandfather (square) and your grandmother (circle). Let us say that your father is one of three children. He is the middle child with an older and a younger sister. In your father's side of the diagram, you connect two circles, one on the left side of your father and the other on the right side. Write down their names and nicknames and their dates and places of birth. The draft of your three-generation family tree is initiated.

The family tree illustrated in Figure 20.2 is fictitious, but the relationships depicted are a composite of actual cases. The historian of this family is Nelly Cruz. Nelly is the third generation in the family tree (see arrow). Nelly and her husband, Jose, left the Philippines in 1982, shortly after their wedding, and moved to Brooklyn, New York. Nelly has identical twin daughters who have reached the age at which they become curious about their relatives in the Philippines. This interest served as a stimulus for Nelly to initiate a family tree.

Nelly began her family tree by diagramming her immediate family, including her parents, her only brother, her husband, and her twins. She soon discovered that she had either forgotten or never known many things about her family. To research her family further, Nelly decided to visit her family in the Philippines. Once in the Philippines, she was able to sit down with her parents and learn more about her family. Her parents were eager to tell Nelly stories about her grandparents, uncles, aunts, and cousins.

Nelly discovered that her Aunt Cecilia was actually the second wife of her Uncle Rene. Rene's first wife, Anna, had been killed in a car accident in 1954. Uncle Rene's sons, Cousin Lito and Cousin Felix, turned out to be a gambler and a drinker, respectively. Both have never married. Felix has been reported to be in a homosexual relationship. Nelly also found out that Aunt Elena's divorced husband, Martin, was living with a younger woman, just slightly older than her cousin Pepe.

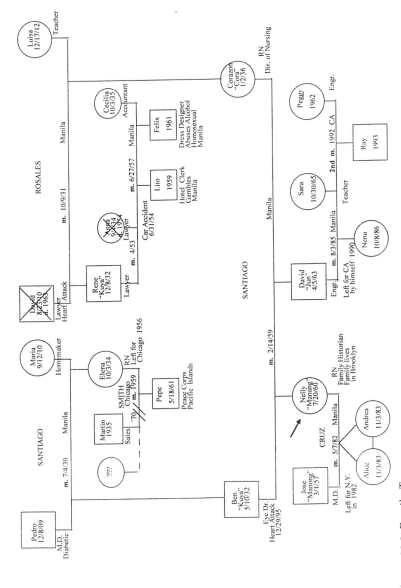

Figure 20.2. Family Tree

293

As Nelly tried to incorporate this new information into her family tree diagram, she found out that she did not have enough space. Nelly solved this problem by elongating the vertical lines for her parents and by making the symbols smaller for some of the individuals who had married into the family.

On her way back home, Nelly paid a surprise visit to the home of her brother, Jun, who was living in California and who had had very little communication with the family for over 3 years. She was eager to show him the pictures she had taken of Jun's wife, Sara, and his daughter, Nena, who were waiting for him to bring them to the United States. Nelly was shocked when she discovered that Jun had met and illegally married an American woman with whom she worked and even had a 3-year-old son by her. No one back in the Philippines had known of this relationship. Nelly had known when she undertook the task of researching her family tree that she might uncover things that might be very difficult to grasp emotionally. The actions of her brother caused her much anger, pain, and sadness, but at least now she understood her brother's lack of communication with the family.

When Nelly arrived home, she was able to sit down with her daughters and enrich their lives with the stories she had been told during her family tree research. She especially recalled the happiness exhibited by her parents as they unfolded the tales of the family. Her daughters enthusiastically traced and identified each member of the family on Nelly's family tree diagram. The daughters expressed interest in visiting the Philippines and connecting with their relatives. Nelly's next step will be to research her husband's family.

Nelly's family tree research is far from finished. She has taken the first steps in data collection. She was fortunate to obtain as much information as she did during one visit home. Most of the time, however, the collection of data is a long and tedious process.

Data Collection

Gathering information about your family is a process that can take years, especially finding information about family members residing in the

Philippines, the United States, and other parts of the globe. Patience, perseverance, and courage are tested virtues in the search for one's identity in the context of the family. Courage and the need to learn the truth are ingredients in this journey. The process is also one of excitement and fun as well as challenge because you are charting unknown areas of your family. Sadness, regrets, resentments, anger, and frustration may also be part of the journey to self-discovery. You may even uncover long-held secrets.

Finding information about your family can be done using a variety of methods such as personal visits, writing letters, telephone communication, and, of course, computer technology. The personal touch in collecting information is recommended. Basic information is supplemented with dates of marriages, separations, divorces, diagnoses, illnesses, hospitalizations, deaths, geographic moves, career changes, educational achievements, and retirements. Birthplaces, current locations, occupations, honors, awards, and other significant facts are recorded. Medical histories, especially those that are genetically based, should be highlighted. Record the dates that have importance to the family. For example, the recent eruption of Mt. Pinatubo may have had significant impact on one or more family members in the Philippines. I know that this date is vivid in my mind because my husband and I had to stay an extra week in Manila when our flight home to the United States was canceled due to the ash fall in Manila.

More subjective information is also collected, such as personality descriptions of family members, as well as values, beliefs, and stories that have been handed down from one generation to the next. Some family stories may be more difficult to obtain. For example, many people are reluctant to recall their lives during the Japanese occupation. Information on shameful events such as suicide, divorce, early pregnancy, out-of-wedlock pregnancy, murder through domestic violence, incest, and drug and alcohol abuse may be hard to get. A very opportune time for collecting information is when parents, relatives, and/or significant others visit the family for a short period of time or stay longer to help out. During this time, information gathering and sharing about members of the family can be initiated. There is a wealth of information about the family, and it takes very little energy to get family members talking about themselves and others. From experience, family history taking is a way of reminiscing the past, sharing oneself, and providing a legacy to future generations, especially the generations that were born in the United

States and may be confused in their identity or have rejected their Filipino American heritage.

Deceased individuals are significant members of the family and are recorded in the family tree. Often the deceased family members are inadvertently not included. Their stories are very important. How and when one becomes a family member are important pieces of information. For example, is it by birth, marriage, or adoption? Poorer relatives are at times taken in by more financially able relatives and become part of the household. The departures of family members through separation, divorce, or death also constitute critical data. Temporary absences of members via a long visit to the Philippines or to the United States, hospitalizations, military service, job transfers, and other circumstances that disrupt the family are written down. The incorporation of a relative into a Filipino American home is common. The length of stay of this relative can vary from a few weeks to a few months to even years. This addition to the family system has both positive and negative impact on the family system and merits documentation.

Communication

Communication is a cornerstone in human relationships. According to Virginia Satir (1976), "Communication is to relationship what breathing is to maintaining life" (p. 20). It is through communication that one is able to express needs, wants, desires, feelings, thoughts, and actions. You can easily identify these processes of communication by observing closely how your family interacts with one another. Pay attention to who calls whom, who writes to whom, and who comes and visits the family. Are individuals able to freely express their thoughts, feelings, and ideas? Is there a free exchange of information among family members? How is the information disseminated? Note the frequency of these behaviors. Is there an individual or family member who serves as the family communicator? The styles of communication used by family members are dependent on many factors, but most depend on the value and belief system of the family.

Another important aspect of family communication is the family ritual and how it is observed and practiced. Family rituals are shared observable and repeated symbolic family activities. They transmit information (values, attitudes, beliefs) about family identity across generations. Rituals clarify family roles and delineate boundaries. All families observe and practice rituals. They may be formal or informal, rigid or flexible, and most are handed down from generation to generation (Bossard & Boll, 1950; Wolin & Bennett, 1984).

Wolin, Bennett, and Jacobs (1988) categorized rituals into three groups. First, there are *family celebrations* or holidays and other occasions observed widely throughout the culture. One example is the exodus of many Filipino Americans to the Philippines during the month of December to spend Christmas with their families. Second, there are *family traditions*, which are less culture specific and more idiosyncratic to particular families. Eating together as a family is an example. Third, there are *patterned routines*, which are frequently enacted but are the least consciously planned of all the family rituals. Saying the rosary is an example of this ritual. For Filipino Americans, the identification, observance, and practice of these family rituals are basic to the development of one's identity as well as to the development of the family identity. The younger generation depends on the older generation to convey these rituals for camaraderie and to instill a sense of belonging and continuity.

In summary, I have given you a starting point for your journey to self-discovery using the family tree as a frame of reference. The process of collecting information and connecting with your family history will serve as a foundation for further enrichment and solidification of your identity and heritage.

The various patterns of communication and transactions in operations in family systems will open opportunities for an improved and higher level of functioning. The documentation of all the information collected will serve as a reference and a legacy to future generations. It is hoped that all the factors and forces enumerated in this chapter will provide the reader with another picture of how to become a proud Filipino American, a productive and significant contributor to this country, our country, the United States of America.

The final hurrah is when each and every Filipino American can truly embrace and celebrate the uniqueness of his or her personal identity and the heart and mind are open so that the richness of the many cultures are integrated in our *Being*.

▓

References

Bossard, J., & Boll, E. (1950). *Ritual in family living*. Philadelphia: University of Pennsylvania Press.

Bowen, M. (1978). *Family therapy in clinical practice*. New York: Jason Aronson.

Bradt, J. (1980). *The family diagram: Method, technique and use in family therapy*. Washington, DC: Groome Center.

Carter, E., & McGoldrick, M. (Eds.). (1980). *The family life cycle*. New York: Gardner.

Guerin, P., Jr. (Ed.). (1976). *Family therapy*. New York: Gardner.

Minuchin, S. (1974). *Families and family therapy*. Cambridge, MA: Harvard University Press.

Satir, V. (1976). *Making contact*. Berkeley, CA: Celestial Arts.

Stine, G. (1989). *The new human genetics*. Dubuque, IA: William C. Brown.

Toman, W. (1969). *Family constellation*. New York: Springer.

Wolin, S. J., & Bennett, L. A. (1984). Family rituals. *Family Process, 23*, 401-420.

Wolin, S. J., Bennett, L. A., & Jacobs, J. S. (1988). Assessing family rituals in alcoholic families. In E. Imber-Black, J. Roberts, & R. A. Whiting (Eds.), *Rituals in family therapy* (pp. 230-256). New York: Norton.

21

The Filipino American Young Turks of Seattle

A Unique Experience in the American Sociopolitical Mainstream

Peter M. Jamero

Although Filipinos have been a part of the American scene since 1763, only in more recent years have they begun to be a visible part of American sociopolitical life. In San Francisco, where thousands of pioneer Filipinos first entered the United States during the 1920s and where 42,652 still reside today (California State Data Center, 1991), it was not until 1989 that the first Filipino American was named department head in the city and county of San Francisco. In neighboring Daly City, where Filipinos constitute 35% of a population approaching 100,000 residents, it was not until 1993 that the first Filipino American was elected to the city council. Even in Hawaii, where the population density of Filipinos is the highest in the nation, it was not until 1986 that a Filipino American was elected to a statewide office.

After the first blush of these victories, the first question usually posed was "Why did it take so long?" A review of the literature suggests that the underlying reasons may be inherent in Filipinos themselves. Some observers attribute the slow ascent of Filipinos to positions of power to the lack of a strong Filipino economic, political, or social base (Cordova, 1973) or to a continuing colonial mentality (Lott, 1976). Others point to the "glass ceiling," regionalism, and factionalism (Takaki, 1989). For example, in San Diego one observer identified the proliferation of community organizations as "divisive and detrimental to Filipino American political effectiveness" (Espiritu, 1995). Still others blame the "crab mentality" of Filipinos as told in the crabs-in-the-pot story: "If one Filipino climbs to the top, other Filipinos try to pull him down" (Boylan, 1991, p. 50; Rodis, 1991). Rodis further noted that the absence of a national identity in the Filipino culture has resulted in political naiveté among Filipino Americans.

This chapter will recount the 1970s experience in Seattle, Washington, where a small group of Filipino Americans was instrumental in bringing visibility and recognition to the Seattle Filipino community as a significant element in the Seattle sociopolitical mainstream. Considering that the proportion of the population that is Filipino in Seattle is only a fraction of the proportion in San Francisco or Honolulu, its sociopolitical accomplishments are remarkable. Thanks in large part to the work of this small group, as early as the 1970s the Seattle Filipino community was able to celebrate a number of Filipino firsts, including the unprecedented election of a Filipino American to the Seattle City Council and the first-ever governor's appointment of a Filipino American to direct a statewide department. This group was the informal but highly effective band of Filipino Americans to which this chapter refers as the Filipino American Young Turks of Seattle (FAYTS). The term was inspired by the then-president of the Filipino Community of Seattle, Inc. (FCSI) who, after a FAYTS-led success in 1970, dubbed the small group "Young Turks." It is hoped that this account of the FAYTS experience during the decade of the 1970s can contribute, in a small way, to greater participation of today's Filipino communities in the American sociopolitical mainstream.

Historical Roots

The seeds of the FAYTS movement were sown in the civil rights decade of the 1960s. Activists who later would become key FAYTS players participated as individuals in marches and demonstrations supporting causes in what then was largely focused on other ethnic group concerns. Their participation gave them valuable lessons in dealing with mainstream America in terms of tactics and strategy. More important, Filipino American participation in the civil rights movement provided early visibility and lasting credibility in working with Seattle's major ethnic minorities—black, Hispanic, Asian, and Native American.

During the late 1960s and into the 1970s, Filipino Americans would take increased leadership roles in civil rights. Bob Santos, who at the time was executive director of CARITAS, an inner-city tutoring program for youth, was the most visible of the Filipino American civil rights activists. As a leader in civil demonstrations, Santos was often arrested. With the consequent media exposure that Santos received, the face of the Seattle civil rights movement began to take on a brown hue.

Systematic exclusion of ethnic-focused programs in higher education was another motivating factor for pre-FAYTS activism. Filipino American students Anthony Ogilvie and Larry Flores led a successful sit-in that, for the first time, established Asian American components within the Ethnic Studies and Equal Opportunity Programs at the University of Washington.

Ensuing antidiscrimination efforts in public education, government, labor, and private clubs drew the energies of other Filipino Americans. A number of advocacy organizations were formed, such as the Coalition Against Discrimination (CAD), the Asian Coalition for Equality (ACE), and the Filipino American Coalition for Equality (FACE). A key player in these coalitions was Andres "Sonny" Tangalin. Filipino American participants in political campaigns of Democratic congressional candidates included Dolores Sibonga and her husband Marty, publishers of a Filipino community newspaper focusing on civil rights.

By the end of the 1960s, a number of Filipino Americans had taken on visible professional and community responsibilities. Bob Santos was appointed to the Seattle Human Rights Commission, Roy Flores became the first director of the Ethnic Cultural Center at the University of Washington, and Anthony Ogilvie was named assistant director of the Office of Minority Affairs at Seattle University.

FAYTS Is Born

If FAYTS seeds were sown in the 1960s, then its bloom began in 1970 with the Tony Baruso campaign for Washington State Representative. A native of the Philippines, Baruso was well-known in Filipino community circles but had virtually no name recognition in the district he intended to represent. Furthermore, he had few people or financial resources at his disposal.

Fresh from their victories at the University of Washington, Anthony Ogilvie and the Flores brothers, Larry and Roy, were eager to support a fellow Filipino. They contacted Fred Cordova, a respected leader in the Filipino community, who was acquainted with Baruso. A small group was called together at the home of Fred and Dorothy Cordova to mount a belated campaign on behalf of the Filipino political unknown. Despite the contributions of the group, Baruso lost.

Ironically, it was in support of a failed political campaign that FAYTS first came together. This group of young Filipino Americans who had come together to help a fellow Filipino they did not know found that they had many things in common, worked well together, were socially compatible, and collectively had access to a rich array of resources, knowledge, and skills.

Common Ground

The Baruso campaign was the first sociopolitical activity in which FAYTS collective knowledge, professional skills, and community networks were focused on a Filipino American issue. By 1970, these Young Turks had developed into a close-knit group who were looking for means to move Filipino Americans onto center stage. Prior to 1970, they played largely supporting roles to other ethnic groups. Now they wanted to open doors for Filipinos to participate in the sociopolitical mainstream. This common concern for Filipino access to, and empowerment in, institutions in the wider community was the single most important defining factor that drew these young Filipino Americans together. It was their major common and sustaining bond. However, the group had other factors in common:

- Most had roots in the Central Area, the inner-city district where Seattle's ethnic minorities were concentrated and where the heart of the initial Filipino community was first situated.
- They attended common schools: Maryknoll and St. Theresa Catholic grade schools, Immaculate and O'Dea Catholic high schools, and Franklin and Garfield high schools.
- Virtually all were well educated and well read. Most had earned at least a bachelor's degree, and some were in the midst of master's or doctorate programs.
- Most were associated as youth with Filipino Youth Activities of Seattle, Inc. (FYA), where they first learned to bond and share an uncommon trust with one another.
- They had strong credibility with other ethnic communities.
- There existed an effective skill level of relating with the dominant white community nurtured through their experience in the world of work and the broader community.
- The group was relatively young; most were in their early 30s.
- All but one were American born, and only one had ever visited the Philippines. They identified themselves as Filipino Americans; their concerns were American issues.

FAYTS Nucleus

FAYTS operated as an informal, loosely structured group. FAYTS did not have officers or a single, consistent leader. It did not have written rules or a formal organization. Instead, it operated within a changing and overlapping set of leadership and supporting roles, depending on the project of the moment. Members kept in close communications with one another. Proposed issues and actions were thoroughly discussed. Developments were routinely "checked out" and verified. Fourteen young men and women formed the core of FAYTS.

- *Dorothy Cordova*, the eldest daughter of a large pioneer family with close kinship ties to the Filipino community, brought instant credibility and support for FAYTS causes. She cofounded Filipino Youth Activities (FYA), which planted the seeds for much of the initial awareness, philosophy, and commitment of FAYTS.

- *Fred Cordova*, a native of California, cofounded FYA shortly after his marriage to Dorothy in 1953. A Seattle University journalist, he not only possessed a gift for writing but also was an eloquent, forceful public speaker. He was particularly effective as a passionate spokesman of the Filipino experience in America.

- *Bob Flor*, son of a University of Washington-educated Filipino father and Caucasian mother, was a doctoral candidate in education during the early 1970s. He provided FAYTS with access to the intellectual segment of the Seattle community as well as linkage to the Democratic Party through his participation in local politics.

- *Larry Flores*, the youngest member of FAYTS, provided access to college-age Filipino Americans. His intimate street knowledge of the inner city was also valuable in opening doors to other ethnic communities. He could be counted on to ring campaign doorbells, develop grant proposals, and march in demonstrations.

- *Roy Flores*, a college administrator, brought quality organizational and analytic skills to FAYTS. He was able to interact with ethnic community leadership while also effectively communicating with the rank and file. His even temperament and insightful approach ensured that issues being explored by FAYTS were thoroughly examined.

- *Pete Jamero*, who came to Seattle in 1970 with the first contingent of a new federal regional office, brought an ability to articulate FAYTS interests to the highest echelons of power. His top-level experience with government broadened FAYTS perspectives and brought additional dollar and technical resources to the community. He was the oldest of the "Young Turks."

- *Terri Jamero*, a native Californian along with her husband, Pete, was one of the few newcomers to the group. She provided a woman's perspective and conscience to an otherwise male-dominated FAYTS agenda. Her ideas, behind-the-scenes support, and commitment to FAYTS causes were critical to the success of FAYTS.

- *Rev. Harvey McIntyre, S.J.*, one of two non-Filipinos in the group, was the lobbyist for the Roman Catholic archdiocese and provided access to the resources of the church. He was intimately knowledgeable and skilled within the rough-and-tumble world of state, local, and church politics. He was also a member of the Seattle City Human Rights Commission.

- *Anthony Ogilvie,* the young, bright, energetic, innovative "idea man" of the group, was often the catalyst in testing new ground for FAYTS. He was a dynamic, charismatic speaker who was key to the early success of the Far West Conventions of the 1970s. The only FAYTS member born in the Philippines, he came to the United States as an infant.

- *Bob Santos,* a tireless advocate for the downtown area where many elderly Filipinos lived, earned the unofficial title of Mayor of Chinatown/International District. He was the consummate demonstrator, and his support of minority causes provided early credibility for FAYTS. Streetwise and smart, he was also skilled in negotiating with top levels of government.

- *Dolores Sibonga,* involved in the publication of a Filipino community newspaper advocating civil rights along with her husband, Marty, became the first Filipino American to pass the Washington State Bar. Articulate and an excellent speaker, she had a successful law practice that evolved into her election to the Seattle City Council in 1978.

- *Andres "Sonny" Tangalin,* born in Chicago of a Filipino father and Polish mother, moved to Seattle as a teenager. Raised in housing projects, he was respected for his concern for poor and disadvantaged populations. He was active in educational politics and had access to school resources. His intellectual, at times hyperbolic, approach was critical in FAYTS deliberations.

- *Dale Tiffany,* a soft-spoken, transplanted Flathead Indian from Spokane, became a community insider in the course of his marriage to Jeannette, a member of a pioneer Seattle Filipino family. Excellent in his organizational skills and attention to detail, he often had responsibility for managing initiatives and political campaigns advocated by FAYTS.

- *Jeannette Tiffany,* an artist by profession, provided critical linkages to Seattle's arts and cultural communities. She also was the principal architect of multimedia communications in the promotion of FAYTS initiatives and political campaigns, as well as having the lead role in the design of FAYTS signs, posters, and letterheads.

Other Seattle Filipino Americans were involved from time to time and provided FAYTS with invaluable skills, talents, services, and access points. They included Mike Castilliano, who was assistant to the vice president for minority affairs at the University of Washington; Peter

Bacho, who went on to a successful career as an author and university professor; Pio De Cano Jr., son of the pioneer Seattle labor leader; Angie Flores, always dependable as a behind-the-scenes worker; Val Laigo, Seattle University professor; and Frank Irigon, a University of Washington student skilled in nonviolent demonstrations.

Sociopolitical Impact on the Filipino Community

Throughout the 1970s, FAYTS was consistent in its focus on working toward Filipino participation in the American mainstream. Because many of its pre-FAYTS activities were in the arena of civil rights and in seeking remedies for discrimination, the Filipino community initially regarded FAYTS as being limited to these causes—causes in which the community had mixed feelings.

This early perception was reinforced by FAYTS association with Larry Itliong, the noted Filipino labor leader and civil rights activist. It was Itliong, along with Philip Vera-Cruz, who led the successful strike of California Filipino farmworkers in 1965 for improved wages, benefits, and living conditions. Shortly thereafter, the Filipino agricultural union combined forces with the Mexican union led by Cesar Chavez to form the United Farm Workers (UFW), which would soon draw national attention for its strikes and boycotts against California agribusiness. Itliong met a number of times with then Seattle Mayor Wes Uhlman, who had taken great interest in the civil rights direction of UFW. Itliong's visits to Seattle were not-to-be-missed opportunities for FAYTS to learn from the legendary Filipino labor leader.

The Filipino community's limited perception of FAYTS was dramatically changed in 1970 with the successful election of a small FAYTS slate to the 25-member governing body of the umbrella Filipino Community of Seattle, Inc. (FCSI). With their subsequent involvement in the business and governance of FCSI, FAYTS members were regarded in a different light. They now were seen as individuals who could make a difference in accessing the resources and privileges of mainstream America.

Although FAYTS was accepted into the governance of the affairs of FCSI, some of its ideas were considered risky, particularly those ideas involving finances. The Filipino community's tepid response to the FAYTS agenda resulted in a change in FAYTS' strategy in working with the community. In developing its new strategy, FAYTS decided to take advantage of its many contacts achieved in the years of working with the broader mainstream community. Essentially, the new strategy called for FAYTS to limit its role to that of making personal connections to funding and legislative resources in the public and private sectors on behalf of the Filipino community. With FAYTS assisting in its role as resources contact, FCSI soon obtained block grant funding from the city of Seattle in 1971 to operate a Congregate Meal Program and a Filipino Elderly Program.

The Filipino community would also benefit from a new program spearheaded by FAYTS in 1971, the Demonstration Program for Asian Americans (DPAA), funded by the U.S. Department of Health, Education, and Welfare. Under the leadership of its executive director, Dorothy Cordova, DPAA subsequently conducted the first study of Filipino demographics in Seattle. DPAA also initiated a groundbreaking study on the plight of Philippine-trained physicians excluded from practicing in Washington State due to difficulties in passing a culturally biased examination administered by the Educational Council for Foreign Medical Graduates.

FAYTS was heavily involved in the 1971 First Filipino Young Peoples Far West Convention, sponsored by FYA. The convention was a huge success, drawing upward of 500 young Filipino Americans from California, Oregon, Alaska, and Washington. Many of the delegates were high school and college students. The convention agenda included virtually every significant issue for Filipinos—from political empowerment, to education and employment concerns, to family issues, to discrimination and identity problems. Important groundwork was laid, in terms of organization and identification of needed resources, to empower Filipino communities on the West Coast. A proposal was subsequently submitted to the federal Community Services Administration (CSA) to establish a networking organization, the Filipino Information Resource Center (FIRC). The FIRC proposal was approved by CSA, only to be canceled by the Nixon administration's order to roll back all newly signed federal contracts.

Subsequent Young Filipino Peoples Far West Conventions were held in Stockton (1972), San Jose (1973), Los Angeles (1974), Seattle (1975), and

Berkeley (1976). However, the high promise of empowerment for Filipino Americans that emerged in 1971 would soon disappear as a consequence of divided loyalties growing out of the anti-Marcos movement.
For many young Filipino Americans, working to overthrow the Marcos
dictatorship was a rare opportunity to express Filipino pride and identity. On the other hand, those affiliated with FAYTS and FYA regarded
their priorities to be the issues of Filipinos in America. Although FAYTS
and FYA were sympathetic to the plight of Filipinos living under the
Marcos regime, they considered it to be a complex problem of a country
not their own. Moreover, to involve themselves in the overseas affairs of
the Republic of the Philippines was seen as severely straining their
limited resources and energies. A deep schism within the ranks of young
Filipino Americans thus developed that effectively resulted in aborting
a promising movement that had all the potential for unifying Filipino
Americans across the nation.

FAYTS again put on its FYA hat in 1972 in helping obtain Model
Cities funding for FYA to operate a bilingual program for Filipino
students. Community based rather than housed in schools, the program
was the precursor to other similar programs.

Also in 1972, the Seattle Filipino community celebrated the appointment of Peter Jamero, by Washington State Governor Dan Evans, to the
post of director of vocational rehabilitation (DVR). As director of a
statewide program with a staff of more than 400, Jamero was cited by
the Washington State Superintendent of Instruction as "the highest
ranking government official of Filipino ancestry in the nation."

With the availability of Comprehensive Employment and Training
Act funds from the U.S. Department of Labor in 1973, FAYTS joined in
the Asian community effort to establish an employment program, the
Employment Opportunity Center. FAYTS successfully advocated for the
center to be located near the Filipino Community Center and for the
inclusion of bilingual Filipino employment counselors.

In 1975, it was FAYTS that coined the catchy acronym *FAPAGOW*
(Filipino American Political Action Group of Washington) for the new
nonpartisan political organization. FAPAGOW was founded by Vic Bacho,
a first-generation leader of the Filipino community who had advocated
for open housing in Seattle in the mid-1960s.

Funding for the International District Health Clinic was secured in
1976 through the resource contacts of FAYTS. An initiative of young

Asian activists, the clinic was established to serve the needs of Asian disadvantaged and elderly residents of the Chinatown area, home to many Filipino elderly single men.

In the late 1970s, young Filipino activists, working in conjunction with FAYTS and Filipino community leaders, provided the leadership for the establishment of the International District Drop-in Center for Filipino Elderly. Again, FAYTS played a major support role by making the personal connections to obtain funding resources.

Political Campaigns

Filipino communities throughout the United States have been described as naively believing that the appearance of closeness to powerful political figures is empowerment itself (Rodis, 1991). In Seattle, the Filipino community's working relationship with FAYTS helped it to become more knowledgeable and sophisticated in dealing with the broader Seattle community. The Filipino Community of Seattle, Inc., whose social functions formerly held little interest for public officials, now found its affairs to be in demand. No longer was it enough for these public officials to eat *lumpia*, wear a *barong Tagalog*, shake a few hands, and expect to get the Filipino vote. No longer were Filipino community leaders content to have their photographs taken with political candidates and public officials. Now politicians came, but they also received demands for access, positions on issues, and jobs.

Close involvement in the Seattle political scene was perhaps the inevitable destiny of a group that sought Filipino inclusion in the sociopolitical mainstream. After its recognition for the professional manner in which the Baruso campaign was operated, FAYTS became a regular participant in the Seattle political scene. It was sought for its input as well as for its personpower by mainstream candidates of both major political parties. Some played key roles in campaign organizational structures. They were on a first-name basis with public officials at all levels of government. These young Filipino Americans became visible in virtually every political campaign in Seattle and King County, as well as in statewide and national races. Theirs were familiar faces in city hall, the county courthouse, the state capitol, and Washington, D.C.

It was perhaps predictable that FAYTS would one day run its own candidate for office. A few had already been approached by the Democratic Party and/or community groups to campaign for office, only to decline because of the lack of dollar resources. In 1973, Bob Santos was offered people and money resources by the Republican Party to run for the state senate. The Republican Governor also assured Santos that his top aides and appointees would be made available for the campaign. The people and money resources were not enough; Santos lost. In retrospect, it should be noted that the state senate district was predominantly Democratic in its registration. Moreover, FAYTS' own political leanings and affiliation were strongly Democratic. Santos ran for the state senate the following year, this time as a Democrat. However, the Democratic Party, unlike the Republicans, did not possess the dollar and people resources that Santos had had in 1973. Santos lost again, in part because of his previous decision to run as a Republican. FAYTS was in charge of both the Santos campaigns. Despite the election outcomes, FAYTS' positive reputation for the conduct of political campaigns remained unblemished.

In 1975, FAYTS became heavily involved in a pan-Asian effort to elect a more sympathetic representative, preferably an Asian, to the Seattle School Board. It was not until June when FAYTS' Peter Jamero was persuaded to campaign for the position. With the primary election scheduled for September and the general election for November, winning the election presented a formidable task from the outset. Moreover, Jamero, relatively new to the district, was unfamiliar with education and school politics. He had the additional disadvantage of having to campaign while working full time in Olympia, 60 miles away. Jamero won enough votes in the primary to qualify for the runoff in the general election but lost to a candidate with greater name familiarity and experience in education circles.

The Filipino community was finally able to celebrate the first successful campaign of a Filipino candidate in 1978 with the appointment and subsequent election of Dolores Sibonga to the Seattle City Council. Articulate and tough but sensitive to social programs and ethnic group concerns, Sibonga won a substantial plurality of the vote. FAYTS involvement, though significant, was not to the same degree as in the campaigns of earlier Filipino Americans. The impetus for Sibonga's candidacy came from the broader Seattle community. The Sibonga campaign organization was a consequent reflection of that support. Nevertheless, long-time associates Fred and Dorothy Cordova and Dale and Jeannette Tiffany were visible campaign confidants. Sibonga would go on to win two additional 4-year terms. Throughout her 13 years as Seattle City Councilwoman, the Filipino community would be well served.

During the remaining years of the 1970s, FAYTS continued its high visibility in virtually every national, state, and local campaign. With the appointments of Terri Jamero and Bob Santos to the Seattle staff of newly elected Congressman Mike Lowry in 1978, FAYTS also became visible in the offices of elected officials at the national level.

Minority Involvement

Minority concerns continued to be a high priority for FAYTS. In the early 1970s, it was involved in demands to include Asian workers in the construction of the Kingdome and in minimizing the adverse impact of construction on Asian residents of the International District. FAYTS marched with black and other minority contractors against the city of Seattle to obtain a fair share of city contracts. Bob Santos supported the Native American leader of Filipino heritage, Bernie Whitebear, in the successful United Indians of All Tribes takeover of Fort Lawton.

With Sonny Tangalin taking the lead for FAYTS, Asian American activists successfully helped to overturn the exclusionary policies of private clubs, such as the Elks, in 1971. Private clubs had long banned Asians from membership. Moreover, private clubs received lucrative price breaks on liquor, which in Washington is state controlled. An executive order issued by the governor subsequently ruled such practices to be discriminatory.

In 1972, FAYTS was involved in the successful effort that established the Governor's Asian American Advisory Committee. FAYTS was prominently represented on the first committee appointed by Governor Dan Evans.

FAYTS activism was not limited to Seattle or the state of Washington. In 1971, FAYTS joined other Asian Americans in a demonstration at a

Seattle conference of social workers to protest the inattention of the national organization to Asian American concerns. The protest resulted in government funding to support the 1972 National Asian American Mental Health Conference in San Francisco. Four additional conferences were funded by the National Institute of Mental Health (NIMH). Of greater significance was the subsequent NIMH funding of the Asian American Community Mental Health Training Center in Los Angeles and the Mental Health Resource Center in San Diego (Morales, 1974). FAYTS was represented on the operating board of each center.

An unexpected but welcome outcome of FAYTS involvement in Asian mental health concerns was the establishment of an unofficial West Coast communication network of activists from San Francisco, Los Angeles, and Seattle. These young Asian Americans would go on to coordinate a host of sociopolitical efforts on a regional and national scale.

The most unusual demonstration in which FAYTS was involved occurred in 1971 against the pastor of the Central Area's St. Theresa Catholic Church. The priest had a long history of racist behavior in a parish that had become predominantly minority. After three marches by a diverse group of demonstrators, the church transferred the pastor.

Epilogue

As the 1970s drew to a close, the fervor that typified FAYTS endeavors began to wane. The 1980s would see two more city council victories for Dolores Sibonga, a political appointment as director of the King County Department of Human Resources for Pete Jamero, the publication of Fred Cordova's (1983) landmark book *Filipinos: Forgotten Asian Americans*, and the founding of the Filipino American National Historical Society (FANHS). However, the passion formerly found within FAYTS had subsided.

Several factors contributed to the change in sociopolitical passion. First, FAYTS itself was undergoing change. Some FAYTS players had gone on to pursue career advancements, family obligations had grown, and the high energy level that had sustained their efforts over the years had decreased as they approached their 40s and 50s. Moreover, many FAYTS members had grown disenchanted with their participation in

Asian American coalitions, particularly at the state and national levels. The Asian American movement they had helped launch was now perceived as disproportionately rewarding other Asian communities at the expense of Filipinos. Gradually, FAYTS members began to drift apart. Political participation became more individual rather than group oriented. Social get-togethers, once regular events, were now rare.

Second, the Filipino community had undergone profound change. Subsequent to the 1965 liberalization of immigration legislation, the population now predominantly consisted of new immigrants. The newly arrived immigrant Filipinos did not personally relate to the history of exclusion experienced by earlier generations of Filipino Americans. Access to jobs, housing, and education was now legally ensured for these new Americans, thanks in part to the civil rights and antidiscrimination efforts of groups such as FAYTS. Moreover, the priorities of the new immigrants were still rooted in the motherland. Unlike FAYTS, their energies went to assisting relatives abroad and in supporting the growing anti-Marcos movement.

Did FAYTS meet its goals and objectives? Certainly, FAYTS was successful in bringing increased access, recognition, and participation to the Filipino community as a significant force in the broader Seattle sociopolitical mainstream. Today, Filipino community concerns and causes are supported by the greater Seattle community. The Filipino community continues to be represented on boards and commissions and continues to be routinely considered in the conduct of major political campaigns. Seattle Filipino Americans continue to be elected to public office or appointed to influential political and administrative power positions. Moreover, programs in which FAYTS was involved continue to serve the present-day Filipino community.

On the other hand, FAYTS fell short of its objectives in several critical areas. First, it was unable to sustain its efforts. The fervent FAYTS efforts of the 1970s are past history. Its contributions in opening access and equal opportunities for Filipinos are unrecognized today by a changed Filipino community with different priorities. And, as noted earlier, FAYTS itself changed. Some members disappeared into the American mainstream. Others pursued new interests.

Second, Filipinos continue to be the "forgotten Asian Americans" (Cordova, 1983). Despite greater numbers, they have not benefited from the Asian American movement to the same degree as other Asian ethnic groups. Recent FAYTS discussions, for example, have considered whether the time has come for Filipino Americans to rethink their continued participation in Asian American sociopolitical coalitions and form their own movement.

What can Filipino American communities learn from the FAYTS experience in terms of greater participation in the American sociopolitical mainstream? I suggest three fundamental lessons:

1. Coalition building and individual participation with mainstream and other minority groups must be actively pursued. FAYTS credibility, networking capacity, and political clout had their roots in FAYTS long-standing working relationships with the diversity that is America.

2. If greater participation in the sociopolitical mainstream is to be accomplished, it logically follows that the primary focus and energies of the community must be directed to deal with Filipino issues of America, and secondarily to issues of the ancestral "homeland."

3. Language, regional, and generational differences among Filipinos must be bridged. FAYTS was able to bridge these gaps through the ability of key players to "fit in" and relate with older or younger Filipinos, Filipinos of mixed ethnicity, and those born and/or raised in the Philippines, regardless of regional affiliation or language facility.

Hopefully, the story of FAYTS can be helpful to other Filipino American communities in their quest for sociopolitical recognition. The experience of the Filipino American Young Turks of Seattle during the 1970s is but one experience. There may be other helpful experiences. If this account of the FAYTS experience encourages studies of other community experiences and strategies that promote increased Filipino community participation in the American sociopolitical mainstream, the basic objectives of this chapter will have been met.

References

Boylan, D. (1991). Crosscurrents: Filipinos in Hawaii's politics. In J. P. Okamura, A. R. Agbayani, & M. T. Kerkvliet (Eds.), *Social process in Hawaii: The Filipino American experience in Hawaii*. Manoa: University of Hawaii at Manoa.
California State Data Center. (1991). *1990 census* (P42, 652). Sacramento, CA: Author.

Cordova, F. (1973). The Filipino-American: There's always an identity crisis. In S. Sue & N. W. Wagner (Eds.), *Asian-Americans: Psychological perspectives*. Palo Alto, CA: Science and Behavior Books.

Cordova, F. (1983). *Filipinos: Forgotten Asian Americans. A pictorial essay, 1763–circa 1963* (D. L. Cordova, Ed.). Dubuque, IA: Kendall/Hunt.

Espiritu, Y. L. (1995). *Filipino American lives*. Philadelphia: Temple University Press.

Lott, J. T. (1976). *Migration of a mentality: The Pilipino community*. Social Casework, 57, 165-172.

Morales, R. F. (1974). *Makibaka: The Pilipino American struggle*. Los Angeles: Mountainview.

Rodis, R. E. (1991). *Telltale signs: Filipinos in America*. San Francisco: INA.

Takaki, R. (1989). *Strangers from a different shore: A history of Asian Americans*. New York: Penguin.

22

Filipino Americans and Ecology
New Challenges in the Global Future

Felix I. Rodriguez

Educators have recognized that solving modern-day ecological problems requires not only global cooperation among nations but also a fundamental transformation in human values—in the way we see ourselves in relation to the natural world, in the way we live, work, consume, produce, and fulfill our needs (Bowers, 1993; Cobb, 1994; Orr, 1992). By changing our values and lifestyle, we will be able to exert less pressure on the earth's resources and thus be able to sustain ecosystems, the biosphere, and the future of civilization itself. Certainly, this will involve simplifying our lives and learning to distinguish between true and false needs.[1] What does this transformation mean for Filipino Americans?[2] How can Filipino Americans reconcile their need for personal economic security and upward mobility with the global need for ecological sustainability? What challenges does this transformation present to Filipino Americans?

316

Colonization and the Myth of Development

Understanding the issue of reconciling needs with ecological sustainability requires an examination of forces that may either strengthen or weaken the project of value transformation among Filipino Americans. The ecological consequences of previous colonizations in the Philippines provide Filipino Americans with a great cause to contribute to a worldwide ecology movement. However, the desire to "make it" in America and to project an image of conventional economic success may drive Filipino Americans to cultivate a lifestyle centered on material acquisition.

The history of the Philippines reveals a pattern of ecological destruction stemming from colonial economic development (Broad, 1993; McLennan, 1982; Ofreneo, 1993; Rodriguez, 1995, 1996; Roth, 1983; Vitug, 1993). Starting in the late 16th century, the building of galleon ships by the Spanish colonial government cleared large forested areas. Spanish colonial policy altered the traditional concepts of land ownership and land use, thereby denying a large segment of the native population access to their resource base. In the 19th century, the opening of the Philippines to global trade stimulated the growth of an export crop economy based on the production of sugar, abaca, indigo, and copra. The expansion of agricultural estates resulted in the disappearance of tropical rain forests in areas such as Negros Island. Commercial agriculture coupled with population growth exerted great pressure on land, so that by 1960, according to Wernstedt and Spencer (1967, p. 78), soil erosion and depletion of soil fertility had already become widespread problems. The American colonial administration stimulated further exploitation of forest resources. The United States encouraged the exportation of wood and timber, which greatly accelerated forest depletion. At the turn of the century, 75% of the Philippines was covered with old-growth forests (Howard, 1993, p. 2). By 1990, this figure had gone down to only 2.3%.

As colonization resulted in adverse ecological consequences, it also exposed Filipinos to a Western, mainly American, standard of living. A largely Western-oriented educational system in the Philippines has promoted the belief that the United States represents the end-state of development for human societies. Colonialism has fostered a perception that achieving the standard of living found in the United States is the mark of a highly sophisticated society. Hence, adults dream of going to the United States as if longing to be reunited with a long-lost parent. Elementary school children, seeing Donald Duck on television, dream of becoming Americans in the hope that they will finally be able to live in Disney's Kingdom. When referring to relatives who have immigrated to the United States, it is not unusual to hear some Filipinos use the expression *"Nasa States na"* (They already are in the States). It is not unusual to hear others make remarks such as *"May McDonald's na sa atin"* (We finally have a McDonald's in the country). The first expression presents an image of the Philippines as a country where the *telos* of life is to go, to be, in the United States. Filipinos look at their own country as a waiting station for their final destination to America. The second suggests that the Philippines is a country where development, and therefore civilization, is understood to mean having or possessing a globally ubiquitous representation of America, which is McDonald's. Becoming an American or a Filipino American, then, means having the privilege of realizing what is generally believed as the highest level of human and economic development possible.

Every year, immigrants from the Philippines join their families in the United States. For many Filipinos, coming to America means the fulfillment of a lifelong dream to partake of opportunities that they feel are limited in the Philippines. Partaking of these opportunities means not only that one can satisfy the most basic needs for housing, clothing, and sustenance but also that one can meet these needs in bigger quantities. The goal of improving their economic position, in contrast to their former life in the Philippines, may drive many Filipino Americans to assimilate uncritically the drive for consumption and wastefulness. The desire to participate in a prosperous culture as active consumers can make them retreat to a life of daily work, unmindful of larger global issues that, in the long run, may affect their very lives, their health, and their environment. The drive to consume reveals itself in many anecdotal stories of one-upmanship. Who has not been to a party where Filipinos and Filipino Americans try to outdo each other in their latest acquisitions, such as cars, clothes, or houses? Indeed, the problem embraces not only ecology but also the stability of families as parents attempt to fulfill material expectations. For instance, it is not uncommon to find dual-income families in which a mother works as a nurse on two shifts while the husband works on two jobs. The desire to own a house and aspirations of upward mobility have driven many to work long hours, creating many problems at home and in the community.

Although Filipino Americans do have rights, just like any other group, to meet their needs as native-born Americans or as older and more recent immigrants, they may find themselves in a position in which they become faithful consumers instead of mindful citizens of the planet. This contradiction parallels the experience of so-called developing countries in their attempt to industrialize or become more like economically developed countries. Critics have charged that resource exploitation in Third World countries has created serious social and ecological consequences such as forest depletion, pollution, disappearance of farmlands, loss of biodiversity, and the impoverishment of women (Rodriguez, 1995; Shiva, 1989, 1993). Governments of developing countries defend their program by arguing that they have the right to destroy their own environment just as developed countries have done on the road to industrialization. The argument goes that development entails a cost and that they are willing to pay the cost to achieve economic prosperity. Immigrants, on the other hand, claim that they have just as much right to own and consume their share of American prosperity. They feel that they are entitled to work just as hard to improve their economic position as earlier generations of Americans did.

Challenges Ahead:
Seeing Connections and Redefining Fulfillment

How can Filipino Americans contribute to the larger goal of transforming values to create a better environment not only for themselves but for everyone in the world? The notion of interrelatedness is at the core of ecology. This implies that what human beings do and what they fail to do have consequences for the life of the earth. A basic step that Filipino Americans need to take is to develop a greater awareness of this interrelatedness. This involves making connections between problems and their causes, between actions and their possible consequences. Moreover, it requires that individuals enter domains previously unknown to them, taking risks in understanding new knowledge, and being part of new territories that require deep commitment to and involvement in social change. It means asking questions about life and their place in the world.

The need to appreciate better the idea of interrelatedness has become a matter of urgency as the world economy becomes increasingly more integrated. A global economy has enabled powerful countries, institutions, and corporations to maintain access to the resources of other nations. The position of Filipino Americans in the United States presents a difficult situation because they end up participating in and benefiting from a society that is subsidized by poor countries such as the Philippines and that continues to consume a larger share of the world's resources (Rifkin, 1991, p. 174). The global future presents a real challenge, especially when we consider that Filipino Americans themselves have been shaped by global processes. The search for economic opportunities has continued to push Filipinos to America and to different corners of the world. It is not unusual to find Filipino American families with members and relatives working in Saudi Arabia, Japan, Italy, Singapore, and Hong Kong. A greater awareness of life's interconnectedness should make Filipino Americans realize that hyperconsumption in the United States poses great harm to those countries that have lost most of their resources to economic development.

Another important challenge for Filipino Americans is to demythologize development by exposing its complicity in creating and perpetuating ecological destruction. Development in the Philippines, principally motivated by the desire of colonial powers to seek economic gains, has resulted in social and ecological damage. Global ecological problems have made it apparent that economic prosperity involves a high cost that ultimately will affect not only the natural world but social relations as well. Although the 20th century has seen unparalleled technological achievements and material wealth, a large portion of the earth's population remains in a state of want owing to the impoverishment caused by environmental degradation.

In the United States, a generation of young Filipino Americans is beginning to question the myths they learned from such sources as their parents, the media, and the educational system. The concern for identity in America has made them examine the reasons for their existence in the United States and especially the prospects of their own future. Young Filipino Americans may feel that they do not share their parents' desire for material betterment. Some may feel that their experience of racism, discrimination, and being perceived as the "other" is not worth the effort involved in achieving success and social conformity, especially when one loses the most important element of one's life—identity.

The conventional meaning of empowerment in America for Filipino Americans has emphasized visibility in political and economic fields— public offices, positions in city and state commissions, and executive positions in large corporations. Demythologizing development demands a reconceptualization of empowerment as a means to restore Filipino Americans as the subjects of their own lives, not the objects, or passive receptors, of someone else's notion of development or progress. They may have to redefine fulfillment in terms of being able to pursue their interests independent of social pressures. In short, they may have to live their lives not on the basis of the larger society's definition of material success but according to a standard of responsibility and caring.

Conclusion

This chapter has only superficially dealt with problems related to ecology by raising questions concerning the possibility of reconciling needs with sustainability. This issue affects all the inhabitants of the earth but is particularly germane to the experience of Filipino Americans in the United States. The ecological consequences of colonization in the Philippines provide Filipino Americans with an important experience that should enable them to take an active part in the global ecology movement. However, the desire to "make it" in a land that to most people represents the highest stage of economic development may drive Filipino Americans to pursue a life centered on material fulfillment.

Filipino Americans, then, need to develop a greater awareness of ecology itself—that everything is connected with everything else. In fulfilling their goal of upward mobility, Filipino Americans will have to avoid becoming simply units of consumption. They have to examine how their own lifestyle can become a means of supporting a society that, as one of the richest in the world, consumes a disproportionate share of the world's resources. Filipino Americans will also have to divest themselves of the myths associated with development, especially the form avidly promoted by Western culture. They may have to face the fact that living in the United States makes them participants in and thus beneficiaries of a lifestyle greatly subsidized by poor nations, one of which is the country they have left behind.

Notes

1. See Marcuse (1964, pp. 4-8). Marcuse distinguished between false needs and true needs. False needs are

> those which are superimposed upon the individual by particular social interests in his repression: the needs which perpetuate toil, aggressiveness, misery, and injustice. . . . Most of the prevailing needs to relax, to have fun, to behave and consume in accordance with the advertisements, to love and hate what others love and hate, belong to this category of false needs. (p. 5)

On true needs, Marcuse has this to say:

> The only needs that have an unqualified claim for satisfaction are the vital ones—nourishment, clothing, lodging at the attainable level of culture. The satisfaction of these needs is the prerequisite for the realization of *all* needs, of the unsublimated as well as the sublimated ones." (p. 5)

2. By *Filipino Americans*, I refer to a diverse group of individuals who consider or identify themselves as Filipino Americans because of birth, immigration, marriage, citizenship, Filipino parentage, or some combination of these possibilities.

References

Bowers, C. A. (1993). *Education, cultural myths, and the ecological crisis: Toward deep changes.* Albany: State University of New York Press.

Broad, R. (1993). *Plundering paradise: The struggle for the environment in the Philippines.* Berkeley: University of California Press.

Cobb, J. B., Jr. (1994). *Sustaining the common good: A Christian perspective on the global economy.* Cleveland, OH: Pilgrim.

Howard, M. C. (Ed.). (1993). *Asia's environmental crisis.* Boulder, CO: Westview.

Marcuse, H. (1964). *One-dimensional man: Studies in the ideology of advanced industrial society.* Boston: Beacon.

McLennan, M. S. (1982). Changing human ecology on the Central Luzon Plain: Nueva Ecija, 1705-1939. In A. W. McCoy & E. C. de Jesus (Eds.), *Philippine social history: Global trade and local transformation* (pp. 57-90). Quezon City: Ateneo de Manila University Press.

Ofreneo, R. E. (1993). Japan and the environmental degradation of the Philippines. In M. C. Howard (Ed.), *Asia's environmental crisis* (pp. 201-219). Boulder, CO: Westview.

Orr, D. W. (1992). *Ecological literacy: Education and the transition to a post-modern world.* Albany: State University of New York Press.

Rifkin, J. (1991). *Biosphere politics: A new consciousness for a new century.* New York: Crown.

Rodriguez, F. I. (1995). *Reconstituting damaged ecologies: Ethics for post-colonial development.* Paper presented at the Conference on Environmental Ethics, Philosophy of Ecology, and Bioethics, Cortona, Italy, August 26-29, 1995.

Rodriguez, F. I. (1996). *Land and the Philippine Revolution: An ecologist's perspective.* Paper presented at the International Conference on the Centennial of the 1896 Philippine Revolution, Manila, August 21-23, 1996.

Roth, D. M. (1983). Philippine forests and forestry. In R. P. Trucker & J. F. Richards (Eds.), *Global deforestation and the nineteenth-century world economy* (pp. 31-49). Durham, NC: Duke University Press.

Shiva, V. (1989). *Staying alive: Women, ecology, and development.* London: Zed.

Shiva, V. (1993). *Monocultures of the mind: Perspectives on biodiversity and biotechnology.* London: Zed.

Vitug, M. D. (1993). *Power from the forest: The politics of logging.* Quezon City, Philippines: Philippine Center for Investigative Journalism.

Wernstedt, F. L., & Spencer, J. E. (1967). *The Philippine island world: A physical, cultural, and regional geography.* Berkeley: University of California Press.

23

Filipino Spirituality
An Immigrant's Perspective

Thelma B. Burgonio-Watson

By the rivers of Babylon—
there we sat down and there we wept
when we remembered Zion.
On the willows there
we hung up our harps.
For there our captors
asked us for songs,
and our tormentors asked for mirth, saying,
"Sing us one of the songs of Zion!"
How could we sing the LORD's song
in a foreign land?
Psalm 137:1-4 (NRSV)

Although there is a diversity of religion in the Philippines, Roman Catholicism is still the major religion, practiced by 85% of the population. The rest are members of the Protestant churches, the Independent Aglipayan or the Philippine Independent Church, the Muslims, the Iglesia Ni Cristo, the Church of the Latter Day Saints, the Jehovah's

Witnesses, or some other sect. Still others are practitioners of or believers in animistic religions involving multiple supernatural beings or spirits.

Growing up Protestant in northern Luzon, a region that claims itself as the bulwark of Roman Catholicism in the country, makes me a minority in my own town. (Every region claims to be the bulwark of Roman Catholicism.) Filipinos in the United States remain mostly Catholic, but there are also many of us Protestants who continue to thrive.

This chapter is an attempt to share my own home-grown spirituality and how it has been a resource for me as a Filipino Protestant immigrant woman in this land. I will focus on how this particular spirituality is claimed for a community struggling to sing a new song in this country. It is my hope that this sharing may illuminate some issues in the Filipino American community, regardless of denomination or belief system. Space constraints will limit the discussion to some issues that Filipino Americans in the greater Seattle area have been confronted with most recently—issues that are probably common to many Filipino Americans across the United States—and the role of spiritual values in helping this particular community in its struggle.

What Is Spirituality?

All of life is spiritual. Even that which is considered material is of the Spirit if one believes, as I do, that everything comes from the Spirit, the Creator, the Giver and Source of all life. Spirituality is more than one's religious convictions; it is a way of life.

As I have mentioned at the outset, there are diverse religious beliefs among Filipinos and among Filipino Americans. These religious beliefs may influence one's spirituality.

Asian women who gathered in Singapore in 1987 at the Consultation on Asian Women's Theology to articulate an emerging Asian theology expressed this spirituality for me when they described Asian women's spirituality as

> faith experience based on convictions and beliefs which motivate our thought processes and behavior patterns in our relationship to God

and neighbor. Spirituality is the integral wholeness of a person con-
cretizing her/his faith through their daily life experience. It is a
response and commitment of a soul infused by the spirit to the
challenge for human dignity and freedom, and a new life of love.
(Women's Spirituality Workshop, qtd. in Kyung, 1990, p. 85)

My own experience in living amidst the diversity of beliefs and
practices of the Filipino people—and by the terms of the definition cited
above, Filipinos are deeply spiritual people—is that it does not matter
whether one is attached to a religious institution or not. Nowhere is
one's spirituality tested more than in the situation of being an immigrant in this country, especially a new immigrant trying to make sense
of a life that has been uprooted and disconnected from that which is
familiar, nurturing, and accepting. In coping with the challenges of
always looking like a "foreigner" or "alien," I find my spiritual resources affirming and undergirding. For me, spirituality is made up of
all that I have experienced in life growing up in an extended family and
in an inclusive caring community in the barrio and in the church, and
out of such experiences grow the commitments and decisions that I
make every day.

As a female Protestant minister working with a predominantly
Roman Catholic Filipino American community, I need to call on what I
believe are our community spiritual resources when my people look to
me for spiritual nurture in the midst of ongoing struggles.

Ongoing Issues

As an immigrant in this country, I am struggling to claim and maintain
an identity as a Filipino woman. These days, this means identifying with
the oppression of women and children, among them Filipino women and
children, by sexual and domestic violence, by tourism and multinational
corporate presence, and by poverty. I must work for freedom from that
oppression in an interreligious, feminist, and global setting.

I finished this chapter on the eve of the sentencing of a man (Timothy
Blackwell) who murdered three Filipino women and an unborn child in

Seattle on March 2, 1995. One of the women, Susana Remerata, was a "mail-order bride"; the other two, Phoebe Dizon and Veronica Laureta, were her friends, who were helping her gain independence from this abusive murderous husband (Blackwell). The unborn child was Susana's. The convicted murderer was charged on three counts of first-degree murder and one count of manslaughter. The jury has two options: life imprisonment without parole or the death penalty. The prosecutors and the victims' families chose the death penalty. Some of us in the Filipino and wider community—friends and supporters of the victims and their families—were torn. Many of us could only whisper to each other that we would support the wishes of the families, although we were against the death penalty.

The death penalty is an issue not only for Filipino Americans but for society as a whole. However, it is the larger issues of racism, trafficking in Filipino women, and domestic violence that continue to confront the Filipino community today. The murder of the three Filipinas and an unborn child is one of the outcomes of this racism, trafficking in Filipino women, and domestic violence. In this tragic case, it all began as a mail-order-bride issue. Timothy Blackwell met Susana Remerata, who later came to the United States as his bride, in a matchmaking catalog that advertises Asian women, many of them Filipino women. Men who obtain their partners in this way are attracted to the racist stereotypes of Asian women as docile, submissive, and compliant. Inherent in this practice of obtaining a woman/wife/partner through a catalog is the racist, dehumanizing way that women are displayed like inanimate objects for sale.

The mail-order-bride industry is a form of trafficking in women. Unfortunately, it is an open and legal practice. But like Susana, immigrant women who come to the United States as mail-order brides are more vulnerable to abuse because of the inequality of the relationship between the partners, which is further compounded by the mail-order bride's immigrant status, race, and lack of or limited knowledge of the culture, language, and society.

Susana was a victim of the mail-order-bride industry and a victim of domestic violence as well. Her husband abused and murdered her. Embedded in the practice of the mail-order-bride industry is race, gender, and class discrimination. The men who resort to this practice are often from more affluent countries, such as the United States. The women who participate in this practice are from poor countries, the Philippines among them.

Undoubtedly, racism, trafficking in women, and domestic violence are all complex issues that face Filipino Americans across the United States. Fortunately, also common to Filipino Americans are the spiritual values that I have found to be helpful in coping with these issues.

The Value of Community

A spiritual value that is common to most, if not all, Filipinos is the value of community life. The extended family is the most basic community. You orient your actions to the needs and betterment of the collective. Sometimes the collective is only family or the extended family that often makes up a barrio. Often, when Filipinos talk about community, they refer to living in a barrio where most of the people are related. At least in the barrio where I grew up and where I learned what community means, no one was hungry, no one was homeless. We shared and pooled resources. We wept with those who mourned; we took time to celebrate. It was in the barrio that I learned that I could not have become what I am now without the whole barrio supporting and affirming me. It was there in the barrio, reinforced in my local church, that I learned that I belong to a caring, nurturing community. In my context, that was the barrio and the church together. Where I go, the spirit of the community goes with me. When I am honored, the community is honored, and when I am shamed, the community is shamed, and vice versa.

As an immigrant, I find that the basic resource of living in a community is often missed or missing. We cope either by re-creating that community through participation in an organized setting or by forming our coalitions with people from the same linguistic or ethnic group. Hence, the proliferation of diverse Filipino coalitions everywhere in the United States.

I believe that the forming of these coalitions is motivated by a longing to re-create that sense of barrio community where people know each other, speak the same dialect, share customs, and come from the same ethnic region. Hence, in Washington State, there are conceivably

Filipino associations of people who grew up in the same town (closest to the context of the barrio).

On the other hand, I believe that not all of these coalitions are motivated by a spirit of community that goes beyond that of the barrio and that not all of them support and nurture relationships, promote and advocate for the good of the collective above the individual, and practice the sharing and pooling of resources. Some coalitions are divisive and at odds with the spirit of true community. The spirit of community needs to transcend the barrio community.

It is a spiritual value to seek your own community for support and nurture. After all, we are in a strange land and a different culture. It does not matter that we were once a colony and have some familiarity with the culture. Many of us still need to be connected with our own people. That makes life in this adopted country more meaningful. Relating to the community gives us a sense of ethnic identity and belonging. That sense of identity might be challenged in times of crisis such as publicized violence within the community, whether gang violence or domestic violence, as in the case of Susana and others after her.

However, in the greater Seattle area, the organized Filipino American communities have become rallying points in times of adversity, and despite the diversity and competition, many people come together in solidarity, as they did in response to the death of Susana Remerata Blackwell and her friends. Such is the spiritual value of the commitment to be in community. It is a shelter in times of storm and a place of feasting and fiesta in times of celebration, as in the annual celebration of Pista Sa Nayon. A truly spiritual resource indeed, for when one member of the body is hurting, the community suffers together, and when the community is honored, all the members celebrate.

However, not all Filipinos choose to go back to the Filipino community as a resource. Many have chosen and have become part of communities other than the Filipino American community, and that is okay, too. They have chosen another means of fulfilling their need for community. I have no reason to believe that they cannot go back any time they want to claim their place in the Filipino community. On the other hand, spirituality is the embodiment of one's faith in daily life. There are occasions on which that faith seeks its fulfillment outside the Filipino community. People need to have the freedom to choose their communities. It is not surprising that some Filipinos can fit in comfortably in the mainstream community. An explanation is Filipinos' exposure to that mainstream community through colonization, whether for good or ill. I feel that in the true spirit of community, Filipino Americans would be eager to include people who claimed or reclaimed their place in the community. There are no gatekeepers. In the current struggle against racism and discrimination, Filipino Americans need to stand together as one big community transcending linguistic, regional, and religious barriers—transcending the barrio.

It is sad to say that despite the shared value of community, Filipino Americans may still be divided by religious beliefs and traditions. Some may even limit their community participation within shared religious beliefs exclusively.

We need a place for solidarity as our people confront racism, violence, and the diminishing resources for immigrant communities. Admittedly, other Filipinos are too busy eking out a living or have adapted to the more individualistic lifestyle of the mainstream American culture.

Hospitality

Another spiritual value that unites Filipinos wherever they are is hospitality. Living in community and hospitality go together. It is a value of being able to share one's life and material resources. Hospitality is welcoming and sharing to all of humanity and all of creation; it is offering one's food to the hungry and expecting nothing in return. Hospitality is lived out in community. It is the ability to be present for the "other," to meet the other's need. It is a gift of generosity. It is a value that is rooted and grounded among people who live close to the land and enjoy and respect the fruits of the land. It is a value that also has some Judaic/ Christian influence. We are reminded that "we were once strangers in the land of Egypt" and therefore are to be hospitable to one another. It is a value that opposes the mainstream value of "every man for himself" and has come into conflict with the way immigrants in this country have been treated and continue to be treated. Racism abounds, and it hurts. So in the midst of racism and the increasing hostility to immigrants and their welfare, Filipino Americans struggle with what it means to be hospitable to each other. This value and the value of community were both tested at the death of Susana Remerata, her unborn child, and friends. The communities came together, grieved together, and supported one another. They committed themselves to coming together to see to it that domestic violence, mail-order-bride issues, and other forms of violence that affected the community were addressed by the community. Above all, the community saw to it that Susana did not get a pauper's burial, although she did not have a family here. The community was her family. They sent her body home. That is hospitality. That is community, and that is honoring life. Such spiritual resources transformed a community tragedy into solidarity.

Filipino Americans are heirs to the faith and spirituality of their ancestors who first arrived here in various ways. Their faith is full of courage, industry, hope, and transformation. We are rooted and grounded by the spiritual sense of reverence for life, community, and hospitality. With hope and courage, we can participate in transforming this society. We are heirs to this spirit from our people who paved the way for us to this our adopted land.

It is in the spirit of community and hospitality that we are able to address the issues of racism, domestic violence, and gang violence in our midst. As long as we remember that what shames the community is not that there is violence but that no one helps, we will be able to work together to educate ourselves for prevention and intervention.

Meanwhile, I struggle to sing my song with renewed hope that I am connected to a community that affirms life and hospitality. A poem of mine expresses this struggle:

> *By the waters of Puget Sound*
> *I sat down and wept*
> *When I remembered that I am in a strange land*
> *that I am a stranger, an alien.*
> *How can I sing my song*
> *When every day I am reminded that I and my sisters am not welcome*
> *on this side of the Rim.*
> *Whereas at one time my people welcomed the missionaries who came*
> *to the other side of the Rim*
> *and taught us their songs.*

I am inspired by the spirit of my people who came here before me, who not only have survived but have continued to flourish because they have not forgotten to live in the spirit of community and hospitality and have remembered that to live in community is to participate in transforming all our communities so we can be free to sing our songs and live free from violence.

In the end, what matters is not that you are part of the Filipino community per se but that you have a sense of identity that is rooted in belonging to a community. The spiritual value of a true community transcends regionalism, religious beliefs, and ethnicity and nurtures you to be in solidarity with those who are oppressed by racism, discrimination, and violence.

Reference

Kyung, C. H. (1990). *Struggle to be the sun again.* Maryknoll, NY: Orbis.

Index

About the Authors

 **Amefil R. Agbayani,** PhD, is Director of Student Equity, Excellence and Diversity at the University of Hawai'i at Manoa. She was born in the Philippines and went to Hawai'i as an East-West Center grantee in the 1960s. She has a PhD degree in political science from the University of Hawai'i at Manoa and conducts research on Filipino and minority higher education. She serves as Chair of the Hawai'i State Commission on Civil Rights, is a board member of the Hawai'i Community Foundation, and is a Hawai'i representative on the Democratic Party National Committee.

 **Peter Bacho** is a teacher and writer. From 1984 to 1989, he was an editorial contributor to the *Christian Science Monitor;* his other essays on politics also appeared in leading foreign policy journals. His novel *Cebu* won the 1992 American Book Award. His collection *Dark Blue Suit and Other Stories* is forthcoming. He was born and raised in Seattle and previously worked as an attorney.

Jacqueline T. Jamero Berganio, BA, is Prevention Coordinator for the Seattle-King County Department of Public Health's Division of Alcoholism and Substance Abuse Services. She manages a countywide program that provides a range of services to help prevent and delay alcohol, tobacco, and other drug use among children and youth. She is a 1996 recipient of an award for leadership in prevention given by the State of Washington Department of Social and Health Services' Division of Alcohol and Substance Abuse. She has been a board member and leader of numerous community organizations: Asian Pacific Partners for Empowerment and Leadership, Washington Asian Pacific Islander Families Against Substance Abuse, Association of County Human Services Prevention Committee, and Filipino Youth Activities. Currently she is President of the Seattle Chapter of the Filipino American National Historical Society. A third-generation Pinay born in Sacramento, California, to Peter Madelo Jamero and Teresa Elizabeth Romero, she counts her blessings for being raised in a tight-knit family with her parents, four sisters, and one brother. The majority of her life has been spent in Seattle, where she resides with her husband, Richard.

Allan L. Bergano, DDS, is the proud son of Fabian Cariaso and Aurora Lagasca Bergano. He has two sisters, Barbara and Cheryl, and is happily married to Edwina Lapa-Bergano. A second-generation Pinoy, born and raised in Seattle, he is a product of Filipino Youth Activities, Inc., of Seattle, Washington and the Educational Opportunity Program of the University of Washington. He is the founder of the Hampton Roads Chapter of the Filipino American National Historical Society (FANHS). A grassroots advocate for the inclusion of Filipino American history in the American history curriculum since 1971, he has passionately lectured to students in Washington, California, Hawaii, Maryland, Illinois, Pennsylvania, New York, New Jersey, Georgia, and Virginia. Currently he is the Chairperson for Pinoys in Motion, a fundraising venue of FANHS. He resides in Virginia Beach, Virginia, where he has been a dentist in private practice since 1983.

Barbara L. Bergano-Kinney is the daughter of Fabian Cariaso and Aurora Lagasca Bergano. She has one brother, Allan, and one sister, Cheryl, and is married to William W. Kinney of Honolulu, Hawaii. Born and raised in Seattle, she is a second-generation Filipina who was actively involved with the Filipino American Baranggay Folk Arts, Inc., as their Vice President and choreographer for 11 years. A University of Washington graduate, she currently works for the Department of Transportation, Federal Aviation Administration, as the Regional Training Manager for the Northwest Mountain Region. Her 13 years of experience in career, management, and executive development include policy direction and guidance of senior management officials on corporate and emerging business requirements in the area of employment development. A member of the International Personnel Management Association, she is a registered career counselor with the state of Washington. She resides in Tukwila, Washington, with her husband and daughter, Briana Lehualani.

Rick Bonus completed his PhD dissertation, *Locating Filipino Americans: Ethnicity and the Cultural Politics of Space in Southern California,* in the graduate program in communication at the University of California, San Diego. He holds an MA in mass communication from California State University at Fresno. He has written and presented essays on the political, social, and cultural dynamics of Filipino American identities. He also teaches in the Department of Ethnic Studies at the University of California at San Diego.

Thelma B. Burgonio-Watson, MDiv, was the first Filipina to be ordained as a Minister of the Word in the Presbyterian Church (U.S.A.) in 1984. She finished her degree at the University of Dubuque Theological Seminary in Dubuque, Iowa. She currently works as a Program Specialist at the Center for the Prevention of Sexual and Domestic Violence in Seattle. She grew up in Santa, Ilocos Sur, and finished her undergraduate degree in public health at the University of the Philippines.

Emilie Gaborne Dearing, MS, is a Certified Nurse Specialist in Psychiatric Mental Health, with a multiethnic private practice in Fairfax, Virginia. She specializes in family research, cross-racial and cross-religious marriages, and biracial and multiracial individuals and families, with an emphasis on mental health and multicultural training and education. She is a consultant to the Indochinese Community Center in Washington, D.C. She is Vice-Chair of the National Asian Pacific American Families Against Substance Abuse and is on the Board of Directors of the Asian and Pacific Islander Partnership for Health. She was a member of the National Steering Committee for the 1992 Secretary of Health to link primary care, HIV, alcohol, and drug abuse treatment. She was born in Barotac Nuevo, Iloilo, Philippines, and spent her college years in Manila. She is fluent in Ilongo and Tagalog.

M. Evelina Galang, MFA, is the author of *Her Wild American Self*, a collection of short fiction (1996). Her stories and essays have appeared in many publications. In 1993, she won the Associated Writers Program Intro Award in nonfiction, and in 1994, she was the John Gardner Scholar in Fiction at Bread Loaf Writers Conference. She received her MFA from Colorado State University, where she was a Graduate Student Diversity Fellow, and her BA in radio, television, and film from the University of Wisconsin at Madison. She has been Assistant Professor and Literary Festival Director at Old Dominion University. She is currently teaching in the MFA Creative Writing Program at Chicago's School of Art Institute. She is at work on both a novel and a screenplay. Born in Pennsylvania, she grew up in Chicago and Milwaukee.

Theodore S. Gonzalves, PhD, received his graduate training at the University of California at Irvine in comparative culture. His research focuses on cross-cultural expressive forms, politics, and history. He has taught courses in American ethnic studies, political and social science, and literature.

Peter M. Jamero, MSW, a "bridge generation" (second-generation) Filipino American, was born in Oakdale, California. He retired in 1995 after 30 years of top-level executive experience in local, state, and federal government and in the private nonprofit sector as Director of the Washington State Division of Vocational Rehabilitation; Director of the King County (Seattle) Department of Human Resources; Executive Director of the San Francisco Human Rights Commission; Executive Director of Asian American Recovery Services (San Francisco); Branch Chief of the U.S. Department of Health, Education, and Welfare (Washington, D.C.); and Vice President of United Way of King County (Seattle). He also served as Assistant Professor of Rehabilitation Medicine at the University of Washington. He earned an MSW from the University of California at Los Angeles and a certificate in public affairs from Stanford University. The Filipino American National Historical Society (FANHS) gave him the VIP Gold Award for Lifetime Achievement in Government in 1994. Following his retirement, he and his wife, Terri, moved near the farm and Filipino labor camp in Livingston, California, where he was raised during the 1930s and 1940s. They have six children and 12 grandchildren. He is a founding member and former Vice President of FANHS.

Christine T. Lipat, the daughter of two Filipino medical professionals, was born and raised in New Jersey. Currently, she is Acting Executive Director of the Asian American Arts Alliance, a board member of the Astraea National Lesbian Action Foundation, and a founding member of Kilawin Kolektibo, a Pinay lesbian-identified collective of women based in New York City. A graduate of Oberlin College, she is currently completing her MS in nonprofit management from the New School of Social Research.

Juanita Tamayo Lott, MA, is President of Tamayo Lott Associates, a public policy consulting firm in Silver Spring, Maryland. Her lectures and publications cover Asian American issues, racial classification, and the implications of demographic shifts. She advises the U.S. Bureau of the Census and other federal agencies, nonprofit organizations, and public school systems. She is also a contributing editor for the first *Asian American Almanac*, a 900-page reference work (1995). As an undergraduate, she was co-chair of the first Pilipino Studies Program in the nation at San Francisco State University in 1969. Born in Ilocos Norte, she grew up in San Francisco.

Martin F. Manalansan IV, PhD, was born and raised in the Philippines. He graduated from the University of the Philippines with a degree in philosophy magna cum laude. He received his MA in anthropology from Syracuse University and his PhD in social anthropology from the University of Rochester. He has worked for more than 6 years in AIDS education, program evaluation, and social research. At present, he is Director of Education of the Asian and Pacific Islander Coalition on HIV/AIDS (APICHA) in New York City. His research interests include critical theory, sexuality and gender, immigration and diaspora, cultural studies, public health, and nationalism. He is currently editing an anthology of ethnographic essays on Asian American communities.

Cynthia C. Mejia-Giudici, MA, is the daughter of first-generation immigrants from Pangasinan Province: Her father came to the United States in 1929 to study, and her mother joined him in 1951 as a war bride. She received her BA in East Asian studies from Fairhaven College and her MA in education of the deaf from Gallaudet University. She is coeditor of *Filipinos in America, 1898-1974* (1975). Born in Ohio and raised in Seattle, she has traveled extensively and speaks Japanese, Spanish, and Sign Language. She taught ESL in Japan, middle school in

Virginia public school deaf programs, and community and adult basic education for the deaf programs in Virginia and Seattle. A Sign Language interpreter for deaf and hard-of-hearing programs at Seattle public schools, she has also been consultant to Prince George County's (Maryland) Asian American studies curriculum and Youth for Understanding. She is the immediate past-President of the Seattle chapter of the Filipino American National Historical Society. She and her husband Carey have three daughters: Monica Teal, Catherine Ligaya, and India.

Concepcion A. Montoya, MDiv, received her degree from Union Theological Seminary in New York City, where she concentrated on ethics and theology. She is also a graduate of New York University, where she majored in political science. A member of the "1.5" generation, she was born in the Philippines and arrived in the United States when she was 14 years old. She is fluent in Tagalog. Her work in immigration advocacy arises from her interest in religion and politics. She frequently writes and speaks about immigration issues.

Jonathan Y. Okamura, PhD, is a researcher with the Student Equity, Excellence and Diversity Office at the University of Hawai'i at Manoa and is a frequent lecturer in the Department of Ethnic Studies. Born and raised on the island of Maui in Hawai'i, he received his PhD degree in anthropology from the University of London and conducted his dissertation fieldwork with Filipino immigrants in the Kalihi area of Honolulu. He has researched and written on minority higher education, ethnic identity and relations in Hawai'i, and cultural minorities in the Philippines, where he taught in Manila at a Catholic university for 3 years in the mid-1980s. His current research interests include the global Filipino diaspora and racialization in Hawai'i.

Trinity A. Ordona, born and raised in San Diego, is a Filipino American from a post-World War II immigrant family of 13 children. She has a 25-year history of civil rights activism in the Asian, women's, and gay communities. She was a founding member of the national Asian/Pacific Lesbian and Bisexual Women's Network and the Asian Lesbian Network- USA; part of an international network of Asian Lesbians in Asia and the Diaspora; and co-coordinator of the Asian/Pacific Islander (A/PI) Parents and Friends of Lesbians and Gays Family Project, a group that supports families of A/PI queers. A PhD graduate student in history of consciousness at the University of California at Santa Cruz, she is writing the first social history of the Asian Pacific lesbian, bisexual, and transgender movement in the United States.

Raquel Z. Ordoñez, MPA, was born in Quezon City, Philippines, the older of two daughters of Generoso Zaraspe and Rosario Sims. She grew up in Lobo, Batangas, a small town in southern Luzon; her mother was the town's first nurse. After completing her BA in English, she taught in the English Department at the University of the Philippines for 8 years. She received several national awards for creative writing and published literary criticism. Her initial work toward an MA as a Rockefeller Foundation Fellow was interrupted when the Marcos regime imposed military rule in the country. Subsequently, her husband, Roberto Ordoñez, a journalist, was imprisoned, and she was placed under house arrest for 2 years. During that time, their first child was born. After those years, she was selected by the United Nations Development Programme to organize the training section of the Bureau of Foreign Trade. She then moved to the National Economic and Development Authority as Assistant Chief of the Economic Information Staff. She migrated to the United States in the early 1980s. In 1993, she founded the Coalition for the Advancement of Filipino Women, a network of over 400 organizations and individuals dedicated to raising the status of women and their communities.

Antonio J. A. Pido, PhD, is retired from the Michigan Jobs Commission Development as a Policy Analyst. He is also an occasional instructor in sociology at Lansing Community College. He was Assistant Professor of Sociology at Bradley University, Peoria, Illinois. Prior to his immigration to the United States, he was a Research Social Scientist at the National Science Development Board (now the Department of Science and Technology); Research Director and later Program Director at the Office of the Presidential Assistant on National Minorities, Office of the President, Philippines; and part-time Assistant Professor of Sociology, University of the East, Manila. He has various publications in the Philippines, the United States, and Japan and a book, *Pilipinos in America* (1986). He was born in Cebu City, Philippines, and immigrated with his wife and children to the United States in 1972.

Linda A. Revilla, PhD, is a 2.5-generation Filipina American, born in Springfield, Illinois, and raised in California, Florida, Maryland, and Japan. She received her BA in psychology from the University of California at San Diego and a PhD in developmental psychology from the University of California at Los Angeles. She was faculty of American Ethnic Studies at the University of Washington before moving to Honolulu. She is currently on staff at the Department of Veterans Affairs Pacific Center for PTSD and a lecturer in ethnic studies at the University of Hawai'i. Her research interests include Asian American mental health and Filipino American identity, family, and veteran issues. She is married to Gregory Mark, and they have one child, Kellen Nainoa.

Nilda Rimonte is the founder of the Los Angeles-based Center for the Pacific-Asian Family (CPAF), the first sexual assault and domestic violence program for Asian Pacific Islanders in the United States, and was its Executive Director for 13 years. She has written on the subjects of domestic violence and sexual assault. She also recently completed her own collection of short stories and has edited an anthology of woman-focused short fiction by Filipina writers, containing some of her own translations from Tagalog to English. She traces her interest in victimization issues to her work with battered women and rape victims at CPAF. She credits Memmi and Freire for lighting her way.

Felix I. Rodriguez, PhD, is an Associate Professor in the Department of Political Science at De La Salle University in Manila, Philippines. He finished his BS in biology at the University of the Philippines at Los Baños in October 1977. After receiving his PhD in social ecology from the University of California at Irvine, he became an Assistant Adjunct Professor in the College of Medicine at the University of California at Irvine. His current research interests focus on issues related to ecology and development and environmental history and ethics. In 1996, he received a C.I.T.E. (Citizens Improving the Environment) Award from the Washington State Department of Ecology. He was born in 1957 in a small town called Las Piñas, Rizal, which is now part of metropolitan Manila.

Maria P. P. Root, PhD, trained as a clinical psychologist, is Associate Professor of Ethnic Studies and Adjunct Associate Professor of Psychology and Women's Studies at the University of Washington and a clinical psychologist. Her interests focus on race relations, trauma, the mental health of minorities and women, and multiracial families and individuals. She has written and edited several books and authored numerous articles and book chapters. She has also been awarded the Washington State Psychological Association's Distinguished Psychologist Award, the Filipino American National Historical Society's VIP Award (Seattle Chapter), leadership awards from the American Psychological Association, and distinguished career awards from the American Psychological Association and the Asian American Psychological Association Born in Manila, Philippines, she and her mother joined her father in Los Angeles in the 1950s.

Cianna Pamintuan Stewart lived in Davao City until she was six years old, when her family returned to the United States after the declaration of martial law. She graduated from Wesleyan University, where she studied theater. She divides her time between theater directing and organizing around Asian/Pacific Islander sexual and gender diversity through the Visibility Campaign, Asian and Pacific Islander Wellness Center: Community HIV/AIDS Services, in San Francisco.

Leny Mendoza Strobel, EdD, received her graduate degree from the University of San Francisco. She teaches at the American Multicultural Studies Department at California State University at Sonoma. She has published several articles and is a contributing editor to a forthcoming anthology, *Geography of Encounters*. She is also editing a forthcoming anthology of essays on Filipino and Filipino American perspectives on decolonization. She is a lecturer and community adviser to Filipino American and Asian American college groups and Filipino American community groups in the Bay Area. She was born and raised in San Fernando, Pampanga.

Leonardo A. Tacata Jr., MPH, is an epidemiologist and Project Director for the Filipino American Community Epidemiological Study (FACES), a research project of Asian American Recovery Services, Inc. in San Francisco. He earned his MPH degree from the University of California at Los Angeles School of Public Health, where he specialized in epidemiology. He is a member of the Filipino American National Historical Society (Vallejo City and Los Angeles chapters), Filipinos for Affirmative Action, and the Pilipino Community Health Task Force in San Francisco. He traces his roots through his father Leonardo Amudo Tacata of Pasuquin, Ilocas Norte, and his mother Azucena Asprer Tacata of Kiamba, South Cotobato. Born in Manila, he immigrated to San Francisco in 1972; he currently resides in Daly City, California.

Antonio T. Tiongson Jr. is currently pursuing graduate studies in ethnic studies at the University of California at San Diego. His interests include community building in an age of multinational corporations and conservatism, hip-hop culture, social movements around the globe and their relevance to struggles in the United States, and reclaiming the narratives of resistance and struggle of Filipino Americans. Born in the Philippines, he immigrated to San Francisco in 1981.

Mary Ann Ubaldo was born and raised in Manila and graduated from the University of the Philippines. She is cofounder of Kilawin Kolektibo, a Pinay lesbian-identified collective of women in New York City, and was also a member of Gabriela Network, a Philippines-U.S. women's solidarity organization. She runs a jewelry business named after the Filipina legendary tribal warrior Urduja, in which she creates unique pieces that incorporate Filipino motifs using the ancient Philippine script called *alibata*. She is also a musician and photographer.